Think, Write, Speak

Think, Write, Speak

Uncollected Essays, Reviews, Interviews,
and Letters to the Editor

VLADIMIR NABOKOV

Edited by Brian Boyd and
Anastasia Tolstoy

ALFRED A. KNOPF NEW YORK 2019

THIS IS A BORZOI BOOK
PUBLISHED BY ALFRED A. KNOPF

Compilation copyright © 2019 by
The Vladimir Nabokov Literary Foundation

Introduction copyright © 2019 by Brian Boyd

All rights reserved. Published in the United States by Alfred A. Knopf,
a division of Penguin Random House LLC, New York,
and distributed in Canada by Random House of Canada,
a division of Penguin Random House Canada Limited, Toronto.

www.aaknopf.com

Knopf, Borzoi Books, and the colophon are registered trademarks
of Penguin Random House LLC.

Library of Congress Cataloging-in-Publication Data
Names: Nabokov, Vladimir Vladimirovich, 1899–1977,
author. | Boyd, Brian, [1952–] editor. | Tolstoy, Anastasia, editor.
Title: Think, write, speak : uncollected essays, reviews, interviews,
and letters to the editor / by Vladimir Nabokov ;
edited by Brian Boyd and Anastasia Tolstoy.
Description: First edition. | New York : Alfred A. Knopf, 2019. |
In English with some text translated from Russian. | Includes almost
a hundred selected interviews with the author from 1932–1977.
Identifiers: LCCN 2018057673 (print) | LCCN 2018059234 (ebook) |
ISBN 9781101874929 (ebook) | ISBN 9781101874912 (hardcover)
Classification: LCC PS3527.A15 (ebook) |
LCC PS3527.A15 A6 2019 (print) | DDC 813/.54–dc23
LC record available at https://lccn.loc.gov/2018057673

Jacket art and design by Chip Kidd

Manufactured in the United States of America
First Edition

Contents

Abbreviations

DN	Dmitri Nabokov
EO	Vladimir Nabokov, trans. and commentary, Aleksandr Pushkin, *Eugene Onegin* (4 vols., 1964; rev. ed., Princeton, N.J.: Princeton University Press, 1975)
LCNA	Vladimir Nabokov papers, Library of Congress
LTV	Vladimir Nabokov, *Letters to Véra*, ed. and trans. Olga Voronina and Brian Boyd (2014; corrected ed., New York: Vintage, 2017)
SM	Vladimir Nabokov, *Speak, Memory: An Autobiography Revisited* (1951; rev. ed., 1967; New York: Vintage, 1989)
SO	Vladimir Nabokov, *Strong Opinions* (New York: McGraw-Hill, 1973)
V&V	Vladimir Nabokov, *Verses and Versions: Three Centuries of Russian Poetry*, ed. Brian Boyd and Stanislav Shvabrin (New York: Harcourt, 2008)
VN	Vladimir Nabokov
VNA Berg	Vladimir Nabokov Papers at The Henry W. and Albert A. Berg Collection of English and American Literature, The New York Public Library Astor, Lenox and Tilden Foundations
VNA Montreux	Véra Nabokov's archive of Vladimir Nabokov's papers, Montreux, as catalogued and transcribed or photocopied by Brian Boyd, 1979–1983

Introduction:
Thinker, Writer, Speaker, Person

Brian Boyd

> I, the man, am a deeply moral, exquisitely kind, old-fashioned and rather stupid person. I, the writer, am different in every respect. It is the writer who answers your last and best question.
>
> (Interview with Helga Chudacoff, 1974)

I

Nabokov famously, and infamously, began *Strong Opinions*, his 1973 selection of his "public prose": "I think like a genius, I write like a distinguished author, and I speak like a child."[1] *Think, Write, Speak* echoes that pronouncement and that volume, offering a comprehensive selection from his remaining interviews, essays, letters to the editor, and reviews.

Soon after preparing *Strong Opinions*, Nabokov selected the tales that would go into his fourth English-language volume of stories, by then all being translated from his early Russian fiction, and joked: "There remain two or three broken crackers and some mouseturdies at the bottom of the barrel; otherwise, *c'est tout*."[2] But what remained of his "public prose" after his selection for *Strong Opinions*, on the other hand, is not the bottom but the bulk of the barrel.

Much loved by Nabokov's readers though it is, *Strong Opinions* was a rushed compromise. Nabokov had recently signed an initially generous-seeming but soon rather onerous eleven-book deal with his new publisher, McGraw-Hill. When the time quickly came to supply yet another volume, he scurried to assemble *Strong Opinions* from material that was in most cases recent, topical, and ready to hand. The interviews run from 1962 to 1972, the essays and reviews almost all from 1963 to 1972.

Think, Write, Speak selects from all the remainder of Nabokov's public prose, essays from 1921, letters to the editor from 1926, reviews from 1927, and interviews from 1932. The more than 150 items here do not cover *all* Nabokov's uncollected output in these modes. Because his critiques of young and mostly forgotten Russian poets for faults in their versification and imagery mean little to readers without Russian, only one such example has been included, the review of the first volume of poems by Boris Poplavsky—"a far violin among near balalaikas," as Nabokov would describe him two decades later in *Speak, Memory*, before admitting that he would never forgive himself for "the ill-tempered review in which I attacked him for trivial faults in his unfledged verse."[3]

But almost everything else is here, except for reporters' scene-setting, which Nabokov excluded from *Strong Opinions*, for long-winded interview questions, which Nabokov retained there, and for repeated answers to repeated questions, which Nabokov also retained. Not that the same questions do not recur here, too (why *Lolita*? why Switzerland? why a hotel? how do you write? what's your daily routine? what language do you think in?), although Nabokov's answers sometimes offer enough novelty to warrant reproducing, despite partial overlaps. Understandably, his own exasperation at repeated questions became more intense after *Strong Opinions*, as is explicit in a note to one interviewer ("I thank you for sending me the list of your questions for an interview in the *Welt des Buches*. You say that 'in some instances' similar questions had been set before. That is an understatement"), and as is implicit in his grumpily curt answers to her questions, except for the last one, cited in the epigraph above.

With *Strong Opinions* as the model, I had expected to order the material generically—interviews, letters to the editor, essays, and reviews—and then chronologically within each genre. But soon a single chronological order came to seem far preferable, allowing the century as well as the person to take a clearer shape. Nearly three items a year over the more than half-century of Nabokov's adult writing life constitute almost a biography of his career, the rolling shadow of the train of his fiction. They mark the changes in him—a fledgling prosaist, an acclaimed émigré, a dislocated and relocating writer, a reviewer and teacher by necessity, a sudden international success, a recognized master—and the changes in his world, from émigré Berlin at its initial peak to émigré Paris crushed by the German occupation, from reorientation to triumph in America, from a Europe distanced for him, after twenty years, to his own settled perch atop the Montreux Palace Hotel. All the way, indeed, from V. Nabokoff—a Cambridge undergraduate signing himself "Vl. Sirin," introducing the university, the town, and his own pangs of exile there to an émigré Russian audience recently landed in Western Europe—to "VN," the world-famous author, but with less than six months to live, gamely trying to look forward to the completion of another novel he probably already suspected he would never finish.

In Nabokov's public prose, context tends to count much more than it does in the invented worlds of his fiction. Often, the material reflects the stage of his life (his first reading tour to Paris, his arrival in New York, his teaching Russian language at Wellesley or European or Russian literature at Cornell, the publication of *Lolita* or later books) or the phase of his writing career (his first hostile review, his needing to display his skills to a new French or a new American reading or academic audience, his recently established or now long-assured fame) or the time when the piece was written (the tenth anniversary of the Bolshevik coup, the centenary of Pushkin's death or the recent deaths of friends closer to home, the desperation of Russian émigrés in occupied France, a defense of democracy under assault from dictatorships, Nabokov's virulent dislike for Germany at war, the social changes of the 1960s). In this public prose, chronology often matters much more than genre, even when Nabokov asserts his independence of his era and his concern for the timeless in human lives.

II

Not only something of a biography, *Think, Write, Speak* also offers a new showcase of Nabokov's variety.

A first essay, signed "Vl. Sirin," a pseudonym just ten months old but already in print more than thirty times, shows Nabokov, still a student, straddling from the outset the Russian and the Anglophone worlds in his art as in his life. For the Russian émigré audience clustering in Berlin, he evokes Cambridge and the impressions it makes on a fellow exile: its exoticism, even in its homeliness; the reverse exoticism émigrés had for native-born students; the nostalgia he feels there, especially for the Russian soulfulness that he misses in English acquaintances.

In his second essay, he straddles the Russian and English worlds in a different way, while simultaneously straddling both this world and the next. He introduces for a Russian audience what has excited him most in recent English literature, the poetry of Rupert Brooke. He admires his recent Cambridge predecessor most of all for celebrating the everyday from the perspective of an imagined afterlife. Literary scholars tend to think of 1922 in terms of the retrospectively fixed milestones of literary history: in poetry, therefore, *The Waste Land*. History in the making does not arrive with its later labels, as Nabokov often stresses, in this volume as elsewhere. He would not refer to T. S. Eliot until 1946, and then in a spirit of challenge. He discovered contemporary literature at his own pace and with his own strong dispositions.

Essays three (by "Vladimir V. Nabokoff") and four (by "V. Cantaboff") change again, not least in being in English about Russian subject matter. Nabokov wrote them after his father's assassination in March 1922, and after he had left Cambridge in June and rejoined the remainder of his family in Berlin, by now still more emphatically the center of the burgeoning Russian emigration. There the Russian cabaret Karussel (a pun on "*Russ*ian," "*rousse*," "*russ*isch" and German "*Karussell*") had presumably approached him to contribute to their magazine: his English, his cosmopolitanism, the intense longing for Russia in his prolific verse made him a perfect person to turn to as a bridge between the Russian cabaret and the Western audience it sought. (Later in the year, Nabokov would start writing sketches for the earliest, most successful and long-lasting of Berlin's Russian cabarets, Sinyaya Ptitsa, the Bluebird.) These commissioned pieces display his eagerness for art and tap aspects of his youthful memories of Russian life and folkloric traditions that he would never return to in his later work with such boyish enthusiasm.

From 1922, Nabokov wrote occasional reviews of the work of young émigré poets, now forgotten even without his rating them forgettable.

Most of these reviews have not been included here, both because the poets have left few traces and because Sirin's criticisms of technicalities of Russian language and versification mean little to an audience without Russian. But the fifth entry here offers an excerpt from a review—not only not commissioned, but apparently never published—of volumes of poetry by Dmitri Shakhovskoy, Ilya Britan, and Lev Gordon, because, in critiquing Gordon, Nabokov introduces Osip Mandelshtam as a foil. Nabokov wrote almost nothing about Mandelshtam even privately, and nothing in public until the late 1960s, when he deplored Robert Lowell's blurrily distorted "imitations" of Mandelshtam. His vivid and original 1924 comments about Mandelshtam are the first signs of his response to a major near-contemporary, and the most detailed comments he made on the poet until near the end of his own career.

By the time of the sixth essay—a year later, in late 1925—Sirin had already written his first novel, *Mashen'ka* (*Mary*). Again he surprises. *Mary* had been set in the Berlin emigration but was fired by, and lingered over, memories of first love in Russia. But this essay, also written in Russian, entitled "Play" in Nabokov's manuscript but "Breitensträter–Paolino" in its published version, although it begins with a uniquely Nabokovian delight in play as a cosmic principle, soon turns specifically to boxing, and then to a particular heavyweight bout in Berlin between the German champion and the Basque giant who would drub his valiant opponent. Nabokov—who had been taught boxing at home as a child and was ready to use it at school to defend victims from bullies, and was an occasional boxing coach in the mid-1920s—here exults in boxing, its traditions, its champions, its artistry, its courage. He exults even in the pleasure of being knocked out. Most surprisingly of all, this non-crowd-lover, this resolute individualist, exalts the crowds who come to watch boxing in a spirit very much like his.

Item number seven, a letter to an editor that may never have been sent, shows a young writer's irritation, a few months later, at receiving a hostile and sloppily or maliciously misquoting review of his first novel.

Over the next few years, Nabokov would compose several talks for the small émigré literary circle organized in Berlin by his friends Raisa and Vladimir Tatarinov and the critic Yuli Aykhenvald. He spoke on a wide array of themes, whether requested by them or proposed by him. The first, long in tiresome preparation but hastily drafted, is an exasperatedly indignant denunciation of the wretchedness of Soviet literature, with astonishing examples of incoherent bombast that were a nightmare to translate (Nabokov would return to the topic and the strategy of damning citation in 1930 and in 1941). It contains in passing an unexpected demotion of Chateaubriand (whom in a 1969 interview featured here Nabokov ranks as among the greatest authors of all time) and an unexpected promotion of Conrad (whom he will soon start to dismiss). The next talk critically resists generalizations, especially about times and places, about periods and countries—a theme that will recur throughout his work, including later pieces here. As in later reviews and interviews, his precise knowledge of distant historical detail allows him to challenge the supposedly unprecedented new features of a particular epoch, especially the present day. A third talk on man and "things"—by which he means human artifacts—has something of the scattershot whimsy and penetration of early essayists like Montaigne and Bacon. Written just before he announced to his mother that he was working on his second novel, *King, Queen, Knave*, it offers insights into Nabokov's preoccupation in the novel with invented automatons and humans turning themselves into automatons or things, and his awareness of the deep origins of automation stretching back millennia, into "gray-haired antiquity."[4]

One could anticipate, from Nabokov's known attitudes, that in 1927 he might denounce the Soviet regime's celebrations of its tenth anniversary, but instead he publicly celebrates the tenth anniversary of the unprecedented cultural freedom of the emigration. Far less expected, indeed quite astonishing, is Nabokov's response to an invitation the next year to speak, before an émigré musical evening devoted to "Spring and Music," on the sounds of Russian spring—so apt a topic, it would seem, for someone whose early work had been as nostalgic as it was alert to sonic detail and pattern. At the last minute, he delivered a talk, instead, on opera.[5] That someone later famous for his amusia—in his autobiography, he would write, "Music, I regret to say, affects me merely as an arbitrary succession of more or less irritating sounds"[6]—should talk on and in defense of the naturalness of opera seems astonishing in itself. All the more so when someone who would also write "*Vive le pédant*,"[7] and act according to that motto, should on this occasion speak so loosely of music ("a Beethoven sonata directly imitates either nature or human life") yet at the same time show a discriminating taste ("only when this harmony is observed is opera beautiful. It is in this sense that *Pelléas and Mélisande, Boris Godunov,* and, in part, *Carmen,* are beautiful").[8]

Although Nabokov's reviews of other émigré writers in the mid-1920s are sporadic and mostly negative, in the late 1920s he began to review frequently and mostly enthusiastically. He reported with glee on another sport or game with which we associate him much more than we do boxing, in his review of a chess book on Alekhine and Capablanca. Two weeks before Alekhine became world champion, Sirin recommended this "thrilling" book as "a most entertaining novel, or rather, the novel's first volume, since its main characters have only now really clashed."[9] He particularly relished the characterization of the contrasting styles of the two grandmasters. About fifteen months later, he would conceive of and rapidly compose his own chess novel, *The Luzhin Defense,* named perhaps with a nod to the famously bold Alekhine Defense, just as the beginning and end of Aleksandr Ivanovich Luzhin's name, if not his chess style, also seem a nod to Alekhine. Like the nonfiction chess reporting that Nabokov extols as a "novel," his own novel would reach a high point in the description of the final tussle between the styles of a Russian master and his Latin opponent (the fictional Turati replacing the real-life Capablanca).

Next month, Sirin wrote an admiring review of the collected poems of Vladislav Khodasevich, and a year and half later, an even more admiring review of the selected poems of Ivan Bunin. Nabokov would soon become a literary ally and, after he began traveling to Paris, also a friend of Khodasevich, whom he admired despite his acidity, and he would become an acquaintance of Bunin, whom he came to find increasingly coarse and unkind.[10] Although he would continue to prefer Bunin's poetry to his more celebrated prose, he would also come to rate Khodasevich's verse, not Bunin's, the finest Russian verse of the early decades of the twentieth century.

In 1928, Nabokov wrote a scathing review of the medievalizing fabulist Aleksey Remizov, and a fascinated appreciation of a translation of the eleventh-century but decidedly unmedieval Persian mathematician, astronomer, and poet, Omar Khayyám. Already a translator himself, in his early twenties, of not only much of Rupert Brooke but all of Romain Rolland's *Colas Breugnon* and Lewis Carroll's *Alice's Adventures*

in Wonderland, Nabokov for the first time here *discusses* translation, as he
would do frequently after his move to America, where he would become
the most renowned translator of Russian verse into English. Here he
shows his thorough knowledge of other versions of Omar Khayyám
in addition to Edward FitzGerald's translation. He also shows he can
separate the *poetry* of FitzGerald and Tkhorzhevsky, both of which he
admires, from their scholarship and translation, which he critiques.

Also in 1928, he wrote the first of four obituaries. His friend Yuli
Aykhenvald, killed by a tram on his way back from a rare party at the
Nabokovs', had been recognized as a critic of rare subtlety in Russia before the Revolution, and in the emigration had been the first
renowned critic to recognize Sirin as a major talent. By the time he did
so, in 1925—after Berlin became expensive again, once the restabiliza-
tion of the mark had punctured the hyperinflation of 1923—the center
of the emigration had moved to Paris. Nabokov's obituary of his friend,
at the very end of 1928, marks the last of his work collected here that
assumes a Berlin focus.

Nabokov would remain in Germany until the beginning of 1937,
partly, still, to protect his Russian undiluted, by living in a country
whose language he barely knew; partly because Véra could easily find
work here, until Hitler's policies affected her employers and then her;
partly because, from 1932, they could share affordable quiet accom-
modation with Véra's cousin Anna Feigin; and partly because, despite
their growing wish to move elsewhere—to France, England, or, as
war loomed, even farther afield—Véra was reluctant to leave until her
husband could establish a financially secure base in a less unwelcoming
country. Germany was deeply affected by the Depression, and the Berlin Russian daily, *Rul'* (The Rudder), in which Nabokov had published
hundreds of poems, stories, plays, reviews, and essays, would fold in
1931. But in 1929, his novel *The Defense* began publication in *Sovremennye zapiski* (Contemporary Annals), the "thick journal" that was the
best-paying, most prestigious, and most eagerly read in the emigration.
Readers in émigré Paris, by now well established as the émigré hub,
had had no reason to buy the high-priced *Rul'* but now realized, in the
pages of *Sovremennye zapiski,* that a writer of genius had emerged in
the emigration. Ilya Fondaminsky, one of the journal's editors and its
main financial prop, came from Paris to visit Nabokov in Berlin in early
1930 and was ready to commit to publishing serially his future novels.

Sirin's suddenly risen reputation in Paris began to spread beyond the emigration. In 1930, he was approached by two Paris journals, one resolutely émigré, the other French but international in scope, to contribute to surveys on modern literature: on Proust, for the émigré journal *Chisla* (Numbers); on literary populism, for *La Grande Revue*. The voice and ideas of the mature Nabokov sound here in both responses, in his sense of the utter and proper individuality of writers, readers, and characters. His last two extended Russian essays appeared in 1930 and 1931: one in *Rul'*; the other, even before the final issue of *Rul'*, in the new Paris journal *Novaya gazeta* (The New Newspaper). The first was a satirically incompetent sales pitch for Freudianism; the second, a critique of Soviet literature for returning to medieval, black-and-white standards of vice and virtue. Both anticipate *bêtes noires* in Nabokov's later fiction and his own increasing predilection for testing readers' moral and psychological judgment. A 1931 French essay, "Les Écrivains et l'époque," for the journal *Le Mois*—solicited by the journal, and with a three-page profile on "perhaps the only great writer that the Russian emigration has so far produced"[11]—shows Nabokov in top form, imagining the present from the vantage of the future, a theme that he had broached in his 1925 story "A Guide to Berlin" and that had also motivated him to write his newest novel, *Glory*, which had just begun to appear serially in *Sovremennye zapiski*, after briefer excerpts in émigré Paris dailies.

Nabokov followed up his damning and later-regretted review of the first book by the Paris-based poet Boris Poplavsky with a review of a novel by Nina Berberova, also based in Paris. He begins in a way that almost leads us to expect another dismissal, even when he quotes as "convincing" the thematically central song, "Long not for darling Russia, Cossack . . . Come to the country of the French," only to make explicit, at the last moment, a ringing endorsement of a vision of the emigration quite unlike his own, and yet a view of the emigration as if seen in epic retrospective that curiously chimes with his essay "Les Écrivains et l'époque" a month earlier.

A memorial tribute for the poet Sasha Chorny shows Nabokov belatedly and publicly voicing the gratitude he regrets not having expressed to Chorny in his lifetime, for helping him publish and improve his youthful poems: "I don't hide from myself that of course he did not value them as highly as I then thought (A.M. had excellent taste), but he was doing a kind deed and he did it thoroughly."

Chorny, already well known as a poet, had mentored the fledgling Sirin in Berlin but, like so many other émigrés, writers or not, had then moved to France. Now, in October 1932, Sirin himself traveled to Paris, for his first triumphal reading tour, and to meet people he had only written about, like Khodasevich and Berberova (recently but amicably separated), Bunin, and Kuprin. On this occasion, he faced his first press interview. His account of his working methods as a writer both connects and contrasts with his later descriptions of his working habits, in content (later in life, he would not work with such abandon) as well as in expression: he shows an unguardedness here despite Andrey Sedykh's comment that Sirin "speaks quickly and with passion. But a kind of prudence prevents him from speaking of himself."[12] Contrast his descriptions of his working methods here, for instance, with the clarity and amplitude of his remarks to Dieter Zimmer in 1966, by which time he was a seasoned reporter on himself.

An obituary of Amalia Fondaminsky, who died in 1935 and whom Nabokov had known for only the month of his 1932 reading trip to Paris, has to skirt his shallow knowledge of her to soothe her devoted husband, Ilya, a fervent supporter of *Sovremennye zapiski* and of Sirin. In 1936, with three of his novels already published in French translation, Nabokov again traveled to France in the hope of finding a literary home there, but to no avail. At the beginning of 1937, Véra promptly sent her husband to France and away from the Germany where one of the right-wing assassins of his father had just been appointed second-in-command of the Nazi government's office for Russian émigré affairs. In this centenary year of Pushkin's death, Nabokov wrote a long essay in French in honor of Pushkin, addressing the subject of biography and of readers' relations to the authors they construct in their imaginations. This major essay echoed Nabokov's multiple explorations of biography and Pushkin in *The Gift*, which he had been working on for four years, and anticipated his future work on biography in both fiction (*The Real Life of Sebastian Knight, Pnin, Pale Fire, Look at the Harlequins!*) and fact (his scholarly work on Chernyshevsky in the 1930s and on Pushkin in the 1950s) and his imminent work as a translator on arriving, after more vicissitudes and historical convulsions, in the United States rather than France. Written with much more care than many of his earlier occasional essays, with the flair and the imagination open on all sides so evident in his fiction, the essay was a pitch for Nabokov to be taken seriously as a writer in French and to be recognized as a bridge between Russian and French literary culture.

An author questionnaire later in 1937 for Bobbs-Merrill, the publisher of "Vladimir Nabokoff"'s first novel to appear in the States, *Laughter in the Dark*, marks another shift in Nabokov's focus, although as yet he could see no way of reaching even England (where translations of *Camera Obscura* and *Despair* had already been published), let alone America. But when his friend the historical novelist Mark Aldanov was offered a position teaching creative writing at Stanford, declined because he lacked confidence in his English, and passed the invitation along to Nabokov, a new world opened up—once he could obtain an exit visa from France, an American visa, and the cost of the passage, at almost the last possible moment to escape from the advancing German army, late in May 1940. An interview from New York's Russian émigré daily, *Novoe russkoe slovo* (New Russian Word), a series of short paragraphs looking back on the European emigration and out on his new American location, and an appeal on behalf of Russians still stranded in now occupied Paris mark Nabokov's first few months in New York.

He needed to switch as a writer, he knew, from Russian to English. As he wrote for *Novoe russkoe slovo*, the Russian emigration as he and others had known it in Europe would never be the same after the German invasion of France. He had been trying for some time to recast himself as a writer in English—when he revamped the translation of *Despair* in 1935, reworked *Camera Obscura* into *Laughter in the Dark* in 1937, and wrote *The Real Life of Sebastian Knight* directly in English in 1938–39. But he still had no publisher for that first English-language novel, and he needed to make himself known. Luckily for him, his cousin the composer Nicolas Nabokov knew the renowned critic Edmund Wilson. Wilson—at this time eagerly reading Russian, especially Pushkin—invited Nabokov to contribute to *The New Republic*, where he was acting editor. Nabokov wrote twelve reviews over the next four years, mainly in 1941, first for *The New Republic*—Wilson was most impressed by their quality—and soon also for *The New York Sun* and *The New York Times*. Whereas his Russian reviews had been of other émigré writers, mostly poets, his splendid American reviews covered all sorts of topics, starting with Russian matters (dancer Serge Lifar's biography of Diaghilev; a history of the Dukhobor sect); historical fiction (Masefield); literary criticism (three books on Shakespeare); philosophy; biography and art (a life of the painter Charles Conder); essays (Belloc); history (England); politics (Soviet repression); and translations of Georgian and Russian literature. They offer a confident cascade of ideas, information, and images that show sides of Nabokov we might not otherwise have glimpsed. On the British poet laureate John Masefield as novelist, in *Basilissa, a Tale of the Empress Theodora:* "This book is a splendid example of false romance and false history; it belongs to a widespread genus of false books, and, to the investigator, its shortcomings are as fascinating as the qualities of real achievement."[13] On philosopher Frederick Woodbridge: "the old pitfall of that dualism which separates the ego from the non-ego, a split which, strangely enough, is intensified the stronger the reality of the world is stressed ... The human mind is a box with no tangible lid, sides or bottom, and still it is a box, and there is no earthly method of getting out of it and remaining in it at the same time."[14] On Hilaire Belloc: "he attempts to be trivial and remote simultaneously, making as it were a slide-preparation of the obvious and then peering at it through a telescope."[15]

In 1941, the writer Klaus Mann, son of Thomas Mann and exiled by Hitler, set up a new magazine, *Decision*, to champion free European culture and encourage U.S. involvement in the war. He marshaled a stellar editorial board and contributors. For some reason, Nabokov was already well enough known to Mann to be asked to write an essay on recent Soviet literature. For the third time in his life, Nabokov forced himself to read Soviet work, in this case material from 1940, for an essay that ended by pointing out, wryly, the decline of German villains in the fiction of the year following the Molotov-Ribbentrop (or Hitler-Stalin) Pact. Although Nabokov's essay was set in type, Hitler's invasion of Russia reshaped the context in which it was written, as Pearl Harbor then undermined the rationale for *Decision*, which itself began to founder. Despite existing in corrected proofs for eighty years, the essay has never before been published. By the time Mann's journal failed, Nabokov had begun his own war effort, the novel *Bend Sinister,* which interlards "bits of Lenin's speeches, and a chunk of the Soviet constitution, and gobs of Nazist pseudo-efficiency,"[16] just as his essay for *Decision* had opened with official remarks on the position of the artist in Nazi Germany and Soviet Russia that eerily echoed each other.

One short letter in response to someone's pointing out an error in his essay "The Art of Translation" (the essay itself appears in *Verses and Versions*)[17] links back to his 1937 French essay on Pushkin and his current work on translating Russian poets (Pushkin, Lermontov, Tyutchev, Fet, and Khodasevich) as another way of putting his talents to work and earning an income and attention. But Nabokov was also trying to establish himself in other ways. A first interview by a student at Wellesley College in early 1941, when he was just a visiting lecturer there, prefigures more student interviews and profiles after he secured an insecure but annually renewed position there, first in comparative literature and then teaching the Russian language. The essay "The Creative Writer," perhaps first prepared for his teaching as a creative writer at Stanford in the summer of 1941, was shaped for delivery at a New England Modern Languages Association meeting late in the year. Again attempting to get himself noticed by a new audience, Nabokov, in this flamboyant, freewheeling, high-energy essay (republished in *Lectures on Literature* but with two pages missing, now reinstated),[18] speaks for the irrationality of the creative imagination and against the rational calculation of the market-oriented writer—partly a reaction to his disgust with the market-oriented advice to American writers he had read in preparation for his Stanford teaching. Markedly different in style is the lecture fragment *on* style, written for his Stanford creative writing class: much plainer than "The Creative Writer," but playful as well as lucid and accessible, with the individuality that he singled out as the true core of style.

While he held a precarious position at Wellesley from 1941 to 1948, Nabokov was also writing other essays as a result of another precarious but annually renewed position as the de facto curator of Lepidoptera at Harvard's Museum of Comparative Zoology. These scientific papers, reprinted in *Nabokov's Butterflies*,[19] do not feature here, but his work as a lepidopterist would become a subject of fascination for interviewers in the years of his post-*Lolita* fame.

Nabokov earned his position at the MCZ on the strength of his earlier scientific publications, and kept earning its renewal by the quality of his new work, but perhaps also because younger scientists were otherwise deployed for the war effort. The war also had an impact on Wellesley College. Wellesley's president, Mildred McAfee, would be summoned to Washington as head of the Women's Naval Reserve, the

WAVES (Women Accepted for Volunteer Emergency Service), and Wellesley's students, too, were ready to throw what weight they could into the war. In a panel discussion at Wellesley in April 1942, Nabokov himself spoke directly, lucidly, and eloquently on democracy ("Ethically, the members of a democracy are equals; spiritually, each has the right to be as different from his neighbors as he pleases . . . the subtle balance between the boundless privileges of every individual and the strictly equal rights of all men"),[20] as he had done more obliquely, ungently, and pungently in his recent anti-Soviet and even more strongly anti-German comments, in his essay on Soviet literature, in "The Creative Writer," and in the book on Nikolay Gogol that he was beginning to write.

In 1943, Nabokov wrote a last obituary, on Iosif Hessen. Hessen had edited *Rul'* in the Berlin of the 1920s, when Sirin was contributing poems, stories, plays, essays, reviews, and even crossword puzzles to the newspaper: "The blue hues of Berlin's twilights, the tent made by the corner chestnut tree, faint light-headedness, poverty, being in love, the mandarin tinge of a prematurely lit neon sign, and the animal yearning for a still fresh Russia—all this was dragged in iambic form to the editorial office, where I.V. would bring the page up close to his face, as though he was latching on to what was written from its hem, from the bottom up, with a parabolic movement of his eye, after which he would look at me with a half-sarcastic benevolence, lightly shaking the page, but he would say only: 'Hmm, hmm.' "[21] Nabokov, who had helped extricate Hessen and his son George, the closest friend of his adult life, from occupied France, recorded his regret that he never had the chance to see Hessen in America before his death soon after reaching New York and safety.

As the war's outcome became clear, Wellesley relaxed its war alertness, and Nabokov's Russian course was allowed to become a regular part of the schedule. His short 1945 essay "On Learning Russian" offers delightfully presented tips that many Anglophones who have learned the language for a year or two might wish they had been taught from the start. His 1948 essay "The Place of Russian Studies in the Curriculum" responds to a particular moment in his life (his imminent departure for Cornell, knowing that a replacement for his own position would soon arrive at Wellesley) and a particular phase in the century's history (the approach of the Cold War). It both tolerates the practical pressures of the moment and makes an eloquent pitch for the disinterested humanities and the timeless value of the best of Russian literary culture: new vistas for the student's imagination, exposure to "a certain unique quality about Russian literature, a quality of truth not rubbed in, of imagination controlled by dignified truthfulness, which has had an ennobling influence on the world literatures."[22]

The next piece marks another new phase in Nabokov's life: his move to Cornell, and a permanent academic position, at first in Russian literature but soon needing to be augmented by the larger classes he could command in teaching Masterpieces of European Fiction. At least in his first year of this course, 1950–51, he seems to have taught Kafka's unsettling *Metamorphosis*, which he would continue to teach happily for the rest of the decade, with the help of a contrast with the false coziness of Thomas Mann's story "The Railway Accident." As an essay this feels slight, but as a lecture it must have been hilarious and damning.

Nabokov had been lured to Cornell by Morris Bishop, a light-verse contributor to *The New Yorker*, where Nabokov's own poems had started appearing in 1942, his short stories in 1945, and his memoirs, in a rapid flow, from the start of 1948. His demonstration of his exceptional mastery in English, even when seen in the company of other contributors to the English-speaking world's best-paying magazine, had persuaded Bishop to seek him out for Cornell as a Russian teacher. Nabokov's exposure in *The New Yorker* also led to his being interviewed in 1951 in *The New York Times*, on the publication of *Conclusive Evidence*, the first name for the memoir that, as *Speak, Memory*, would earn him acclaim as one of the greatest of autobiographers.

His interviewer of course did not know, and Nabokov had no inclination whatever to tell, about *Lolita*, the work that was preoccupying his imagination even as he began teaching his course in European fiction and researching his provocative translation of and massive commentary to Pushkin's *Eugene Onegin*. The atmospheric disturbance that would generate Hurricane Lolita on its August 1958 American publication started in 1955, with the novel's publication in English in Paris. *Lolita*'s endorsement by Graham Greene as a book of the year, its denunciation by a British defender of moral standards, its banning and unbanning and rebanning by the French government, and the campaign on its behalf by the New York publishing-and-literary establishment from 1956, ensured, along with its originality of subject matter, character, and style, that the novel would cause literary havoc in the season when it was launched.

Lolita was, among much else, Nabokov's proof that he was a decidedly American author. Ironically, the first of the *Lolita* interviews, even before its American publication, was for a Russian audience—American, European, and Soviet—in the Voice of America's Russian program, a radio interview by his longtime friend, the ex-wife of his cousin Nicolas, Natalia Nabokov (née Shakhovskaya), with whom he and his family had briefly stayed when they first arrived in America. Unlike his other interviewers over the next few years, she also knew about the other work that had been haunting his decade, his *Eugene Onegin* opus. Other interviews soon flooded in from New York, from *Life*, from local newspapers in upstate New York in and near Ithaca—where Nabokov, financially secure at last, could denounce what he thought was the betrayal of Russian language teaching by linguists at Cornell who knew how to analyze Russian into morphemes and phonemes but not how to teach the language that his prospective advanced literature students would have needed.

Interviewers obscure and famous (the latter including Lionel Trilling, John Wain, Alain Robbe-Grillet) tracked Nabokov's progress from upstate New York. He left there on a sabbatical from Cornell in February 1959 that soon turned into permanent retirement, headed for the American West, then to Paris and London for the launch of the French and British editions of *Lolita* at the end of 1959. Nabokov managed to lie low in the French Midi and then while working in Hollywood on the screenplay for *Lolita* in 1960. When he returned to Europe after finishing the screenplay, and was working on *Pale Fire*, he was exuberant and relaxed in interviews in Nice. But his recoil from seeing his casual conversation in print, his rising status—as the author not only of *Lolita* but also of the utterly different *Pale Fire* and the rich pickings from the start of his Russian backlist, *Invitation to a Beheading* (1959), *The Gift* (1963), *The Defense* (1964)—and therefore his increasing need to protect his privacy and his time, soon led him to become more guarded, more controlling, and more purposefully aloof in his interviews.

He began to demand written questions sent well in advance, and to prepare written answers before his interviewers came. He even insisted he be allowed to see and correct drafts of interview write-ups that were more than verbatim question and answer, and often sought to eliminate the reporting of some of the casual chitchat he could easily slip into when he met an interviewer he found engaging or simply when his mood was especially exuberant. Despite such impediments, the Swiss media switched on to his presence in Montreux, and interviewed him again and again between 1963 and 1967. American, German, Italian, and French interviewers increasingly sought him out—five Italian interviewers in one day in late 1969, as the rush job of the Italian translation of Nabokov's longest and most complex novel, *Ada*, was about to appear. The price of fame rose: an interview with his first biographer, Andrew Field, when they were still on speaking terms; interviews with other academics, including his former Cornell students, and now Nabokov scholars, Alfred Appel, Jr. (see *Strong Opinions*), and Stephen Jan Parker; and interviews with other major media from the North American and European television, radio, newspaper, and magazine press.

The first few decades of the pieces in *Think, Write, Speak* tend to reflect the circumstances Nabokov found himself in—emigration in Berlin, partial reorientation to the new émigré center, Paris, a sudden desperate lurch aside to New York, war, teaching at Wellesley and Cornell—before inspiration and luck combined to make him famous enough for his own circumstances and imagination to become the target of endless interviewers' questions. The voice throughout is almost unmistakably Nabokov's, but the focus of the last, post-*Lolita* bulk of the book shifts from others' or his own prompts in multiple directions to interviewers' prompting him to talk almost exclusively about himself, now that *he* had become news.

III

Two-thirds of the items in this collection are interviews, all except a handful from the last third of Nabokov's adult writing life, from his post-*Lolita* years of world fame. The collection's title foregrounds the seeming arrogance of Nabokov's opening remark in *Strong Opinions*, "I think like a genius," and therefore also foregrounds the question of his personality.

Nabokov's control of his interviews was partly a consequence of his modesty. He really thought very little of himself as a speaker of sustained speech: "I am a shy, retiring person, I feel stupidly confused to have my book provoke such attention and ask so much of my readers";[23] "I admire people who can speak and it all comes out in well-ordered, beautifully rounded sentences. I cannot do that. I can't speak that way. I am an idiot in conversation";[24] "I'm not a dull speaker, I'm a bad speaker, I'm a wretched speaker"—and here comes the decidedly written continuation—"The tape of my unprepared speech differs from my written prose as much as the worm differs from the perfect insect."[25]

For good reason, Nabokov has often been considered the finest prose stylist in English. He knew that if he worked at what he wrote he could make it sing, sometimes with the complex amplitude of choral polyphony. But in sustained speech, he often spoke like almost any of us, with the hesitations, redirections, and incompletions of ordinary speech that discourse analysts have discovered with their tape recorders, giving the lie to the considered, emphatically *written*, dialogue that novelists of earlier centuries so often imagined for their characters. "Examples," Nabokov has written, "are the stained-glass windows of knowledge."[26] Here's a glimpse of his spontaneous speech, from a transcript of his first live television interview: "Well, it seems to me that all worthwhile novelists after all are concerned with passion and love and apart from Humbert and nymphets there does exist, always has existed, in novels as well as in life—if you take a novel, take *Anna Karenin*, you know, Tolstoy's *Anna Karenin* with Kitty and Levin—which have a relationship you see, we all see, how in ordinary life in Europe and in America, which may be termed passionate love, amorous love within the terms of a normal marriage. So we have that too."[27]

Speaking in a sustained way was all the more difficult for someone who saw so many possibilities in words and their ordering, and who stressed the power of revision in writing and the fact that he wore out his erasers faster than his pencil lead. Nabokov was also simply not enough of an egotist—he excoriated the egotism of a Hermann, a Humbert, a Kinbote, a Van Veen—to think that his life mattered because it was his. He wrote an autobiography only when he could see how to make an account of his life into a work of art in terms of its structures, its strategies, its sentences. Despite the worldwide interest in him in his years of fame, he could never see a sufficiently artistic form for shaping a continuation of his life beyond the point in May 1940 where *Speak, Memory* so elegantly suspends itself, and therefore could not bring himself to write a continuation just because it was *his* life and because it would sell well.

Yet Véra Nabokov treasured her husband's originality in everything he said as well as in all he wrote. Alfred Appel, Jr., himself an irrepressible wit, thought Nabokov "the most fun to be with of any person I have ever known."[28] And in interviewers' reports we can often hear Nabokov injecting a twist of surprise wherever he could into his spontaneous remarks, as long as he did not have to speak in oral paragraphs. His brief bursts of patter, of twisting words, of imagery, humor, or ironic self-consciousness, animate his casual speech and disclose not another Nabokov but a less guarded, a more spontaneous one. Once, when he was asked what he thought was his principal failing as a writer, he answered, "Lack of spontaneity; the nuisance of parallel thoughts, second thoughts, third thoughts; inability to express myself properly in any language unless I compose every damned sentence in my bath, in my mind, at my desk." To which the interviewer responded: "You're doing rather well at the moment, if we may say so." Nabokov shot back, or seemed to: "It's an illusion."[29] Indeed, introducing this interview in *Strong Opinions*, he had already disclosed, "Great trouble was taken on both sides to achieve the illusion of a spontaneous conversation."[30]

In one interview below, Nabokov declares, apropos of *Pale Fire*, "The clearest revelation of personality is to be found in the creative work in which a given individual indulges":[31] he has in mind Shade's verse and Kinbote's commentary. His dictum has its value: in a creative work, we can see depths and sides of personality that we can discover in no other way. But there are many sides to personality, and personality as the controlled projection of carefully considered words discloses only some.

In his written answers to written interview questions, Nabokov wishes his portrait for the photo gallery of history to be taken from a certain fixed angle. But other angles and other environments allow new features to show. For that reason, my selection is not what Nabokov's would have been: I include not only the prepared responses but also selections from vivid casual remarks, "spontaneous rot," as Nabokov described it to one of the interviewers in *Strong Opinions*.[32] Personality is a characteristic individual range of responses to circumstance, and the changing circumstances of different interviews, of encounters with different individuals, on different occasions, in different moods, with different degrees of spontaneity, allow us a Nabokov in the round.

Exasperated with Helga Chudacoff's asking him so many questions already asked in *Strong Opinions*, Nabokov directed her to his answers there, and responded with irritated curtness, sometimes almost stone-walling, to whatever questions she offered that had *not* been asked before. But when she reached him she found him different: "Now in Zermatt he looks me over critically and remarks dryly: 'You don't look like a hiker.' And I cannot help but notice that he underestimates his gift for conversation. He talks openly and unhesitatingly in American with a slight Russian accent and not without charm."[33] He quickly picks up on the alertness and openness of Robert Boyle or the erudite intelligence of Penelope Gilliatt. In his breaks from the creative concentration of composing *Pale Fire* in early 1961, Nabokov freewheels with Anne Guérin, relaxes playfully with Janine Colombo, almost chatters away to Rosalie Macrae. He pulls the legs of an interviewer who doesn't get him: James Salter unwittingly reports that he likes "bright people, 'people who understand jokes.' Véra doesn't laugh, he says resignedly. 'She is married to one of the great clowns of all time, but she never laughs.'"[34] (In serious mode, he would say, "She has the best sense of humor of any woman I have ever known."[35]) To Gaetano Tumiati's aggressive first question he responds even more aggressively. Despite their deep shared interest in art and science, he bristles at what he seems to see as Jacob Bronowski's attempt to put words or opinions in his mouth. Yet with another highly opinionated writer, Alberto Ongaro, also attempting to push him into agreement, Nabokov takes the time to answer fully and thoughtfully, to engage in a rare two-way debate over ideas: ideas about love and sex in the modern world, not framed as he would ever have framed them, but nevertheless ideas preoccupying him in his own way as he wrote *Ada*, yet never expressed in this manner, with this directness, or with this wealth of examples, anywhere else in all his voluminous work.

IV

In 1976, when I settled on my doctoral topic, I began to send out for interlibrary loans of Nabokov's uncollected reviews, essays, and interviews. I was repeatedly dazzled by what turned up: the grainy photocopies allowed me to see writer and man from new angles and with a new clarity. I have been puzzled, ever since, that other Nabokov scholars, so appreciative of *Strong Opinions*, have so rarely sought out these revelations and illuminations. And ever since, too, and with even more eagerness after I began to catalogue Nabokov's archives for his widow in 1979 and discovered still more, I have wanted to compile a volume like this.

The material here would make it even harder for some prominent Nabokov scholars to maintain some of their positions. Alexander Dolinin, in an essay on "Nabokov as a Russian Writer," tried to insist, in 2005 and later, that Nabokov, in the years after *Lolita*, engaged in a consistent process of "tricky mythmaking," downplaying his Russianness and his Russian works to "present himself as a born cosmopolitan genius who has never been attached to anything and anybody";[36] he "sends all [his] Russian writings downhill, relegating them to a secondary role of immature, imperfect antecedents," "downgrading them to the rank of apprenticeship."[37] Although there has always been ample evidence against Dolinin's claims,[38] *Think, Write, Speak* presents much more: "As a child, I was Russian, my first muse was Russian. We speak only Russian in my family today";[39] "The language of my ancestors is still the one where I feel perfectly at home. . . . It goes without saying that I adore Russian";[40] "my knowledge of Russian is infinitely greater than my knowledge of English."[41] Asked what language he would have preferred to have been born with, he answered in one word: "Russian."[42] In 1959, asked which of his books he liked most, he said there were three on the same level, naming *Lolita*, *The Gift*, and *Invitation to a Beheading*.[43] In 1962, he told *Newsweek*: "As a writer, I am better in Russian."[44] A few years before his death, he declared to another interviewer, "I have written in Russian the kind of books I wanted to write."[45]

Maurice Couturier, the leading French Nabokovian, in a book entitled *Nabokov, ou la tyrannie de l'auteur*, writes, in keeping with his title, that Nabokov "has done all he could to put the reader in an uncomfortable position, indeed to tame him"; or: "Nabokov perfectly mastered his text and imposed his lasting law (and his ideal self) on his reader. Proof too that a good reading of his novels is a pre-empted one, for the spaces of interpretation they leave are extremely restricted. Interpretation, like translation, is already treason!"[46] Nabokov's own comments could not be further from these assertions: readers "of course are welcome to any interpretation they desire";[47] "the reader has no business bothering about the author's intentions, nor has the author any business trying to learn whether the consumer likes what he consumes";[48] "For whom do I write? I write for the good reader. And you know, I have had some wonderful readers. Some of my readers have read my books better than I have written them."[49] In one interview, he puts the case with sublime simplicity: "I write what I like and some like what I write—that about sums it up."[50] Not much sign of tyranny here from this lifelong champion of individual freedoms.

What I have valued most in compiling these essays, reviews, and interviews, which may not be what others appreciate most, has been discovering aspects of Nabokov's mind and thought I have never quite seen before, especially his sense that the aim of art is to capture what is eternally true in human experience, "the everlasting reality of human passions":[51] "Every country lives in its own way, and every person in his own way. But there's something eternal. Only the portrayal of this eternal element is of value. Proust's characters have lived everywhere and always."[52] Nabokov rejects the communist sense of distinct bourgeois and proletarian consciousnesses, ironically agreeing to the conclusion that "a self-restrained communist and born member of the proletariat, and an unrestrained landowner and born nobleman, respond to the simplest things in life in different ways: the pleasure from a sip of cold water on a hot day, the pain from a hard thump on the head, the discomfort caused by ill-fitting footwear, and many other human experiences which are equally familiar to all mortals. It would be pointless for me to claim that a Soviet executive sneezes and yawns in the same way as an irresponsible bourgeois."[53] No, he says, this time without irony, "love has always been the same. Love now is no different from in Catullus's day. . . . If by this question you want to know if I believe people still fall in love and in the same way as before, I will answer yes. You see, I have taught for a long time in universities. I know young people well, I have seen couples who loved each other, couples who break up painfully, others who break up painlessly, as always, as always. The young people I've known were no different in love from the way I was nor from how young people are today or will be like tomorrow. Love and sex, I repeat, are always the same."[54]

Yet Nabokov also has a sense of the precious uniqueness of any era's particulars, of the combinations that the inhabitants of any time take for granted, not realizing how exotic they will look in retrospect. Having singled out such a cluster of present details that he does not expect still to coexist decades hence, he adds, in "Writers and the Era": but "then one tells oneself that after all, among the things that seem to us to group together in a unique order, forming present reality, there are some that will exist for a long time—the jerky twittering of sparrows, the green of the lilacs falling over the railings, the white breastpiece and the gray rump of a cloud gliding proud through the damp blue of a June sky."[55] But along with Nabokov's sense of the constants of nature, including human nature, he also has a sharper and fuller sense than I had realized of history's particulars not only in his own age but across hundreds and thousands of years.

One final comment. As I have noted, almost two-thirds of the items selected for *Think, Write, Speak* are Nabokov interviews after *Lolita*. Nabokov had strong opinions, often consistent over sixty years or more, but he could also contradict himself. One of the pleasures of *Think, Write, Speak* is to notice how thoroughly and how fascinatingly he contradicted himself on the subject of his most famous novel. Enjoy discovering and making sense of these contradictions yourself—and much, much more.

Note on Texts

The texts follow Nabokov's manuscripts, where available, or otherwise the earliest published editions. The sequence follows the order of composition, where it can be ascertained, not of publication, which can on occasions be years later.

Interviews are selected from so as to present as much as possible of Nabokov verbatim that he has not written or said elsewhere. To that end, questions and circumstantial reporting by interviewers or remarks by them or others are often either omitted or truncated and are always placed in italics. Answers partially overlapping what Nabokov has said elsewhere may be reproduced to provide the context for a valuable new detail, disclosure, opinion, or formulation. Where Nabokov provided written answers to interview questions, these will be followed, but they are often supplemented with selections from casual oral remarks recorded by the interviewers.

All translations from the Russian are by Brian Boyd and Anastasia Tolstoy, with suggestions by Stanislav Shvabrin, unless otherwise indicated. All other translations are by Brian Boyd.

Think, Write, Speak

1

Cambridge (Essay, 1921)[*]

There's a lovely saying: abroad, even the stars are tinny. Isn't that true? Nature may be beautiful overseas, but it is not ours, and we find it soulless and artificial. One needs to gaze at it persistently to begin to feel it and love it, whereas at first something of the greenhouse wafts from the unfamiliar trees, and all the birds seem as if on springs, and the sunset looks no better than a rather dry watercolor. So I felt when I rode into this provincial little English town, where, like a great soul in a small body, an ancient university lives its proud life. The gothic beauty of its numerous buildings (called colleges) stretches gracefully upward; gold clock-faces glow atop precipitous towers; through gaps in age-old gates decorated with stuccoed crests, rectangles of lawn gleam sunnily green; while opposite these very gates modern shopwindows have their multicolored displays, blasphemous as colored-pencil doodles sketched in the margins of a sacred book.

Back and forth along the narrow streets dart bicycles covered in mud, ringing their bells, motorcycles cackle, and, wherever you look, all around swarm the kings of Cambridge town—the students: their dress ties flicker like striped crossing barriers, their extraordinarily crumpled, sinuous trousers flicker in all shades of gray, from whitish and cloud-colored to wild dark-gray trousers wonderfully matching the color of the neighboring walls.

In the mornings, grabbing notebooks and regulation cloaks in a

---

[*] Vl. Sirin, "Kembridzh," *Rul'*, Oct. 28, 1921, 2. At the time of publication, VN was early in his third and final year at Cambridge. His family had moved to Berlin in 1920. There, late that year, his father, Vladimir Dmitrievich Nabokov, helped to found and edit the liberal daily *Rul'* to serve the hundreds of thousands of Russian émigrés settling in Germany. In Jan. 1921, VN had adopted the nom de plume "Vladimir Sirin" to distinguish his work from his father's, since they both published so often in *Rul'* and elsewhere in the émigré press.

heap, these doughty lads hurry to their lectures, making their way single file into the lecture halls, sleepily listen to the mumblings of a wise mummy on the rostrum, and, awakening suddenly, signal their approval through the pulsating stamping of their feet when, amid the dull flow of academic speech, a flash of wit splashes like a fish. After lunch, pulling on their lilac, green, and blue jackets, they fly off like crows in peacock feathers to the plush fields where balls will thwack until dusk; or to the river, which flows with Venetian languor past the gray and tawny walls and cast-iron lattices—and then Cambridge empties for a while. The burly policeman yawns, leaning against a lamppost, two old women in funny black hats prattle at the crossing, a shaggy dog snoozes in a rhombus of sunlight. . . . By five o'clock everything wakes up again, crowds throng to the tea shops, where toxically bright pastries glisten on every little table like fly-agaric mushrooms.

Sometimes I sit in a corner and look out on all of these smooth, no doubt very pleasant faces, but somehow always reminding me of a shaving soap advertisement, and then I suddenly become so bored, so weary, that I almost want to howl to break the windows. . . .

There's a kind of glass wall between them and us Russians. They have their own round and solid world, like a scrupulously colored-in globe. Their souls lack that inspired whirlwind, that throb, that radiance, that dancing frenzy, that anger and tenderness, which carries us, God knows, to what heavens and what abysses. We have moments when the clouds are on our shoulders, the sea knee-high—and our souls roam free! To an Englishman this is incomprehensible, novel, perhaps even alluring. If he does get drunk and riotous, his riotousness is banal and hearty, so that even the observers of order look at him and simply smile, knowing he will never cross a certain line. And on the other hand, not even the headiest drunkenness will make him flow with feeling, bare his chest, throw his hat on the ground. . . . At any time signs of frankness jar him. You might be speaking to a friend about this or that, about strikes and steeplechases, when you ingenuously blurt out that you feel you'd give every drop of blood to see again some bog near Petersburg—but to utter such thoughts is indecent; he'll look at you as if you'd whistled in church.

It turns out that in Cambridge there's a whole list of the simplest things that by tradition a student must not do. You shouldn't, for example, take a rowboat on the river—hire a punt or raft; you shouldn't wear a hat in the street—the city is ours after all, there's no need to stand on ceremony; you shouldn't shake people's hands, and God forbid you greet a professor—he'll only smile confusedly, mumble something, stumble. There is no shortage of these rules, and a newcomer will inevitably put his foot in it from time to time. If a wild foreigner nonetheless behaves in his own way, at first people will marvel at him—what an oddball, a barbarian—but then they will start to avoid him, to not recognize him on the street. Sometimes, it is true, a kind soul with a weakness for exotic creatures will come your way, but he will only approach you in a secluded spot, fearfully looking around him, and, having satisfied his curiosity, will disappear forever. This is why, at times, your heart swells with sorrow, feeling that it won't find a true friend here. And then everything seems dull: the eyeglasses of the nimble old woman whose room you rent, and the room itself, with its dirty-red sofa, gloomy fireplace, absurd little vases on their absurd little shelves, and the sounds rising from the street, the cry of the newspaper boys: Paypa! Paypa! . . .

But one can get used to anything, adapt, and learn to notice beauty in what's strange. Wandering on a smoky spring evening around the town, becalmed, you sense that there exists, beyond the speckle and bustle of our life, an altogether different life in Cambridge, the life of beguiling bygones. You know its large, gray eyes pensively and dispassionately look upon the caprices of a new generation, just as a hundred years ago they looked upon that limping, effeminate student Byron, and on his tamed bear, who remembered all too well his native pine forest and that cunning little peasant in fabled Muscovy.

Eight centuries have flown by: the Tatars swooped down like locusts; Ivan thundered; turmoil stirred across old Rus', like a portentous dream; and then new tsars rose up like golden mists; Peter toiled, hacked with abandon and emerged from the forest into the great wide world;—and here all the while these walls, these towers, stood immutable. And in just the same way, year in, year out, smooth-faced youths gathered to the chiming of the bells in the dining halls, where, just as today, rays of light would stream through the stained glass of the high windows, daubing the tiles with pale amethysts, and these youths would joke around in just the same way, except perhaps that their talk would be fierier, their beer headier. . . . I think about this, as I stroll along the hushed streets on a smoky spring evening. I come out onto the river. I stand for a long time on a little pearl-gray arched bridge, and not far off, another little bridge just like it forms a complete circle with its crisp, charming reflection. Weeping willows, old elms, festively luxuriant chestnut trees rise up here and there, as though embroidered in green silk on the canvas of a fading and tender sky. It smells faintly of lilacs and slimy water. . . . And now bells begin to chime through the whole city. . . . Round, silvery sounds, distant, near, drift by, intercrossing in the sky; and, having hung like a magic net above the crenellated towers for a few moments, they disperse, melt lingeringly, near, distant, into the narrow, misty lanes, into the beautiful night sky, into my heart. . . . And, gazing at the tranquil water, where subtle reflections bloom like designs on porcelain, I begin to think still more deeply, about much, about the whims of fate, about my homeland, and about the fact that my best memories grow older every day, and so far nothing can replace them. . . .

2

Rupert Brooke (Essay, 1921)[*]

I watched them; I admired them for a long time; barely flashing, they swam, swam tirelessly back and forth behind the glass barrier, in the haze of the still water, pale green, like slumber, like eternity, like the inner world of a blind man. They were huge, round, colorful: their porcelain scales seemed as if painted in bright colors by a meticulous Chinaman. I looked upon them as in a dream, spellbound by the mysterious music of their flowing, delicate movements. In between these gently shimmering giants darted multicolored fry—tiny specters, reminiscent of the softest butterflies, the most translucent dragonflies. And in the half-gloom of the aquarium, as I watched all these fantastical fish, gliding, breathing, staring wide-eyed into their pale-green eternity, I recalled the cool, meandering verses of the English poet who sensed in them, in these supple, iridescent fish, a profound symbol of our existence.

Rupert Brooke . . . This name is not yet known on the Continent, let alone in Russia. Rupert Brooke (1887–1915) is represented by two slim volumes, in which around eighty poems are collected. His work has a rare, captivating quality: a kind of radiant liquidity—not for nothing did he serve in the navy, not for nothing does his very name mean "brook" in English. This Tyutchev-like love for everything streaming, burbling, brightly chilled, is so strikingly, so convincingly expressed in most of his poems that you want not to read them, but, rather, to suck

---

[*] Vl. Sirin, "Rupert Bruk," *Literaturnyi al'manakh: Grani* (Berlin: Grani, 1922), 211–31. Holograph, VNA Berg, dated Sept. 1921, although VN wrote to his parents (May 11, 1921, VNA Berg) that he was sending an article to Alexander Glikberg (Sasha Chorny), the editor of *Grani*, who indeed published "Rupert Bruk" at the beginning of 1922. Apart from the essay "Cambridge," no other early essay by VN is known. Perhaps he began an essay on Brooke in May that took him all summer to finalize.

them up through a straw, to press them to your face like dewy flowers, to lower yourself into them as into the freshness of an azure lake. For Brooke, the world is a watery deep, "A fluctuant mutable world and dim, / Where wavering masses bulge and gape / Mysterious. . . . The strange soft-handed depth subdues / Drowned colour there, but black to hues, / As death to living, decomposes— / Red darkness of the heart of roses, / Blue brilliant from dead starless skies, / And gold that lies behind the eyes, / The unknown unnameable sightless white / That is the essential flame of night, / Lustreless purple, hooded green, / The myriad hues that lie between / Darkness and darkness."[1] And all of these colors breathe and stir, producing those scaly creatures that we call fish; and thus, through his subtly eerie poems, the poet conveys all the tremble of their lives.

> Fish (fly-replete, in depth of June,
> Dawdling away their wat'ry noon)
> Ponder deep wisdom, dark or clear,
> Each secret fishy hope or fear.
> Fish say, they have their Stream and Pond;
> But is there anything Beyond?
> This life cannot be All, they swear,
> For how unpleasant, if it were!
> One may not doubt that, somehow, Good
> Shall come of Water and of Mud;
> And, sure, the reverent eye must see
> A Purpose in Liquidity.
> We darkly know, by Faith we cry,
> The future is not Wholly Dry.
> Mud unto mud!—Death eddies near—
> Not here the appointed End, not here!
> But somewhere, beyond Space and Time,
> Is wetter water, slimier slime!
> And there (they trust) there swimmeth One
> Who swam ere rivers were begun,
> Immense, of fishy form and mind,
> Squamous, omnipotent, and kind;
> And under that Almighty Fin,

The littlest fish may enter in.
Oh! never fly conceals a hook,
Fish say, in the Eternal Brook,
But more than mundane weeds are there,
And mud, celestially fair;
Fat caterpillars drift around,
And Paradisal grubs are found;
Unfading moths, immortal flies,
And the worm that never dies.
And in that Heaven of all their wish,
There shall be no more land, say fish.[2]

In this poem, in this trembling drop of water, the essence of all earthly religions is reflected. And Brooke is himself a "dreaming fish" when, cast on a tropical island, he promises his Hawaiian sweetheart the perfection of a land beyond the clouds: "There the Eternals are, and there / The Good, the Lovely, and the True, / And Types, whose earthly copies were / The foolish broken things we knew; / There is the Face, whose ghosts we are; / The real, the never-setting Star; / And the Flower, of which we love / Faint and fading shadows here; / Never a tear, but only Grief; / Dance, but not the limbs that move; / Songs in Song shall disappear; / Instead of lovers, Love shall be. . . ."[3] But then, suddenly coming to, the poet exclaims: "How shall we wind these wreaths of ours, / Where there are neither heads nor flowers? / Oh, Heaven's Heaven!—but we'll be missing / The palms, and sunlight, and the south; / And there's an end, I think, of kissing, / When our mouths are one with Mouth. . . . / Hear the calling of the moon, / And the whispering scents that stray / About the idle warm lagoon. / Hasten, hand in human hand, / Down the dark, the flowered way, / Along the whiteness of the sand, / And in the water's soft caress, / Wash the mind of foolishness, / Mamua, until the day. / Spend the glittering moonlight there / Pursuing down the soundless deep / Limbs that gleam and shadowy hair, / Or floating lazy, half-asleep. / Dive and double and follow after, / Snare in flowers, and kiss, and call, / With lips that fade, and human laughter / And faces individual. . . ."

No other poet has so often, and with such heartrending and artistic acuity, looked into the twilight of the beyond. In trying to imagine it, he moves from one conception to the next with the fevered haste of a man looking for matches in a darkened room while someone knocks menacingly at his door. One minute it seems to him that, having died, he will wake up on a "long livid oozing plain / Closed down by the strange eyeless heavens" and see himself as "An unmeaning point upon the mud; a speck / Of moveless horror; an Immortal One / Cleansed of the world, sentient and dead; a fly / Fast-stuck in grey sweat on a corpse's neck,"[4] while in the next he foresees infinite bliss. That presentiment pulsates most ardently in his poem "Dust."

Here it is in its Russian translation:

> *Kogda, pogasnuv, kak zarnitsy,*
> *uydya ot dal'ney krasoty,*
> *vo mgle, v nochi svoey otdel'noy,*
> *istleyu ya, istleesh' ty. . . .* *

When the white flame in us is gone,
And we that lost the world's delight
Stiffen in darkness, left alone
To crumble in our separate night;

When your swift hair is quiet in death,
And through the lips corruption thrust
Has stilled the labour of my breath—
When we are dust, when we are dust!—

Not dead, not undesirous yet,
Still sentient, still unsatisfied,
We'll ride the air, and shine, and flit,
Around the places where we died,

---

* As those who know Russian will notice, VN was at this stage a very free translator. A literal prose version of his translation of this first quatrain would read: "When, extinguished, like summer lightning, / going away from distant beauty / into darkness, into our separate night, / I turn to ash, you turn to ash." He keeps rhyme (though, as here, usually only on lines 2 and 4) and adds his own sound harmonies, like, here, "*ot dal'ney . . . otdel'noy*" ("from distant . . . separate").

And dance as dust before the sun,
And light of foot, and unconfined,
Hurry from road to road, and run
About the errands of the wind.

And every mote, on earth or air,
Will speed and gleam, down later days,
And like a secret pilgrim fare
By eager and invisible ways,

Nor ever rest, nor ever lie,
Till, beyond thinking, out of view,
One mote of all the dust that's I
Shall meet one atom that was you.

Then in some garden hushed from wind,
Warm in a sunset's afterglow,
The lovers in the flowers will find
A sweet and strange unquiet grow

Upon the peace; and, past desiring,
So high a beauty in the air,
And such a light, and such a quiring,
And such a radiant ecstasy there,

They'll know not if it's fire, or dew,
Or out of earth, or in the height,
Singing, or flame, or scent, or hue,
Or two that pass, in light, to light,

Out of the garden, higher, higher. . . .
But in that instant they shall learn
The shattering ecstasy of our fire,
And the weak passionless hearts will burn

And faint in that amazing glow,
Until the darkness close above;

And they will know—poor fools, they'll know!—
One moment, what it is to love.[5]

Between these two extremes unwinds a string of more tranquil
images. Here, on the banks of Lethe, among mythic cypresses, the
poet encounters his dead mistress, and she, this carefree Laura, "toss[es
her] brown delightful head,"[6] so amused is she by the sight of the dead
ancients—a snub-nosed Socrates, a puny Caesar, an envious Petrarch.

Or else, having run up a blossoming hill, somewhere near Cambridge, Rupert, cheerfully panting, exclaims that his soul will be resur-
rected in the kisses of future lovers. At other times the clouds caress
his imagination:

> Down the blue night the unending columns press
>   In noiseless tumult, break and wave and flow,
>   Now tread the far South, or lift rounds of snow
> Up to the white moon's hidden loveliness.
> Some pause in their grave wandering comradeless,
>   And turn with profound gesture vague and slow,
>   As who would pray good for the world, but know
> Their benediction empty as they bless.
>
> They say that the Dead die not, but remain
>   Near to the rich heirs of their grief and mirth.
>   I think they ride the calm mid-heaven, as these,
> In wise majestic melancholy train,
>   And watch the moon, and the still-raging seas,
> And men, coming and going on the earth.[7]

This isn't far from a complete reconciliation with death, and indeed
the fourteenth year of our century inspired Brooke to write five colorful
sonnets, lit up, as if from within, by a wonderful humility:

> These hearts were woven of human joys and cares,
>   Washed marvellously with sorrow, swift to mirth.
> The years had given them kindness. Dawn was theirs,
>   And sunset, and the colours of the earth.

These had seen movement, and heard music; known
    Slumber and waking; loved; gone proudly friended;
Felt the quick stir of wonder; sat alone;
Touched flowers and furs and cheeks. All this is ended.

There are waters blown by changing winds to laughter
And lit by the rich skies, all day. And after,
    Frost, with a gesture, stays the waves that dance
And wandering loveliness. He leaves a white
Unbroken glory, a gathered radiance,
    A width, a shining peace, under the night.[8]

Here's another sonnet from the same series. Its rough copy is on display beneath glass in the British Museum, between a Dickens manuscript and Captain Scott's diary:

If I should die, think only this of me:
    That there's some corner of a foreign field
That is for ever England. There shall be
    In that rich earth a richer dust concealed;
A dust whom England bore, shaped, made aware,
    Gave, once, her flowers to love, her ways to roam,
A body of England's, breathing English air,
    Washed by the rivers, blest by suns of home.

And think, this heart, all evil shed away,
    A pulse in the eternal mind, no less
        Gives somewhere back the thoughts by England given;
Her sights and sounds; dreams happy as her day;
    And laughter, learnt of friends; and gentleness,
        In hearts at peace, under an English heaven.[9]

In these examples I wanted to show the diversity of those colored panes of glass through which, flitting from one to another, Brooke gazes into the distance, trying to discern the features of approaching death. It seems to me he is so persistently troubled not so much by the thought of what he will find there, as by the thought of what he will leave behind *here*. He loves the earth passionately. For him, earthly life is like first love, and even though he senses that other love affairs will follow, nothing for him will be able to replace the splashes of sun, the howls of the wind, the pricking of the rain, the glittering majesty and glittering agony of that first love—not the cold kisses of the heavenly stars, or the sadistic caresses of snoutless death, or the serenades of angels, or spectral beauties wandering over Lethe. The same idea glimmers in a short, very subtle poem about the Virgin Mary: the Archangel Gabriel disappears like a golden speck into the sky; Mary, for the first time, feels within Her body the beating of a second heart, a divine beating, separating Her from the world, illuminating Her with a celestial light, but . . . "The air was colder, and grey. . . ."[10] In that moment She has, most likely, understood that Her earthly life is over, that never again will She play or sing or pet little white goats, among the crocuses, under the olive trees.

I repeat: Rupert Brooke loves the world, and its lakes and waterfalls, with a passionate, penetrating, head-spinning love. He would like to smuggle it with him beneath his coattails at the hour of his death, and later, somewhere in some limit beyond the sun, to examine it in his idle hours, to palpate this imperishable treasure endlessly. Yet he knows that even if he finds an inexpressibly beautiful paradise, he will still be leaving behind his damp, living, brilliant earth forever. Sensing the end is nigh, he writes an inspired testament—he counts up his riches and hurriedly compiles a muddled list of all that he has loved on earth. And there is a lot he has loved: "White plates and cups, clean-gleaming, / Ringed with blue lines; and feathery, faery dust; / Wet roofs, beneath the lamp-light; the strong crust / Of friendly bread; and many-tasting food; / Rainbows; and the blue bitter smoke of wood; / And radiant raindrops couching in cool flowers; / And flowers themselves, that sway through sunny hours, / Dreaming of moths that drink them under the moon; / Then, the cool kindliness of sheets, that soon / Smooth away trouble; and the rough male kiss / Of blankets; grainy wood; live hair that is / Shining and free; blue-massing clouds; the keen / Unpassioned beauty of a great machine; / The benison of hot water; furs to touch; / The good smell of old clothes; and other such—/ The comfortable smell of friendly fingers, / Hair's fragrance, and the musty reek that lingers / About dead leaves and last year's ferns; [. . .] / Sweet water's dimpling laugh from tap or spring; / Holes in the ground; and voices that do sing; / Voices in laughter, too; and body's pain, / Soon turned

to peace; and the deep-panting train; / Firm sands; the little dulling
edge of foam / That browns and dwindles as the wave goes home; / And
washen stones, gay for an hour; [. . .] / Sleep; and high places; footprints
in the dew; / And oaks; and brown horse-chestnuts, glossy-new; / And
new-peeled sticks; and shining pools on grass . . ."[11]

And here Brooke finds momentary solace in the thought of glory:
"My night," he says, "shall be remembered for a star / That outshone all
the suns of all men's days. / Shall I not crown them with immortal praise
/ Whom I have loved, who have given me, dared with me / High secrets,
and in darkness knelt to see / The inenarrable godhead of delight?"[12]

And having once more forgotten that "The laugh dies with the lips,
'Love' with the lover,"[13] the poet in his quivering iambs merges life and
death into a single fervent rapture:

> Out of the nothingness of sleep,
>   The slow dreams of Eternity,
> There was a thunder on the deep:
>   I came, because you called to me.
>
> I broke the Night's primeval bars,
>   I dared the old abysmal curse,
> And flashed through ranks of frightened stars
>   Suddenly on the universe!
>
> The eternal silences were broken;
>   Hell became Heaven as I passed.—
> What shall I give you as a token,
>   A sign that we have met, at last?
>
> I'll break and forge the stars anew,
>   Shatter the heavens with a song;
> Immortal in my love for you,
>   Because I love you, very strong.
>
> Your mouth shall mock the old and wise,
>   Your laugh shall fill the world with flame,
> I'll write upon the shrinking skies
>   The scarlet splendour of your name,

Till Heaven cracks, and Hell thereunder
  Dies in her ultimate mad fire,
And darkness falls, with scornful thunder,
  On dreams of men and men's desire.

Then only in the empty spaces,
  Death, walking very silently,
Shall fear the glory of our faces
  Through all the dark infinity.

So, clothed about with perfect love,
  The eternal end shall find us one,
Alone above the Night, above
  The dust of the dead gods, alone.[14]

But for Brooke, woman does not always appear as the eternal companion, the guarantor of immortality. Just as in his poems dedicated to the "great Maybe,"[15] Brooke in his depictions of women and of love is unstable, changeable, like the beam of a torch which lights in passing here a puddle, there a blooming bush. He shifts from the divine madness that inspired "Dust" and "The Call" to some kind of anguished sketches, drawing "unsatisfied / Sprawling desires . . . / Fantastic shape to mazed fantastic shape, / Straggling, irregular, perplexed, embossed, / Grotesquely twined, extravagantly lost / By crescive paths and strange protuberant ways."[16]

Brooke can just about reconcile himself to the "fantastical" human body when that body is young, headstrong, pure, but the poet recoils in anger and disgust from feeble old age, with its toothless, slobbering mouth, its red eyelids, its late lasciviousness. . . . And the prehistoric device of juxtaposing spring and decay, dreams and reality, roses and thistles, is renewed by Brooke unusually subtly.

The following two sonnets can serve as an example:

Hot through Troy's ruin Menelaus broke
  To Priam's palace, sword in hand, to sate
  On that adulterous whore a ten years' hate
And a king's honour. Through red death, and smoke,
And cries, and then by quieter ways he strode,

Till the still innermost chamber fronted him.
He swung his sword, and crashed into the dim
Luxurious bower, flaming like a god.

High sat white Helen, lonely and serene.
He had not remembered that she was so fair,
And that her neck curved down in such a way;
And he felt tired. He flung the sword away,
And kissed her feet, and knelt before her there,
The perfect Knight before the perfect Queen.

So far the poet. How should he behold
That journey home, the long connubial years?
He does not tell you how white Helen bears
Child on legitimate child, becomes a scold,
Haggard with virtue. Menelaus bold
Waxed garrulous, and sacked a hundred Troys
'Twixt noon and supper. And her golden voice
Got shrill as he grew deafer. And both were old.

Often he wonders why on earth he went
Troyward, or why poor Paris ever came.
Oft she weeps, gummy-eyed and impotent;
Her dry shanks twitch at Paris' mumbled name.
So Menelaus nagged; and Helen cried;
And Paris slept on by Scamander side.[17]

This disgust with decrepitude reveals itself even more strongly in the poem "Jealousy," addressed, probably, to a young bride. In it, the poet is so carried away with his depiction of the future aging of the rosy, dashing husband, whom he already sees as bald, and fat, and dirty, and God knows what else, that only in the thirty-third—the final—line does he suddenly realize: "Oh, when that time comes, you'll be dirty too!"[18]

It seems to me that both in this poem, and in that other one, dedicated to a remarkably detailed and rather disgusting examination of seasickness, whose manifestations are here directly compared to memories of love,[19] Brooke slightly flaunts his ability to clasp and snatch up, like a spillikin, any image, any feeling; to slightly blacken the underside of love, just as he blackened (in his poem about the "fly / Fast-stuck in grey sweat on a corpse's neck," mentioned above) the view of a region beyond the grave. He knows perfectly well that death is only a surprise; he is the singer of eternal life, tenderness, woodland shades, clear streams, sweet smells; he ought not to compare the searing pain of parting to heartburn and belching.

After all Brooke was not happy in love. It is telling that he can imagine a completely cloudless blissfulness with a woman only by transporting both himself and her beyond the limit of earthly life. Loving infinitely the beauty of the world, he frequently feels that clumsy, disorderly passion disturbs with its prosaic tread earth's chiaroscuro and soft sounds. He expresses the incursion of this goose's prose into the garden of poetry in the following way:

> Safe in the magic of my woods
>   I lay, and watched the dying light.
> Faint in the pale high solitudes,
>   And washed with rain and veiled by night,
>
> Silver and blue and green were showing.
>   And the dark woods grew darker still;
> And birds were hushed; and peace was growing;
>   And quietness crept up the hill;
>
> And no wind was blowing . . .
>
> And I knew
> That this was the hour of knowing,
> And the night and the woods and you
> Were one together, and I should find
> Soon in the silence the hidden key
> Of all that had hurt and puzzled me—
> Why you were you, and the night was kind,
> And the woods were part of the heart of me.
>
> And there I waited breathlessly,
> Alone; and slowly the holy three,

The three that I loved, together grew
One, in the hour of knowing,
Night, and the woods, and you——

And suddenly
There was an uproar in my woods,

The noise of a fool in mock distress,
Crashing and laughing and blindly going,
Of ignorant feet and a swishing dress,
And a Voice profaning the solitudes.

The spell was broken, the key denied me
And at length your flat clear voice beside me
Mouthed cheerful clear flat platitudes.

You came and quacked beside me in the wood.
You said, "The view from here is very good!"
You said, "It's nice to be alone a bit!"
And, "How the days are drawing out!" you said.
You said, "The sunset's pretty, isn't it?

. . . .

By God! I wish—I wish that you were dead![20]

Or else the poet complains that his beloved does not understand him:
he asks her to be meek—she kisses him on the lips; he asks for earth-
shattering ecstasies—she kisses him on the forehead. He himself con-
fesses that he belongs to those who are "wanderers in the middle mist,
/ Who cry for shadows, clutch, and cannot tell / Whether they love at
all, or, loving, whom: / An old song's lady, a fool in fancy dress, / Or
phantoms, or their own face on the gloom."[21] And one of these specters
appears to him once:

I came back late and tired last night
  Into my little room,

To the long chair and the firelight
  And comfortable gloom.

But as I entered softly in
  I saw a woman there,
The line of neck and cheek and chin,
  The darkness of her hair,
The form of one I did not know
  Sitting in my chair.

I stood a moment fierce and still,
  Watching her neck and hair.
I made a step to her; and saw
  That there was no one there.

It was some trick of the firelight
  That made me see her there.
It was a chance of shade and light
  And the cushion in the chair.

Oh, all you happy over the earth,
  That night, how could I sleep?
I lay and watched the lonely gloom;
  And watched the moonlight creep
From wall to basin, round the room.
  All night I could not sleep.[22]

At other times, however, Brooke feels as though his own body hinders him from loving, and in beautiful lines he depicts that strange, sudden coldness which once made a Venetian woman feel so offended by bashful Rousseau.[23] He could savour unbridled happiness, if only woman were a blossoming tree, a sparkling stream, a wind, a bird. But as soon as the person obscures the goddess in her, as soon as the shriek of a cheap violin disturbs the silence of the radiant night, Brooke suffers, is tormented, and curses this agonizing dissonance. And the effect of all his strivings, downfalls, disillusionments, and failures in love is a feeling, not just of a personal, but of a cosmic loneliness, though one which he feels only in the godforsaken hours of insomnia when the captivating visible world is shrouded in dusk.

> The stars, a jolly company,
>   I envied, straying late and lonely;
> And cried upon their revelry:
>   "O white companionship! You only
> In love, in faith unbroken dwell,
> Friends radiant and inseparable!"
>
> Light-heart and glad they seemed to me
>   And merry comrades (*even so*
> *God out of Heaven may laugh to see*
> *The happy crowds; and never know*
> *That in his lone obscure distress*
> *Each walketh in a wilderness*).
>
> But I, remembering, pitied well
>   And loved them, who, with lonely light,
> In empty infinite spaces dwell,
>   Disconsolate. For, all the night,
> I heard the thin gnat-voices cry,
> Star to faint star, across the sky.[24]

We should remark, by the way, that Brooke likes to depict God with a beard, in a cloak, upon a golden throne (just as fish are represented as some kind of scaly, tailed Jupiter, swimming in the Heavenly Creek). But here's what happened once:

> Because God put His adamantine fate
>   Between my sullen heart and its desire,
> I swore that I would burst the Iron Gate,
>   Rise up, and curse Him on His throne of fire.
> Earth shuddered at my crown of blasphemy,
>   But Love was as a flame about my feet;
>   Proud up the Golden Stair I strode; and beat
> Thrice on the Gate, and entered with a cry—

All the great courts were quiet in the sun,
  And full of vacant echoes: moss had grown
Over the glassy pavement, and begun
  To creep within the dusty council-halls.
An idle wind blew round an empty throne
And stirred the heavy curtains on the walls.[25]

The meaning of this sonnet is not entirely clear: has earthly love vanquished and overthrown God, or did the poet wish to express the thought that the external God of Sabaoth is inextricably linked with the God "within us," and therefore disappears as soon as man begins to deny him, or is the meaning that God is simply dead and has long ceased ruling the world? Equally dark is the symbol in another poem, similar in spirit to the sonnet above:

Slowly up silent peaks, the white edge of the world,
  Trod four archangels, clear against the unheeding sky,
Bearing, with quiet even steps, and great wings furled,
  A little dingy coffin; where a child must lie,
It was so tiny. (Yet, you had fancied, God could never
  Have bidden a child turn from the spring and the sunlight,
And shut him in that lonely shell, to drop for ever
  Into the emptiness and silence, into the night. . . .)

They then from the sheer summit cast, and watched it fall,
  Through unknown glooms, that frail black coffin—and therein
  God's little pitiful Body lying, worn and thin,
And curled up like some crumpled, lonely flower-petal—
Till it was no more visible; then turned again
With sorrowful quiet faces downward to the plain.[26]

Both of these poems belong to the poet's earliest works (they were written in 1906), and even though they are picturesque and majestic in themselves, they are scarcely distinctive of Brooke. He so keenly senses the divine in surrounding nature,—to what end, then, does he need this prop-room eternity, these Vrubelesque angels,[27] this potentate with a cottonwool beard? Let fireflies believe in electrical beacons, dragonflies in the Antoinette monoplane, flowers in the gigantic *Victoria regia*,[28] moles in a blind, velvety monster; let the good folk in some little provincial town snuffle, and mumble, and blow their noses into huge checkered handkerchiefs, as they crowd around the body of a dead girl, the fleeting lover of a wandering poet—"They will put pence on your grey eyes, / Bind up your fallen chin," "and their thoughts will creep / Like flies on the cold flesh" . . . but "I," says the poet, "I shall not hear your trentals, / Nor eat your arval bread"[29]—and from the stifling little white town he walks to the top of a hill, full of exultant recollections, and there, alone among the stars and the wind, he keeps her Ambarvalia.[30] Now he is happy: his beloved has become one with the eternal, hundred-colored, hundred-sounding nature that he so fervently loves. But, then, even in his love of nature, Rupert Brooke is capriciously narrow, as are all poets of all times.

Kipling writes somewhere: "God gave all men all earth to love, / But, since our hearts are small, / Ordained for each one spot should prove / Beloved over all."[31] So Pushkin loved "two rowans before a small isba,"[32] and Lermontov "twin birches gleaming white."[33] And Rupert Brooke, in talking of his love for the earth, secretly has only England in mind, and not even all of England, but only the little town of Grantchester, a magical little town. Sitting in Berlin's Café des Westens on a stifling summer's day, Brooke rapturously recalls that hazily green, that shadily cool river flowing past Grantchester.[34] And he speaks of it with exactly the same expressions he used to speak of a fragrant Hawaiian lagoon, for that lagoon was in essence the very same dear, narrow little river, bordered by willows and hedges, whence here and there "an English unofficial rose" peers out. In a sequence of untranslatable, burbling lines, he forces a hundred spectral Vicars to dance on the fields in the moonlight; fawns furtively peep through the greenery; a Naiad swims up, her head crowned in reeds; Pan quietly pipes. With deep tenderness the poet sings praise to his little fairy-tale town, inhabited by people clean in body and soul, and so wise, so refined, that they shoot themselves as soon as dull old age approaches. . . .

I once rode through Grantchester on my bicycle. The fences, the complicated iron gates, the barbed wire in the surrounding fields all tormented the eye. The dirty little brick houses all reeked of resigned boredom. A tomfool wind whirled up a pair of underpants hung up to dry between two green stakes, above a wretched vegetable patch. From the river came a little tenor on a crackly gramophone.

I have tried to give the general outline of Rupert Brooke's poetic persona. Death, which he had been so intently watching for, caught him unawares in the violet Aegean Sea, on a calm, sunny day. He did not live a long life, and the motley nature of his moods arises partly from the fact that he somehow did not quite have time to sift all his riches, did not quite have time in his life to fuse all the world's colors into a single color, a radiant whiteness. And yet, it is not difficult to discern the main characteristic of his art—his passionate service to pure beauty. . . .

3

Laughter and Dreams (Essay, 1923)[*]

Art is a permanent wonder, a wizard with a trick of putting two and two together and making five, or a million, or one of those gorgeous giant numbers which haunt and dazzle the delirious mind writhing through a mathematical nightmare. Art snatches at the simple things of the world and twists them into wonderful shapes, drenches them in color, making Madonnas out of Florentine flower-girls and transforming into great symphonies the tiny sounds of birds and brooks. Commonplace words, our petty dreams and worries, become magic on the stage when Art, the whimsical wizard, touches with rouge the lips of life. For Art knows there is nothing so plain or absurd, or ugly, that cannot in a certain light swell into beauty, and Russian Art among all others has been especially successful at proving this.

When I say so I am not referring to writers such as Gogol, that genius of the grotesque who would find the secret of sublime comedy in the mud pool of a dismal little town or in the bloated features of a provincial clerk; neither am I thinking of Dostoevsky's dark wanderings through the realms of the distorted and the mad. It is of a certain byway of the stage that I wish to speak.

The Russian soul is endowed with the power of breathing its own life into those various forms of Art, which it finds in other nations; so it happened that the French "cabaret" (a rendez-vous of poets, actors and artists), without losing anything of its lightness and brilliancy, acquired in Russia a distinct national flavor. Folklore, songs and toys were magically recalled to a new life, producing the effect of those

[*] Vladimir V. Nabokoff, "Laughter and Dreams," *Karussel/Carousal/Carrousel* 2 (1923), 4–6; also in *Carrousel: Three Texts by Vladimir Nabokov* (Aartswould: Spectatorpers, 1987), 9–15. *Karussel* was published by the Berlin Russian cabaret Karussel, which had opened in 1922.

lacquered curves and patches of rich color which are associated in my mind with the first blue days of a Russian spring.

Well do I remember those days,—and that merry fair, the "Verba," a living symbol of earth's quivering gladness.[1] Wet bunches of fluffy, pearl-gray catkins cut from the countryside sallows have been brought to town and are being sold on the boulevard along which stretches a double row of wooden stands put up for the occasion. Between these circulates an endless flow of buyers and the glossy purple mud under their feet is all speckled over with spilled confetti. Aproned hawkers cry out their wares—tiny cotton devils pricked onto a cardboard shield, and red elongated balloons blowing out with a particular squeak, and glass tubes filled with colored alcohol in which dances a bottle-green imp when an india-rubber membrane is pressed at the bottom. And on the stands, under the drip-drip of the brown birch trees glistening in the March sun, other wares are displayed,—cream wafers and Eastern Delight, goldfish and canaries, artificial chrysanthemums, stuffed squirrels, gaudily embroidered shirts, sashes and kerchiefs, harmonicas and balalaïcas,—and toys, toys, toys. Among those my favorite was a set of a dozen round wooden "babas" (peasant women) each one a shade smaller than the next and hollow inside, so that they fitted one into another.

Much did I love too a toy consisting of two carved wooden figures, that of a bear and that of a peasant. These two could be made to hit by turns a wooden anvil in the middle. And there were also queer brightly painted round-bellied little dolls loaded with lead so that no force on earth could make them lie quietly on one side,—they would always turn up straight again with a brisk oscillating movement. . . . And over all this rolls the glossy blue sky, and wet roofs glisten like mirrors, and the golden ding-dong of the church bells mingles with the shrill cries of the fair. . . .

This world of toys, color and laughter—or better to say the condensed impression of that world—has been magically revived on the stage of the Russian "cabarets." I have spoken of the "Verba" only to show what I mean by the romance of Russian folklore expressed in bright smooth wooden toys. These toys have been made to live and dance on the stage. Art has disclosed the very soul of their shining hues. But this is not all. There is yet another deep beauty, another enchantment in the inmost self of Russia. And the "cabaret" being essentially an artistic variety, an expression of different moods, of laughter and dreams, of sunshine and dusk,—this other kind of beauty has likewise been rendered by art. For if Russian headgears and cupolas are marvelously bright-colored there is another side of the Russian soul which has been expressed by Levitan in painting and by Pushkin (and others) in poetry. It is that misty sorrowful sway of national songs, "the tenderest on earth"—as an English poet put it. They ring, those songs, along lonely roads and at sunset on the banks of great rivers. And then there is the strange charm of the pale northern night gliding ghostlike through a dream-city. And perhaps deeper than anything else in the mystical intensity of its passion—there is the melody of gypsy love.

Thus the spectator is made to laugh and dream alternatively. Wooden soldiers, ruddy-faced dolls, moujiks looking like bearded samovars pass and dance before his eyes, and, then, pale-faced Romance sweeps by singing of sleepless nights and distant lands.

And what is life itself—if not another "cabaret" where tears and smile are weaved into one wonderful many-colored tissue?

4

Painted Wood (Essay, 1923)[*]

Japanese butterflies, those splendid tailed creatures with splashes and ripples of color on their delicately veined wings, always seem to have fluttered off Japanese fans or screens, just as the dove-gray volcano of that country looks as if it was acutely aware of its penciled image. And there is something in the fat little bronze idols, in their placid curves and eastern chubbiness, that makes one think of those round staring fishes that dream in a rainbow-haze—gleaming ghosts of a tropical sea. Thus, art and nature mingle together in such a wonderful way that it is difficult to say for instance whether sunsets made Claude Lorrain, or Claude Lorrain made sunsets. What strikes me too, is the connection between wooden Russian toys and the bright damp mushrooms and berries found in such profusion in the dark rich depths of northern forests. I seem to see the Russian peasant unconsciously drinking in their purple, blue, scarlet hues and remembering them afterward when carving and painting a plaything for his child.

I have read somewhere that several centuries ago there was a glorious variety of the pheasant haunting Russian woods: it remained as the "fire bird" in national fairy tales and lent something of its brightness to the intricate roof decorations of village cottages. This wonderbird made such an impression on the people's imagination that its golden flutter became the very soul of Russian art; mysticism transformed seraphim into long-tailed, ruby-eyed birds, with golden claws and unimaginable wings; and no other nation on earth is so much in love with peacock feathers and weathercocks.

Cranberries, red mushrooms and an extinct pheasant combined to

---

[*] V. Cantaboff, "Painted Wood," *Karussel* 2 (1923), 9–10; also in *Carrousel: Three Texts by Vladimir Nabokov* (Aartswould: Spectatorpers, 1987), 19–24. See n. on "Laughter and Dreams."

produce a most cheerful kind of art. In its beginning it had possibly a trace of genius in it, just as there is genius in the exquisite animal-pictures left by a prehistoric artist on the walls of his cavern—a cavern discovered in the southern part of France. And compare those leaping stags and red-haired buffaloes delicately painted in ochre, black and vermilion—compare them with the banal animals in modern picture-books! That subspecies of *Homo sapiens* knew how to make his family happy.

The same thing occurred in the case of national Russian art. Year after year, through long generations the moujik carved and painted dolls, boxes, cups and a hundred other things till at last the primordial image that laughed and sparkled in his brain grew dim and distant, because he found needless to keep his inspiration glowing, when he had only to copy the work of his predecessors. So life went out of this art, leaving behind only curves and angles of brightly painted wood. It became somewhat "bad taste" to decorate houses in the national style, in the "cock-style" as people would call it—with a contemptuous sniff. Russian attire—embroidered kerchiefs, sashes, high boots, bead neck-laces and so on—were just laughed at. Russian children preferred teddy bears and golliwogs and clockwork trains to the painted stare of silly little wooden toys; and no one would dream of keeping his cigarettes or her needlework in one of those lacquered boxes (with the picture of a troika on it) for which an Englishman would gladly pay several pounds: yes, that was the curious thing about it.

And then, all of a sudden, there blew a marvelous wind, a merry, invigorating wind, that made the sunshine leap, and that tossed up dry leaves, making them look like little bright birds. . . . Wooden toys and the dead heroes of Russian songs woke up, stretched themselves and lo! here they are again, laughing and dancing, glossy-new. A man walking along the street in some great stone-gray town, would suddenly come across the name of their new home—"Russian Theatre-Cabaret." And if he entered, there he would be, gaping at the whirling wonders of a foreign art. Wonders to him, not to us. We have grown a little tired of our playthings, they do not personify our true idea of Russia. We wink at each other behind the curtains, while the foreigner is taking in the delightful lie. Art is always a little slyish and Russian art particularly so.

Taking everything in consideration it is not very strange that people of other countries are so attracted by our wooden dolls coming to life on the stage. Parisian "Cabarets" could produce long-haired poets in velvet jackets droning beautiful verses about cats, parrots and tropical lands, Italy would be more given to serenades and concetti, Germany has its bursts of gruff, simple humor—but the Russian "Cabaret" alone is endowed with the power of making the wildest dreams come true, of disclosing bewildering vistas full of dancing grotesque figures.

5

On Poetry (Review Excerpt, 1924)[*]

...After the robust wild tastelessness of Ilya Britan it is somehow strange to move to the nervous and dryish Lev Gordon. But if the banality of the former wins the reader over by its frankness, the hidden banality of the latter provokes a certain irritation. Here's why. There is a splendid poet called Mandelshtam. His work is not a new stage of Russian poetry: it's only an elegant variant, one branch of poetry at a given moment in its development, when it has extended many such branches to left and to right, while its growth at the top has been almost imperceptible after the first fresh spurt of the Symbolists.[1] In this sense, Mandelshtam is important only for his individual pattern. He sustains, he adorns poetry, but he does not advance. He is a charming dead end. To imitate him is to fall into a certain kind of plagiarism. The rather dull Tsekh poets[2] partly imitate him. And Lev Gordon imitates him *and* the rather dull Tsekh poets.

Mandelshtam's image, his cool refinement, is expressed in his special, almost glassy, poems, in his tenderness toward material trifles, in his sense of weight and weightiness: thus, adjectives expressing lightness or heaviness almost completely crowd out the sensory adjectives predominant in other poets. Hence his poetry's coldness, its arrowlike harmony, in which the most tender earthly words, such as a "swallow" or the names of goddesses, turn into the sound of a needle falling onto a bed of crystal. Lev Gordon's banality consists in his imitating this. In Mandelshtam, the heaviness creates a feeling of pressure and airlessness, and the lightness, a feeling of faint nausea and dizziness. And here in

[*] V. Sirin, "O poezii," review of poetry books by Dmitri Shakhovskoy, *Pesnya bez slov* (*Song Without Words*, 1924), Ilya Britan, *Raznotsvet* (*Variegation*, 1924), and Lev Gordon, *Ottepel'* (*Thaw*, 1924). Apparently unpublished. Corrected holograph manuscript, VNA Berg.

Gordon we read lines like these, which we have read somewhere long ago, if not in Mandelshtam, then in the Tsekh poets: "the smoke of the cheap, light cigarette, headier than wine, makes my head spin." A little further on and we find the familiar swallow: "swallowlike summer traverses the translucent, brooding distances . . . ," or this image (not bad at all): "and my glass spheres dance in a sonorous semicircle." In passing, Gordon advises the poet to be a "smith of the golden word" or in other words to write a sonnet correctly, as he does himself: "honoring one's vow." But he honors it badly—it is impossible to rhyme *slóva* ("of a word") and *okovy* ("shackles") in a sonnet, just as it is unacceptable to omit a supporting consonant in "impoverished" masculine rhymes.[3]

6

Play (Breitensträter–Paolino)
(Essay, 1925)[*]

Everything in the world plays: the blood in a lover's veins, the sun on water, and a musician on a violin.

Everything good in life—love, nature, the arts, and homespun puns—is play. And when we actually play—whether we're knocking down a tin battalion with a pea or meeting over the barrier of a tennis net—what we feel in our very muscles is the essence of the play engaged in by the marvelous juggler who tosses from hand to hand, in an unbroken sparkling parabola, the planets of the universe.

People have played as long as they have existed. There are eras—humanity's holidays—when people particularly take to games. So it was in bygone Greece, in bygone Rome, and so it is in the Europe of our own day.

A child well knows that in order to play to his heart's content he must play with someone else or at least imagine somebody, he must become two. Or, to put it another way, there is no play without competition; which is why some kinds of play, such as those gymnastic festivals in which fifty-odd men or women, moving as one, form patterns across a parade ground, seem insipid, since they lack the main thing which gives play its ravishing, thrilling charm. That's why the communist system is so ridiculous, since it condemns everyone to performing the same tedious drills, not allowing that anyone should be fitter than his neighbor.

---

[*] "Braytenshtreter–Paolino," *Slovo* (Riga), Dec. 28–29, 1925. Holograph, VNA Berg, entitled "Igra" ("Play"), dated Oct. 3, 1925. *Slovo* text discovered and republished by Boris Ravdin, "Braytenshtreter–Paolino," *Daugava* (Riga) 3 (1993), 166–69; he notes that the *Slovo* version is probably the reprint of a Berlin émigré publication. Translated by Anastasia Tolstoy and Thomas Karshan as "Breitensträter–Paolino," *Times Literary Supplement*, Aug. 3, 2012, 14–15; translation revised by Brian Boyd.

Not for nothing did Nelson say that the Battle of Trafalgar was won on the football and tennis grounds of Eton.[1] And the Germans, too, have lately realized that the goose step won't take you far, and that boxing, football, and hockey are more valuable than military or any other drills. Boxing is especially valuable, and there are few sights healthier or finer than a boxing match. A highly strung gent, who dislikes washing stark naked in the mornings and inclines to surprise that a poet working for two and a half connoisseurs earns less money than a boxer who works for a crowd of many thousands (a crowd which, by the way, has nothing in common with the so-called masses and is filled with a delight far more pure, sincere, and good-natured than that of the crowd welcoming home its civic heroes), this highly strung gent will feel indignation and disgust toward a fistfight, just as in Rome, probably, there were people who frowned at the sight of two huge gladiators demonstrating the very best in the gladiatorial arts, slugging each other with such iron blows that not even the *pollice verso*[2] was necessary, they'd finish each other off anyway.

What matters, of course, is not at all that a heavyweight boxer is a little bloodied after two or three rounds or that the white waistcoat of the referee looks as though red ink has leaked out of a fountain pen. What matters is, first, the beauty of the very art of boxing, the perfect accuracy of the attacks, the side jumps, the dives, the range of blows—hooks, straights, haymakers—and, second, that fine manly excitement this art arouses. Many writers have depicted the beauty and the romance of boxing. Bernard Shaw has a whole novel about a professional boxer.[3] Jack London,[4] Conan Doyle,[5] and Kuprin[6] have all written on the subject. Byron, that darling of all Europe, except exacting England, eagerly befriended boxers and loved to watch their fights, just as Pushkin and Lermontov would have loved it, had they lived in England. Portraits have survived of the professional boxers of the eighteenth and nineteenth centuries. The famous Figg, Corbett, Cribb[7] fought without gloves and fought skillfully, honorably, tenaciously, more often to utter exhaustion than to a knockout.

And it was not at all the commonplace of humaneness that led to the appearance of boxing gloves in the middle of last century, but, rather, a desire to protect the fist, which could otherwise be too easily broken in the course of a two-hour bout. They have all long since stepped down

from the ring, those famous, champion pugilists, having won their sup-
porters quite a few pounds sterling, and lived to a ripe old age, and in
the evenings, in taverns, over a pint of beer, they would talk with pride
of their former exploits. They were followed by others, the teachers of
today's boxers: the massive Sullivan, Burns, with his looks of a London
dandy, and Jeffries,[8] the son of a blacksmith, "the white hope," as they
called him, a hint that black boxers were already becoming unbeatable.

Those who had hoped that Jeffries would beat the black giant
Johnson[9] lost their money. The two races followed this fight closely.
But despite the furious enmity between the white and black camps (the
event took place in America twenty-five or more years ago),[10] not a
single boxing rule was broken, even though Jeffries, with every one of
his blows, kept repeating, "Yellow dog . . . yellow dog." Finally, after a
long, splendid fight, the enormous Negro struck his opponent so hard
that Jeffries flew backward from the ring, over the surrounding ropes,
and, as they say, "fell asleep."

Poor Johnson! He rested on his laurels, gained weight, married a
beautiful white woman, began appearing as a living advertisement on
the music-hall stage, and then, apparently, ended up in jail, and only
briefly did his black face and white smile flash out from the illustrated
magazines.

I was lucky enough to see Smith, and Bombardier Wells, and Goddard, and Wilde, and Beckett, and the wonderful Carpentier, who beat
Beckett.[11] That fight, which paid the winner five thousand, and the
runner-up three thousand pounds, lasted exactly fifty-six seconds,[12] so
that someone who had paid twenty pounds for his seat had only enough
time to light a cigarette, and when he looked up at the ring, Beckett
was already lying on the boards in the touching pose of a sleeping baby.

I hasten to add that in such a blow, which brings on an instantaneous
blackout, there is nothing terrible. On the contrary. I have experienced
it myself, and can attest that such a sleep is rather pleasant. At the very
tip of the chin there is a bone, like the one in the elbow which in English is called "the funny bone," and in German "the musical bone."
As everyone knows, if you hit the corner of your elbow hard, you immediately feel a faint ringing in the hand and a momentary numbing
of the muscles. The same thing happens if you are hit very hard on the
end of the chin.

There is no pain. Only the peal of a faint ringing and then pleasant instantaneous sleep (the so-called knockout), lasting from ten seconds to half an hour. A blow to the solar plexus is less pleasant, but a good boxer knows just how to tense his abdomen so that he won't flinch even if a horse kicks him in the pit of the stomach.

I saw Carpentier this week, on Tuesday evening. He was there as trainer to the heavyweight Paolino,[13] and the spectators seemed not to recognize immediately, in that modest, fair-haired young man, a recent world champion. His fame has faded now. They say that after his fearsome fight with Dempsey he sobbed like a woman.

Paolino appeared in the ring first and sat down, as is customary, on a stool in the corner. Huge, with a square dark head, and wearing a magnificent robe down to his heels, this Basque resembled an Oriental idol. Only the ring itself was lit, and in the white cone of light falling on him from above, the platform looked like silver. This silvered cube, amid a gigantic dark oval, where the dense rows of countless human faces called to mind kernels of ripe corn strewn against a black background— this silvered cube seemed lit up not by electricity, but by the concentrated force of all the gazes fixed on it out of the darkness. And when the Basque's opponent, the German champion Breitensträter,[14] stepped onto the bright platform, fair-haired, in a mouse-colored robe (and for some reason in gray trousers, which he immediately began to pull off), the enormous darkness trembled with a joyful roar. The roar did not die down when the photographers, jumping onto the edge of the platform, pointed their "monkey-boxes" (as my German neighbor called them) at the fighters, at the referee, at the seconds, nor when the champions "pulled on their boxing gloves" (which reminds me of "the young *oprichnik* and the valiant merchant").[15] And when both opponents threw off their robes (and not "velvety furs") from their mighty shoulders and rushed toward each other in the white gleam of the ring, a slight moan went through the dark abyss, through the rows of corn kernels and the misty upper tiers, for everyone saw how much bigger and stockier the Basque was than their favorite.

Breitensträter attacked first, and the moan turned into a rumble of delight. But Paolino, hunching his head into his shoulders, answered him with short uppercuts, and from almost the first minute the German's face glistened with blood.

With every blow that Breitensträter took, my neighbor took in air with a whistle, as if he himself were taking the blows, and all the darkness, all the tiers croaked a kind of enormous supernatural croak. By the third round it became noticeable that the German had weakened, that his punches could not push off the hunched orange hill moving toward him. But he fought with extraordinary courage, trying to make up with his speed for the fifteen pounds by which the Basque outweighed him.

Around the luminous cube, across which the boxers danced with the referee twisting between them, the black darkness froze, and in the silence the glove, shiny with sweat, smacked juicily on the live naked body. At the start of the seventh round Breitensträter fell, but after five or six seconds, jerking forward like a horse on black ice, he stood up. The Basque fell upon him immediately, knowing that in such situations you must act decisively and swiftly, put all your strength into your punches, for sometimes a blow that is stinging but not firm will, instead of finishing off your weakened opponent, enliven him, wake him up. The German bent away, clinging to the Basque, trying to win time, to make it to the end of the round. And when once more he went down, the gong did in fact save him: on the eighth count, he got up with great difficulty, and dragged himself to his stool. By some sort of miracle he had survived the eighth round, to mounting peals of applause. But at the start of the ninth round Paolino, striking him beneath the jaw, hit him just the way he wanted. Breitensträter collapsed. The darkness roared furiously, chaotically. Breitensträter lay twisted like a pretzel. The referee counted down the fateful seconds. He kept lying there.[16]

So the match ended, and when we had all emptied out onto the street, into the frosty blueness of a snowy night, I was certain that in the flabbiest family man, in the humblest youth, in the souls and muscles of all this crowd, which tomorrow, early in the morning, would disperse to offices, shops, factories, there would be one and the same grand feeling, for the sake of which it was worth bringing together two excellent boxers, a feeling of dauntless, flaring strength, vitality, courage, inspired by the play in boxing. And this playful feeling is, perhaps, more valuable and purer than many so-called higher pleasures.

7

Letter to the Editor,
Zveno (1926)[*]

In connection with a vicious article in *Zveniya*, Paris 1926 (or 1927)†

Dear Mr. Editor, Sir,

I will allow myself the liberty of noting several factual inaccuracies in Mr. Mochulsky's rather blockheaded article on my novel.[1] Here they are: in my novel there are no "sleepy lakes," no "walks through the forest to the sound of rain," no "stormy summer nights." Nor do I employ the words "groundless," "steeped," or "analysis" and so on, which Mr. Mochulsky cites in quotation marks. In general, I would advise that a critic:

1. actually reads the book he is analyzing
2. refrains from an "ideological" approach to literature while doing so and turns his critical gaze to the remarkable things present in the stories and poems that *Zveno* publishes.

---

[*] From holograph draft, VNA Montreux. Whether the letter was sent or published is not known. The review of *Mashen'ka* (*Mary*) by K. Mochulsky appeared in *Zveno* on April 18, 1926, 2–3.
† In VN's later (late-1960s?) hand.

Nabokov's draft letter to the editor of *Zveno*, protesting an inaccurate review of his first novel *Mary* (*Mashen'ka*, 1926)

8

A Few Words on the Wretchedness of Soviet Fiction
and an Attempt to Determine Its Cause
(Essay, 1926)[*]

Lermontov has a wonderful poem that opens like this, "The year shall come, Russia's black year . . . ,"[1] and goes on to depict this year, Russia's black year, when the "crown will fall" and great calamities overtake the country. In hindsight, we can see prophecy in this poem, although it is of course less likely that the poet was seized by prophetic terror than that he fell upon this terrifying image by the chance caprice of inspiration. Nor did his prophecy entirely come to pass. The poet mistook the color. The year that has arrived for Russia is not black but gray, and not the gray of stone or ash, but that shade of gray the French have in mind when they say that all cats are gray at night. This gray year, this gray night of Russia, which, as we shall see, has drained the color from Russian literature, among other things,[2] is not a dreadful phenomenon, it will pass, this gray time,—its tedium will be grasped particularly well by schoolchildren of ages to come when they have to learn by rote those five or six pages of their middle school and secondary school textbooks, those five or six pages assigned to Russia's gray year. And anyone who thinks that I am somehow excluding this current Russian epoch from the general flow of Russian history is mistaken. Russian literature has

---

[*] V. Sirin, "Neskol'ko slov ob ubozhestve sovetskoy belletristiki i popytka ustanovit' prichiny onogo," June 11, 1926. Holograph, VNA Berg. Written for an informal talk VN gave on June 12, 1926, to the Aykhenvald-Tatarinov literary circle, which he had belonged to since its founding in émigré Berlin in late 1925. Though he had been forcing himself for some time to persist with the preparatory reading in recent Soviet literature, he composed the talk only the day before, writing nonstop all day (see also *LTV*, 70–73). VN often did not indicate omissions from his source. First published, ed. Alexander A. Dolinin, with the same title, in *Diaspora* 2 (2001), 8–23.

known such gray periods before, although perhaps less protracted. There were such years at the end of the last century, right before the dawn of Symbolism—there were such years, when a righteous gray sludge of socially conscious "literature" flowed copiously and unstoppably through our "thick journals."[3] But it seems that never before has this gray righteous sludge flowed with such copiousness and aplomb as it does through the pages of contemporary writers in Russia.

Before I embark on an analysis of this literature, I want to warn my listeners, first, that this[4] analysis will by no means be exhaustive (although I will simultaneously try to show that this kind of analysis does not need to be comprehensive), and, second, that the present lecture is not the fruit of cheerful creative playfulness, but the fruit of the arduous, bloated boredom sitting like a hunchback on me as I read the works of the few writers I'll talk about. And so that both you and I can get a taste for this at once, to set the right tone at once and show at once what pearls I've found during my laborious plod along the paths of contemporary Russian literature, I suggest that we linger on one writer, who is not well known among the so-called emigration, but whose brilliance has been boomed out in more than one article in Russia.

The writer's name is Gladkov and his principal novel is called *Cement*.[5] The plot is as follows: A certain Red Army soldier called Gleb comes back from the front to a factory in one of the southern provinces where he used to work. He finds that it has all gone to rack and ruin: the factory is closed, the workers have taken on goats, the whole place is desolate. Gleb meets his former comrades Savchuk and Loshak, and tells them this (please pay special attention to the tone of this factory worker): "Hello there, fellers! What a hell of a mess you've made of the factory, my friends! You ought all to be shot, my dear comrades." Savchuk replies: "Gleb! Dear comrade! Loshak, my hunchback friend, don't you see? It's our Gleb! Once dead and now alive . . . Look, Loshak." "Loshak was sitting like a black idol and looked at Gleb with the whites of his eyes."[6] I'd like to note, by the way, that, among the other physiological curiosities enacted by Gladkov's characters, they look not with their eyes, but without fail with the whites of their eyes. One of them even manages to sit in them: "Loshak continued to sit in the whites of his eyes like a stone idol."[7] Gleb appears at the factory like some kind of guardian angel, and the workers, after many conversations in a heightened tone, with many a "dear comrade," "hunchback friend," "my good friend," and so on, agree that production at the factory needs to be raised. In a word, Gleb is the embodiment of virtue, which, as we shall see later, triumphs over all sorts of dark powers. Having spoken to Savchuk and Loshak, he heads over to his wife, and this is where the drama starts to show. His wife, Dasha, has somewhat changed over the years of his absence. An unpleasant conversation takes place. Here's how Dasha responds to Gleb's reproaches: "Do you want cute little flowers curling up on the windowsills, Gleb, and the bed to be billowing with down-filled pillows? No, Gleb, I spend the winter in an unheated room[8] (we've got a fuel crisis, remember), and I eat in the communal canteen. As you see, I'm a free Soviet citizen." Gleb asks: "And Niurka? Maybe you've thrown our daughter out, too? That's a fine pickle." (Again, please take note of the tone. That "fine pickle," is especially fine, a smack of Odessa jargon.)

No, answers Dasha, their daughter is in the children's home. Gleb threatens to drag her back from there. "'Fine, Gleb. I don't have anything against that. But since I haven't got me any free time, it'll be you who sits with her and feeds her with all due care.' And Dasha did not snuff out her smirk, and the smirk bounced off the wall back onto her face and her face fired (or firéd, I don't know) with a dull glow between the black patches in the hollows of her eyes. Gleb recovered and crushed his heart. He smirked, too, and gulped his Adam's apple down with saliva. But his heart burst with a burning shudder, tearing at his muscles. Tamed, he gnashed his teeth from the splinter in his brain, he was large-boned, dashing, his jaws clenched so that his cheeks fell in."[9]

Having performed all these extraordinary feats with his body parts, Gleb leaves to continue his virtuous exhortations among the workers. He finds Savchuk fighting with his wife, Motya: "Gleb came in and laughed, like one of the familiar."[10] Having laughed like one of the familiar, he says: "Savchuk, my dusty friend! What mad dog has bitten you, dear comrade?" That's when his wife, Motya, steps in: "So as to get a handful of flour, have I not looted our nest, and stripped myself naked like a wanton?"[11] (This is now less Mayne Reid[12] than Old Testament.)

Savchuk says: "'The factory . . . what used to be and what's left now, Gleb, my friend. Remember, how the saws used to sing like girls in springtime.[13] Ah, old friend! . . . I was hatched from an egg here, you see. I haven't known any other life outside this hellhole.' He pumped his fists full of blood and gnashed his teeth."[14]

Continuing on his excursions, Gleb finds himself at a Party cell meeting. This is in the fourth chapter already, which is called "Comrade Zhuk Who Scolds." Finding himself in the corridor, Gleb meets two more comrades. "Both cut themselves out distinctly like one-dimensional profiles into matte tiles."[15] (It is only we mere mortals who cut cards, or cut ourselves up over exams. But to cut oneself like a one-dimensional profile—that's beyond us. These people even have some other special possibilities in this line.) Gleb meets his old friend Zhuk, and greets him in his typically idiotic and pretentious tone. "'Greetings, buddy! Yelling and denouncing as usual? When will you stop denouncing? One should take charge, while all you do is whine, you pug nose.'—Zhuk stared in amazement, and his face gasped[16] and crumbled like broken crockery."[17] Finally, Gleb meets up with another nice[18] character, the engineer Kleist. This meeting is sheer cinema. For example, imagine this: a rich banker defames his daughter's impoverished admirer, and the admirer is shipped off to hard labor. Then, one fine day, would you believe it, the admirer, unshaven and all the rest, returns like some kind of Nemesis in male form, and the banker is done for. Gladkov, on the other hand, deals with this as follows. Once, before Gleb's departure for the front, the engineer Kleist committed a major crime: When the Cossacks attacked the factory and began to catch the communists, the engineer Kleist let Gleb be caught too. The officers whipped Gleb. Gleb ran away, ended up at the Red Army front, and with some more grinding of his teeth vowed vengeance on Kleist. And now he runs into him. The engineer, meanwhile, is living in his own home, as bourgeois as can be (how he manages this is a mystery, since he's surrounded by communist workers, who are no fools and of course must know that he helped the Whites back then), but in any case, he lives, as is fitting, with his faithful servant Yakov. Gleb interrupts this idyll. When he unexpectedly walks into his study, the clever engineer asks: "Why didn't my servant Yakov warn me of your arrival?" Gleb, no less shrewdly, replies as though he's reading from Margot's book on French grammar:[19] "I sent your Yakov to the cooperage factory to chop firewood," and, he adds, "Lackeys are not suited to our way of life. You ought to remember me, Comrade Technician-Leader." Kleist replies:

"Yes, I remember you. Maybe so, but what of it?"[20] Gleb clamped his jaws and arranged to meet the engineer that night. When Gleb turned up, the engineer became frightened. "The engineer Kleist stood paralyzed, his back leaning right up against the parapet, while his head jerked his hat up and down in sporadic, halting jolts."[21] Whether this astonishing trick works on Gleb, or whether, as the author implies, he understands that the engineer will be useful to the factory and everything personal should be forgotten, I don't know, but Gleb forgave the engineer Kleist. After that Gleb convinces the authorities to reopen the factory, he goes to work, he fights off the Whites, and in his spare time hangs around his wife, marveling at what is happening to her: "He smiled at her with the moisture in his eyes. And in that brief moment of her silence he saw two forces sink their teeth into each other in her soul. Her eyes shimmered like a hard-cut gem."[22] Ladies and gentleman, there is no need to prolong this analysis. The author will prove that the private life is not what matters, Gleb will resurrect the factory, and the novel will end with a speech by Gleb and a wave of the red flag. Communist virtue has triumphed, and there's no point clunking on any longer[23]—as the virtuous Gleb might put it. What's important is that this is the kind of literature that's a tuning fork for all Russian production in this field.

If we now turn our attention to Seifullina,[24] we find in her "Virinea"[25] the same dead, false Dasha, while in the manner of her writing, in her conveyance of peasant dialogue, we find the same unbearable, self-satisfied talentlessness. Seifullina is below the level of Nagrodskaya or Charskaya,[26] although it is the same kind of philistine women's fiction. Let us extract a few sentences from a penny dreadful, for example: "The young officer walked into the luxuriously appointed boudoir at a buoyant pace. Princess Zizi met him with a wearied wanton gaze, and it seemed that all of her—from her wily lips down to the little heel of her nervously tapping foot—was surrendering herself to the man walking in." And now let us take the following little sentence from Seifullina: "The untouched and hugely fertile steppe lay enveloped by the hills, which for the first time were being disturbed by explosions. And the earth, which had been significantly full of languor,[27] breathed with one spring after another, waiting to be germinated. And from the whores, and the gentlemen building the road, a shameful ailment spread visibly through the region, the women had grown restless without their husbands during the war."[28] Or this gem: "And now, in this sweet and secret hour, fondling couples concealed themselves in the silent darkness, celebrating this light hour, among the unwieldy days, day after muffled day, all alike as twins, stretched over the earth, over the collective farm."[29] This illiterate, pompous vulgarity with which Madame Seifullina teems, is worse than the lavish forms of "Princesses Fifi," and at any rate they are harder to read. A wonderful thing is happening, a new type of novel is emerging, which I would call the village dreadful. The novel by Gladkov I just touched upon belongs to this village dreadful type. Everything that Seifullina has written, and will write, belongs to this type. Her Virinea/Dasha character, after a turbulent career, meets a soldier called Pavel (the action takes place at the very start of Bolshevism), who cannot be distinguished at all from the soldier Gleb. In village dreadfuls, engineer gentlemen replace the shady dealers, bankers, and theater directors of the ordinary penny dreadful. Seifullina has pages, to my taste, highly comical, about how Virinea, who has wound up at the factory, finds herself lured by the old engineers into working as a cook. There is no need to recount the plot of the novel; the examples adduced will serve to warrant how unnecessary all this is. Wait a moment—someone might cry out—but how can that be? Doesn't Seifullina depict the peasant way of life; doesn't she penetrate into this way of life, and illuminate it? Doesn't she open up different and, at times, new aspects of the peasant soul to us, the peasant way of life today, which we, as émigrés, do not know and cannot know? Of course not. If some second-rate writer X[30] writes a book about the Niam Niam tribe, unknown to me, then I, knowing absolutely nothing about the Niam Niam tribe, will conclude from the mere talentlessness of X's book, that everything in it is false, that he has endowed his depictions with his own highly boring theories and feelings. For the same reason I am not going to read the Far East adventures of Pierre Loti, or the American adventures of Chateaubriand, since I feel that the Parisian boulevards ruined Loti, and unrestrained romanticism ruined Chateaubriand. Whereas, having never been to India, I nonetheless immediately feel that Bunin or Conrad are speaking a profound artistic truth to me. A talentless writer remains a talentless ethnographer, if he presents his ethnographic observations in the form of fiction. And if you delve into

Seifullina's folklore, you'll be hit by such a pungent dose of the "âme slave à la Dostoevsky," that Claude Anet[31] and other lovers of exoticism don't even come close.

However, before I develop this double-dyed "Slavic soul" theme in Soviet literature, I would like to touch briefly, speaking of Seifullina, on a question, which in its turn I will also address more broadly: that is the question of how today's Russian writers become perfectly unbearable when they try to examine the psychology of the simplest human relationships. I laughed, I choked with laughter, I bent over double, as I read the profound short story "On a Weekday" by this same Seifullina. This short story condenses a motif found in the work of almost all contemporary writers, namely this: a cuckolded husband finds solace in working for the Party. Here we find hysterical jealousy, an honest communist friend, the hero himself—but you have to read the entire yarn to truly appreciate its side-splitting wretchedness. It is a mini-paradise for the critic. But I don't have the book to hand, so I shall limit myself to an excerpt. Here it goes: she leaves, he immerses himself in Party work. And the story ends like this: "'Goddamn it,' he said, 'we have huge economic opportunities.' The dreary dullness left his eyes. They were alive."[32]

But let's go back to "the Slavic soul," and for[33] this we will turn to the writer Zoshchenko.[34] Here is a writer who is harmless, grayish, mawkish; even his cussing is sentimental—in other words, "crewcut" literature. He won't say "Petersburg"—that reeks of the White Guards—but he won't say "Leningrad," either—that's a little too shameful. But it's fine to write "Piter"—left-leaning students as well as housemaids especially loved to say "Piter." We read Zoshchenko's story "Love."[35] Stupidly false. A certain Grishka, a worker, loves someone else's wife. This love isn't without communist flavor, but nor does it lack the notorious "I love her, I pity her"—i.e., a simple Russian man says, "I pity her," instead of "I love her." Grishka punches a bell-bottomed sailor in his muzzle—that is, his mug—for talking mockingly about politics. Grishka readily kisses the dirty snow on "sweetie's"—that is, his beloved's—boot, and no less readily gets into drunken rows. Oh, those Russians, with their worshipping of women, and their rows, and their murders! . . . An amazing nation![36] While Seifullina, in "Humus," has a man who has bumped off a landowner pet a goat that wanders in.[37] Deep move!

Amazing people! So there's Grishka. It is vulgarized Dostoevsky, a saccharine style, with its "e'en"s and "swain"s, and then, suddenly, we have the dear, old-fashioned, and intelligentsia-like "She sat deep in thought. Dusk always deepens sorrows." Let's take another little story by Zoshchenko: "Lial'ka Fifty." Maksim robs and kills a market woman, in order to take money to the prostitute Lial'ka. On his way to her, he himself gets robbed. He comes to Lial'ka with empty hands, she kicks him out. The writer seems to think that the reader should feel pity for Maksim at this point, but why pity when there isn't a living word in the story. "Do you have a heart?" asks Maksim. "Do you pity the bird? Do you pity the parrot?"[38] In a word, "the Slavic soul" is alive and well. There are other Zoshchenko stories I'd like to talk about, such as "The Last Master," which features a wonderful landowner, whose behavior alone supposedly justifies a thousand revolutions. A lackey reads Pushkin to this landowner from a neighboring room (so that the landowner doesn't have to see the serf). The whole story's lackeyish. I would also have talked about the stories "The Goat" and "Apollo and Tamara,"[39] but I'm afraid of boring you. All of it is very elementary as fiction. The author pretends to be an idiot, but why isn't clear. It's impossible to talk seriously about the artistic value of his short stories. And, strangely enough, their air is not Russian, but, rather, some kind of Western Slavicism, some kind of Serbian or Bulgarian folklore. . . . Let's pass on. . . .

Like Zoshchenko is Panteleimon Romanov, whose stories *Rul'* so readily publishes. Unfortunately, I did not make notes as I read—I was relying on my memory—but now I have a horrible feeling that I can't say anything more about him other than that I found him immensely boring to read. He is a small-scale writer, that's something else I remember, and he can write only about one thing—he overhears one or two conversations, and that's the story. And if I'm confessing, let me confess everything. I recently read Leonov's *The Badgers*,[40] and again didn't take notes, and gave the book away, and again I must confess that it's all become surprisingly jumbled in my head. Yet Leonov and, I suppose, Fedin[41] are now the only two writers in Russia you can read, if not with artistic rapture, then at least without the disgust evoked by Gladkov, Seifullina, Bystrov, Puzanov,[42] etc. All the same, *The Badgers* in some way strongly resembles "Virinea," with the same kind of strong, virtuous man who knows exactly what to do and how to help. Perhaps the wave of all this garbage has made me deaf, and I simply no longer have the strength to look for anything good. And how can you not become despondent when even in a writer like, for example, Pilnyak,[43] where you really want to find something good—if only because he at least has a certain magnitude—how can you not become despondent when[44] you read such a clumsy, unnecessary, and false "grand" story as, for example, his "Mother Earth"? The main character of this tale "of the forest and the peasants," as Pilnyak writes in a kind of clichéd lyrical digression "(apart from Anton Ivanovich Nekuliev, the forest ranger, apart from the tanner Arina/Irina Sergeevna Arsenieva, apart from the summer, the ravines, the whistling and warbling), the main character is the little wolf cub."[45] However, it turns out that this little wolf cub, purchased by Irina, not only is not the main character at all but merely flashes here and there, like a tiresome digression; it turns out he's not a wolf cub at all,[46] but, rather, a fox cub. What the point of all this is, God knoweth. Here's what the story is really about. In these parts of the Volga that Pilnyak depicts, the peasants are mercilessly chopping down the forest. Following the violent death of the forest ranger, his deputy, Nikulin,[47] arrives. I went out to meet him through the thicket of Pilnyak's prose, and what did I find, good God, but our old dear friend—Gladkov's Gleb, Seifullina's Pavel—with that same honesty, that same grinding of the jaw, that same sternness, the same loyalty to communism. This old friend of ours begins to confront the timber thief. He's almost killed by the peasants a few times, but in the end everything turns out all right. Incidentally, he gets together with Irina Sergeevna, a tanner. Here's a description: "People like Nekuliev (read: honest communists), are shy in love; they are chaste and honest in everything. Sometimes—for the sake of politics or for the sake of life—they lie, but this isn't dishonesty and hypocrisy, but, rather, a strategic maneuver with themselves;[48] they are chastely honest, straightforward, and exacting. Then, on that day, the sun crashed into the office and things were very cheerful; and then, after a few days, in the same moonlit week, in a moonlit and dew-soaked haze, Nekuliev said—with all the sun and all that is most beautifully human on his side—'I love, I love'—so that in this love there was only the sun and man: then it smelled drunkenly of lindens and the moon was red . . . and there remained only the moon, only the damp Mother Earth, and she gave herself to him, still a virgin at thirty, having given away all that was gathered over those thirty springs."[49]

I think that this bombastic verbiage is not by any means literature. Be that as it may, Nikulin alias Gleb alias Pavel soon notices that the tanner Irina smells of leather, and here, by the way, the Whites advance. Gleb-Nikulin says: "Comrades, I'm leaving you for the Red Army. Do as you know how to. If you want to, you can come with me." He leaves a note for Irina. "Forgive me, Arina. I was honest—with you and with myself. Goodbye, farewell forever, you've taught me how to be a revolutionary." The Cossacks attack, rape Arina, and impale her on a stake.

At this point I would like to point out the following: Soviet writers do not always present the Whites as beasts. Here's a subtle move. Of course, the general sense is always one of indignation against the counterrevolutionary, but occasionally comes this subtle move, in one part of the novel, to show the Cossack has human pity—subtle, of course, for the reader concludes: Such even-handedness! Where is the communist bias? Look, after all, the author even manages to find kind souls among them. Gladkov has a kind Cossack of this type in *Cement*. The Cossack lets Dasha go, although, true, three other officers, saved till the end, rape her. That same device, except in reverse, is used by Krasnov in his infamous novels.[50] For pity's sake, says the die-hard émigré reader, how can he possibly be an anti-Semite when he has a Jewess save the life of a White officer! But this device, this military tactic, cannot fool the perceptive critic.

I'm going back[51] to the type of the honest communist (Gleb, Pavel, Nikulin). I would like to point out that the emergence of this type is the culmination of the following line: the philosophizer of the old plays, then Chekhov's Lvov, and finally, the honest communist. A direct and natural development. This same line might also slightly touch Bazarov and Sanin.[52] So it's a mistake to think that the Russian Revolution gave literature a new hero. Since it is a "product of the masses," that is, of mediocrity, it is incapable of creating anything; instead, it has latched on to and naturally developed the most mediocre character type in all of Russian literature, a line, I repeat, that goes from the old-world *raisonneurs*, through Lvov in *Ivanov*, to our friend Gleb-Pavel-Nikulin.

I will say more about the amazing monotony of the themes[53] of all these writers, but since I have already compared Gladkov's Gleb to Pilnyak's Nikulin, let me underline the interchangeability of the development of this theme now: one has the workers selling off steel, and Gleb stops this in the name of the factory's production; the other has peasants cutting down the forest, and Nikulin stops this in the name of forestry.

And another thing: you cannot leave a woman alone with any of these writers. Dasha, Virinea, Arina—all of them are raped at the first handy opportunity. Vsevolod Ivanov (who has something either of the good old *Caucasian Sketches*[54] or Charskaya's *The Princess Dzhavakha*),[55] nevertheless has a story entirely predicated on the fact that practically an entire regiment has its eye on the same woman, while she not only saves herself but kills three of the most aggressive lechers. This story, which is called "The Desert of Tuub" (which in itself is already a notorious testament to its exotic vulgarity), takes place in a Turkmenistan setting and is utterly laughable and utterly talentless. It begins: "Behold the stubborn grass. . . ."[56] I think it's not worth continuing.

But women are pursued not only in the southern steppes, they have no peace even in the Arctic snows. I'm referring to Pilnyak's story "Beyond the Portage." Its epigraphs are made up of an excerpt from a learned treatise and a line from Dahl—"Polundra!"—which to the Pomors means "Beware."[57] In fact, epigraphs from Dahl wouldn't go amiss before all of Pilnyak's stories.[58] In this story, Pilnyak describes a polar expedition. He grips the reader through fear. Horrors are piled one on top of another like ice floe on ice floe, and for some reason this brings to mind Leonid Andreev.[59] In fact, some of the descriptions are undoubtedly rather good; however, things look rather worse on the psychology front. We meet a Professor who, in spite of all the dangers, spends a great deal of time playing with a kitten. Here we remember the wolf cub from not so long ago and grow bored. There is one woman on the expedition. From the very first sentence in which she is mentioned, I already knew with perfect certainty what was waiting for her in the Arctic snow. Among the people abandoned on Spitsbergen, some kind of irresistible hunger stirs, the woman sows discord among them, and the Captain—also a sort of honest communist—kills the woman (i.e., the individual) in the name of the expedition (i.e., the masses). Does Pilnyak really have so little artistic flair that he doesn't understand that such a[60] kind of "Arctic drama" hopelessly ruins his story? Of course, something like this could have taken place, but his flair should have hinted to the writer that to write about it would mean bringing something terribly false into his story, which has otherwise been truthfully written. In this respect he could learn a lot from the English.

And here, now that I've mentioned the North Pole and the English, the time has come to drag my lecture out of the ruts of the Russian landscape, out of the realm of folklore, village dreadful fantasies, and internal Soviet politics. The time has come, for a moment (since I'll have to come back to all this again), to drag it to other realms, and in fact to turn to the depiction of foreign lands by these Russian writers. Putting aside the fact that in his so-called English stories, Pilnyak foppishly calls a bus a "bess" (with two "s"s!), although if you're going to write the English name, then you should write "bus" with one "s," while he calls cars[61] "carr,"[62] with two "r"s, even though one would suffice,— putting all this aside—we can note at once that these Pilnyak stories exude the naïvest provincialism. I myself am a firm believer that the most cultured country in the world, despite its notorious Bolshevism, is Russia. But I cannot stand it when a Russian, let alone a writer, finds himself in a foreign country and begins to look around with that kind of condescension and to judge the hypocrisy or the dim-wittedness of this or that nation, and in any way at all reveals that cheap pretentious provincial chauvinism, which is so like simple human stupidity. Pilnyak moves through England smirking and snickering, and even when he praises something, there's a certain shade of scorn in his praise. I won't cite concrete examples; one needs to read the whole book. Fedin's novel *Cities and Years* is guilty of the same provincialism in his descriptions of Germany, of a small German city such as Nuremberg. His observations are based on clichéd prejudice. The German translator Groeger[63] told me that Germans reading Fedin reasonably object: why should we care at all[64] about this fantasy created by some Fedin fellow? For an artist to portray the Germans as sausage makers and honest burghers lowers the artist, and when Fedin, or Fedin's hero Andrei, is horrified to the point of nightmare that the Germans have public executions, that the head of a famous outlaw is kept in a glass jar in a museum, and that at a fair a burgher can throw a ball at a painting of this very head—when Fedin is horrified at all this, one must assume either that there are no executions in Fedin's homeland, or that Fedin is simply making a fool of the reader. On top of these horrors, he also presents us with the inevitable dim-witted military cadets and drunken students, and, just like Pilnyak in England, keeps snorting away either in praise or in condemnation, and, in short, plays the fool. The novel gains nothing from this, and a juxtaposition of the German parts of the novel with the Russian parts produces the most comical impression. I have to admit, however, that Fedin is a literate and, perhaps even more, a talented writer. Some of his images are pleasantly striking. But the plot of the novel, its ridiculous coincidences, the vagueness of the hero, who is trying to be Gleb Pavlovich Nikulin without quite making it, and finally its melodramatic end, when the heroine, Fräulein Marie, rolls unexpectedly into St. Petersburg—this whole unwieldy, confused, and shallow plot deprives Fedin's novel of any kind of significance. At the very beginning of the novel I marked and wrote out the following: a professor in St. Petersburg is returning home from work at night singing "The Marseillaise" ("a song without equal") and then exclaims: "Oh, to be born again! A hundred years from now! To see people weep at the very mention of these years, to bow one's head somewhere before the tattered remnant of a banner, to read an operations report from the headquarters of the Worker-Peasant Red Army! This newspaper (he points to the newspaper in his hand), in a hundred years humanity will preserve a fragment of this sheet as a relic, as the holy of holies. . . ."[65]

I think the Professor is gravely mistaken. And this thought leads me back to the thesis I set out at the beginning of this lecture—namely, that it's precisely our years that are Russia's gray year, and our descendants, especially schoolchildren, will think of them with a completely understandable yawn. I doubt there is anyone in France today who cherishes as a relic an issue of *Mercure de France* from 1789. In the same way, I doubt that our descendants will cherish *Izvestia* or *Pravda*, all of these organs of philistine communists. And I doubt, especially, that any of the names I have mentioned in the course of this lecture will drag themselves all the way to those far-off days. For the gray year of Russia has given birth to a rather gray literature. All of these writers share the point of view that the revolution is some kind of apocalyptic event, that it will turn the world upside down, that the Great War has altered certain paths, certain values. This kind of point of view ruins an artist, and it is here that I detect the primary reason for the unartfulness of Russian literature. The artist is someone who operates with constant values. And then: these writers have lost their sense of mankind and replaced it with a sense of class. To put it another way, man is moved not by ordinary human feelings, so extraordinary in their everydayness, but, rather, by some kind of extraneous class and mass sensations, which castrate art. In this I see the second reason for their poverty of spirit.

Further: Their field of observation is remarkably narrow. Just as in old comedies we always find the same old faces—the male guardian, the maidservant, the suitor, the suitor's servant, etc.—so, too, in the narrow field of vision of Soviet novelists the very same characters are always in motion. A peasant, inclined to communism, or simply a communist, an honest communist, a Red Army soldier; a peasant woman, inclined to communism, or simply a communist, and so on, alongside natives of the old regime—engineers, officers, professors, etc. The combinations that can be made from this limited material are also limited. Hence the oppressive monotony of situations, relationships, and conclusions. Here's my third reason.

And then: the lack of culture, the lack of education of the writers. I am sure that 99 percent of them have not read Balzac or Flaubert. I am not even sure that most of them have read Chekhov, Shchedrin, Leskov, or Bunin. Hence the exceptional naïveté of their style and the exceptional monotony of their verbal flow. They lack not only literary culture, but culture in general; not just, for instance, knowledge of world history, but that elusive shade of culture whose presence, even in someone not well educated, immediately allows you to call him cultured. But there's not even much of a basic education in them. It's not enough to know that in the provinces of the Volga a *vylazina* is the name for the skin a snake sheds. And it is in this deficiency, or even absence, of all culture that I find the fourth reason for the wretchedness of Soviet literature.

Finally, there is a fifth and, so to speak, an external reason. It lies in that heavy, secret censorship dissolved in the very air, which I would say is the most surprising, indeed the only gifted accomplishment of the Soviet regime. I must, however, add that Messrs Gladkov and Bystrov, etc., and Mesdames Seifullina and Forsh[66] would hardly write any better, or more "White-ly," even if censorship were to disappear.

It seems to me that these five reasons—the belief in historical cataclysms, the class take on the world, the narrow field of vision, the lack of culture, and censorship—are the essence, the most undoubted and central reasons, for the temporary decline of Russian literature. I don't believe that this is an entirely negative phenomenon. It is a kind of respite. Men, even very great men, sometimes experience a time like this on the brink between boyhood and youth, when they become unbearable to those around them—rather rude, rather awkward, rather pimply. This is the kind of period that I think Russian literature is going through at the moment, having forgotten its wonderful nursemaids and those moments in its wondrous childhood, when it was so good, so fine, so joyous, so sensitive to every trifle. But that's all right. Its youth still lies before it, and a literature with that kind of childhood cannot have anything but a brilliant and entrancing[67] youth. And who knows, perhaps those who continue the work of the first fosterers of the Russian muse will come from an altogether different milieu from the one the Gladkovs and the Seifullinas have emerged from. I sometimes imagine that these future writers might be created from the wonders of exile and the wonders of a return. With that I will end my lecture. I repeat once more, it is far from complete. For instance, I haven't even mentioned Lidin[68] or Yakovlev,[69] even though I have read both. But no matter what reproaches of this sort are thrown my way, and no matter what new names are suggested to me for investigation, I resolutely declare that for a long time to come—perhaps for a whole year—I shall not touch Soviet literature, for the kind of scornful[70] boredom I experienced in the time I read these Soviet writers, one after another—I have no intention of living through such boredom again.

9

On Generalities (Essay, 1926)[*]

There is a very tempting and very harmful demon: the demon of generalizations. He captivates human thought by marking every phenomenon with a little label, and carefully placing it next to another, also meticulously wrapped and numbered phenomenon. Through him a field of human knowledge as unstable as history is turned into a neat little office, where this many wars and that many revolutions sleep in folders, and where we can pore over bygone ages in complete comfort. This demon is a lover of words such as "idea," "tendency," "influence," "period," and "era." In the historian's study this demon combines phenomena, influences and tendencies of past ages, reducing them to one with hindsight. With this demon comes appalling tedium, the consciousness (utterly mistaken, by the way) that, however humanity plays or fights, it follows an implacable course. This demon should be feared. He is a fraud. He is a salesman of centuries, pushing his price list of history.

And the most awful thing happens perhaps when the temptation of completely comfortable generalizations seizes us in contemplation not of those past, spent times, but of the time we live in. No matter that the spirit of generalization, in its striving for ease of thought, has christened a long series of in no way innocent years the "Middle Ages." That is still pardonable; it has perhaps saved modern schoolchildren from worse

---

[*] "On Generalities," holograph, VNA Berg, presumably of a talk given in the Aykhenvald-Tatarinov circle, not necessarily in 1926 (VN's remembered dates were often approximate). First published, ed. Alexander Dolinin, "On Generalities," *Zvezda* 4 (1994), 12–14. Translated by Luke Parker, "On Generalities," *Times Literary Supplement*, May 13, 2016, 17–18, lightly revised here. Four decades after he wrote this essay, VN added the English title "On Generalities," and the place and time of composition, "Berlin 1926," on the previously untitled Russian manuscript. A better title might be "On Generalizations."

disasters. No matter that in five hundred years the twentieth century, plus several other centuries, will also in turn fall into a folder with some ingenious little label or other: for example, the "Second Middle Ages."[1] This does not concern us, although it is amusing to dream of the twentieth century that will present itself to the imagination of a history professor in five hundred years, and of the Homeric laughter that would seize us were we to glance through future textbooks. But one wonders, are we really obliged to name our century in some way, and will these attempts of ours not play a nasty joke on us, when in thick books they begin to inflame the imaginations of future sages?

One such sage, a penetrating historian,[2] was working one day on the description of some ancient war when, suddenly, a noise from the street reached his ears. A crowd was separating two fighting men. And neither the very sight of the fight, nor the expressions of the fighting men, nor the expostulations of the onlookers could give the curious historian an accurate picture of what exactly had happened. He pondered the fact that it was impossible to get to the bottom here even of a chance street fight, of which he himself was a witness; he reread the description of the ancient war that he was working on and understood how unsubstantiated and haphazard were all his profound arguments about that ancient war. Let us admit to ourselves, once and for all, that history as an exact science is just for convenience, "for the simple folk," as the museum guard used to say, showing two skulls of one and the same criminal, in youth and old age.

If every human day is a sequence of chances—and in this lies its divinity and power—then all the more so is human history, too, only chance. You can combine those chances, tie them into a neat bouquet of periods and ideas; but the aroma of the past is lost in the process, and we now see, not what was, but what we wish to see. By chance a general has an acutely upset stomach—and a long-lasting royal dynasty now gets replaced by the dynasty of neighboring powers. By chance a restless eccentric wants to sail across the ocean—and trade now gets transformed and a maritime nation gets made rich. Why indeed should we take after those paradoxical enemies of risk, who sit for years at the green table in Monte Carlo calculating how many spins will fall on red and how many on black, in order to find a fail-safe system? There is no system. History's roulette wheel knows no laws. Clio laughs at our clichés, at us speaking boldly, adroitly, and with impunity about influences, ideas, trends, periods, and eras, and deducing laws and divining the future.

That's how history is treated. But I repeat, it's a hundred times more frightening when the demon of generalizations penetrates our judgments about our own era. And what exactly is our era? When did it begin, in which year, which month? When people use the word "Europe," what exactly do they have in mind, which countries: only those at the "center," or are Portugal, Sweden, and Iceland also central? When newspapers with their peculiar love for sloppy metaphors head an article "Locarno,"[3] I see only mountains, sun glinting on the water, an avenue of plane trees. When people pronounce the word "Europe" with the same metaphorical, generalizing intonation, I see precisely nothing, since I cannot imagine simultaneously the landscape and history of Sweden, Romania, and, say, Spain. And when, in connection with this nonexistent Europe, people talk about some era, then I lose myself in guesses, trying to understand when exactly this era began, and how it could relate in the same way to me, and Ivanov, and Mr. Brown, and Monsieur Dupont.

I am bewildered. I am forced to conclude that my interlocutor is speaking about the last two or three years, that the action is taking place in the town where he himself lives, say, Berlin, and that the barbarism under discussion dates only to the dance halls on the Kurfürstendamm. And as soon as I understand this, everything at once becomes simpler. We are not talking, then, about something general, misty, and aggregated. We are talking about the dance hall in the city of Berlin in the twenty-fourth, -fifth, or -sixth years of this century. Instead of a whiff of the cosmos, simply a chance fashion. And this fashion will pass as it has already passed many times before. It is interesting that these faux-Negro dances[4] were in fashion in the days of the French Directory. . . . Now, as then, there is no more eroticism in them than there was in the waltz. It is curious that in those days, when ladies wore strange feathers in their hats, morality bemoaned Negroid ugliness. And so, if we talk about fashion, the conversation could be interesting and informative. We could talk about the haphazardness of fashion, about how fashion is in no way tied to other phenomena in human life, about the fact, for example, that in the days when Madame de Sévigné wrote her letters, so-called Bubikopf haircuts were worn.[5]

"Chance, Doña Anna, chance," as it is said in *The Stone Guest*.[6] Fashion is haphazard and capricious. The fashion in Berlin does not at all resemble the fashion in Paris. An Englishman seeing so many Berliners stroll about in plus fours is confused: surely half of Berlin is not playing golf all day? And again, if our talk turns to sport, then we need to establish which people, which country, exactly which years we have in mind. And here one should call on someone who knows the history of sport well. He will explain that in Germany sport is only now coming into being, and somewhat rapidly, and for that reason is so striking. Football is taking the place of the goose step; lawn tennis is replacing war games. If we turn our attention to sport in other countries, we find, for example, that in England football has been exciting the crowd in exactly the same way for five centuries now; and that in France they have still kept the huge halls where they played tennis starting in the fourteenth century. The Greeks played hockey and hit a punching ball. Sport, whether hunting, a knightly tournament, a cockfight, or good old Russian *lápta*,[7] has always amused and entertained humankind. To search for signs of barbarism in it is inherently senseless, because a real barbarian is always a terrible sportsman.

We should not slander our time. It is romantic in the highest degree, spiritually beautiful, and physically comfortable. The war, like any war, damaged many things; but it has passed, the wounds have healed over, and by now one can hardly perceive any particularly unpleasant consequences, with the possible exception of lots of bad French novels about the *jeunes gens d'après-guerre*.[8] As for the whiff of revolution, it, too, having appeared by chance, will disappear by chance, as has already happened a thousand times in human history. In Russia, simpleminded communism will be replaced by something more intelligent, and in a hundred years only historians will know the very boring Mr. Ulyanov.[9]

But, meanwhile, let us savor our time like pagans and gods: with its marvelous machines and huge hotels, whose ruins the future will cherish, as we cherish the Parthenon; with its very comfortable leather armchairs, unknown to our ancestors; with its extremely refined scientific investigations; with its smooth speed and good-natured humor; and, most important, with its tang of eternity, which has always been and will be present in every century.

10

A. Znosko-Borovsky, *Capablanca and Alekhine*
(Review, 1927)[*]

Lovers of the art of chess will find this small book a most entertaining novel, or, rather, the novel's first volume, since its main characters have only now really clashed, and the future holds no shortage of entrancing tussles. Znosko-Borovsky, a talented player himself, writes about chess in a masterly way. The book begins with the story of how the bright, intoxicating combination play of former years (Anderssen, Pillsbury, et al.) turned into positional play under the influence of Steinitz, Schlechter, Rubinstein, Lasker, cold masters, admirers of rigor and dryness in chess.

"Capablanca," the author writes, "brought chess back from the province of severe science to the sphere of jolly and joyful art," and goes on to describe his wonderful career, his defeat of Lasker, triumphs, triumphs, an unexpected period of weakness, and again triumphs. There's "play in space," characterized by a concern for the safety and strength of every position, and "play in time"—i.e., a play of motion, of development. And this is Capablanca, a dynamic player, the "knight of fast-flowing time." Znosko-Borovsky is just as accurate in describing Alekhine's game. Comparing him with Capablanca, he refers to the latter as classical and technical, and Alekhine as romantic and tactical. Capablanca is calm, and in his play there's the harmony of genius; Alekhine is fiery, his imagination knows no limits, his combinations are fantastical. "His game spreads out like a fan, which will snap shut only at the moment of the final blow."

[*] V. Sirin, "A. Znosko-Borovskiy. Kapablanka i Alekhin. Parizh," *Rul'*, Nov. 16, 1927, 4. The author's name was in fact Evgeny Alexandrovich Znosko-Brovosky, and the book's full title *Kapablanka i Alekhin: Bor'ba za mirovoe pervenstvo v shakhmatakh* (*Capablanca and Alekhine: The Fight for the World Chess Championship*).

The text comes furnished with some interesting diagrams, and at the end of the book there are fourteen selected chess Capablanca-Alekhine games with splendid brief commentaries.

I would like to mention the unusual vividness of some of the author's expressions, and the brisk, heady pace of the whole narrative. Znosko-Borovsky writes about chess with gusto, juicily and aptly, just as a master should write about his art. The undersigned, a humble but ardent admirer of Caïssa,[1] welcomes the appearance of this thrilling book.

11

Anniversary (Essay, 1927)[*]

In these days when there wafts from over there the cadaver stench of an anniversary, why not celebrate our anniversary, too? Ten years of contempt, ten years of loyalty, ten years of freedom—does this not deserve at least one anniversary speech?

You have to know how to be contemptuous. We have learned the science of contempt to perfection. We are so sated with it that at times we're too lazy even to mock its cause. A slight trembling of the nostrils, a momentary squint of the eyes—and silence. But, today, let us speak.

Ten years of contempt . . . I feel contempt not toward a person, not toward the worker Sidorov, an honest member of some kind of Kompom-pom, but toward that ugly, obtuse little idea that turns Russian simpletons into communist nincompoops, which turns people into a new species of ant: *Formica marxi* var. *lenini*.[1] I cannot bear the saccharine taste of philistinism that I sense in everything Bolshevik. A philistine boredom wafts from the gray pages of *Pravda*, a philistine anger sounds in the Bolshevik's political outcries, philistine nonsense has swelled his poor head. They say Russia has grown more stupid, which is hardly surprising. . . . It has grown thick with backwoods backwardness: with its rapacious provincial accountants, its young ladies who read Verbitskaya[2] and Seifullina, its wretchedly whimsical theater, and its placid drunkard, sprawled in the middle of the dusty street.

I despise the communist faith as the idea of the basest equality, as a dull page in the festive history of humanity, as a denial of earthly and unearthly beauty, as something idiotically encroaching on my free "I," as a promoter of ignorance, obtuseness, and complacency. The strength

[*] V. Sirin, "Yubiley," *Rul'*, Nov. 18, 1927, 2. Holograph, VNA Berg.

of my contempt lies in the fact that I, in feeling contemptuous, do not let myself think about the blood that has been spilled. Its strength lies also in the fact that I do not regret, in bourgeois despair, the loss of my estate, my house, the gold bullion not hidden skillfully enough in the depths of a toilet. An idea doesn't commit murder, a person does—and will face a special reckoning—but whether I forgive or not, that is a question of a different order. Thirst for revenge should not get in the way of the purity of the contempt. Indignation is always helpless.

And not only ten years of contempt . . . We're celebrating ten years of loyalty. We're loyal to Russia not just in the way you remain faithful to a memory, we don't only love it, as you love your fleeting childhood, your fugitive youth—no, we're loyal to that Russia we could be proud of, a Russia created slowly and measuredly and a vast state among other vast states. But what is it now, where is she to go now, this Soviet widow, this poor relation of Europe? . . . We are faithful to her past, we are happy with it, and a wonderful feeling grips us when, in a faraway country, we hear how admiring talk repeats names we have loved from childhood. We are a wave of Russia that has overflowed its shores, we have flooded the whole world, but our wanderings are not always cheerless, and our valiant yearning for our homeland does not always prevent our enjoying an alien country, a refined solitude in the alien electric night on a bridge, in a square, in a station. And even though it is now clear to us how different we are, and though it sometimes seems that there is not one, but a thousand thousand Russias wandering the earth, at times wretched and spiteful, at times warring among themselves, there is nonetheless something linking us all, some kind of common drive, a common spirit, which the future historian will understand and appreciate.

And at the same time we are celebrating ten years of freedom. Such freedom as we know perhaps no other nation has known. In that peculiar Russia, which invisibly surrounds us, which animates and holds us, which saturates our souls and colors our dreams, there isn't a single law other than the law of the love we feel toward it, and there is no ruler apart from our own conscience. We can say anything about it, write anything about it, we have nothing to hide, and there is no censorship to place obstacles before us, we are the free citizens of our dream. Our scattered nation, our nomadic state, is fortified by this freedom, and someday we will be grateful to blind Clio for giving us the chance to partake of this freedom and to understand deeply and to feel our homeland acutely in exile.

In these days when the gray anniversary of the USSR[3] is being celebrated, we celebrate ten years of contempt, loyalty, and freedom. Let's not take to reproving exile. Over these days, let us repeat the words of that ancient warrior of whom Plutarch writes, "At night, in deserted fields far from Rome, I pitched my tent, and my tent was Rome to me."

12

Vladislav Khodasevich, *Collected Poems*
(Review, 1927)[*]

"Adriatic waves, / O, Brenta!"[1] How much is embedded in this agitated exclamation. . . . But Pushkin's Brenta does not exist. The Brenta is simply a "rusty little stream."[2] . . . That is how Vladislav Khodasevich saw it with his own eyes and, having understood the deception of the romantic dream, came to love the prose "in life and in verse."[3] I hasten to note, however, first: this "rusty little stream" of Khodasevich's is no less beautiful in its own way (and beautiful precisely because it is cloudy and rusty) than the Brenta dreamed up by Pushkin; and, secondly, the "prose" Khodasevich refers to is not at all ordinary prose. If we understand poetry in verse to signify poetic beauty, narrow traditional poeticism, then prose in verse means the poet's complete freedom in his choice of themes, images, and words. A daring, intelligent, shameless freedom plus regular (i.e., in some sense restricted) rhythm is what constitutes the special charm of Khodasevich's poetry.

"Adriatic waves, / O, Brenta! . . ." Pushkin's melodious howl (I'm talking here only of the sound—the babble of the first line,[4] the sigh of the second) acts as a kind of leitmotif in many of Khodasevich's poems. His favorite meter is iambic, measured and weighty. It doesn't matter that at times it can be severe to the point of dryness; unexpectedly, it bursts into the most intoxicating paean, a sharp melodiousness breaks off the coldish coursing of the verse. The quivering of his trochees is astonishing. The poet has gasped, woken up at the very moment he seemed to be slipping into sleep. "My heart beats out of rhythm" (which is wonderfully expressed by the half-rhyme *tol'ko/stolika*

[*] V. Sirin, "Vladislav Khodasevich. Sobranie stikhov. I-zo 'Vozrozhdenie.' Parizh" ("Vladislav Khodasevich. *Collected Poems*. Vozrozhdenie Pub. House. Paris), *Rul'*, Dec. 14, 1927, 5.

("only"/"bedside table"), and "still sensing (*oshyshchen'em*) the steep slope, you tremble (*trepeshchesh'*) all over, my dear, light, falling soul."[5] The effects of palpitation, of tenderness, and of falling are achieved (and with what mastery!) through the half-stress on the second foot of the first line, the tickling repetition of the letter *shch*, and the lightness and multitude of vowels in the last two lines. The musicality of the poem "The Mill" is wonderful.[6] It is written in an entirely regular and yet totally unexpected, unprecedentedly beautiful meter. Each of the six stanzas contains five iambic trimeter lines, of which the second and fifth lines rhyme (a simple masculine rhyme) while the others are lengthened by a dactylic ending (with the faintest shadow of assonance in the adjacent lines). It is impossible to describe the singsong patter of this poem, and it would be a pity to quote only an extract. Lastly, in "Ballad," written in amphibrachic trimeter, Khodasevich has in my opinion reached the height of poetic mastery.[7] The poet is sitting in his room illumined by the dry glare of an electric light when he suddenly begins to rock back and forth and to sing (and it is at this point that a dactylic rhyme replaces a feminine one): "and then melody, melody, melody / blends my accents and joins in their quest."[8] It goes on: "And the room and the furniture slowly, / slowly start in a circle to sail, / and a great heavy lyre is from nowhere / handed me by a ghost through the gale."[9]

Such are the astonishing rhythms of Khodasevich's poetry. What's strange is that this craftsmanship and the acute unexpectedness of the imagery produce a kind of hypnotic effect on the reader, and, having bewitched his ear and engaged his attention, they prevent him from "experiencing" along with the poet, from sympathizing in a human way with this or that mood of the poet. In the last section of the collection, there are several poems with a "civic" undertone. Thus, the poem "Windows onto a Courtyard" (with a stanza allotted to each window) evokes a so-called petit-bourgeois atmosphere.[10] However, so splendid is the glassy charm of these images that the reader is simply not in a position to be imbued with that atmosphere, to feel sorry for these wretched inhabitants, to lament their gray lives (and that's a good thing). The same thing can be said about another poem (which describes an armless man accompanying a pregnant woman to the cinema). The poet, overcome with indignation and pity, exclaims: "Then I take out a belt with a drawn-out / lingering cry and beat the angels with swinging blows /

and the angels fly up to the city heights through the wires / just as from Venetian squares / the pigeons skittishly scattered / from the feet of my beloved."[11] If the poet was trying to arouse pity, sympathy, etc., in the reader, then he has failed. We become intoxicated by his imagery, his music, his craftsmanship, and feel absolutely no human feelings toward those who have been pummeled by fate.

There are no bounds to Khodasevich's freedom in choosing his themes. At times, it seems that he is being mischievous and playful, taking a perverse pleasure in his gift of praising the unpraisable. The sacred lack of squeamishness of his muse is expressed especially sharply in the poem "Underground."[12] Here I find myself in a strange quandary: I cannot write out the whole poem, there's not enough space; to simply give a quotation would be unfair to the author; yet I cannot describe the theme of his poem,[13] for the reason that when expressed in bare prose this theme takes on a shade of the crudest and most explicit smuttiness. It is enough for me to say that these sorts of passages can be found in treatises on sexual problems. And yet Khodasevich manages to create a bold and beautiful poem out of this pitiful degradation (for a moment the thought did flash through my mind—what if the muse is offended after all?—but only for a moment).

What is particularly interesting about Khodasevich's art is the somewhat optical-pharmaceutical-chemical-anatomical tinge that many of his poems have. Typically, he uses this as a concluding device: "in my soul and world there are gaps / as though some acid had been spilled" (this is how the poem "The Automobile"[14] ends). Another poem ends like this: ". . . a bright cosmos comes into being / beneath the trembling canopy of lashes; / it swirls and blossoms / like a star of bicycle spokes."[15] The numerous allusions to reflections in mirrors, windowpanes, etc., also belong to this optical realm. "Cain walks past unrecognized / with eczema between his brows,"[16] and "and what a comfort that the chemist / has some acidic headache pills,"[17] are also good examples of Khodasevich's closing chords. There is a whiff of the medicinal about these images: "and on my chest you will timidly replace / the ice bag,"[18] or "the spirit starts to cut its way through / like a tooth from below swollen gums,"[19] and how characteristic is the comparison of the soul to iodine,[20] the soul which corrodes the body just as iodine corrodes cork.

It wouldn't even be worth mentioning the very few and insignificant slips that Khodasevich makes were it not for the fact that absolutely special standards are expected of a master like him. I am talking about such baggy lines as "to draw my heights nearer to me,"[21] and "I hear my own ravings in my sleep";[22] awkward lines such as "exhausted by a dull languor, in which I languished,"[23] and "what signifies the sign of his shaggy back";[24] weak lines such as "and with a slightly frightening smile"[25] and "many times I beheld (*videl*) and then abhorred (*voznenavidel*)";[26] and finally the use of the hideous word "brolly" (*zont*) instead of "umbrella" (*zontik*).[27]

Curiously, a faint influence of Blok can be detected in Khodasevich's blank verse: "I bowed down low to / Pyotr Ivanych, his work, his coffin, / and to all the earth, and the sky, / reflected azure in the glass"[28]—the intonation here is typical of Blok. And a spurt of Tyutchev wafts through other poems: "you'll say: a tall angel there / trod upon the waters weightily"[29] or "the eye rests, the ear hears not, / life is mysteriously good, / and the almost free soul / breathes in the sky unhindered."[30]

Khodasevich is a great poet, but not, I think, a poet for everyone. He repels the person looking for repose and moonlit landscapes in poetry. For those who can enjoy a poet without rummaging through his "worldview" and without demanding rapport, Khodasevich's poetry collection is a ravishing work of art.

13

Man and Things (Essay, 1928)[*]

The title of my talk, "Man and Things," may, perhaps, confuse you. It may seem to you, for example, that, paying homage to the devil of generalization, I intend the word "man" to mean some kind of composite, extraordinarily convenient *Homo sapiens*, a representative of humanity. You might think that for me a "thing" has some kind of definite meaning, which I intend to juggle with philosophical ease. Moreover, the very word "thing" may call up in your imagination something domestic, not very valuable, a thing of comfort or decoration. Incidentally, we might recall that Chekhovian doctor from, I think, *Three Sisters*, who, not knowing how to characterize a gift that was being proudly shown to him, twists it about in his hands and mumbles: "Hmm, yes . . . a thing."[1] In fact, he then, out of clumsiness, drops this thing, a mantel clock, I think, causing resounding repercussions. And still another intonation can be heard in the word "thing." I once had an acquaintance, a jeweler, in whose mouth the highest praise for a bracelet or a *rivière*[2] was precisely this word "thing," pronounced weightily, with a loud voice, over and over, in time with the weighing movement of the palm on which the precious object lay. Finally, the heading of my talk might produce yet another quid pro quo. For the words "man and things" perhaps suggest to another mind the image of a man in an alehouse, a lackey, a waiter,[3] as a result of which, the word "things," too, will hatch out of its fog and take on the image of things for which the management bears no responsibility.

[*] V. Sirin, "Chelovek i veshchi," night of Jan. 13–14, 1928. Holograph, VNA Berg. That night was the "Old New Year's Eve"—when magical things might happen—of the Old Style calendar, which émigrés still kept in mind for festive occasions. This piece was presumably a talk for the Aykhenvald-Tatarinov circle. Published and edited by Alexander Dolinin, "Chelovek i veshchi," *Zvezda* 4 (1999), 19–24.

By listing these possible misinterpretations, I hope to eliminate them. Of course, when I say "man," I mean only myself. Just as the things I am going to talk about won't pass without name tags into the fog of the commonplace. For by the word "thing" I mean not only a toothpick, but also a steam engine. Everything made by human hands is a thing. That is the only general definition I will allow myself.

A thing, a thing made by someone, does not exist in itself. A seagull flying over a cigarette case forgotten on a beach cannot distinguish it from a stone, from sand, from a scrap of seaweed, since in the absence of man a thing immediately returns to nature's bosom. A rifle lying in the depths of a tropical jungle is no longer a thing, but a lawful part of the forest; today already a red stream of ants pours over it, tomorrow it will grow moldy, perhaps even flower. A house is only a stone block when man leaves it. Should he leave it for five hundred years, the house, like a silent, cunning animal running for freedom, will return to nature imperceptibly, and indeed, look, it's just a pile of stones. And note, by the way, how eagerly and how adroitly the very slightest thing strives to slip away from man, and how inclined it is to suicide. A dropped coin, with the haste of a desperate fugitive, traces a wide arc on the floor and disappears into the farthest corner under the farthest sofa. And not only is there no object without man, but there is no object without a definite relationship to it from the human side. This relationship is slippery. Take, for example, a framed painting, the portrait of a woman. One person looks at it and, with the cold admiration of a connoisseur, analyzes the colors, the chiaroscuro, the background. Another, a craftsman, filled with a certain complex sensation, in which images of his craft mix—the glue, the yardstick, the decorative molding, the firmness of the wood, the gilding—looks at the frame with a professional eye. A third, a friend of the woman depicted, discusses the likeness or, pierced for a moment by one of those faint recollections that are like the street urchins of memory, sees and hears with great clarity (albeit for a moment) that very woman put down her handbag and gloves on the table and say: "Tomorrow is the last sitting, thank God. The eyes have come out well." And, finally, a fourth looks at the painting with the thought that today the dentist will cause him a great deal of pain, so that each time he sees this painting, he will recall the buzzing of the drill and how the dentist's breath smelled. What does all this come to, then? There is not one thing, albeit mathematically there is only one thing, but four, five, six, a million things, depending on how many people look at it. What do I care about a pair of boots left by my neighbor outside his door? But were my neighbor to die tonight, what human warmth, what pity, what live and tender beauty would these two old, shabby boots, with their eyelet flaps sticking out like little ears, left standing at the door, radiate over me. In my desk, in a crumpled envelope, I found five matches, their heads blackened. Why I had put them there to keep, what memory is linked to them, I have forgotten, forgotten entirely. I'll still keep them for a time for the sake of that memory, which I know is connected to them, loving them with some kind of secondary love, but then I'll throw them out. Thus do we betray things. At a fair, in a remote little town, I won a cheap porcelain pig at target shooting. I abandoned it on the shelf at the hotel when I left town. And in doing so, I condemned myself to remember it. I am hopelessly in love with this porcelain pig. I am overcome by an unbearable, slightly silly tenderness when I think of it, won, and unappreciated, and abandoned. With much the same feeling, I sometimes look at some trifling, inconspicuous ornamentation, at the flowers on the wallpaper in a dark corner of a corridor, which, perhaps, no one but me will notice. In someone else's house, on the writing desk, I saw the exact same ashtray I have on my desk, and yet this one is mine, the other someone else's. I remember, when I was about ten years old, my uncle died from diphtheria. His rooms were being disinfected. Perhaps they didn't quite explain disinfection well enough to me: I understood that this man had died and now what they were doing was making it so that his things weren't his anymore, removing from them the dust, the smell, all that which made these things precisely his.

I don't like hearing when people talk of machines: oh, our mechanical age; oh, robots; oh, this and that. Machines, instruments, have served us all. In this sense a penknife is no different from some very complicated factory machine. The point is, there's no complexity here. We take the number of parts as complexity, but the parts themselves are simple, and in the end they connect together simply. When a man looks at a steam engine, its mechanism seems to him unbelievably intricate, because in his notion of it he has disconnected the object from the mind that conceived it. The mind is intricate and complex, human ingenuity is astonishing, but the creation itself is of course simple. The charm of machines is precisely the fact that every intelligent, dextrous man can create a machine. No, we have not moved much further on than our ancestors. In the fifth century, a clever Chinese man invented the submarine. The Mongols in days of yore stunned their Western foes with poisonous gases. I read an advertisement, for instance, for some firm producing all kinds of automated devices for the vending of goods, the latest word in technology, so to speak. Yet automated devices were already being used in gray-haired antiquity. Egyptian priests used them to play on the superstitions of their people. Magical urns stood outside the Temples of Isis. They supplied the faithful with the goddess's blessing in the form of a few drops of holy water. All that was needed to make this happen was to drop a five-drachma coin into a slot in the urn, just as a young lady would do at an underground station to get a box of almonds. It turns out that this is a sacred and immortal gesture. Those auto-functioning Egyptian urns brought the priests a good profit for several centuries in a row, and of course the secret behind their mechanism was guarded by strict laws, even by the threat of capital punishment. This is how it must have worked: a dropped coin fell along a wired tube onto the well-balanced shoulder of a lever; this would cause a valve in the bottom of the vessel filled with water to open up for a moment, and a little water would pour out through a discharge pipe into a cup, placed there by a gullible Egyptian, sweating with stupefaction. And several centuries later, on the streets and even on the main roads of ancient Rome, there were automats for vending wine, just like the gadgets we have. Thus, a Roman, leaving home, would always take a drinking goblet. If I were a good artist, I would paint the following picture: Horace, thrusting a coin into a slot machine.

Man is God's likeness; a thing is man's likeness. A man who makes a thing his God comes to resemble the thing. Thus, one comes full circle: thing, God, man, thing—and a full circle is pleasing to the mind. An automat is in many ways most similar to man. You push it, it responds. You grease its palm, and it brings you pleasure. You give it money, it gives you goods. But in all other kinds of things I feel a certain resemblance to man. Underpants drying in a brisk wind launch into an idiotic, but quite human, dance. An inkwell stares at me with one black eye, with a glint in its pupil. A clock whose hands are at ten to two brings to mind a face with Wilhelm's whiskers,[4] while a clock with its hands at twenty past seven brings to mind a face with whiskers turned down Chinese-style. Between the rounded bell-glass of a lamp and the bald head of a philosopher filled with luminous thought there is a soothing resemblance. We have christened the parts of things, weapons, machines, with words we use for different parts of our bodies, making these diminutives as if we were talking of our children. "Toothlet, eyelet, earlet, hairlet, noselet, footlet, back, handle, head."[5] It is as though I am surrounded by little monsters, and it seems to me that the little teeth of the clock are gnawing away at time, that the "ear" of the needle stuck into the curtain is eavesdropping on me, that the teapot spout,[6] with a little droplet poised on its tip, is about to sneeze like a man with a cold. But with larger objects, in houses, trains, automobiles, factories, the human element sometimes becomes startlingly unpleasant. In villages in the Schwarzwald there are sneering houses: the little window in the roof is elongated like a sly eye. Automobiles, too, can be extremely eyelike, the more so because we give them not three, not one, but two headlights. Little wonder that in our fairy tales and in our spiritualist séances things literally come to life.

I think that, by deepening these analogies, and by going into what I admit is a certain anthropomorphic ardor, we can lend things our feelings. In the lazy positioning of a woolen shawl draped over the back of a chair there's something moping: oh, how the shawl longs for someone's shoulders! In an open but still perfectly blank notebook there's something cheerful, joyous, and sincere. A pencil is, by its nature, softer, kinder than a pen. The pen speaks, the pencil whispers.

Finally, there are children among things. These are, of course, toys. They imitate grown-up things, and the more accurate the imitation, the dearer they are to a human child. In childhood I was troubled by the question: Where will my toys go when I grow up? I imagined a huge museum, where they gradually gathered the toys of children who were growing up. And often now, when I go into a museum of antiquities where there are Roman coins, weapons, clothes, chain mail, it seems to me that I have entered that very museum of my dreams.

We fear letting—not for anything do we want to let—our things return to the nature they came from. It is almost physically painful for me to part with old trousers. I keep letters I will never reread. A thing is a human likeness, and sensing this likeness, its death, its destruction, is unbearable for us. Ancient kings were laid in their coffins with their armor, their implements; they would have taken their palaces with them if they could. Flaubert wished to be buried with his inkwell. But the ink-well would be bored without a quill, the quill without paper, the paper without a desk, the desk without a room, the room without a house, the house without a town. And, no matter how hard man tries, he, too, decays, and his things decay, too. And better than lying like a mummy in a painted sarcophagus in a museum draft, it is far more pleasant, and somehow more honest, to decay in the ground to which in their turn toys, and linotypes, and toothpicks, and automobiles will return.

14

On Opera (Essay, 1928)[*]

It would be curious to ascertain whether opera is a natural art. By natural art, I mean the kind of art that finds its likeness or correspondence in nature, just as, for instance, a Doric column or a Beethoven sonata directly imitates either nature or human life; as, for instance, painting or theater do. The question of the naturalness of opera is, of course, complicated by the fact that opera is itself a blend of several art forms, which is why it is necessary to establish whether this blend is something natural, or, more precisely, what conditions are needed for this combination to be natural.

Let us begin *ab ovo*. I am not concerned now with the actual origins of opera, but, rather, with how it might have originated. Could it originate from life itself, from a desire to imitate life, to represent it with that inner accuracy with which, for instance, a sculpture represents life? In other words, does or could opera exist outside of the stage, in nature itself, in life itself? I think, yes. Let us imagine a person who works and sings. What is important here is from where exactly does song, the desire to sing, arise? I suppose that a person is most inclined to break into song when there's the fullest correspondence between his inner state and the outer environment, nature outside him. A workman sings along with his work in exactly the same way a prima donna sings along with music. A plowman returning home in the evening sings along with the lightness and calm of evening, the evening bell, the soft

[*] VN wrote "Ob opere" for an émigré musical evening on "Spring and Easter" organized by the society Vo Dvore, vo Fligele (In the Yard, in the Wing: a phrase from Chekhov's story "The Darling," 1899) and held in Berlin's Augusta-Schule on April 16, 1928. Holograph manuscript, VNA Berg, and program, VNA Montreux. The program and a report in *Rul'*, April 23, 1928, 2, identify Sirin's contribution as an introductory talk on "The Sounds of Russian Spring," but on one copy of the program, VN crossed this out and wrote "Ob opere."

tread and lowing of the cattle. A street urchin, who has thrust his hands into the pockets of his trousers, walks, and whistles (the whistle is a kind of lip song, as distinct from a throat or chest one), finds himself in perfect accord with the pleasant clatter of the city, and it is thanks to this harmony that his whistle, his song, comes into being. In all of these cases there's already the essence of opera. Transport this plowman or this whistler to the stage, replace that nature—that environment which was unwittingly causing them to sing—with music, and what you get is opera. But one must keep in mind here that occasions when a person expresses his feelings through song, and the singing feelings themselves, are limited. So what is happening? When a shoemaker sings as he works—rather, to the tune of his work—where the work is equivalent to the music, we're not surprised, but when a fat old tenor expresses his love not through spoken language but through musical howls, we deem this to be unnatural. I think that the fault lies not with opera, but with that mysterious spirit which has governed mankind from time immemorial—a mysterious spirit or, as in my opinion, pure chance. It is perfectly by chance that we express our usual thoughts in words and not in song. Algebra triumphs over music. If the semantic meaning of language lay not in words, not in signs, but in this or that rising or falling of the voice, then we would converse like birds—that is, by means of song. It is of course too late now to learn to sing and unlearn how to speak, but I repeat that it is perfectly by chance that mankind followed the path to speech. A playful imagination will take a certain pleasure in the following picture: a land where all books are written in musical notes, and shop assistants respond with an aria to the aria of the shopper. And that's why I think that opera, being completely natural in its origins—every day we see a little opera in the street, in the field, in the tavern—remains natural in its further developments, because it provides us with a picture of how people would express their feelings if they always sang, rather than just at work or in the bath. And if correspondence and harmony are always observed between environment and song in everyday life, then this harmony must also exist in opera, and only when this harmony is observed is opera beautiful. It is in this sense that *Pelléas and Mélisande*, *Boris Godunov*, and, in part, *Carmen*, are beautiful.

15

Omar Khayyám Translated by Ivan Tkhorzhevsky
(Review, 1928)*

Omar Khayyám, Persian poet, astrologer, freethinker, and sage, was born in 1040 and died in 1123 AD. He wrote in *rubāʿī* (a *rubāʿī* is a quatrain written with a single rhyme, the third line most often being unrhymed). The original of Khayyám's poems did not survive; all that remained were copies made several centuries after his death and residing in dusky libraries until England "discovered" Omar Khayyám in the nineteenth century.

In 1859, the brilliant English poet FitzGerald published a collection of poems, which he called translations from Omar Khayyám.[1] Undoubtedly, FitzGerald consulted the Persian manuscript, yet it is impossible to consider this book in any way a translation. Despite the abundance of "Eastern" images, these wonderful poems are suffused with the spirit of English poetry; only an Englishman could have written them. They have about the same relation to Persian poetry as, say, Pushkin's translations of the poetry of the Western Slavs have to the actual songs of the latter.

A little later, a number of other translations from Omar Khayyám appeared (for instance, the French translation by Nicolas,[2] who was determined at all costs to make a mystic out of Khayyám, for which he was subtly mocked by FitzGerald at the time). Each translated it in his own way, selecting from the Persian *rubāʿī* what was most to his own liking. Notwithstanding all this, the system employed by the Russian translator Ivan Tkhorzhevsky (who has published over 200 *rubāʿī*) hardly seems right: he used not only the so-called Bodleian text but

* V. Sirin, "Omar Khayyam, v perevodakh Iv. Tkhorzhevskogo. Parizh," *Rul'*, May 30, 1928, 4.

also the works of various other translators, losing sight of the fact that, by taking on the poems of FitzGerald, he was in reality translating not a Persian poet but a very original English one, that FitzGerald, unlike the others, needs to be translated in a very particular way, and in any case without changing or concealing anything. The result of all this is something strange (and I would say unconvincing), since it is impossible to draw on such nonequivalent sources and then present them all as a kind of composite Omar Khayyám. Moreover, the author hasn't added any footnotes, or indicated from where this or that quatrain has been taken—from FitzGerald, from Nicolas, or from Claude Anet (for, alas, it turns out that poor Claude Anet, known for his naïvely vulgar depictions of the "Russian soul," has also "translated" Omar Khayyám . . . before). The result, then, is a very complex combination of intercrossing translations, imitations, and (at times successful) personal refinements, which are difficult to untangle. As far as I could determine, Tkhorzhevsky translated around thirty *rubāʿī* from FitzGerald (not including the short poem about "earthenware," placed at the end of the book). The translations are fairly inaccurate and at times simply incorrect. So, for example, Tkhorzhevsky makes a mistake common to all translators from the English. It concerns the color purple. FitzGerald talks of "flowing purple" seas; Tkhorzhevsky translates "the seas exhale, burning with a scarlet tremor" (which, besides, recalls Balmont); yet the English "purple" is not the same as the Russian (or French) *pourpre* (scarlet, vermillion); but rather, it means "lilac," "violet," at times (in poetry) even "dark blue." Another error: FitzGerald talks of a rose "that blows about us," where "blow" can also mean not bloom but gust—and so the Russian translator introduces into his poem a totally unnecessary wind ("the little wind blows off my silk," his rose says), and with this he dilutes the tender stringency of FitzGerald's lines. The demands of the rhyme scheme (and it really isn't easy to think up a sonorous masculine rhyme for three lines!) often forces the translator to resort to unnecessary refinement. FitzGerald puts it simply: "Morning in the Bowl of Night / Has flung the Stone that puts the Stars to Flight" (there is apparently an Eastern tradition of throwing a stone into a bowl, thereby issuing the order to mount the horses); Tkhorzhevsky has this: "a caravan of stars sets off. / The darkness is exhausted." The image has become runny and confused. FitzGerald has:

"Oh, the brave Music of a distant Drum!"; Tkhorzhevsky has the drum drumming "right beneath the ear." FitzGerald says wonderfully: "For in and out, above, about, below, / 'Tis nothing but a Magic Shadow-show, / Play'd in a Box whose Candle is the Sun, / Round which we Phantom Figures come and go"; Tkhorzhevsky has it: "There in the blue, heavenly lantern / the sun blazes: gold upon the campfire (!?)" and so on. FitzGerald's expressive and, at the same time, warlike musicality is not conveyed at all by the following lines: "Nor shall they ask us; but take and cast us into the world; the heavens deciding who goes where," whereas FitzGerald has: "And He that toss'd Thee down into the Field, / He knows about it all—He knows—HE knows!" In a footnote to this line, FitzGerald provides (let's hope faithfully) the original line: "O dánad O dánad O dánad O—" (which breaks off). Indeed, all comparisons between the original (FitzGerald's) and Tkhorzhevsky's translation reveal many such infelicities, commonplaces, and accommodations to the rhyme scheme; two lines are regularly translated accurately, and two approximately. As Pushkin wrote about rhyme, "Two will come by themselves, the third will be brought in," but at times the third is obstinate.

The mystery and fragrance of FitzGerald's verse evaporates under Tkhorzhevsky's attempt to convert them into Russian sounds. There are also several strange inaccuracies in his translations of Nicolas (for instance, in the poem which begins, "You flew down, O Lord, onto the hurricane"), but here, of course, the translator's task demands less: Nicolas is no FitzGerald. As for the third "source"—unfortunately, I could not establish what bit the notorious Claude Anet had added, what material he had provided our author. There are, it's true, two or three suspiciously "French" quatrains (about love), and I am similarly suspicious about another quatrain which begins, "Monasteries, mosques, synagogues," too simple and distinct a list, which could hardly have been made by a Persian poet of the eleventh century. I leave this, however, to the conscience of Professor Minorsky, who gave the author the necessary references.

If one pays no attention to all this confusion of "sources" and simply reads these *rubāʻī* as the poetry of a good Russian poet, one is frequently astonished at their elegance, the precision of their definitions, and the charm of their murmur. So what if at times we meet expressions overly reminiscent of our own early Symbolism ("blue distances," "somewhere in the distance," "enliven with wine the turning of a page," "a face's briefly given lunar luster," and so on), and so what if we sometimes come across such poor words as "oriole," "discrepancy," "plan," and "climate"—all the same, one cannot help smiling with pleasure, reading this or that quatrain. How delightful, for instance, is this: "All the world's kingdoms for a glass of wine! All the wisdom of books for the tang of wine! All honors for the luster and velvet of wine! All music for the gurgle of wine!" I daresay that, although Omar Khayyám may never have written such lines, he would nonetheless be flattered and delighted.

16

Aleksey Remizov, *The Star Above Stars*
(Review, 1928)[*]

Every fairy tale or saga, like every chess problem, must have what is called a *pointe*—in other words, some salt or spice. Reading Remizov's sagas,[1] one is astounded by how hopelessly flavorless they are, since they lack the very thing that alone might justify this literary genre. And it's no justification that Remizov is supposedly imitating ancient Apocrypha, the legends of traveling pilgrims. Apocrypha and legends have an antiquarian charm, mystical perspectives on ancient thought, landscapes ennobled by distance, symbols which in their time were full of fragrancy and meaning. One would need an especially inspired imagination and an extraordinary mastery to compose such artless fairy tales as were composed in ancient times.

Neither special imagination nor special mastery is to be found in Remizov's work. The fairy tales in this book create an impression of something unsteady, irresponsible, and accidental. When the author presents a sequence of images (and sequences, enumerations, and descriptions are endless), the reader fails to sense that internal law which, deeper than rhythm and truer than meaning, governs the quality and quantity of the given images. "Judas ran to the rivulet—the river flowed away; he ran to the forest—the forest leaned away." The reader is overcome by a kind of mental tickle and doesn't know why the author limited himself to forest, rivulet, and river, and didn't add anything more—say, "He ran to the hill—the mountain flattened," and so on. Or as here, when Remizov enumerates the parts from which God made man: "from the earth—the skeleton, from the sea—blood,

[*] V. Sirin, "Zvezda nadzvezdnaya. Y.M.C.A. Parizh," *Rul'*, Nov. 14, 1928, 4.

from the sun—beauty," and so on. One could add or subtract and the impression wouldn't change. On top of all this, the author abuses astronomy, though he sins less against it than against taste when, as in one story, he talks of the star brought by the Virgin Mary, in another he maintains that the sun is "God's tear," and in a third has God taking beauty from the same sun so as to give it to man. Worst of all is that once again nothing would change if the Virgin Mary brought "the sun above suns" rather than "the star above stars," and if the star and not the sun turned out to be "God's tear." For good measure, the author throws in, "Hell thunders with thunder, the tempest tempers" and the reader automatically adds: "the burn burns." The author is playing a game of building blocks. The author is playing with lists. The author is playing a very boring game.

It would be one thing if Remizov's style were faultless. But, alas, how careless, what an accidental combination of words, and what awkwardness of style at times . . . "The first days on earth gave way to the gloomy, eerie night," or "The cruel twilight clothed the city in moonless silence." But even better is "the shot-wounded insulted heart" and "The heart bled, searched for an exit" (the heart of the Virgin Mary, which "searches for an exit," is, at least stylistically, somewhat blasphemous). And the following already belongs in the realm of impermissible oddities: "They got down on their knees, and the serpent with them." No, this isn't simple ignorance (the author knows that a serpent does not have knees on which it could stand), but nor is this sacred ingenuousness. It is, rather, a sign of the carelessness which marks the whole book.

17

In Memory of Yuli Aykhenvald
(Obituary Essay, 1928)[*]

To get to know a person is to create the person: his traits and signs accumulate in our soul, his image grows, develops, and gains color, and each new encounter with him enriches our soul; and the more harmony and truth there is in this creation, the more we love that person. And when we, still as imperceptibly, grow close to him, when we get used to him, his image becomes so alive in us, so quivering and bright, that it seems as if our work is done, we have created that person, and years go by, and that person has become part of our souls. And as sometimes happens, that person, the very person whose image we have so painstakingly assimilated into our soul, suddenly dies, and then . . . what then? Bewilderment, absurdity, a feeling of some shocking inner incongruity, for the image of the person that we loved, that we created through persistent and joyous labor, of course continues to live on; his name, just as yesterday, is full of life, our lips pronounce it as living, and so the heading on the obituary, destroying all that is human, everyday, habitual-sounding, appears to be a lie.

Yuli Isaevich Aykhenvald has died. The run-up of his existence has been abruptly cut short, but in us the reflection of his life continues to speed on, and its slowing down, its cooling down, will be very gradual. For me, as for many who knew him well, he is as alive today as he was on that Saturday, half an hour before the tragedy, when, as I locked the front door, I could see his slightly stooped back moving away through

[*] V. Nabokov-Sirin, "Pamyati Yu. I. Aykhenvalda," *Rul'*, Dec. 23, 1928, 5. Aykhenvald, long distinguished as a critic in Russia, had become a friend and the most prominent admirer of Sirin in the Berlin emigration. On Saturday, Dec. 15, 1928, he was returning from a party at the Nabokovs' when he was hit by a tram. He did not regain consciousness and died on Monday, Dec. 17.

the glass. His voice reverberates in my ears, the cautious persuasiveness of his intonations, the particular emphasis on the "not" parts of speech, when, in calling one thing beautiful, he would call something else not beautiful. I can see him as he modestly and shortsightedly makes his way through a crowded room, his head slightly tucked into his shoulders, his elbows pressed to his sides, and, having reached the person he has been looking for, suddenly stretches out his narrow hand and touches him by the sleeve with the most fleeting and lightest of gestures.

Oh yes, there is an earthly possibility of immortality. The deceased continues to live a detailed and varied life in the souls of all the people who knew him; some knew him closely, others must make do with an outer impression, the hoard of two or three encounters, and then there are those who saw him only once. And every one of them grasped the man in their own way, so that numerous images of the deceased remain on this earth, at times harmoniously complementing one another. But those who knew him personally will die; thus shall the first stage of this extended life come to an end, so already people will know about him only by hearsay; in writing, his image will endure, but it will be meager and cold. And it pains us to anticipate that future coldness, when only the name still lives. As well it might . . . No matter how we philosophize, no matter how we console ourselves with the responsiveness of our five senses, all the same, all the same the real person, that unique exemplar, is no longer here. He left for home late at night, and was walking deep in thought, the course and content of which no one, no one will ever know. So that from the tram platform only the tram driver and a chance German student saw a stooped man trustingly step onto the rails. And I feel so sorry for him, I feel so sorry for this tender man, that suddenly the line I am writing seems to slip into mist.

18

Ivan Bunin, *Selected Poems*
(Review, 1929)*

Bunin's poems are the best the Russian muse has created for several decades. Once, in Petersburg's loud years, the radiant rattle of modish lyres drowned them out, but that poetic brouhaha passed without a trace and those "blasphemous creators of words"[1] have been dethroned or forgotten. We are left cold by the dead slabs of Bryusov's poetry; Balmont's poetry, which deceived us with its new melody, now seems out of tune; and only the throb of one lyre, the special throb that belongs to immortal poetry, stirs us as before, stirs us more than before, and it seems strange that in those Petersburg years not everyone could distinguish, not every soul was amazed by the voice of a poet whose equal we have not had since Tyutchev's time. Nonetheless, I suppose that even today, among the so-called reading public, especially that part of it inclined to see new accomplishment in the illiterate mutterings of a Soviet poetaster, the poetry of Bunin is not in high regard or, at best, is looked on as the not entirely lawful pastime of a man fated to write prose. It's not worth disputing such a view.

Among Bunin's "selected poems," many one would like to reread are not there. They are printed alongside the writer's stories, in the shadow of his prose, and they exist only in old journals, in supplements to *Niva*,[2] and in a separate little book poorly and sloppily published also by *Niva*. It would be good to see them all collected; every line of Bunin's is worth being preserved. But we must be thankful even for this collection (very elegantly presented, by the way), for these two hundred Bunin poems.

It's easy to pounce on a poet, it is easy to fish laughable mistakes,

* V. Sirin, "Literaturnoe obozrenie: Iv. Bunin. Izbrannye stikhi. Izdatel'stvo 'Sovremennye zapiski.' Parizh. 1929," *Rul'*, May 22, 1929, 2–3.

monstrous stresses, bad rhymes out of his doggerel. But how does one speak of the works of a great poet, where everything is beautiful, everything smooth, how does one express the charm and depth of his poetry, the novelty and strength of his imagery? How can one extract citations when behind a citation the poem stretches whole onto the page? And there are other difficulties: the music and the thought in Bunin's poetry are so merged into one that it's impossible to talk separately about theme and rhythm. You get drunk on these poems, and it's a pity to disrupt their enchantment with empty cries of rapture.

So I have read this book and set it aside, and am beginning to listen to the blissful, throbbing echo it has left behind. And, gradually, I make out the special Buninesque leitmotif, whose simplest expression is repetition, the languid repetition of a single word: "sing, sing, crickets, my night-time friends . . .";[3] "and the ballroom floats, floats in drawn-out / songs of happiness and yearning . . .";[4] "the tumbler pigeons amble, amble, as they coo . . .";[5] "the ringing of little bells [. . .] / flows, flows. . . ."[6] And, finding this rhythmic key, catching this sound, I already feel its further development, the musical enumeration of actions or objects, an almost incantatory exclamation, two lines beginning identically: "Only your morning bells, Sofia, / Only the voice of Kiev . . ."[7]

The key mood in Bunin, corresponding to this key rhythm, is perhaps the very essence of the poetic feeling of his work overall, the purest, most divine feeling a person can experience, looking at the painted world, listening to its sounds, breathing in its scents, being imbued with its fierce heat, its dampness, its cold. It is that desire, sharp to the point of torment, languid to the point of fainting, to express in words the inexplicable, mysterious, and harmonious that make up the broad conception of beauty, the beautiful. "O, torment of torments," the poet himself says, "what do I need, what does *it* need" (the bare maple "against the pure and azure emptiness"), / "the goldfinches, the leaves? And will I ever understand / why I must encompass the joy of this torment— / *this* sky here, and this chime, / and the dark meaning it's full of / —into consonances and sounds?"[8] Bunin's greatness as a poet lies precisely in the fact that he finds these sounds, and his poems not only breathe with that special poetic thirst—to encompass everything, express everything, preserve everything—but also quench that thirst.

Returning to the concept of "beauty," one can note that for Bunin "beauty" is "what passes," but "what passes" he feels as "eternally repeating." In his world, as in the rhythm of his poems, there are sweet repetitions. And this world is unprecedentedly spacious. In the poem "Dog" (which begins so characteristically: "Dream, dream . . .") the poet himself says that he is "like God, fated / to know the yearning of all lands and times."[9] Russia's estates and Russia's fairy-tale heartland— "the Russia of the Princes of Kiev, bears, elks and aurochs";[10] the valleys of Jordan and the "dusty road to Nazareth";[11] Italian wisteria and ruins "and the fires and songs of Catania . . .";[12] "a forgotten portico of Phoebus" on an island in the Aegean sea;[13] the Nile and "the living and clear-cut trace of a footprint"[14] preserved in a thin blue layer of dust, increasing by five thousand years the allotted life of the poet; the smoke of the Bosporus mixed with the cold water, smelling of honey and vanilla; the Indian Ocean, where "like a great cane, the unsteady foresail / staggers from star to star . . ."[15] and Ceylon, "the end of the world"[16]—Bunin felt all this, and conveyed all this. "Earth, earth! Innumerable footprints / I have left on you. . . . But I shall not, I shall never quench the torment / of my love for you!"[17] And Bunin's poems about other countries are not merely "descriptive poems," and not the "Eastern melodies" so soundlessly flaunted by second-rate poets. There is no "exoticism" in them. Bunin feels the dream of a foreign people, a foreign legend, and the detail of a landscape unnoticed by the tourist just as vividly and as keenly as the "creak of a rotting floorboard"[18] in his own estate, the damp garden lit up by night lightning, or a simple, somewhat coarse Russian fairy tale, which he knows like no other how to give life to with his creative breath.

To this richness of themes there corresponds a richness of rhythm. Bunin has an amazing mastery of every poetic meter and every kind of poetry. His sonnets—in the brilliance and naturalness of their rhymes, in the lightness and imperceptibility with which he clothes his thought in such complex harmony—Bunin's sonnets are the best in Russian poetry. His unusual eyesight notices the edge of a black shadow on a moonlit street, the special density of blue sky through leaves, the spots of sun slipping like lace across the backs of horses—and, capturing this harmony of light in nature, the poet transforms it into a harmony of sound, as if keeping the same order, observing the same sequence. "The little Negro boy in a dirty Turkish fez / hangs in a tub overboard, painting the forecastle— / and from the water onto the fresh red varnish / mirrory arabesques rise up. . . ."[19]

I have already said that beauty for Bunin is "passing" (which is why he has so many poems dedicated to tombs, ruins, deserts . . .). After exclaiming "O joyous moment!" he adds: "O deceitful moment!"[20] The cockerel on the church cross that "floats, flows, runs like a rook" (a wonderfully Buninesque repetition of verbs!) "sings that all is deception, / that only for a moment does fate give us / our father's home, and a dear friend, / and a circle of children and a circle of grandchildren. . . ."[21] On Rachel's tomb there are "no name, no inscriptions, no marks. . . ."[22]

One would think that such a profound sensation of transience must breed a feeling of illimitable grief. But the yearning of great poets is a happy yearning. A wind of happiness blows from Bunin's poems, although he has no shortage of gloomy, threatening, and ominous words. Yes, everything passes, but: "Earth, earth! Sweet call of spring, / is there really happiness even in loss?"[23] And Christ tells his Mother (who is mourning that heat will destroy some flowers, others will be scythed down): "Mother! night's darkness covers only the earth, not the sun: / death does not destroy the seed, but only cuts off / the earthly seed's flower. / And the earthly seed will not dry up. / Death mows, love sows again. / Rejoice, my love! You'll be / consoling yourself till the end of the age!"[24] Everything repeats itself, everything in the world is a repetition, a change, with which the poet "unchangingly consoles" himself. This blessed quivering, this languorously repeating rhythm, is perhaps the main charm of Bunin's poetry. Yes, everything on earth is loss and deception, where there were cathedrals there are now stones and poppies, everything living dies away, everything turns into satiny dust upon the flagstones of crypts. But is the loss itself not imaginary, if what's fleeting in the world can be enclosed in an immortal, and therefore a happy, poem?

19

Alexander Kuprin, *The Glade: Short Stories* (Review, 1929)[*]

"... You have to believe in bays and chestnuts. And I won't say a bad word against black horses, either. Only they're unnecessarily hotheaded and quickly work up a lather. This is partly true, too, of dark bays and liver-chestnuts. . . ." How wonderful when a great writer has a passion for something. He writes superbly of everything, but there are some things on earth he writes especially well about. Sight and smell, always highly attuned in a writer, then reach a state of extreme feeling, and the usual level of keenness of observation at once soars, since here constant creative sharp-sightedness is ennobled by expert experience. Kuprin[1] himself notes that, when a Russian talks of his habitual and favorite pursuit, we're astounded by the precision and purity of his language, by the compact freedom of his speech and the easy obedience of the necessary words. But when not just an ordinary Russian, but a Russian writer, who has received a generous gift from God, speaks about what he knows and loves, about a passion endlessly tender and strange, then you can imagine the precision and purity of his expression, how his words move us. This is how Kuprin writes of a horse's charm, of its hot, strong breath and of its marvelous smell, and, reading the first short story in this collection, you feel the whole time the warm, silky skin of the horse beneath its lips, the tender hollow above the nostril, not to be compared to anything else. What, for example, isn't this worth: "The failure of a race can depend on many more reasons: the horse was unwell, but this wasn't seen to in time; it woke up in a bad mood, perhaps it had had a bad dream." And our imagination is immediately

[*] V. Sirin, "Kuprin. 'Elan' (rasskazy). 'Russkaya Biblioteka.' Belgrade," *Rul'*, Oct. 23, 1929, 5.

ignited at the mention of the dream the horse might have had, and you can't help feeling that Kuprin knows even this—a horse's dream—and that this knowledge for him is as easy and natural as the knowledge of the colors of horses' coats. But this longing for an outlet . . . What can the writer do with—and how can he explain to himself—this agitation, this passion. . . . For in this case the man has been created as if solely to write books, and write them beautifully, but "all his life he has been dreaming of training thoroughbred racehorses." Rousseau fancied himself a botanist (he was a dreadful botanist, by the way, but he wrote about plants with great exaltation); it's very possible that, had Kuprin given up writing books, he would have made a wonderful horse trainer, but the loss to Russian literature would have been huge.

In this small collection there are stories not only about horses, but also about dogs, the circus, a magic violin, a flying carpet. And they are all, of course, very Kuprinesque. The author's talent bursts forth from every, even a careless, sentence; yet for some reason some pages seem only quick jottings, simply material—rich and vivid material—for more harmonious and stricter works.

But reproach would be a sin; after all, this is very good, *very* good.

20

Questionnaire on Proust (1930)*

The editors of Chisla *(Numbers) approached a number of writers, asking them to answer the following questionnaire:*

  1. *Do you consider Proust to be the most powerful spokesman of our epoch?*
  2. *Do you see the heroes and atmosphere of his epoch in contemporary life?*
  3. *Do you think that the peculiarities of Proust's world, his methods of observation, his spiritual experience, and his style must have a decisive influence on world literature in the near future, and on Russian literature in particular?*

1. I think that this is impossible to judge: an epoch is never "ours." I have no idea what epoch some future historian will dump us into and what markers he will find for it. I am suspicious of the markers contemporaries find.

2. Again, it's hard for me to imagine contemporary life en bloc. Every country lives in its own way, and every person in his own way. But there's something eternal. Only the portrayal of this eternal element is of value. Proust's characters have lived everywhere and always.

3. Literary influence is a dark and murky thing. We can imagine, for example, two writers, A and B, who are completely different but both under the influence of Proust in some very subjective

---

* V. Sirin (and others), "Anketa o Pruste," *Chisla* 1 (1930), 272–74; Sirin on p. 274.

way; this influence is imperceptible to reader C, since each of the three (A, B, and C) has grasped Proust in his own way. Sometimes a writer will exert influence indirectly, through another, or some kind of complex blending of influences occurs, and so on. It is impossible to foresee anything in this direction.

21

The Triumph of Virtue (Essay, 1930)[*]

To a superficial mind it may appear that the author of this article is better placed than any Soviet critic, who, keenly sensing the class under-pinnings of literature, draws a distinct line between bourgeois and proletarian literature. My advantage over him may seem to lie in the fact that I am an element perfectly devoid of any class-consciousness, and feel no class hatred toward people living better than I, toward the golden-toothed stockbroker who quaffs champagne from morning, or toward the well-fed doorman who nevertheless, like all doormen in Berlin, is a member of the Communist Order, and as a result, I can approach politics, philosophy, or literature without bourgeois or any other kind of prejudices. However, the perspicacious and honest Soviet critic answers that the idea of a human and non-class approach is absurd, or, rather, that the impartiality of appreciation is itself already a hidden manifestation of bourgeois tendencies. This assertion is extraordinarily important, for it follows that a self-restrained communist and born member of the proletariat, and an unrestrained landowner and born nobleman, respond to the simplest things in life in different ways: the pleasure from a sip of cold water on a hot day, the pain from a hard thump on the head, the discomfort caused by ill-fitting footwear, and many other human experiences which are equally familiar to all mortals. It would be pointless for me to claim that a Soviet executive[1] sneezes and yawns in the same way as an irresponsible bourgeois; it's the Soviet critic who is right, and not I. The thing is, class conscious-ness is a kind of spectral luxury, something highbrow and ideal, the one thing that might save from understandable despair the proletarian man,

[*] V. Sirin, "Torzhestvo dobrodeteli," *Rul'*, March 5, 1930, 2–3.

anatomically constructed along the same lines as the bourgeois model and doomed not just to live beneath the bourgeois blue sky and to work with his bourgeois five-fingered hands, but also to carry inside himself to the end of his days that bony character which bourgeois scientists call by the bourgeois word "skeleton."

And here's a curious thing: just as Marx's teachings suddenly acquire a shade of unexpected spirituality when placed against the low bourgeois anatomy of the Marxist himself, so Soviet literature, compared with Russian literature, with world literature, is pervaded by high idealism, profound humanism, and strict morality. What's more, no literature of any country has ever glorified virtue and knowledge, humility and piety, or advocated morality, as Soviet literature has done from the start of its existence. If we were to look for a weak analogy we would have to turn to the innocent infancy of European literature, to that very far-off time when people produced guileless mystery plays and rather crude fables. Devils with horns, misers with their sacks, quarrelsome wives, fat millers, and rogue clerks—all these literary types were simple and sharply defined to the utmost degree. People were fed morality to the bursting point, by the spoonful. Animals soliloquized—domestic livestock and forest creatures—and each one of them represented a human characteristic, was a symbol of vice or virtue. But, alas, literature was not able to hold on to such didactic heights; its fall from grace was the first love song.

Fortunately, there's no reason to think that Soviet literature will divert from this path of truth any time soon. All is well, virtue has triumphed. And it's perfectly unimportant that the good being extolled and the evil being punished are the good and evil of class. In this small class world, the relationships between moral strength and the means of struggle are the same as in the big world, the human one. All of the familiar literary types starkly and simply expressing either good or bad in man (or in society), those bright characters who never darken, and the dark characters destined never to see the light, all our old friends, the philosophizers, the villains, the righteous ruffians, and the cunning flatterers, crowd together again in the pages of Soviet books. Here we find echoes of *Uncle Tom's Cabin*, and a peculiar repetition of some theme from the old supplements of *Niva* (a young princess becomes involved with her father's secretary, an honest *raznochinets*[2] who has populist tendencies), the search for a rose with no thorns along the beaten track that runs from political ignorance to Bolshevik revelation, and the torch of knowledge and the knightly adventures, in which the Red Knight singlehandedly crushes the enemy horde. These elements, common to all human literature up to now, that still persist one way or another in the work of moralizing lady writers and writers for adolescents, and which, probably, will persist until the end of the world, are repeated in Soviet literature as something new, with aplomb, with passion, with rapture. We return to the very mainspring of literature, to a simplicity not yet enlightened by inspiration, and to a moral teaching that has not yet lost its zeal. Soviet literature rather recalls those sanctimonious handpicked libraries found in prisons and correctional facilities for the enlightenment and pacification of inmates.

We don't remember their names; they have no names. The sailor depicted by a second-rate writer and the sailor depicted by a third-rate writer are no different from one another, and only a proletarian critic maddened by loyalty can scrape out heresy here and there. In this literature, at best second-rate (the first-rate kind is not on sale), the sailor type is as clear-cut as, say, the age-old figure of the simpleton. This sailor, much beloved by Soviet writers, says things like "We're done for," swears virtuously, and reads "all sorts of books." He is a ladies' man, like any good, healthy fellow, but this sometimes gets him snared in the net of some bourgeois or partisan siren, and for a time he is knocked off the course of class good. He inevitably gets back on track, however. The sailor is a positive character, although a little dense. Somewhat like him is the "soldier" type, that other darling of Soviet literature. The soldier, too, likes to squeeze village girls filled with all sorts of juices, and to blind female village teachers with his white-toothed smile. Just like the sailor, the soldier often gets himself into trouble over women. He is always brimming with life, well versed in politics, and lavish with cheerful exclamations such as "Come on, then, lads!" The peasants choose him as chairman, and some old peasant invariably grins into his beard and says approvingly, "How big the lad talks" (i.e., the old peasant has seen the light). But the popularity of the sailor or the soldier is nothing compared with the popularity of the Party member. The Party member is sullen, doesn't sleep much, smokes a lot, sees women for the time being as fellow comrades, and is very straightforward in his manner of address, so that everyone feels calmed by his composure, his glumness, and his businesslike air. A childlike smile nevertheless sometimes suddenly breaks through that Party glumness, or in an emotionally difficult situation he might squeeze someone's hand, and at once the eyes of a comrade-in-arms will well with tears. The Party member is rarely handsome, but on the other hand his face seems as if it's hewn from stone. You will simply not find a more luminous type than this. "Eh, brother," he says in a moment of frankness, and with this the reader is given a glimpse into a life full of sacrifices, exploits, and suffering. The literary connection between him and the Count of Monte Cristo or some Red Indian chief is obvious.

This type of Soviet executive never washes. The female Soviet executive, about whom more later, splashes her face with water, and with that her ablutions are over. The non–Party member rubs himself with cold water. The professional of bourgeois origins rubs himself not with water but with eau de cologne, following the example of Chichikov's Sunday extravagances.[3] Not one of the character types so beloved by the Soviet writer is familiar with a bath, and this asceticism is clearly connected to the well-known disgust that bashful virtue has felt toward washing since the dawn of time.

Strolling on through the gallery of literary types, we come across the type of the senior worker (or sometimes a bureaucrat). This person usually speaks with a provincial accent and has a playful slyness about him. The writer makes him a non–Party member only so as to expose the sham or superficial Party affiliation of the other lads, the fraudsters and the hooligans. "Why should I join the Party," he says, "when I'm a Bolshevik as it is. It's not about the rituals, it's about faith." The other type of non–Party member (the one who rubs himself down with cold water) is a suspicious character, from the former intelligentsia, and his White bones practically protrude from him. He is unmasked and booted out; or, with the help of a woman, a virtuous communist, he suddenly begins to comprehend just what a nobody he is. With him opens up a series of villains. Such as, for instance, the *kulak*[4] (who for some reason is most often a miller). He has a fat belly; he is cunning and greedy; first he exploits the poor and later, when the revolution hits him like a bolt from the blue, he joins the Kadet Party and rather fearlessly—in his sinful blindness—upbraids to their faces the Bolsheviks, who have come to requisition his flour and his mill, so duly dies from a bayonet thrust into his fat belly. Next an even bigger fish, the professional or the chairman of the trust, living in opulence with his wife (who shouts at the servants) and his canary (who sings in the kitchen). Descending still lower, we find the old Countess. The old Countess says *"Merci,"* curtsies affectedly, and extends her pinkie when she drinks tea. Once in a while we catch glimpses of ruddy White Guard officers, generals, priests, etc. The academic or the musician—the intellectual type—is also worth noticing. He's somewhat boring, suffers from various illnesses, is weak-willed, and looks at his children, who have joined the Communist Youth League, with secret jealousy. At the very worst, politically speaking, he's a Menshevik.

The female types are even simpler. Soviet writers genuinely idolize women. These appear in one of two main varieties: the bourgeois woman who loves soft furnishings and perfume and suspect professional men, and the communist woman (a Soviet executive or passionate neophyte) whose depiction makes up a good half of all Soviet literature. This popular woman has supple breasts, is young, buoyant, takes part in parades, and is astonishingly hardworking. She is a mix of the revolutionary, the sister of mercy, and the provincial miss. But, above all this, she is a saint. Her random love interests and disappointments don't count; she is betrothed but to one man, the betrothed of her class, Lenin.

It isn't difficult to imagine the kind of story that gets turned out given the available types. If we're speaking the metaphysical Soviet language, then the gender setup of the novel reveals the heroine's relationships with the sailor, the soldier, the rural pauper, the *kulak*, the suspect professional, and with her over-perfumed rival, the wife of the professional. Just as the simple but nonetheless saintly sailor sometimes unwittingly sins against his class by his healthy but imprudent attraction to a bourgeois woman, so, too, the saintly heroine, Katya or Natalia, is sometimes led into devilish error, and the object of her tender affections turns out to be a heretic. But, just like the sailor, the heroine finds the strength to break free from these fiendish intrigues and to return to the bosom of her own class. The Party member shoots dead his unworthy lover, while on the other street corner the female Komsomol[5] member shoots dead her unworthy suitor. The other type of novel is the denunciatory one: officials who are caught stealing face severe retribution; or a gloomy Soviet executive subtly uncovers the terrifying heresy hidden beneath the seductive words and actions of a non–Party member. Young people, too, are depicted, how they should and shouldn't behave, or elsewhere the village teacher diligently searches for the truth and finds it in communism. The better writers admire that theme of the unbelieving intellectual against the backdrop of joyful, calico-red Soviet life.

Virtue's triumph is absolute, on all fronts, to speak again in the appropriate language. If heresy is to be found, it is imperceptible to the layman, and one needs to be a proletarian critic versed in these lofty matters in order to detect the secret stamp of the devil. I deliberately do not address whether this service to virtue is good or bad. I am merely concerned with the question of whether it was worth mankind's while to spend century after century deepening and refining the art of writing books—and Russian writers worked a lot on this—was it and is it worth the labor, when it proves so easy to return to the long-forgotten models of mystery plays and fables, which, though they might summon a yawn from simple folk, praise virtue and scourge vice with due force? Let us instead slam shut our sinful, bourgeois books and drag the righteous Soviet censor out of his humble monk's cell; he is far too cramped in his little world of class and deserves more space. . . . Let us drag him out and bestow universal rights on him. Let him, with the sternness of a film director, place us on the path of good, punish evil mercilessly, condemn bribery, hypocrisy, and human pride, and unite in a marvelous kiss the lips of a simple girl and a pious lad against the backdrop of a dawning day. And you, you talented sinners, keep quiet!

22

International Survey on Populism
(Questionnaire, 1930)*

V. Nabokoff-Sirine

It seems to me that, from the point of view of art, there is no difference between the painting of a "noble" milieu and that of "the people." It's the way one treats the subject and not the subject itself that matters. A description of supper, with flowers on the tablecloth, and the glitter of the seductive Marquise X's rare jewels, is to my taste as soporific as certain country scenes with plump wenches and lots of cider. Bad taste, affectation, and excess psychologizing can be found as much in an image of country romps as in the depiction of the Daedalian adventures of a vicious ephebe, for everything depends on the talent of the writer and only talent counts. The truth is generally bizarre, the bizarre is sometimes true. It's the conventional that's always false.

I dislike all literary movements. From the moment that a novelist goes in for a trend, a school, he argufies, and when a novelist argufies, he's lost. Push this trend to the extreme and you'll have the present case of literature in Russia, where themes and theses are dictated to writers by communist doctrinarians, who tell them, "Give us the description of a collective farm, or else a novel on the role that a bourgeois origin plays in passion." They do it. They do it terribly badly. . . .

---

* In response to the manifesto by Léon Lemonnier and André Thérive in *L'Oeuvre*, Aug. 27, 1929, and Lemonnier's *Manifeste du roman populiste* (Paris: La Centaine, 1930), Jacques Cossin began an "Enquête internationale sur le populisme," in *La Grande Revue*, targeting writers from England, Germany, Belgium, Portugal, Romania, Poland, Russia, Switzerland, Spain, the United States, Norway, Italy, and Greece. The results were published in *La Grande Revue* from Oct. 1930 to Feb. 1931; the Russia section appeared in Dec. 1930, with VN on pp. 227–28.

23

Boris Poplavsky, *Flags*
(Review, 1931)[*]

Rarely, very rarely, does poetry waft through the poems of Poplavsky. "Day descended, in extreme decline, and the finger of rain turned the transparent globe around."[1] The second line is splendid—hard to say why it's splendid, but it is, it is. "The dead fir tree went away. Sledges scrape / ironing the road with the green manes of hands. . . ."[2] That's not bad, either. "We're still so young. Rain poured all summer, / but rowing boats rocked beyond the wet glass. / Pistols cracked in the green garden."[3] Beautiful lines—it's damp, it's green, one breathes freely. However, finding such examples is no easy task, and the ones I've listed are almost the only instances of poetry in Poplavsky's poems (I say "almost" because I also like the first poem in the collection, which is funny and tasteless, but also, as is sometimes the case with Pasternak, somehow captivating). Occasionally, the ear is also seduced by a fleeting tonality, such as, for instance, the beautiful sound of the following line, which is nevertheless rather meaningless: "Go to sleep, O, Morella, how awful are aquiline lives. . . ."[4] Pathos, thunder, tension . . . "Go to sleep, O, Morella, how awful are aquiline lives . . ." You could repeat it all day. . . . And yet, when you read such sonorous and glossy lines as "Don Quixote's jade flies up onto the porch / along with scented Sancho on a red donkey,"[5] you already begin to feel doubt and a faint nausea. Let me specify (as the critic Adamovich is fond of saying, incidentally): what is good and genuine is so rarely met in Poplavsky, it's just a matter

[*] V. Sirin, "Boris Poplavsky. *Flagi*. Izd. Chisla," *Rul'*, March 11, 1931, 5. In his autobiography, VN recalled decades later: "I did not meet Poplavski who died young, a far violin among near balalaikas. 'Go to sleep, O Morella, how awful are aquiline lives.' His plangent tonalities I shall never forget, nor shall I ever forgive myself for the ill-tempered review in which I attacked him for trivial faults in his unfledged verse" (*SM*, 287).

of happy chance. To be frank, Poplavsky is a bad poet, his poetry is an unbearable blend of Severyanin, Vertinsky, and Pasternak (the latter at his worst), on top of which it is seasoned with a kind of awful parochialism, as though the man were permanently living in the same little Estonian town where the book was printed, and printed very badly at that.

"Motors burst out laughing, monocles tumbled,"[6] and "the days turned blue, turned lilac,"[7] vividly remind us of the poet of "moiré dresses" and "lacy forests"[8] (who also loves all the trips to Mars, dirigibles, *Titanic*s, etc., so dear to Poplavsky's heart), while all of these tinsel little angels of Poplavsky's—his blue boys, pink girls, little hares, dwarves, steamships, female travelers, and youths—remind us no less vividly of the sickly sweet nonsense in those notorious songs about "handsome boys," and about how "the plumes on the blind horses swayed, / the old priest ardently swung his incense. . . ."[9] Indeed, Poplavsky is so laughably helpless as a poet (so random are the four lines of his stanza) that at times it seems as though four not particularly literate people have been playing Bouts-Rimés. But, like many poets of his type, Poplavsky is simultaneously prone to sportive verbal refinement: "This game of words could break a donkey, / but I am an iron donkey made of jelly. / I've always felt pity yet I've turned to jelly."[10] I'd like to note that, despite a very superficial knowledge of the Russian language, an un-Russian mode of speech, and poor vocabulary and turn of phrase, Poplavsky harbors a strange predilection for the living, folk word *an*[11]: "and only the pipe on the armchair burns,"[12] or "While a cow is flying in the sky,"[13] or "but then disappears through our fingers. . . ."[14] It sounds sweet and courtly. He also likes the word "chic": "Africa chic,"[15] "Wild chic of operetta divas,"[16] "the chic little hall."[17] The epithet "beautiful," of doubtful quality, is popular with him. One comes across unbearable stresses: *magázin* (shop), *svadébnyi* (wedding), *pozhúryu* (rebuke), and so on. Since he lacks a feel for language, some fairly unpleasant things happen to him from time to time, for example: ". . . people lean towards happiness along with the vessel."[18] He is incapable of composing a more complex sentence and fitting it into a line: "two goddesses with whom I am in love. . . ."[19] Blunders of cadence are extremely common, schoolboy blunders: for instance, the carelessness, that slovenliness of cadence, which doubles the final syllable in a word that ends in two consonants and assigns it two beats in a line: *oktyaber'* (October), *pyupityr* (lectern), *dirizhabel'* (dirigible), *korabel'* (ship).[20] Talking of ships. Poplavsky hasn't avoided the craze for voguish images—there are seafaring and roses galore. It's a curious fact that, after many years when poets left the rose alone, considering it banal and in bad taste to mention it, young poets appeared who judged thus: "Ah, but it's become totally new, it's rested, its vulgarity has disappeared, and now the rose in poetry sounds recherché. . . ." It would be one thing if this idea had struck just one head, but, alas, the rose has been taken up by them all, and, honest to God, I don't see how these roses are better than K.R.'s.[21] Ladinsky, needless to say, is an exception.[22]

With all this in mind, it is difficult to take Poplavsky's poems seriously. It is especially unpleasant when he begins to color them with angelic epithets; it's like some kind of colored marzipan or a colored photographic postcard with mother-of-pearl spangles. The thought even strikes me that perhaps this is all an empty amusement—perhaps it would be better for Poplavsky to try his hand at prose? I hesitate to give any advice, for every pure-hearted suggestion of this sort is usually taken as tactlessness. And yet . . . How good it is at times to go deep into oneself, to refrain piously from writing poetry, to force the muse to fast a little. . . . "O, Morella, go to sleep, how terrible are aquiline lives. . . ."[23] It has a ring to it, there's no way around it, it has a ring—and yet it's such nonsense. . . .

24

What Should Everyone Know?
(Essay, 1931)*

Our epoch, gentlemen, is an epoch of great upheavals, anxieties, and quests. We stand before an approaching future, pregnant with changes, and along with that, like Orpheus, we must clean out the Augural Stables of the past. Before the war, people had morals, old morals, but now they have killed their morals and buried them and written on their gravestone: people had morals, old morals, but they have killed the morals and buried them and written on their gravestone: people had morals, but they killed them and buried them and written nothing on their gravestone. In their place something new has appeared, the beauteous goddess of psychoanalysis, and in her own way (to the great horror of decrepit moralizers) she has explained the real reason for our suffering, our joys, and our torments. Anyone who tries our "Velveteen" shaving soap will never use other brands again. Anyone who looks at the world through the prism of "Freudianism for all" won't regret it.

Gentlemen, the deepest truth can sometimes be expressed in a shallow joke. Let me offer the following example: *Son:* "Daddy, I want to marry Granny. . . ." *Father:* "Don't be silly." *Son:* "But why, Daddy, can you marry my mommy and I can't marry yours?" Silly, you'll say. Yet here, in this little piece of silliness, there's already the whole essence of the theory of complexes! This boy, this pure and honest youth, whose father (a stupid stickler) has denied him the satisfaction of a natural desire, will either conceal his desire and be unhappy for the rest of his life (*Tantalus* complex), or kill his father (hard-labor complex), or, at last, fulfill his desire in spite of everything (happy-marriage complex).

---

* V. Sirin, "Chto vsyakiy dolzhen znat'?," *Novaya gazeta*, May 1, 1931. Translation by Stanislav Shvabrin, Anastasia Tolstoy, and Brian Boyd.

Or take another example: Let's say a man experiences an attack of incomprehensible fear when he meets a tiger in the forest. How can we explain this fear? Gentlemen, an elegant and simple answer is provided by psychoanalysis: undoubtedly, in his early childhood this man was frightened by a picture or by a tiger skin under Mommy's grand piano; this terror (*horror tigris*) continues to live in him subconsciously, and later, in ripe adulthood, is then expressed, as it were, when he encounters the actual beast. Had he a knowledgeable doctor with him in the forest, he would have teased out of his patient the scrap of fateful memory, and would have reminded the tiger, in simple terms, how he, the tiger, had at some point tasted human flesh, so had become a man-eater. The outcome of this conversation is clear.

Gentlemen, submit your dreams to psychoanalysis! Who among us hasn't "screamed in the thrall of a nightmare" after the feast following a fast, or seen Lake Lucerne in our dreams after a trip to Lake Lucerne? But why does this happen? Here's why. A man who has eaten three-quarters of the Easter butter, only to fight that night with a cross between a satyr and a mastodon, is suffering under the burden of his own unfulfilled (erotic) desires. The lake means the same thing.

So, the more comfortable a man's life, the more he favors his least desires, the more happily and thoroughly he indulges them, the less often does he have bad dreams, the healthier is his soul. Indeed, science has established that some ancient Roman emperors (Decameron, for instance) did not dream at all.

Gentlemen, you won't make out the motley fabric of life if you don't master one thing: sex rules life. The pen, with which we write to a sweetheart or a debtor, represents the male organ, while the mailbox where we drop our letter is the female organ. That's how to understand everyday life. Children's games, for example, are all based on eroticism (keep this especially firmly in mind). A boy furiously whipping his spinning top is a subconscious sadist; a ball (preferably large) pleases him because it reminds him of a woman's breast; a game of hide-and-seek is really an emiratic (secret, deep) longing to return to the mother's womb. The same Oedipus complex is reflected in several of our folksy curses.

Wherever we cast our eyes, everywhere, sex is the basis. Turn to the best-known professions, and there it is: the architect makes houses (read: makes love), the cameraman rolls film (read: rolls her over), the lady doctor looks after a sick man (read: the sick man recovers and "looks after" the lady doctor). Philologists will confirm that such expressions as "mercury falling," "falling leaf," "fallen horse" are all (subconscious) hints at a fallen woman. Likewise, compare "sexagenarians" and "sextet" and the "sex drive." Same goes for such words as "sextuplets," "sextant," "sexton," and so on. Many names are steeped in eroticism: Honey, Bunny, Desirée (from "desire"), Mary (from "marry"); the Spanish even have the name Juan (from "Don Juan").

Whatever you do, whatever you might think about, remember that all your acts and deeds, ideas and thoughts may be perfectly satisfactorily explained as shown above. Use our patented remedy "Freudianism for all," and you will be satisfied. We have grateful testimonials from many writers and artists, three engineers, educators, midwives, and so on, and so forth. Acts immediately, pleasant to take. Every modern man should stock up. Highly interesting! Astonishingly cheap!

25

Writers and the Era
(Essay, 1931)[*]

I try sometimes to suppose the idea that twenty-first-century man will have of our epoch. It would seem that we have this advantage over our ancestors, that our technology has found certain means for the more or less permanent conservation of time. People like to say to themselves that the most impersonal writer, making the best possible portrait of his century, cannot tell us as much as the little gray gleam of an old-fashioned film. Wrong. Contemporary cinematographic methods which seem to our eyes to give a perfectly exact image of life will probably be so different from the methods used by our great-great-nephews that the impression that they will give of the movement of our era (the wan quivering of a street corner swarming with vehicles forever vanished) will be rendered false by the very style of the photography, by that antiquated and awkward air that engravings showing the events of a past century have for our eyes. In other words, our descendants will not have a direct sensation of reality. Man will never be the master of time—but how curious it would be to be able at least to stop it to examine at leisure the nuance that escapes us, the ray that's out of place, that shade whose ungraspable velvet isn't made for our touch.

A sunny day, perhaps too hot; there will be rain. I look out my window, I lean out, I try to get out of my era and to envisage this street here in the retrospective fashion that will be so natural to our descendants and that I am so jealous of. A blue car has stopped near the pavement. The sky, a bluish wash, is reflected in the lacquered roof, and the broken chessboard of the paving stones climbs and tilts in the varnished depths

[*] Vladimir Sirine, "Les Écrivains et l'époque," *Le Mois* 6 (June 1–July 1, 1931), 137–39.

of the door. This car, these paving stones, the clothes of the people passing by, the way in which the fruits and vegetables of the corner shop
are arranged, these two big chestnut draft horses attached to a moving
van, the hum of a plane above the roofs—all these things put together
give me the sensation of a certain present reality, of a combination that
will still be possible tomorrow, but which will not be in twenty or so
years. I try to imagine all this as a past resuscitated, I force my eyes to
find the passersby dressed in a bygone style, I almost succeed in seeing
in this car that poor and drab something or other that strikes us when
we see a carriage in a historical museum. Experiments in vain, provoking a slight vertigo, a strange displacement, as when, lying on the sand,
your head back, you look upside down at how people walk (the knee
bends, the foot seems to push the ground back), you have for a moment
a visual sensation of gravity. But these moments are short; the mind is
immediately caught up again by the habits of daily life. And then one
tells oneself that, after all, among the things that seem to us to group
together in a unique order, forming present reality, there are some that
will exist for a long time—the jerky twittering of sparrows, the green
of the lilacs falling over the railings, the white breastpiece and the gray
rump of a cloud gliding proud through the damp blue of a June sky.

Our eagerness to surprise and possess time is conveyed by the stress
we put on the word "our" when we speak of "our era." An ephemeral
possession, for time flows between our fingers, today's generalization
is no longer true tomorrow.

It's the snows of yesteryear and not the marbles that I want to see
and touch. For we really possess only the pale image, the inert body of a
past forever gone. We study it so. We dress it up in so many systems, and
give it such handy labels, that we almost come to the point of believing
that men of the thirteenth century knew as well as we do that they lived
in the Middle Ages. What a surprise it would be to know the label the
future historian will attach to the twentieth century.

It's the man of tomorrow who will examine what will be left of the
remains of the man of today, but it's indeed this latter who sees the
movement, the colors, and the lineaments of his living body, of which
the other sees only the skeleton. The historian of his own time, the
historian of times past are none the wiser. All that we can say of our
century is always more art than science. That philosopher who, two or

three years ago, wrote a big book taking the short skirt as the symbol of our era, must today pull a funny long face if he happens to read fashion magazines or simply to look out the window. There are on the other hand poets who seem to think that the skyscraper is the best mark of the present—whereas architects (and it's always the specialist's opinion that counts) tell us that the trend of the time is to construct smaller and lower houses. That's why I always have a terrible fear of the symbols or symptoms of what people are pleased to call "our era." All the more so since each country seems to have its favorite fetishes.

The blue car has gone, the sky is gray, it's going to rain. A brawl in a street in Algeciras, a submarine gliding toward the Pole, a man in shirtsleeves killing his wife with ax blows in a peaceful little provincial town, a secret political meeting in England, an explorer lost in the mountains of Tibet, drops of rain, one, two, three, and then all together tapping on my window.

No, there's nothing of the systematizer in me, and my mind isn't delicately enough constituted to grasp the ideas and currents of my century. It doesn't seem to me, this century, worse than another; it has its share of courage, goodness, genius, it plays football marvelously well, it thinks and works a lot, in a word, it is. . . .

But there I am, surprising myself fixing an inscription of doubtful validity, a street name the next government will change, a colored hotel sticker fading on an old suitcase. . . .

26

Nina Berberova, *The Last and the First*
(Review, 1931)[*]

"On September 20, 1928, between the hours of nine and ten in the morning, three events took place which marked the beginning of this story: Alexei Ivanovich Shaibin, one of its numerous heroes, turned up at the Gorbatovs' house; Vasya, a son of the Gorbatovs' (the child of Stepan Vasilievich and Vera Kirillovna, and the stepbrother of Ilya Stepanovich), received a letter from Paris from his friend Adolf Kellerman, with important news about his father; and, finally, an impoverished blind wanderer and his guide arrived at the Gorbatovs' farm, in a broad valley of the Vaucluse department."

This wanderer was about to sing a song, which was to "give us an answer, the clearest and most modest answer for the Russian people," but he was interrupted: Shaibin arrived from Africa, and here the story begins its powerful course: the trip of Ilya and Shaibin, and then Vasya, to Paris, and their spiritual adventures there. As a result, the reader does not learn at the beginning of the novel what song the "terribly thin" old man was going to sing; it is merely promised us as the revelation of some secret. Yet the song, delayed and sung only at the end of the book, contains the central idea of the story. The entire plot is only a series of artful variations on this main theme promised at the start and gradually revealed to us in keeping with the musical progression of the plot, and sounding, finally, with simple and convincing force from the lips of the dying stranger:

---

[*] V. Sirin, "N. Berberova, Poslednie i Pervye. Izd. Ya. Povolotskiy. Parizh," *Rul'*, July 23, 1931, 5.

Grieve not in the strangers' land, Cossack,
Long not for darling Russia, Cossack—
Have you not been given free will
And a pathway across the earth?
Walk all along that pathway,
Come to the country of the French.
Build your house on a steep hill,
Draw a boundary around a small field.
Weep not in the strangers' land, Cossack,
For the graves of father and mother.
Take strength from your fate, Cossack,
From the foreign land that you own.

You would think that to settle in the land of strangers would mean to disown your own forever, to cut yourself off from the last tie to Russia maintained by the restlessness of the nomad. Paradoxically, however, it is precisely in toiling on a small foreign field that the author—or the hero—sees the salvation and strengthening of the Russian soul. For there lies something especially Russian in the very notion of "land," and by living on that land, by taking to living plainly, by pushing aside the culture of the city, by doing all this you can preserve the timeless way of life of your homeland. Such is the thesis advanced.

The reader demanding a certain satisfaction from the author, what in everyday life is called making ends meet, and in art, consistency, wholeness, and harmony, will receive an unusually full satisfaction from *The Last and the First*. The book is beautifully wrought. This is the first novel in which the image of the émigré world is presented from an epic and a quasi-retrospective angle, and whose hero is just a little above human height. In some sense one could imagine a Russian writer of the coming century trying to re-create artistically the distant past, managing with only an intent and inspired imagination, and writing a novel about us very similar in spirit to Berberova's.[1] The conventional and stylized nature of this book is due not to any shortcomings but, rather, to the unavoidable nature of epic. What a gifted writer of the twenty-first century will create involuntarily, owing to his distance from us, Berberova creates consciously. From the crumbling, crookedness, and cacophony of all everyday émigré life that she has singled out, she raises to the status of epic just one aspect of our lives that she has rounded off and locked in on in her own way: our longing for land, our longing for a settled way of life. Some of Berberova's techniques would have been simply unbearable in a novel purely about everyday life, but the torturous tension of the dialogues (in places very reminiscent of Karamazovian cries) and some of the strangeness of coincidences and encounters are redeemed by the overall order of this unique, well-formed, and brilliant book. The language is unusually strong and pure; the images are magnificent in their weighty and precise force. This is not ladies' needlework, or a thoughtless fraternization with the abyss, or a made-to-measure response to the ills of the present: this is literature of the highest quality, the creation of a true writer.

27

In Memory of A. M. Chorny
(Obituary Essay, 1932)*

He seems not to have a single poem where at least one zoological epithet couldn't be tracked down—in the same way you might sometimes come across a soft toy under an armchair in a drawing room or a study, a sure sign that there are children in the house. A small animal in the corner of a poem is as definite a marker of Sasha Chorny as an elephant on an eraser.[1] But it is not his books that I want to remember now.

As repulsive as I find all such "personal statements" (and the affectation of those guilty quotation marks), I nonetheless consider it my indispensable duty to speak of the help which A.M. gave me eleven or twelve years ago. One of our finest poets wrote recently of the deaf-and-dumb inattention of the established toward those starting out. There exist two forms of help. There is praise signed off by a loud name, and help in the direct sense: the advice of an elder, his corrections on the novice's manuscript (the wavy line of consternation, the carefully corrected grammatical slip), his beautiful restrained encouragement, and then not at all restrained assistance. It was this second—and most important—kind of help that I received from A.M. He was then twice as old as me and famous; tidings of him had spread from "White Sea to Black"[2] (on the shores of the latter there were even those claiming to be him). He lived in Charlottenburg, at 60 Wallstrasse, I think; a brick wall towered outside his window, his room was darkish; I would bring him poems, which I now recall without any embarrassment but also without any pleasure. With his help I was published in *Zhar-ptitsa*, *Grani*, and elsewhere.

* V. Sirin, "Pamyati A. M. Chornogo," *Poslednie novosti* (The Latest News), Aug. 13, 1932, 23.

Not only did he arrange the publication of a little book of my youthful poems, he also ordered the poems, thought up a name for the collection,[3] and edited the proofs. Yet I don't hide from myself that of course he did not value them as highly as I then thought (A.M. had excellent taste), but he was doing a kind deed and he did it thoroughly. I find it unpleasant, I repeat, to stick my own autobiography in here, and it seems I am not the only one who can recall receiving his help; I just wanted to express somehow my belated gratitude, now, when I can no longer send him the letter whose writing for some reason I put off; now, when it's all over; now, when all that's left of him are a few books and a quiet, lovely shadow.

28

Interview with Andrey Sedykh
for *Poslednie Novosti* (1932)*

(Sirin has a long, thin, noble face, a high forehead. He speaks quickly and with passion. But a kind of prudence prevents him from speaking of himself.)

Your interests?
Setting aside the work of writing, which for me is very arduous and meticulous, then all that remains is zoology, which I studied in Cambridge, the Romance languages, and a great love of tennis, football, and boxing. I seem to be not a bad goalkeeper.

You have been accused of being "un-Russian."
Ridiculous! I've been accused of having been influenced by German writers whom I don't even know. In fact, I read German very badly. It would be more accurate to talk of a French influence: I love Flaubert and Proust. It's curious, but I felt a closeness to Western culture while I was still in Russia. Here in the West, on the other hand, I haven't consciously learned anything, yet I've felt most keenly the fascination of Gogol and, closer to us, Chekhov.

Why are all the heroes of a physically and morally healthy, sporty individual so messed up?
Messed up? . . . Yes, perhaps you're right. It's hard to explain. Perhaps there's more significance and interest to be found in a person's suffering

* "U V. V. Sirina [At V. V. Sirin's]," *Poslednie novosti*, Nov. 3, 1932, 2. Interview by Andrey Sedykh (Yakov Tsvibak), in both the leading émigré newspaper, Paris's *Poslednie novosti*, and the leading newspaper of the Baltic emigration, Riga's *Segodnya* (very slightly reworked, as "Vstrecha s V. V. Sirinym" ["Meeting with V. V. Sirin"], Nov. 4, 1932, 8), before Nabokov-Sirin's first public reading in Paris.

than in a tranquil life. Human nature reveals itself more fully—I think that's it. There's something enthralling about suffering. Right now I'm writing a novel, *Despair*. It's narrated in the first person by a Russified German. It is the story of a crime. One more person "messed up."

What are your working methods?
In what I write mood plays the central role, while everything that comes from pure reason recedes into the background. The idea of my novel forms unexpectedly, it's born in a minute. That's important. All that remains is to expose the photographic plate, which has been fixed somewhere deep inside. Everything's there already, all the main elements; I need only to write the novel itself, to do the hard technical work. An author in the course of his work never identifies himself with the main characters of the novel; his hero lives an independent, autonomous life; everything in this life is predetermined, and no one has the capacity to alter its measured course.

The initial impetus is paramount. There are writers who look upon their work as trade: each day a certain number of pages must be written. But I believe in a kind of inner intuition, in writerly inspiration. Sometimes I write without a break, twelve hours in a row; I'm sick while this goes on, I feel terrible. Yet at other times I have to rework and rewrite innumerable times; there are stories I've worked on for two months. And then trifles take a lot of time, the details of the treatment—some landscape or other, the color of the trams in the provincial town where my hero ends up, all the technical minutiae of the work. Sometimes I have to rewrite and rework every word. This is the only area where I'm patient and not lazy. For instance, in order to write *Luzhin*, I had to spend a lot of time on chess. Incidentally, Alekhine claimed that I had it in mind to depict Tartakower.[1] But I don't know him at all. My Luzhin is the purest fruit of my imagination. Just like Aldanov's Semyon Isidorovich Kremenetsky,[2] in whom people try at all cost to find the features of some well-known Petersburg lawyer now living in the emigration. And, of course, they did find them. But Aldanov is too careful a writer to copy his portrait from a living person. His Kremenetsky was born and lived in Aldanov's imagination alone. Glory and praise to the writer whose heroes seem to be people living our everyday lives among us.

29

In Memory of Amalia Fondaminsky
(Obituary Essay, 1937)[*]

In October 1932 I came to Paris for a month. I had known Ilya Fondaminsky for several years already, but it was the first time I met Amalia Fondaminsky. There are rare people who enter our lives so simply and freely, with such a smile, as though a place has been prepared for them for a long time now, and from then on it is impossible to imagine that only yesterday we had been strangers. The whole past seems to rise at once to the level of the moment of meeting, and then, receding again, takes with it, for its own use, the shadow of the living image, mixes it with shades of our life that has really been and passed, so that it turns out that for the sake of that one person (who by their very nature was a priori dear to us) a kind of false time is created, which retrospectively explains the feeling of natural closeness, the solid tenderness, the experienced warmth, which overcomes us at such meetings. That was the atmosphere of my meeting with Amalia Fondaminsky. The night before we met, I remember my first visit to Rue Chernoviz; I didn't catch Amalia there, and while I conversed with Ilya, I admired her Siamese cat. He was dark beige, with paler shades at the joints, with chocolate-colored paws and the same color tail (relatively short and fattish, which in combination with the coloring of his short-haired fur made his backside rather kangarooish). He looked on at God knows

---

[*] V. Sirin, untitled memoir, in *Pamiati Amalii Osipovnoi Fondaminskoi* (In Memory of Amalia Osipovna Fondaminsky) (Paris: privately printed, 1937). As VN writes here, he had known Ilya Fondaminsky—an editor and the chief funder of a major émigré journal, *Sovremennye zapiski*, based in Paris—since 1930, but he had met Fondamnisky's wife, Amalia, only on his Oct. 1932 trip to Paris. When Fondaminsky decided to publish a small memorial volume in honor of his wife, who had died in 1935, VN could not resist his imploring, despite his brief knowledge of her.

what with his clear eyes, filled to the brim with sapphire water; and this strange azure, his muteness, and the mysterious cautiousness of his movements made him look like a sacred temple creature. It was most likely about him that Amalia Osipovna and I first spoke. Her face shone with a welcome; an intelligent smile played across her lips, her eyes were alert and youthful, her graceful voice tender and quiet. There was something infinitely touching about her dark dress, her short height, and her very light tread. Like all newcomers to an unfamiliar city, I greedily made use of other people's telephones, and so now, too, I asked permission to phone out. When I sat back down at the tea table, Amalia Osipovna, silently and without archness, passed me a letter which I could not have supposed to be in her possession. It was my letter to Stepun,[1] who had once asked me to look over the English translation of his *Pereslegin*,[2] a translation which had seemed inexact to me, and to which I had responded hypercritically, driven by an overscrupulous fear of missing anything. Since one of the two translators had been Amalia Osipovna, Fyodor Avgustovich had passed on to her my letter, with its unflattering report, having told her, apparently, that I was unaware of who had made the translation. This turn in the conversation immediately ushered it out into an expanse of jovial frankness, and it became clear that Amalia Osipovna was a fine appreciator of what could be called the art of the gaffe. We discussed the ones I had already had time to commit in Russian Paris, through absentmindedness, through a lack of everyday sense, or just like that, for no reason. Meanwhile, a saucer with milk, like a full moon, was lowered down to the cat, who began to lap, observing a dactylic rhythm. And the cat, and the whole décor of the apartment, all its objects—from Amalia Osipovna's writing set to the large mat by the door, under which Russian Parisians trustingly hide their keys—all carried the elusive but indubitable stamp of kindness and cordiality that marks things in the homes of people radiant, and generous in their radiance. Amalia Osipovna's heartfelt kindness, transparent to its depths, was combined with a feeling of tenderness toward the world, a love for what Baratynsky called "fanciful nicknames,"[3] the urge to name everything in the world anew, in a special, personal way, as though she believed, perhaps rightly, that by improving the name you can improve its bearer.

I began to visit the Fondaminskys almost every day, and by the end of my stay in Paris I had moved in with them entirely. Amalia Osipovna, with a touching and at the same time unquestioning attentiveness toward me, had decided that I was "worn out," that I needed to "rest" before the public reading which she and her friends took part in organizing, something I had done nothing to deserve. And how I remember the charming, quiet room, with its overhanging bookshelves, where every detail was thought through with care, from the bottle of mineral water, to the hair lotion, to the scented talcum powder. And the ardor with which she sold tickets; and how distinctly I remember the following picture: Amalia Osipovna in the quiet, warm sitting room, is typing up for me several pages from *Despair*, while the cat sits warming himself on the fireplace. And with what a keen sense of shame, of remorse, I can't define it, do I recall how much I smoked in the apartment, not knowing that the smoky air was bad for her, while she of course said nothing to me. I fear that in general I was a difficult lodger, yet she graciously forgave me everything. Once, for instance, having come back very late when everyone in the house was already sleeping, I wanted to switch off the light in the hallway, but there were several switches and I didn't know which was the right one. I tried one, then another, and the lamps in the adjoining rooms started waking up. I was alarmed that I was going to light up the whole house this way, and, having left the light on in the hallway, went off to bed. But then my conscience troubled me. I got up, went back to the hallway, and began to test the switches carefully, and it was worrying that one of them seemed to have no visible effect. It later turned out that on my first attempt I had turned on, and then successfully turned off, the light in Amalia Osipovna's bedroom, and when I returned to the hallway, I lit her bedroom up once more and then left it that way; and she later woke up and turned it off herself, reacting with perfect humor to this nightmarish illumination.

Soon afterward I left Paris, and my final memory was of the small, dark figure of Amalia Osipovna on the platform; she had come to see me off. I would never see her again. And so now I want to keep hold of all this with feeble human hands for a few moments longer—all this which is so wondrous and so unsteady, ready at any moment to tumble silently into the dark and soft chasm of oblivion (but something essential will stay in one's soul forever, no matter how much life tries to conceal the traces, no matter how unreliable the brightness of these details, still memorable today, turns out to be).

30

Pushkin, or the True and the Seemingly True
(Essay, 1937)[*1]

Life sometimes proffers invitations to festivities that will never occur, and illustrations for books that will never be published. On other occasions it presents us with something for which we shall discover an unexpected use only much later.

I once knew an odd character. If he still exists, which I doubt, he must be the pearl of some lunatic asylum. When I met him he was already teetering on the verge of madness. His dementia, presumably precipitated by a fall from horseback in his earliest youth, was of a type that erodes the brain, giving it an artificial sensation of age. My patient not only believed he was older than he was, but was convinced he had taken part in the events of another century. Fortyish, husky, ruddy, glassy-eyed, this man related to me, with that little nodding motion characteristic of dreamy oldsters, how my infant grandfather used to clamber onto his lap. My rapid calculations, as he talked, yielded a fabulous age. The most fascinating and bizarre part was that, as his malady progressed year by year, he retreated into an ever more distant past.

When I saw him again some ten years ago, he spoke of the fall of Sebastopol.[2] A month later he was already regaling me with General Bonaparte. Another week and we were in the middle of the Vendée.[3] If he is still alive, my maniac, he must be far off indeed, among the Normans and their Conquest perhaps, or even—who knows—in the

* Vladimir Nabokoff-Sirine, "Pouchkine, ou le vrai et le vraisemblable," *Nouvelle revue française*, March 1937, 362–78. Written for the centenary of Pushkin's death. Translated into English by DN as "Pushkin, or the Real and the Plausible," *New York Review of Books*, March 31, 1988, 38–42 (see endnotes for DN's note on his translation). Since VN focuses on "truth" more than "reality" in the essay, I have amended DN's English title as above, and one or two phrases in the text that echo the title.

arms of Cleopatra. Poor, itinerant soul, rolling away ever faster down the slope of time! And, all the while, what an abundance of words, what verve, what roguish and knowing smiles.

He remembered the real events of his own lifetime perfectly, only he transplanted them in a bizarre way. Thus, when speaking of his accident, he kept shifting it back in time, progressively altering its setting, as in those classical dramas whose costumes are idiotically updated to suit a given period. One could not name a single personage from the past in his presence without his adding, with an old codger's formidable loquacity, some recollection of his own. Yet he had been born in a poor, provincial milieu, had served in some unspecified regiment, and the education he had picked up rather than received had remained extremely skimpy. Ah, what an overwhelming spectacle, what an intellectual feast it could have been had a refined culture, a good knowledge of history, and a modicum of natural talent accompanied his peripatetic dementia! Just think what a Carlyle would have extracted from such madness! Sad to say, my chap was fundamentally uncultured and woefully underequipped to profit by this rare psychosis, and was reduced to nourishing his imagination with a hodgepodge of banalities and general ideas that were more or less erroneous. Napoleon's crossed arms, the Iron Chancellor's[4] three lone hairs, or Byron's melancholy, plus a certain number of those so-called historical anecdotes historians use to sweeten their texts, provided, alas, all the detail and color he needed, and all the great men he had known intimately resembled each other like brothers. I know of no stranger spectacle than a mania whose very nature seems to demand a whole world of knowledge, inspiration, and refinement, but which finds itself obliged to orbit in a vacant head.

The recollection of this poor invalid returns to haunt me every time I open one of those curious books customarily called "fictionized biographies." I find he had the same compulsion as does a voracious but limited mind to appropriate some tasty personage, the same audacity as that of the self-confident know-it-all who strides off along the boulevard, evening paper in his pocket, to stroll in a very distant past. The formula is a familiar one. One begins by sifting through the great man's correspondence, cutting and pasting so as to fashion a nice paper suit for him, then one leafs through his works proper in search of character traits. And God knows one is pretty unfastidious about it. I have had occasion to find some rather curious items in these accounts of eminent lives, such as that biography of a famous German poet, where the content of a poem of his entitled "The Dream" was shamelessly presented in toto as if it had actually been dreamt by the poet himself. Indeed, what could be simpler than to have the great man circulate among the people, the ideas, the objects that he himself described and that one plucks from his books in order to make stuffing for one's own?

The fictionizing biographer organizes his finds as best he can and, since his best is generally a little bit worse than the worst of the author he is working on, the latter's life is inevitably distorted even if the basic facts are there. Then, hallelujah, we get the subject's psychology, the Freudian frolics, the bedaubed descriptions of what the protagonist was thinking at a given moment: a jumble of words akin to the wire holding together a skeleton's poor bones, a literary vacant lot where, amid the thistles, languishes an old piece of furniture that no one ever saw arrive. To give himself a rest after his labors, the biographer calmly proceeds to don his subject's waistcoat with its heart-shaped cutout, and smoke the great man's pipe. That lunatic I mentioned—he, too, would recount anecdotes from the lives of emperors and poets as if they had lived on his block. A Russian cigarette dangling from the corner of his mouth, he spoke with relish of Tolstoy's bare feet, of the venerable Turgenev's silvery pallor, of Dostoevsky's chains, to arrive at last at Pushkin's love affairs.

I do not know if in France there exists the type of calendar we had in Russia in which, on the reverse of each page, you found fifteen seconds' worth of reading matter, as if, by providing you with that handful of instructive and amusing lines, the unknown authors of the calendar wished to compensate you for the loss of the day whose number you were about to crumple. What you generally got was, in that order, the date of a battle, a verse of poetry, an idiotic proverb, and a dinner menu. Poems by Pushkin frequently appeared—and that was where the reader found the finishing touch for his literary education. These few unlucky lines, half-understood, half-toothless like an old comb, brutalized from repetition by sacrilegious lips, would probably be all that the Russian petit bourgeois would ever know of Pushkin, if we did not have a handful of operas, all very popular, presumably based on his works.

It is fruitless to reiterate that the perpetrators of the librettos, sinister individuals who sacrificed *Eugene Onegin* or "The Queen of Spades" to Tchaikovsky's mediocre music, criminally mutilated Pushkin's texts. I use the term "criminally" because these really were cases that called for legal action; inasmuch as the law prohibits an individual from defaming his fellow man, how, in the name of logic, can you allow the first comer to assault the work of a genius, pillage it and mix in a generous portion of his own—making it hard to imagine anything more totally fatuous than the stage adaptations of *Eugène Onéguine* or *Pique Dame*.[5]

A third and final element, in the simplistic reader's mind, joins the calendar and the operas: hazy recollections of elementary-school compositions—always the same ones—that one used to write about Pushkin's characters. Mix in a few off-color wordplays one often attributed to him, and we have a pretty accurate idea of the Pushkinian erudition of an immense number of Russians.

On the other hand, those of us who really know him revere him with unparalleled fervor and purity, and experience a radiant feeling when the richness of his life overflows into the present to flood our spirit. Everything about it is a source of joy: every one of his enjambments, as natural as the bend of a river; each nuance of his rhythm; as well as the most minute details of his existence, even the names of those who passed close to him, for an instant blending their shadows with his. As we pore over the splendor of his drafts, we seek to unravel in them all the intermediate phases through which his imagination hurtled to arrive at the finished masterpiece. To read his works, without a single exception—his poems, stories, elegies, letters, plays, reviews—and to reread them endlessly is one of the glories of earthly life.

Exactly one hundred years have elapsed since that twilight duel amid the snow, during which he was mortally wounded by a handsome lout who was courting his wife, one Georges d'Anthès, a young adventurer and total nonentity who later returned to France to survive Pushkin by half a century and die, an octogenarian and a senator with an untroubled conscience.

The life of Pushkin, all romantic spurts and blinding lightning bolts, offers temptations as well as traps for the hack biographers in vogue today. In Russia, of late, many have tried their hand. I have seen a couple of such efforts, and they are pretty revolting. But there also exists the pious and disinterested labor of a handful of elite minds who poke through Pushkin's past, gleaning the precious detail with no intention of using it to fabricate tinsel for vulgar tastes. And yet the fatal moment arrives when the most chaste of scholars almost unconsciously begins fictionizing, and in creeps literary prevarication, just as blatant in the erudite and conscientious man's work as it was in that of the shameless compiler.

It seems to me, in short, that by dint of palpating and frisking in search of the human side one reduces the great man to a macabre doll, like those pink cadavers of defunct tsars that used to be skillfully touched up for the funeral ceremony. Is it possible to imagine the full reality of another's life, to relive it in one's mind and set it down intact on paper? I doubt it: one even finds oneself seduced by the idea that thought itself, as it shines its beam on the story of a man's life, cannot avoid deforming it. Thus, what our mind perceives turns out to seem true, but not to be true.

And yet, what blissful reveries await the Russian who plunges into the world of Pushkin! The life of a poet is a kind of pastiche of his art. The passage of time seems inclined to re-evoke the gestures of a genius, imbuing his imagined existence with the same tints and outlines that the poet had bestowed on his creations. After all, what does it matter if what we perceive is but a monstrous hoax? Let us be honest and admit that if our mind could reverse direction and worm its way into Pushkin's age, we would not recognize it. What is the difference! The joy that we derive is one that the bitterest criticism, including that which I direct at myself, cannot destroy.

Here, then, is this brusque, stocky man, whose small swarthy hand (for there was something Negroid and something simian about this great Russian) wrote the first and most glorious pages of our poetry. Here is the blue fire of his gaze, in striking contrast with the dark chestnut hue of his frizzy hair. In those days—around 1830—masculine dress had not yet broken with equine considerations; a man still looked like a horseman rather than an undertaker. In other words, the purpose of the costume had not yet disappeared (for beauty disappears together with purpose). One really did travel on horseback, and one did require those top boots and that ample cloak. Hence it is but imagination that bestows a certain elegance on Pushkin, who, incidentally, in keeping with a whim of the period, liked to disguise himself—as a gypsy, a cossack, or an English dandy. A fondness for the mask, let us not forget, is an essential trait of the true poet.

Laughing heartily, extending his small frame to its full stature, stamping his heel, he suddenly flashes past me like those people you see emerging in a whirlwind from some nightclub (their faces, which you will never see again, obliquely illumined by a reflection, and their voices, which one will never again hear, repeating some merry joke): for is not the past itself a *boîte de nuit*,[6] a boxful of night that I open with impatience? I am quite aware that this is not the real Pushkin, but a third-rate thespian whom I pay to play the part. What is the difference! The ruse amuses me, and I catch myself beginning to believe in it. I see him, successively: on the Neva embankment, in a dreamy state, an elbow propped on the parapet of massive granite whose grains glisten from the moonlight and the frost; at the theater, holding up his double lorgnette amid a rosy light and the din of violins, behaving with fashionable insolence, jostling his neighbor as he makes his way back to his seat; then at his country place, banned from the capital for some overly brash gibe—in his nightshirt, hairy, scribbling verse on a scrap of gray paper of the kind used to wrap candles, as he munches on an apple. I see him walking along a country road, browsing in a bookshop, kissing the delicate foot of a female friend. Or else I see him on a torrid Crimean afternoon, pausing in front of a wretched little fountain trickling in the depths of the courtyard of what was once a Tartar palace, while the swallows dart back and forth beneath the vault.

The images are so rapid that at times I cannot distinguish whether it is a riding crop he holds in his hand or the metal bar he would carry to strengthen his wrist, for, like his contemporaries, he had a predilection for the pistol. I try to follow him with my gaze, but he vanishes, only to reappear, one hand behind his frock coat, walking beside his wife, a pretty woman taller than he, her black velvet hat adorned by a white feather. And, finally, there he is with a bullet in his belly, sitting crosswise in the snow and aiming at d'Anthès for a long, long time—so long that the other can stand it no longer, and slowly shields his heart with his forearm.

There, if I am not badly mistaken, we have some nice fictionized biography. One could continue in this fashion and write an entire book. Yet it is not my fault if I get carried away by these images, images common to Russians who know their Pushkin, and a part of our intellectual life in the same inextricable sense as multiplication tables or any other mental habit. These images are probably false, and the true Pushkin would not recognize himself in them. Yet if I inject into them a bit of the same love that I feel when reading his poems, is not what I am doing with this imaginary life somehow akin to the poet's work, if not to the poet himself?

When pondering the era that we Russians traditionally call the Pushkin period, i.e., the years from 1820 to 1837, one is struck by a special phenomenon, optical rather than mental. The life of those times seems to us today—how shall I put it?—less cluttered, less populous, with nice unobstructed areas of architecture and sky—like one of those old prints, in rigid perspective, where one sees the city square, not teeming with people and devoured by buildings with aggressive angles as it is today, but very spacious, orderly, harmoniously empty, with two gentlemen, perhaps, standing on the cobblestones engaged in conversation, a dog scratching its ear with a hind paw, a woman passing with a basket on her arm, a beggar with a wooden leg, and nothing more: just an abundance of air and calm, a quarter past noon on the steeple dial, and, in the pearl-gray sky, a solitary cloud, elongated and naïve.

One has the impression that everybody knew each other in Pushkin's time, that every hour of the day was described in some gentleman's diary or some lady's letter, and that Emperor Nicholas Pavlovich was privy to every detail of his subjects' existence, as if they were a bunch of more or less rowdy schoolchildren, and he the vigilant and stern schoolmaster. A quatrain that was a bit too flippant, a quip repeated at a gathering, a hastily penciled note passed from hand to hand in the great granite classroom that was Petersburg—everything assumed the proportions of a major happening, everything left its precious mark on the century's young memory. I really think Pushkin's era is, chronologically, the last within which our present-day imagination can still roam passportless, lending to the detail of each day traits borrowed from pictorial art, which still had a monopoly on illustration.

Imagine—if Pushkin had lived another two or three years we would have had his photograph. Just one more step and he would have emerged from the night, rich in nuance and filled with picturesque implications, wherein he resides, to stride firmly into the wan daylight that is now a whole century old. This, I believe, is an important point: around 1840 photography—those scant square centimeters of light—marked the beginning of a visual era that has lasted to the present day. And ever since that time, which neither Byron, nor Pushkin, nor Goethe lived to see, the ambience has been so familiar to our present-day sensibilities that latter-nineteenth-century celebrities assume the appearance of distant relatives—shabbily dressed, all in black as though they were in mourning for the iridescent life of yesteryear, invariably relegated to corners of somber, melancholy rooms, against a background of dust-laden drapery. Henceforth it is a flat domestic light that guides us through the century's grayness. Quite possibly a day will come when this era of sedentary photography will itself seem to us a kind of artistic prevarication with its own special flavor, but we are not yet at that point and—what a stroke of luck for our imagination!—Pushkin has not aged and has never had to wear that heavy fabric with its grotesque folds, that funeral clothing of our grandparents, with a little black cravat devoured by the mandibles of a stiff collar.

I have done my best to define the nearly insurmountable difficulties confronting the most confident mind when it attempts to resurrect, within the confines not of fictional plausibility but of unalloyed truth, the image of a great man who died a century ago. Let us admit defeat, and turn our attention instead to the contemplation of his work.

There is certainly nothing more boring than describing a great work of poetry, except perhaps for listening to the description. The only valid method of study is to read and ponder the work itself, to discuss it with yourself but not with others, for the best reader is still the egoist who savors his discovery unbeknownst to his neighbors. The urge I have at this moment to share my admiration for a poet with others is basically a pernicious feeling that bodes no good for my chosen subject. The greater the number of readers, the less a book is understood; the essence of its truth, as it spreads, seems to evaporate.

It is only after the first gleam of its literary fame has tarnished that a work reveals its true character. But with hard-to-translate writings that secrete their treasures in the darkness of a foreign language matters grow singularly complex. You cannot say to the French reader, "If you wish to familiarize yourself with Pushkin, take his works and lock yourself up with them." Our poet is decidedly unappealing to translators. Tolstoy, who happens to belong to the very same race as Pushkin, or good old Dostoevsky, who is vastly inferior, enjoys in France a fame of the same cloth as many native writers. Yet the name of Pushkin, which to us is so replete with music, remains prickly and shabby to the French ear.

It is always harder for a poet than for a proseman to cross borders. But in Pushkin's case there is more profound cause for that difficulty. "Russian champagne," a refined littérateur said to me the other day. For let us not forget that it is precisely French poetry, and an entire period of it, that Pushkin put at the service of his Russian muse. As a result, when his verse is translated into French, the reader recognizes both the French eighteenth century—rose-tinted poetry thorny with epigrams—and the artificially exotic romanticism that lumped together Seville, Venice, the Orient with its babooshes,[7] and sweet-honeyed Mother Greece. This first impression is so wretched, this old mistress so insipid, as to discourage the French right away. It is a platitude to say that, for us Russians, Pushkin is a colossus who bears on his shoulders our country's entire poetry. Yet, at the approach of the translator's pen, the soul of that poetry immediately flies off, and we are left holding but a little gilded cage. The other day I took a crack at this ungrateful toil. Here is an example, a famous fragment of verse in which the Russian seems to gurgle with the joy of life, but which, when translated, becomes a mere reflection:[*]

THE THREE SPRINGS

Dans le désert du monde, immense et triste espace,
trois sources ont jailli mystérieusement;
celle de la jouvence, eau brillante et fugace,
qui dans son cours pressé bouillonne éperdument;
celle de Castalie, où chante la pensée.
Mais la dernière source est l'eau d'oubli glacée. . . .

(Amid the world's expanse, morose and boundless,
there surged mysteriously forth three springs.
The spring of youth, a rapid spring, and riotous,
it shimmers, babbling, on its frothy course.
Castalia's spring, with inspiration welling,

---

[*] DN note: "The brackets enclose lines that Vladimir Nabokov omitted, for reasons of his own, in his French translations."

[slakes exile's thirst amid the world's expanse.]
The last spring is the cold spring of oblivion—
[sweetest of all it quells the passioned heart.])

Even though all the words are there, I do not believe these lines can give an idea of the ample and powerful lyricism of our poet. But I must admit that I gradually began enjoying the task, not with the evil intent of putting Pushkin on exhibit for the foreign reader, but quite simply for the exquisite sensation of plunging, heart and soul, into this poetry. Now I was no longer trying to render Pushkin in French, but to put myself into a kind of trance so that, without conscious participation on my part, the miracle of total metamorphosis might occur. At last, after several hours of these internal mutterings, of those borborygmi of the soul that accompany the composition of poetry, I felt the miracle had been accomplished. But as soon as I had written these brand-new lines in my poor foreigner's French, they began to wither. The distance separating the Russian text from the translation I had at last completed was now evident in all its sad reality. For example, I had chosen a piece of verse that, in Russian, has a divine simplicity; the words, in themselves perfectly straightforward, slightly larger than life, as if, at Pushkin's touch, they had regained their original amplitude, the freshness they had lost at the hands of other poets. Here is the dim reproduction that resulted:

SING NOT, MY FAIR
Ne me les chante pas, ma belle,
ces chansons de la Géorgie,
leur amertume me rappelle
une autre rive, une autre vie.

Il me rappelle, ton langage
cruel, une nuit, une plaine,
un clair de lune et le visage
d'une pauvre fille lointaine.

Cette ombre fatale et touchante,
lorsque je te vois, je l'oublie,

mais aussitôt que ta voix chante,
voici l'image ressurgie.

Ne me les chante pas, ma belle,
ces chansons de la Géorgie;
leur amertume me rappelle
une autre rive, une autre vie.

(Sing not, my fair, when I'm with you,
the songs of melancholy Georgia.
They make me recollect anew
another time, a distant shoreline.

They make me recollect, alas,
those melodies that you sing cruelly,
the steppe, the night, a poor, far lass,
her face illumined by the moonlight.

The phantom, ominous yet dear,
is, at the sight of you, forgotten;
your singing, though, makes it appear
again before my eyes to haunt me.

Sing not, my fair, when I'm with you,
the songs of melancholy Georgia.
They make me recollect anew
another time, a distant shoreline.)

What I found rather curious during these efforts at interpretation was that each poem I selected found its own special echo in one French poet or another. But I soon understood that Pushkin had nothing to do with this: I was being guided by my personal literary recollections, not by that false French reflection one has the impression of finding in his verse. Guided by these obliging recollections, I was, if not satisfied, at least not overly irritated by my translations. Here is one I find a little more successful than the rest:

POEM COMPOSED AT NIGHT DURING
A SPELL OF INSOMNIA

Je ne puis m'endormir. La nuit
recouvre tout, lourde de rêve.
Seule une montre va sans trêve,
monotone, auprès de mon lit.
Lachésis, commère loquace,
frisson de l'ombre, instant qui passe,
bruit du destin trotte-menu,
léger, lassant, que me veux-tu?
Que me veux-tu, morne murmure?
Es-tu la petite voix dure
du temps, du jour que j'ai perdu?

(I can't sleep—there is no light;
all is murk and irksome slumber.
All I hear is that clock near me,
ticking in a monotone.
Lachesis, you babbling beldame,
tremor of the sleeping night,
mouselike scampering of life—
why must you upset me so?
What's your meaning, tedious whisper—
a reproach or else the murmur
of the day that I have lost?
[What is it that you want from me?
Do you call, or prophesy?
I would like to understand,
I would like your sense to find.])

I also attempted to translate some excerpts from Pushkin's longer poems and his dramas. For curiosity's sake, here is one of the most beautiful stanzas of *Eugene Onegin*. I would have given a great deal to achieve a good translation of these fourteen lines:[*]

---

[*] DN note: "See my introduction [see notes p. 498]."

EXCERPT FROM "YEZERSKI"

Pourquoi le vent troublant la plaine
va-t-il virer dans un ravin,
tandis que sur l'onde sereine
un navire l'attend en vain?
Demande-lui. Pourquoi, morose,
fuyant les tours, l'aigle se pose
sur un chicot? Demande-lui.
Comme la lune aime la nuit,
pourquoi Desdémone aime-t-elle
son Maure? Parce que le vent,
le coeur de femme et l'aigle errant
ne connaissent de loi mortelle.
Lève ton front, poète élu;
rien ne t'enchaîne, toi non plus.

(Why does the wind revolve in the ravine,
sweep up the leaves and bear the dust,
when avidly on stirless water
wait for his breath the galleon must?
From mountains and past towers, why
does the dread heavy eagle fly
to a sear stump? Inquire of him.
Why does young Desdemona love
her blackamoor as the moon loves
the gloom of the night? Because
for wind and eagle
and maiden's heart no law is laid.
Poet, be proud: thus are you too:
neither is there a law for you.)

I nurture no illusions about the quality of these translations. It is reasonably plausible Pushkin, nothing more: the true Pushkin is elsewhere.
Yet, if we follow the riverbank of this poem as it unfolds, we do note, in
the bends I have managed to comply with here and there, something
truthful flowing melodiously past, and that is the sole truth I can find
down here—the truth of art.

What an exciting experience it would be to follow the adventures of an idea through the ages. With no wordplay intended, I daresay that this would be the ideal novel: we would really see the abstract image, perfectly limpid and totally unencumbered by humanity's dust, enjoying an intense existence that develops, swells, displays its thousand folds, with the diaphanous liquidity of an aurora borealis. One could select, for instance, the idea of beauty, follow its historical tribulations, and turn it into something vastly more vivid than an adventure novel.

How truly dramatic is the fate of such an oeuvre as Pushkin's. He was not yet dead when the narrow mind of the critic Belinski picked a quarrel with him. The reproach, you see, was that he was insufficiently concerned with the squabbles of his day. Hegelian philosophy came to no good in our parts. Yet there was not a single moment when Pushkin's truth, as indestructible as conscience, ceased to glitter somewhere. I feel it within me now, and it is what forces me to repeat something Flaubert knew as well as Shakespeare, and Shakespeare as well as Horace—that for a poet only one thing counts: his art. It is high time we remembered this, for I would say we are floundering, so far as literature is concerned. What is known as a "human document," for example, is already enough of a farce in itself, while all the sociology that struts through the contemporary novel is as nauseating as it is laughable.

I do not mean to say that the century in which we live is worse than any other. On the contrary, the divine spirit seems now to be more firmly established in the world. When, among other men, one finds a man, his radiant plenitude is no less valid than that of the best minds of the past. Of course the philistine may have the impression that the world is going from bad to worse: either it is the old refrain about machines becoming our masters, or else the fear of some catastrophe that our newspaper predicts. But the philosopher's eye surveys the world and sparkles with satisfaction as it notes that the essential things do not change, that goodness and beauty retain their place of honor. If at times life appears pretty dim to us it is because we are nearsighted. For someone who knows how to look, everyday existence is as full of revelations and delights as it was to the eyes of the great poets of the past. Who on earth, one asks oneself, can be this artist who suddenly transforms life into a small masterpiece? How many times, in a city street, I have suddenly been dazzled by this miniature theater that unpredictably materializes and then vanishes. It can be a coal-laden truck rolling along a sun-dappled avenue and the coal vendor with his black-smeared face, bouncing on his lofty seat, holding in his teeth, by its stem, a linden leaf of heavenly green. I have watched comedies staged by some invisible genius, such as the day when, at a very early hour, I saw a massive Berlin postman dozing on a bench, and two other postmen tiptoeing with grotesque roguishness from behind a thicket of jasmine to stick some tobacco up his nose. I have seen dramas: a dress-maker's dummy with its torso still intact but with a lacerated shoulder, sprawling sadly in the mud amid dead leaves. Not a day goes by that this force, this itinerant inspiration, does not create here or there some instantaneous performance.

One would therefore like to think that what we call art is, essentially, but the picturesque side of reality: one must simply be capable of seizing it. And how entertaining life becomes when you put yourself into the frame of mind where the most elementary things reveal their unique luster. You walk, you pause, you watch people pass, and then the hunt begins. And when you notice a child in the street transfixed by the sight of some incident that he will surely recall one day, you have the sense of being time's accomplice, for you see that child storing away a future recollection that already seems to adorn him. And how enormous is the world! Only in the penumbra of a store's back room can one imagine that voyages offer no mysteries; in reality the mountain wind is as thrilling as ever, and to die pursuing high adventure remains forever an axiom of human pride.

Today more than ever a poet must be as free, savage, and solitary as Pushkin intended a hundred years ago. Occasionally, perhaps, the purest of artists is tempted to have his say, when the clamor of his century, the screams of those being slaughtered, or the snarling of some brute reach him. But it is a temptation to which he must not succumb, for he can be sure that if something is worth saying it will ripen and eventually yield unexpected fruit. No, the so-called social side of life and all the causes that arouse my fellow citizens decidedly have no business in the beam of my lamp, and if I do not demand an ivory tower it is because I am quite happy in my garret.

31

Bobbs-Merrill Author Questionnaire (1937)[*]

First experiences in writing
As a child I loved writing imaginary stories using a white pencil which being invisible on paper afforded magical possibilities. At 13, when a cousin of mine suggested that we should each write a poem and see who did it better, I chose a volume of verse in the library and discreetly copied out a couple of pretty stanzas. My cousin's amazement at my proficiency stung my pride, prompting me to try whether I could not surprise him with something of my own making. So I retired to the smallest room in the house and there composed my first poem. It fell rather flat.

Other personal experiences I consider remarkable or unusual
The mysterious fact of my having managed somehow to smuggle out of Russia, which I hastily left at the tender age of 19, a sufficient amount of word material to write my books in exile amid a babble of foreign tongues.

Idiosyncrasies, if any
The squeak of cotton wool, the touch of satin.

Personal preferences
Hot sun, bathing, first cigarette before breakfast, writing in bed, boxing matches.

---

[*] Answered Nov. 19, 1937. Publicity questionnaire for VN's first novel published in America, *Laughter in the Dark* (1938; *Kamera obskura*, 1932–33) (Bobbs-Merrill note: "If it were not for the fact that there is a direct relationship between the information you give us and the sale of your book we would not bother you at all"). In *DLB Yearbook 1985*, *Biographical Documents*, II, 28–30, reproduced from Bobbs-Merrill manuscripts, Lilly Library, Indiana University, Bloomington; "[Laughter in the Dark] Answers to Publicity Questionnaire," VNA Berg.

Personal dislikes
Books with a Message. Studs. Dictators. East Wind. Oysters. Wireless sets; voluble conversation about same.

Superstitions
Once, in London, I dreamt of a green wall and the very next day, I was introduced to a person whose name turned out to be Greenwall. I never met him again, nor did that meeting in any way affect the course of my existence but several years later I picked up a book from a stall and its title was *Dreams and Their Meaning* by A. Greenwall.

The vocation I was advised to follow
The one I followed.

World War service. Army, Navy, Red Cross, etc.
I was too young for the War. Sometimes I can imagine myself going to a small informal war in a warm hilly place, just for a lark, as I should go big game hunting—say. But on the whole, war, especially the popular international kind, seems to me a pastime for solemn fools and slaves.

Clubs, fraternities, organizations, etc.
I dislike clubs, I hate organizations, and I loathe fraternities.

Hobbies, collections, etc.
The study and collection of butterflies and moths.

My favorite outdoor sports
I played football up to 1933, keeping goal; was sometimes brilliant and always unsound. I also played a good deal of tennis.

My favorite indoor sport
Chess, and especially the composing of chess-problems some of which I have published. I was the first Russian to compose a crossword puzzle, inventing, too, its Russian name which has now entered the language so thoroughly that people laugh when I say it is the child of my brain.

Favorite book and why
The book I shall write someday. Also: *Eugene Onegin, Hamlet, Madame Bovary, The Shropshire Lad*. Generally speaking, I like books that are well written—I don't mind what they are about.

Favorite author and why
Don't know—I prefer books to authors.

[Questions on the forthcoming novel, still untitled in its English version]

[What was its source?]
None. All my novels are inventions pure and simple. I am never interested in my characters. It is just a game and the playthings are put back into the box when I have finished.

[Where and how did you write it?]
I wrote it in Berlin. First (as I always do) I composed it completely in my mind, which is a very exhausting business, but quite indispensable in my case. This took me about half a year (my other books went through a longer incubation period), after which I had the book perfectly clear, so that I felt every page of it, much as a botanist feels the flora of a given place mentioned in his presence—a compound impression which he knows he can at once put down in full detail if he chooses. The next stage—the actual writing of the book (which I always do by hand and generally lying in bed)—was comparatively an easy matter (and took about two months). I had only to copy out in ink the sentences ready in my mind and then to correct very carefully anything that might have got blurred or distorted in the act of copying. This done, I dictated the book to my wife, who typed it. All this refers to the Russian original. When translating it, I again had to rewrite it by hand, changing a lot, because I saw it all in another, English, rhythm and color.

[Did you do any unusual research for your book?]
Well, I did go to an oculist to discuss my hero's blindness, but I don't think that is very unusual.

32

Interview with Nikolay All
for *Novoe Russkoe Slovo* (1940)[*]

Vladimir Vladimirovich Sirin-Nabokov was one of two Russian writers living in Paris exclusively on the income from his literary works.

The other such writer was Aldanov, who, apart from his literary works, also earned money from his role on the staff of *Poslednie novosti*. His main income, of course, came from translations of his work, since sales of books in Russian were rather weak.

New York

I wouldn't put New York last in terms of beauty, perhaps even in second place. What surprises and delights me most here is the stillness, the harmony and symmetry. In my opinion there's no "rushing around"; life's slower here than in Paris. Of course, compared with Paris, people here live more comfortably. There's an astonishing quietness in the streets, which I explain by the uniformity of sounds. In Europe, the sounds are more multifarious and for that reason significantly noisier.

Here, Vladimir Vladimirovich is primarily "enchanted" by the "freedom of movement" and conversation, by the wonderful straightforwardness and kindness of relationships.

As early as the steamship dock, I was startled by the customs officers. When they opened my suitcase and saw two pairs of boxing gloves, two officers put them on and began boxing. A third customs man was intrigued by my butterfly collection and even suggested that I name

[*] "V. V. Sirin-Nabokov v N'iu Iorke chuvstvuet sebia 'svoim'" ("V. V. Sirin Feels 'at Home' in New York"), *Novoe russkoe slovo*, June 23, 1940, 3. On VN's arrival in the United States.

one species "Captain." When the boxing and the chat about butterflies were over, the customs officers told me to close my suitcase
and be on my way. Doesn't that show the simplicity and kindness of
Americans?

On escaping Europe

A few days ago I got a letter from friends in Paris. They write that
the house where I had been living with my wife and son before we
left had been hit by a bomb from a German plane and was completely
destroyed. But our voyage was without adventure, unless you count the
minor panic on board the *Champlain* when we saw a strange stream of
steam on the surface of the ocean. Many thought with horror, "It's a
submarine," but to everyone's delight it was only a whale.

Leaving France was very difficult for other Russians, and I would
hardly have got out without the kind help of Countess Alexandra Tolstoy. The greatest obstacle was getting a visa. But once you have a visa,
the French let you out without any delay. They even said to me, "You're
right to leave."

On the fate of the Paris emigration

Russians felt no urge to leave Paris. Probably partly from their love for
the city, partly habit, and partly due to that typically Russian fatalism—
what will be will be.

Russian writers were seriously impoverished in Paris. Not long
before I left I met Bunin and the Merezhkovskys at Kerensky's. Bunin
still has some means, but the Merezhkovskys live in great poverty, like
almost all the rest of the Russian émigrés. The only options for earning
any kind of income—literary evenings, newspapers, and journals—came
to an end with the war. And it's hard to conjecture what it must be like
now.

I think that France's defeat marked the end of a certain era of the
Russian emigration. Now its life will take on some entirely new forms.
We'd have to count the period from 1925 to 1927 as the best moments
of the life of that emigration. But it wasn't too bad before the war, either.
Rudnev, the editor of *Sovremennye zapiski* (Contemporary Annals), told
me that he had enough money to publish two issues. And that really
meant something. But now there's nothing left.

On adjusting to America

All the same, you need to learn how to live here. I once was at an auto-mated restaurant for a glass of cold chocolate milk. I put in the coin, turned the handle, and saw the chocolate flow right onto the floor. In my absentmindedness I forgot to put a glass under the tap. So here, too, one needs to learn to put the glass in the right place.

One time I walked into a barber's. After a few words with me he said, "I can see right away that you're an Englishman who's just come to America and you work in newspapers."—"How did you reach that conclusion?" I asked, surprised at his penetration. "Because you speak with an English accent, you haven't yet managed to wear down your European shoes, and because you have the large forehead and head of someone who works in the press."

"You're a veritable Sherlock Holmes," I flattered the barber.

"Who's Sherlock Holmes?"

33

Definitions (Essay, 1940)[*]

1.

On last winter in Paris. It was like the dream of someone in a spell, who, in his sleep, sensing the threat of disaster, the need to wake up, cannot free himself from his dream. The sides of monuments were mechanically lined with bags of sand, the lampposts mechanically turned into blue night-lights, workers mechanically dug bomb shelters in the square, where a disabled veteran mechanically watched as before to make sure that children didn't dig holes in the paths. The Russians, meanwhile, racked their brains for nine months over what exactly the word *prestataire* might mean in the edict affecting them.[1]

2.

A radiant, intelligent, endlessly beautiful country, where every stone is full of nobility and grace, where every cloud over a hill overgrown with chestnut trees is already a work of art—this is how the émigré has come to feel about France, and no temporary disaster could alter that feeling. Regardless of who was to blame for France's fatal helplessness, the fragility of an empire is not always a vice, just as strength is not always a virtue. Moreover, here was a country where thinking of Russia was easiest and pleasantest of all: Paris served as a worthy frame for the play of Russian memories, and I know people who wouldn't swap a cheap all-night seat over an empty shot glass in a corner café for any other foreign wonders at all.

[*] Vladimir Nabokov-Sirin, "Opredeleniya," *Novoe russkoe slovo*, c. June–July 1940; typescript, LCNA, box 8, folder 7.

3.

On rumors, on the thirst for news. To a free person who rarely reads newspapers, is indifferent to politics, and is not remotely equipped for the communal mood—what an unbearable humiliation to depend on headlines and to be immersed, against one's will, in the leveling slough of shared anxiety. The very ubiquity of contemporary warfare lies in the sense that the penetration of its rules already mimics the natural order of a totalitarian regime; the war tragedy of a "democratic" country consisted precisely in the fact that its imitation of the authentic original was only superficial. For something more than all the pacts tied Russia and Germany together, something as powerful as *poshlost*[2] and lust. But the most important thing that organically unites dictatorships (irrespective of the differences in economic character and whatever their primordial impetus, devotion to the fatherland, or devotion to humanity) is that of rhythm—the rhythm of the marching masses.

Here, let us recall with a smile the three nations who have given the world the finest music.

4.

Method, a parasite on the ideal, bloats and then takes possession of it. Spirit and purpose dissolve in method, which gradually asserts its sinister supremacy until complete satiation, i.e., to that point at which militarized citizens can no longer be especially interested in the theoretical foundations of state tyranny. We are currently witnessing a process in which the meaning of catchcries—Nazism, communism, democracy—is defined no longer by the ancient ideals which gave birth to them, but by the degree to which this or that government is able to turn its population, one and all, into rosy-cheeked slaves.

5.

On indisputable things. In some future Lives of Great Men, our descendants will find Hitler's biography, too. But you can't fool the classifiers of "human greatness." That term presupposes a multitude of gradations, which depend as much on the profession of the given giant as on the degree to which his personality approaches the fullest spiritual scale. National leaders, generals, historical public favorites, typically belong to the lowest rank of great men. Take away da Vinci's freedom, his Italy, his eyesight, and he will remain great; take away Hitler's cannon and he becomes nothing more than the author of a rabid pamphlet, i.e., a nonentity. Geniuses of war have no metaphysical future. Napoleon's shade is bored, finding that the Elysian Fields are only a continuation of St. Helena; and I doubt that the souls of Shakespeare, Pascal, or Marco Polo will find (after satisfying their initial curiosity) the company of Julius Caesar particularly appealing.

6.

On literature. The term "émigré writer" has an air of tautology about it. Any true author emigrates into his art and exists within it. The love of a Russian writer for his homeland has always been nostalgic, even if he never left it. Not only Kishinev[3] or the Caucasus,[4] but even Nevsky Prospekt[5] have seemed like far-flung exile. Over the course of the last twenty years our literature, developing abroad beneath the impartial European sky, has taken the high road, while literature produced in Russia itself, deprived of its right to inspiration and sorrow, has been growing sunflowers in the back alleys of its soul. An "émigré" book is to a "Soviet" one as a metropolitan phenomenon to a provincial one. You shouldn't kick a man when he's down, so it would be a sin to criticize a literature against whose background an oleograph, a cheap, shameless historical print,[6] seems a masterpiece. For other, special reasons, it's awkward for me to expatiate on our metropolitan literature, too. But here's what I can say: in the purity of its designs, in its high standards, in its asceticism, and its sinewy strength, our literature, even though its first-rate talents are not numerous (but in what times have there ever been many?), is worthy of its past. The poverty of living conditions, printing-press difficulties, the unresponsiveness of readers, the savage ignorance of the average émigré crowd—all this was compensated for by an incredible opportunity, untried in Russia—to be free of censorship of any kind at all, state or social. I use the past tense, for the twenty-year European period of Russian literature really came to an end after the events that for a second time have shattered our lives.

34

Diaghilev and a Disciple (Review, 1940)[*]

Serge Diaghilev: An Intimate Biography, by Serge Lifar.
New York: G. P. Putnam's Sons, 413 pages. $5.

The Russian Renaissance is a curiously lovely thing to look back at over one's shoulder, blending as it does priceless artistic magic with a touch of eerie futility and the pathos of its impending doom. Starting some fifty years ago with a revolt against the Russian "Victorian" era, it came to an end twenty-five years later; and the utilitarian and didactic tendencies of the sixties and seventies that had retreated for a short time, like a wave that leaves the wet sand aglow with painted pebbles, came rolling back with far greater force.

Among the many names connected with the Russian Renaissance, that of Diaghilev deserves honorable mention. Although not a creative genius in the precise sense of the term, his perfect taste in art, allied to a fascinating personality and to fiery energy in the promotion of what was finest in art, gives him a prominent place in the history of Russian culture. For this reason, Mr. Lifar's book is worth reading.

The book consists of two parts, the first dealing with the bare facts of Diaghilev's life—and for serious students of the Russian ballet, it will be quite sufficient to dip into these first 246 pages, where compilation prevails over original effort. True, there is too much of the good thing, and I for one have never been able to stomach these minute details of a biographee's infancy. But there is worse: Mr. Lifar's style is so pompous and long-winded that it runs away with him. Such expressions as

---

[*] V. Nabokov, "Diaghilev and a Disciple," *New Republic,* Nov. 18, 1940, 699–700. The first review commissioned by Edmund Wilson, acting editor of *The New Republic,* whom VN had been put in contact with through his cousin Nicolas Nabokov.

divine, sublime, quest for the Holy City, memory of a distant heaven, applied to an irascible gentleman in top hat and silk muffler, who happened to possess a wonderful flair in the matter of dancing, may be put down to the devotion of a pupil to his master; but I refuse to be told that "childish memories persisted in Diaghilev all through his life" and that "in Benois' decor for the 'Götterdämmerung' [with which Diaghilev was not directly connected] it is as though some tiny corner of the Perm province haunts him [Diaghilev]."

His real achievement was that he knocked into shape and then showed the world that exquisite combination of movement, color and sound, the Russian ballet. His portly appearance was so "gentlemanly and aristocratic" that people turned back to look at him. The habit he had of smashing crockery and hotel furniture when slightly annoyed was partly responsible, perhaps, for the foreign conception of the Russian ego as exported abroad. His morals were frankly abnormal. He could be charming when he chose to smile. He bullied his dancers, blandly betrayed his friends and vilely insulted women. In later years he developed a mania for book-collecting, which Mr. Lifar deplores, but which seems to have been the most lovable trait in the man's character.

The second part of the book is devoted to what the author considers to be Diaghilev's best find: Serge Lifar. The meticulous noting of petty intrigues, the settling of private feuds, and a smirking, pretty-pretty, love-in-the-mystical note hardly make pleasant reading, while the "intimate" details of the author's relations with Diaghilev (depicted, for instance, as an enormously fat old man clad in an old-fashioned nightgown and imitating for Mr. Lifar's benefit ballet steps in a double-bed hotel room) are revolting not merely in themselves, but also by reason of the clumsiness of Mr. Lifar's pen. Under these circumstances, the translator's task must have been arduous in the extreme, and no wonder his version lacks distinction—though on the whole it is a trifle less trite than the original Russian text. Still, I do not think that he ought to have been so misled by the elephantine shape of the word "compendious" as to use it in the sense of "large"; on the other hand, it is not his fault, but the author's, if certain other phrases come to grief. It is Mr. Lifar himself who says of a first-night success: "I was inundated with flowers, objects, fruit and letters."

35

Crystal and Ruby (Review, 1940)[*]

The Knight in the Tiger's Skin, by Shot'ha Rust'hveli.
New York: International Publishers, 347 pages. $4.50.

Tariel, the sunlike, the cypress-formed, may be inferior, spiritually and intellectually, to his Western brethren, King Arthur's knights, but, otherwise, he puts them rather into the shade. Matched with this mournful, moaning, "mad-minded" rover, great Lancelot of the Lake would seem almost perky, and romantic Sir Tristram a very lukewarm lover. The mysterious Meskhian bard, Shot'ha Rust'hveli, who sometime between 1184 and 1207, in remote Georgia, where the vine in the valley looks up at the snow of the heights, composed a 60,000-word poem, certainly had both genius and leisure.

An author's worth is tested by his manner of introducing his characters. Rust'hveli's approach is enchanting. "They [the King and his hunters] saw a strange knight weeping on the bank of a stream"—no, this is not Keats, and the fair ladies here are anything but "sans merci." Fate, court intrigues and two purple-black Negroes who smuggle a moon-pale princess to a land beyond the sea, these are the instruments of a lover's woe. The poem is unrolled like an Oriental rug. Such symbols as "cleft roses" and "opening pearl" are delightfully used for defining the action of speech when lovers or friends converse. More often, however, Tariel and his boon companion, those two "pale lions," those raven-haired knights, shed torrents of ruby tears, scratch their violet cheeks, and swoon at the mere mention of the fair one's name; but between fits they are tough customers, demigods in subtropical

[*] V. Nabokov, "Crystal and Ruby," *New Republic*, Nov. 25, 1940, 733–34.

forests, slaughtering beasts and men with Homeric ease and gusto (note that splendid passage where Tariel tries to kiss a roaring tigress before killing her). And, as the tale proceeds, and adventures, feasts, deceits and disguises accompany the quest for the moonlike crystal-ruby-faced Nestan-Daredjan, "crystal and ruby become bluest indigo" and "the aloe-tree opens not its pearl," and dazzling metaphors are heaped and scattered this way and that, with the poet finding voluptuous delight in the paradox of blending variety with repetition, more than one reader will exclaim (falling into the style of the poet): this is like a drunken florist fighting a mad jeweler!

But we succumb in the end to the writer's charm. I have especially enjoyed such details as Rust'hveli's fondness for describing eyelashes (which are such a prominent feature in Persian miniatures), and all the comparisons he finds for them: they "droop like the tail-feathers of the raven" and rise "like a host of dusky Hindus" (which, again, reminds one of that other Oriental poet—was it Hafiz?—who called the dark eye of his mistress, "you cruel Negro"). "The Knight in the Tiger's (or rather Panther's) Skin" can be likened as a whole to that giant gem of whose radiance Rust'hveli says that "before it at night a painter could have painted a picture."

Has the original Georgian, perchance, passed into English via the Russian medium? I wonder. Anyway, Mrs. Marjory Scott Wardrop's translation looks beautifully done, and the tone sounds right everywhere. In regard to the incredibly cheap illustrations by J. M. Toidze, my roses would prefer to glue together. Then there is the preface by Comrade Pavle Ingorokva. Containing as it does some valuable information about Georgian poetry, it would have been much more to the point (though much less amusing) had it not advertised with such primitive pomp "the land of the Soviets where mankind's dream of freedom has in truth been realized . . . the land of emancipated labor and free thought." . . . By the way, I have a queer inkling that readers of the Russian version are supposed to understand that the hero of Rust'hveli's poem is really St'halin, the sunlike, the cypress-formed.[1]

36

Help, People! (Appeal, 1940)[*]

The fate of nations is unscrupulous in its means, uneconomical, stupid, and brutish. One could award mankind the following grades: A with a wonderful + for natural history or drawing, but for some reason always a C– in history and conduct. It turns out that those who become ringleaders are the most backward, malicious, and ungifted, and it turns out so because we have long wings and yet weak feet, it's all in the feet, for certain dreams should sit on telegraph wires and not come down to earth.

Over the last quarter-century, three states, ours, the German, and the Italian, have fallen into a stinking chasm and greedily, readily, and almost gleefully (with the megalomania of martinets, with megaphones and gala performances on the squares of subjugated cities) they have dragged a dozen other countries along with them. All these are tragic truisms it wouldn't be worth tallying, if in this case I was not guided by a definite purpose. The fact is that, through the unthriftiness of history, the Russian people have been treated twice to Tyutchev's notorious feast, where they were served not only the *okroshka*[1] of the Russian Revolution, but a second course, German blood sausage. The people of the 1880s might think that we lived in an oh-so-fascinating period, that we must have seen so much, and so on, but most of my contemporaries will surely agree with me that aside from a diabolical tedium, a humiliating dulling of the spirit, being forced to listen to the most vulgar choking out of the most vulgar phenomena at the fair of great men, and a completely unbearable quantity of utterly unjustified human suffering, history has given us nothing at all. Let us pause on this suffering . . . on this black ice under thought, where thought slips

[*] V. Sirin, "Pomogite, gospoda!," *Novoe russkoe slovo*, Dec. 1, 1940, 3.

and falls. Safety is sweet, all agree,—and there's even a cursed comfort in moaning and sighing—with a glass of tea, in the warmth of an American apartment, between the radiator and the radio—over the troubles in Europe. But (to return to the main point of these urgent lines), we now have a concrete opportunity to mend our ways—i.e., to quit our sympathizing sighs and offer those far off some real help.

We're talking about the Russians in France, who have been caught unawares by grim elements essentially no different from the elements of hunger, oppression, and beastly law they've already endured once, twenty years ago. Many of them no longer have the strength to repeat what they've gone through, and one's heart breaks when one thinks of these people, in most cases no longer young, for whom stoic contempt toward self-satisfied violence alone is no guarantee of survival. They are short of many of the usual things of life, growing scarcer with each day in the depleted air of a ravaged country; and besides all this, they need freedom—they must be rescued. The Tolstoy Foundation is holding an evening of Russian ballet for their benefit. They say watching the ballet is bliss for many—but it's especially good when it glides against the blazoned background of a good deed.

37

Mr. Masefield and Clio (Review, 1940)[*]

Basilissa, a Tale of the Empress Theodora, by John Masefield.
New York: The Macmillan Company, 307 pages. $2.50.

What is history? Dreams and dust. How many ways are there for a novelist of dealing with history? Only three. He can court the elusive Muse of verisimilitude by doing his best to unearth and combine all pertinent facts and details; he can frankly indulge in farce or satire by treating the past as a parody of the present; and he can transcend all aspects of time by entrusting a mummy selected at random to the sole care of his genius—provided he has genius. As neither of the first two methods seems to have been adopted by Mr. John Masefield in his new book, it may be assumed that he relied upon inspiration to transform a certain remote epoch into the everlasting reality of human passions. Unfortunately, his art is not up to the task; and this being so, a problem of appreciation is set: when the magician alone is deceived into seeing his charms working, must the onlookers stare at the stick which has not burst into blossom?

They must. This book is a splendid example of false romance and false history; it belongs to a widespread genus of false books, and, to the investigator, its shortcomings are as fascinating as the qualities of real achievement. Theodora, the "cast mistress" of Hekebolos, is stranded at the Daphne Hotel in Antioch, whither she came upon the advice of a mellow old monk (well known family-solicitor type). The jewels given her by her lover turn out to be worthless, and with her hotel bill unpaid and her passage back to her hometown unbooked, Theo has "a very

---

[*] V. Nabokov, "Mr. Masefield and Clio," *New Republic,* Dec. 9, 1940, 808–9.

unpleasant twenty minutes thinking of these things" (and presumably looking at a wristwatch which is fourteen centuries slow). Luckily she happens to meet a ballet girl whom she had done a good turn in the past by saving her from the attentions of an elderly philanderer (which goes to show that the morals of maidens were as sound in Byzantium as in Victorian novels). Thanks to this friend, she finds work with a ballet-company that, judging by sundry hints, has come to the East all the way from white and blue Monte Carlo.[1] Theo, we learn, knows a few words of French (*livre rouge, remplaçant*, etc.) current in the profession. It is also pleasant to note that round about the year 520 AD hotels already charged for another day if one did not leave until noon. Then she takes ship for Constantinople.

Up to this point Mr. Masefield's style has been of a cool and dainty sort which may fool the unsophisticated into mistaking a stale imitation of Anatole France for the perfume of bygone days. The trick of ending a sentence with the words "and very lovely," letting it melt away, as it were, may pass for exquisite delicacy of style; but a closer inspection reveals that this purring purity is a poor counterfeit, full of telltale repetitions.

In Byzantium the story increases its pace. It does so in an alarming way. Before the reader is really prepared, Theo, who despite the Hekebolos affair had seemed a prude and a bore, is explaining to the crusty old colonel of an Emperor and his dull-witted nephew, Prince Justinian, the intricacies of current politics. In the meantime, a riotous election is taking place in the City. Theo turns into that familiar figure, the clever girl of detective romance; and at last, with the story zooming now at top speed and no time for niceties, the villains are routed, and Theodora marries the Prince.

It is psychologically interesting to inquire why on earth Mr. Masefield should have imagined that he needed Byzantium for the spinning of this kind of yarn. Even if the crude accusations of Procopius' "Anecdota" be disregarded, there is plenty of evidence for believing that the real Theodora was anything but the gentle young governess that Mr. Masefield's heroine suggests. The recent boom in historical novels has evidently exerted its attractive force on Mr. Masefield. If this be Byzantium, well, all one can say is that it has been annexed by Ruritania. The same atmosphere of falsity, the same faults, though generally more subtly concealed than Mr. Masefield's self-conscious anachronisms, are to be found in all historical romances produced by the second-best modern writers, so that whether their heroes be called Peter the Great or Goethe, Marie Antoinette or Nero, or whether they be minor gallants that leap onto the screen out of fat best sellers, all these characters have, inevitably, something in common: the curious family likeness that links Mme. Tussaud's waxworks figures.

38

Prof. Woodbridge in an Essay on Nature Postulates the Reality of the World (Review, 1940)[*]

Perhaps the main charm of *An Essay on Nature*, by Frederick J. E. Woodbridge[1] (Columbia University Press, $3), is its verbal integrity, the author's splendid determination to stand no nonsense from words. However often he may have wondered what sort of uniform Nature's messenger boy wears, he is not to be taken in by the imp of ambiguity in a messenger boy's disguise.

His pronounced dislike for what has been dubbed in philosophy "dualism" is somewhat akin to a chess-problem composer's attitude toward "duals"; what distresses a philosopher of Professor Woodbridge's type is the possibility of solving a philosophical problem in more than one way just because this or that term involved is ill defined and thus polymorphic—a flaw invalidating the problem itself. Such is his wariness in dealing with a given term (whether it be "knowledge," "light" or "matter"), so repellent to him is the chance of some second sense being smuggled in under the belly of an innocent looking noun, that he finds it preferable to shear the whole flock. In result a certain crisp dryness of expression is attained, and thought goes about almost naked, shuddering a little on its way, but unmistakably genuine.

MAN WITHIN NATURE

The major assumption is (and his wisdom would appreciate my using the present instead of the past) that man being within nature, there

[*] V. Nabokov, "Professor Woodbridge in an Essay on Nature Postulates the Reality of the World" (review of Frederick J. E. Woodbridge, *An Essay on Nature* [New York: Columbia University Press, 1940]), *New York Sun*, Dec. 10, 1940, 15.

cannot be any independent explanation of what we do and of the world in which we do it. This is an example of the author's very refreshing common sense, but it does not quite manage to put the solipsist into the fool's paradise which it assigns to him. Every monistic philosophy must somehow avoid (or ignore, as Prof. Woodbridge does) the old pitfall of that dualism which separates the ego from the non-ego, a split which, strangely enough, is intensified the stronger the reality of the world is stressed.

True, natural death achieves a natural fusion ("... to die and to remain somewhere and somehow in Nature's embrace," as Prof. Woodbridge beautifully says in another connection), but while the brain still pulses one cannot escape the paradox that man is intimately conscious of Nature because he is walled in himself and separated from her. The human mind is a box with no tangible lid, sides or bottom, and still it is a box, and there is no earthly method of getting out of it and remaining in it at the same time. Prof. Woodbridge finds the world so real and analyzes the reality with such masterful vigor that the question whether our knowledge of the world is real, too, has no time to interest the fascinated reader; one recalls it only afterward, just as one wonders after a journey whether that picturesque scene in the Old Town was not staged perhaps for the tourist's benefit. I particularly liked Prof. Woodbridge's "optical structure of the universe."

That philosophers are essentially diurnal creatures (no matter how late into the night their inkpots and spectacles glitter) and that space would not be space if color and outline were not primarily perceived are suppositions that transcend the author's "naïve realism" just at the point where he seems to be most securely hugging the coast. But is visibility really as dominant as that in all imaginable knowledge of Nature? Though I personally would be satisfied to spend the whole of eternity gazing at a blue hill or a butterfly, I would feel the poorer if I accepted the idea of there not existing still more vivid means of knowing butterflies and hills.

MEMORY AND IMAGINATION

Then again there is Prof. Woodbridge's suggestion that memories and imagination are consequences of retrospective and prospective events of

Nature and not vice versa. One would have liked him to have explained in that light what "growth" is, because in the course of his very close reasoning one is disappointed not to find discussed the connection so naturally felt by the layman of Nature between the idea of time and that of development. Philosophers are born to be criticized, and the fact that some passages in Prof. Woodbridge's book make one a little cross with his dynamic common sense, is in no way detrimental to his work. The clarity of his style, his mental inclinations, his art of selection, the rich store of wisdom which lies behind the assorted samples displayed all go to make a work of permanent value, a monument to the memory of a fine scholar and, as one may infer, of a kindly man. Taken as a piece of writing, it is a good instance of the author's contention that language is not applied to Nature but is really made in Nature, and one thinks of the way a creative writer must feel, namely that trying to set down his sentence in the best possible state—of conservation rather than creation—is but an effort to materialize something which already exists in the somewhere which Prof. Woodbridge obligingly terms "Nature."

39

Homes for Dukhobors (Review, 1941)[*]

Slava Bohu, The Story of the Dukhobors, by J. F. G. Wright.
New York: Farrar and Rinehart, 438 pages. $3.50.

Nu (as the author would say), this is a highly entertaining account of what the Dukhobors did, or declined to do, in Caucasia and Canada. Although the first chapters dealing with the history of the movement are anything but dull, the real fun starts when the bearded babes have been shipped to the remote wood selected for them by hopeful humanitarians. King Lear and his Fool lost on a Heath, the Little White Cows in *South Wind,* Northern fairy tales, the glamorous, albeit fast, colors of modern journalism—such are some of the various impressions and associations suggested by Mr. Wright's work.

The exact recipe (a little flogging and lots of Siberia) which the Russian government used in trying to cure a remarkably obstinate sect of its aversion for military service was doubtless a nauseating affair; but when another, more patient, state saw its own laws ignored by those difficult people and solemnly herded them into air-conditioned prisons, persecution remained persecution from the Dukhobor point of view. Indeed, they must have preferred the *ispravnik* to the sheriff, as a sock on the jaw must have conveyed a plainer mode of martyrdom than did the unintelligible exigences of a foreign police force.

A queer flaw in the morality of a movement cannot help affecting its faith in some queer way, and in the Dukhobors' case there was a flaw, which Mr. Wright defines very neatly. It is one thing to refuse obedience to the state because "we have no master except God"; but

[*] Vladimir Nabokov, "Homes for Dukhobors," *New Republic,* Jan. 13, 1941, 61–62.

the situation is entirely different when this assertion is a deliberate falsehood. For there was a definite man behind God, and that man was Peter Verigin.

The secret of this leadership was kept with remarkable care and success. Verigin, an exile in Siberia, happened to come across the teachings of Tolstoy and, without acknowledging his sources, infused a few Tolstoyan ideas into the sermons he sent to his distant flock. Tolstoy, who was quite unaware of Verigin's existence, experienced a pleasant shock when casual contact with some Dukhobors revealed the amazing fact that his own views were being naïvely professed by ignorant muzhiks. Without Tolstoy's help, the exodus to Canada would hardly have taken place. There were among the Dukhobors, to be sure, many fine fellows and staunch Christians; but when one reads of their childish behavior and futile feuds, one feels somehow that the whole trend of the movement would have been historically far more important had not that initial cunning (inspired by practical purposes) subtly corrupted its core.

Such passages as the descriptions of the voyage and of stark-naked Russians flaunting God's white uniforms in the shocked silence of Main Street, are very vividly done; so is the picture of Verigin Jr., who succeeded to the Dukhobor throne after his father had been killed by an anonymous bomb, and who was far more interested in the last syllable of his name than in religious matters.

An irritating feature of the book is Mr. Wright's dismal trick of sticking in Russian words, all of which are misspelled or misplaced, or ridiculously wrong. It is always rather perilous for a writer to try to toy with a foreign idiom. I like to recall the case of the famous Russian writer Herzen, who, living in Putney and knowing very little English, illustrated a brilliant essay on the Britisher's innate contempt for poverty by the unfortunate remark that the worst invective commonly heard in London streets was the word "beggar."

SOVIET LITERATURE 1940

by V. NABOKOV

"THE PERSONALITY OF THE ARTIST SHOULD DEVELOP freely and without restraint. One thing however we demand: acknowledgment of our creed." Thus spoke the Nazi, Dr. Rozenberg.

"Every artist has the right to create freely; but we, Communists, must guide him according to plan." Thus spoke Lenin.

Both are textual quotations and their similitude would have been highly diverting had not the whole thing been so very sad. What was the freedom of which Lenin spoke? A further quotation supplies the answer. "It will be a free literature because neither greed nor ambition, but the ideas of Socialism and sympathy for the workers will bring more and more writers to our ranks." The subtle shade of the term "freedom" will be fully appreciated if it be remembered that one of the points of the Communist creed is that all foreign writers are either the lackeys or the victims of Capitalism and therefore cannot be called "free."

"We guide your pens." This, then, was the fundamental law laid down by the Party and supposed to produce "vital" literature. The round body of the law had delicate dialectical tentacles. The next step was to plan the writer's work as thoroughly as the economic system of the country, and this promised him what Communist officials called "an endless variety of themes"; for every turn of the economic and political path implied a turn in literature. One day the lesson would be factories, the next, farms; then wreckers, then the Red Army—and so on, with the Soviet novelist puffing and panting, and dashing about from model sanitarium to model mine, always in mortal fear that if he were not nimble enough he might praise a Soviet rule or a Soviet hero that would be abolished on the day of his book's publication.

When tackling the job of examining the Soviet literary output for 1940, I comprehended the dreariness of my task; but fortunately the material obtainable here did not prove too extensive. The features corresponding to the program for the given year turned out to be as follows: praise of Stalin, praise of the literature of the Soviet minorities, a benevolent attitude towards nature lyrics, certain allowance for romantic emotions, illustrations of the spiritual health of *homo sovieticus*, Polar expeditions, absence of new talent, and absence of the former "villain"—the Fascist wrecker.

These points are continuations or developments of the 1939 problems, and the general luridly patriotic atmosphere is also not new. Let us examine these features one by one.

Perhaps the most humorous aspect of Stalin-worship is that any present-day writer describing events of the Lenin period, for instance the Civil War, is expected to show Stalin as Lenin's equal, Lenin's boon companion and best adviser, the twin idol of revolutionary Russia in the early twenties. This retrospective myth makes a farce of history, for in point of fact the present dictator in those days was a far less conspicuous figure, both in the public eye and in Lenin's *entourage*, than any specimen of the lot later withdrawn from circulation by the dictator. Famous witnesses of his obscurity, former successful rivals, demi-gods of past propaganda in prose and verse, were thus very neatly removed and now, twenty years later, a prudent and well-meaning writer, when he looks back and sees the once brilliant figures blotted out by today's censor, automatically picks out the burly, heavily moustached hero whom the others once screened from view. But what is funnier still, is that in the literature of that distant period no mention was ever made of Lenin's Best Friend.

A good instance of the retrospective myth may be found in Alexis Surkov's poem "Childhood of a Hero" (*Novy Mir*, June 1940) where the soldiers who "shook the world" twenty-three years ago are made to fire a young boy's imagination by enthusiastic references to Lenin's Companion.

All this, as a Russian saying goes, are mere flowers—now come the berries.

The corrected galley proofs of Nabokov's 1941 essay, "Soviet Literature 1940," for *Decision*, a high-level but short-lived journal, which folded before the essay could be published

40

Soviet Literature 1940
(Essay, 1941)[*]

"The personality of the artist should develop freely and without restraint. One thing however we demand; acknowledgment of our creed." Thus spoke the Nazi, Dr. Rosenberg.[1]

"Every artist has the right to create freely; but we, Communists, must guide him according to plan." Thus spoke Lenin.

Both are textual quotations and their similitude would have been highly diverting, had not the whole thing been so very sad. What was the freedom of which Lenin spoke? A further quotation supplies the answer. "It will be a free literature because neither greed nor ambition, but the ideas of Socialism and sympathy for the workers will bring more and more writers to our ranks." The subtle shade of the term "freedom" will be fully appreciated if it be remembered that one of the points of the Communist creed is that all foreign writers are either the lackeys or the victims of Capitalism and therefore cannot be called "free."

"We guide your pens." This, then, was the fundamental law laid down by the Party and supposed to produce "vital" literature. The round body of the law had delicate dialectical tentacles. The next step

---

* "Soviet Literature 1940," unpublished essay, written Feb. 1941, from proofs corrected by author, VNA Montreux. Commissioned for *Decision: A Review of Free Culture*, ed. Klaus Mann, who founded the magazine to strengthen the rapport between European and American intellectual and literary culture; its first issue, in Jan. 1941, included Sherwood Anderson, W. H. Auden, Stephen Vincent Benét, Aldous Huxley, Christopher Isherwood, and Stefan Zweig. VN wrote his essay after the Molotov-Ribbentrop Pact (or Nazi-Soviet Nonaggression Pact) of Aug. 23, 1939, had been strengthened by the German-Soviet Commercial Agreement of February 1940. But after Germany invaded Russia on June 22, 1941, the emphasis on the similarity of Nazi and Soviet tyrannies was less welcome to many, and the planned July issue was in any case deferred for other reasons. By the time of *Decision's* second and final issue, a double issue in Jan.–Feb. 1942, the United States was an ally of the USSR against Germany and Japan, and there was no place for this essay.

was to plan the writer's work as thoroughly as the economic system of the country, and this promised him what Communist officials called "an endless variety of themes"; for every turn of the economic and political path implied a turn in literature. One day the lesson would be factories, the next, farms; then wreckers, then the Red Army—and so on, with the Soviet novelist puffing and panting, and dashing about from model sanitarium to model mine, always in mortal fear that if he were not nimble enough he might praise a Soviet rule or a Soviet hero that would be abolished on the day of his book's publication.

When tackling the job of examining the Soviet literary output for 1940, I apprehended the dreariness of my task; but fortunately the material obtainable here did not prove too extensive. The features corresponding to the program for the given year turned out to be as follows: praise of Stalin, praise of the literature of the Soviet minorities, a benevolent attitude toward nature lyrics, certain allowance for romantic emotions, illustrations of the spiritual health of *Homo sovieticus*, Polar expeditions, absence of new talent, and absence of the former "villain"—the Fascist wrecker.

These points are continuations or developments of the 1939 problems, and the general luridly patriotic atmosphere is also not new. Let us examine these features one by one.

Perhaps the most humorous aspect of Stalin-worship is that any present-day writer describing events of the Lenin period, for instance the Civil War, is expected to show Stalin as Lenin's equal, Lenin's boon companion and best adviser, the twin idol of revolutionary Russia in the early twenties. This retrospective myth makes a farce of history, for in point of fact the present dictator in those days was a far less conspicuous figure, both in the public eye and in Lenin's *entourage*, than any specimen of the lot later withdrawn from circulation by the dictator. Famous witnesses of his obscurity, former successful rivals, demigods of past propaganda in prose and verse, were thus very neatly removed and now, twenty years later, a prudent and well-meaning writer, when he looks back and sees the once brilliant figures blotted out by today's censor, automatically picks out the burly, heavily mustached hero whom the others once screened from view. But what is funnier still, is that in the literature of that distant period no mention was ever made of Lenin's Best Friend.

A good instance of the retrospective myth may be found in Alexis Surkov's poem "Childhood of a Hero" (*Novy Mir*, June 1940), where the soldiers who "shook the world" twenty-three years ago are made to fire a young boy's imagination by enthusiastic references to Lenin's Companion.

All this, as a Russian saying goes, are mere flowers—now come the berries.

In the May issue of the *Krasnaia Nov* the reviewer of the "Collection of Hymns to Stalin" expresses an official warning of a kind which I think has never been matched at any time in the annals of hero-worship. "One must oneself possess the brush of a genius in order to convey the greatness of this man who has fulfilled the fondest hopes of mankind"—the satanic point being that authors are henceforth forbidden to produce "trite formal portraits of the Man": their innermost thoughts and feelings in regard to Him must find expression "in deep and vivid images." The Party now tells the poets (with a grim smile): "Well, let us see what you really think: if your poem about Stalin turns out to be of a ready-made type, then the adoration you express is insincere." One has to go back to the Dark Ages to find something similar, and even then casuistry was not so sophisticated and the test by fire not so exact. It is a spiritual fire that is now tried, and the test is reversed; if you burn, you are saved. When the poet Stiensky writes that "any words of mine are eclipsed by the greatness of his achievement," the author, as the reviewer darkly observes, is "somewhat inaccurate" because he (the miserable Stiensky, who by now is shaking in his miserable shoes) "mentions only the great task accomplished, but not the greatness of the man who accomplished it."

With this extravagant "inquiry into the spirit" ruthlessly applied, the difficulties which a flatterer encounters attain nightmare absurdity. In Lenin's time, at least, a pundit was quite satisfied with the most banal words of praise, provided this praise was abundant.

In regard to the vogue enjoyed today by the writings and songs of Soviet minorities (especially of the Eastern tribes) one cannot help feeling that it is also connected with hero-worship, being based upon the Hero's racial antecedents and not merely upon that crude form of imperialism which the Soviet Government has recently developed. We learn that "in the matter of attaining wonderful heights" the poetry of the East-Russian tribes Ashoogui, Jirshi and Akyni (of whom the present writer, being a poor ethnologist, hears for the first time) is remarkable in every way. Marietta Shaguinian writing of Azerbaijan prose, and more particularly, about the short story "The Letter-Box" by someone called Mamed-Kuli-Zade, observes that "it is hardly possible to find in the literature of the whole world many stories that attain the same level of artistic force and social truth." The story in question is about a peasant who quarreled with the postman because he thought that the latter had no right to take letters out of a box where people put them; it is a mere anecdote interesting only from the point of comparative folklore. The Usbekistan and Tajikistan poets are also doing well as was predicted by a poor Yorick[2] at the Congress of Writers in 1934, when among other things he (Radek) so wisely said: "Our way does not lie through Joyce but along the highroad of Socialist Realism."[*]

Now comes a bright spot. Even in former years it could be noticed that short nature lyrics about stones and stars had a better chance to be published than a novel or short story that avoided social considerations. Perhaps the Party thought that the reader ought to enjoy a little relaxation now and then; it also believed (basing its opinion on the absurd dualism of "form and content") that Soviet literature ought to show what it could do in the Verlaine line. Incidentally, this leniency toward poets who dared seek inspiration in nature and natural suggestions resulted in Pasternak being able ten years ago to publish his exquisite verse in Russia (it may be noted here that by far the two greatest Russian poets of recent years are Pasternak and Hodassevitch; the latter died in Paris in 1939). Thus, it is very refreshing to find among the official rubbish already mentioned, a delicate little poem about a nightingale holding a caterpillar in its beak or a very minor poet's chat with the sea in the good old style: "Thy cool kiss has left its salt upon my lips."

On the other hand, the fiction represented in the monthlies I have examined is of incredibly poor quality. I could not force myself to plod through a serial novel by Alexis Tolstoy, but I tackled a story by Fedin who has long been considered a promising writer. The story deals with a lung sanitarium in Davos. Being under the fatal spell of Capitalism, the doctor managing the establishment "discovers" tuberculosis in

---

[*] *VN note:* Being under the impression that the action in *Ulysses*—"that dung heap of creeping obscurities that cannot be understood without a special dictionary"—took place in 1916, he fiercely attacked the author for ignoring the Irish insurrection.

healthy people so as to avoid bankruptcy. The style is about that of, say, Vicki Baum. The characters are drawn according to the so-called Monte Carlo tradition (as for instance in *Grand Hotel*).[3] There is the emotional girl, the rich capricious widow, the English clergyman and so on. The hero is a Soviet engineer of the strong silent type with a humorous twinkle, the quiet he-man imposed by the myth of Lenin's personality. Thanks to his Communism, he steadily improves at Davos, in spite of Capital and quacks.

The health motive based on the syllogism: Communism is sound, I am a Communist, I am sound, appears to be very popular lately. "Nowhere does the spiritual health of the Soviet citizen express itself so thoroughly as in his behavior when confronted with trees in a wood," says one writer—and this does not mean, translated into bourgeois language, that the citizen enjoys climbing trees; it means that he has the sacred satisfaction of knowing that every tree in every wood, just as every hair on every head, is counted and checked by the Perfect State.

Because they provoke such healthy emotions, stories about forest life and wild creatures are well represented in these periodicals. "His (the stag's) mighty horns rocked slightly, and the young aspens bowed before him as if they were grassblades"—that kind of stuff—and then follow some sound facts about the preservation of wildlife in the Soviet Garden of Eden. Polar expeditions are welcome, too, with a full list of the grub taken:

```
chocolate. . . . . . . . . . 40 kg.
biscuits. . . . . . . . . . . 250 kg.
white flour. . . . . . . . . 150 kg.
condensed milk. . . . . 500 kg.
```

and so on, in order to show how generous the State is, if a fellow shows his Soviet pluck. A holiday dessert is also described:

Cake Napoleon
Biscuits "Pot-Pourri"
Chocolates "Derby," "Swan" and "Tennis."

Note the delightful names.

That the Soviet citizen's mouth must water when he reads this is confirmed by a very pathetic reflection in the late Ilf's notebook:[4] "It is always pleasant to read in books of discovery the list of provisions taken by the explorer."

But the average citizen wants something more than candy; he wants Romance. In the Perfect State where all are happy, where boy-gets-girl and vice versa, where sexual disaster is impossible, because there can be no social conflict, neither Werther, nor Hedda Gabler, nor Madame Bovary may appear in the flesh, and thus cannot be described from Soviet examples. If the citizen is permitted to read *Madame Bovary* (which is very popular at present in Russia), it is because he is expected to enjoy the book from an artistic and historical angle: "bourgeois literature gives us form, we provide matter." But the Soviet citizen pounces upon the artistic and historical *roman* because here at least he finds an emotional outlet, a tale of wonder and woe, a boy-does-*not*-get-girl story. Here, too, as in the lyric department, the management allows a good cry and then points out the lesson: the does-not-get theme is reactionary because it is only in capitalistic countries that the upper classes develop laws that produce love-conflicts and romantic tragedies. Curiously enough, the idea that a healthy Soviet girl may not care for the particular healthy Soviet boy who cares for her is absolutely ignored. So when a new Russian novel, Freierman's *First Love*,[5] was allowed to appear and became last year's best seller, the Government achieved two ends: it gave the child a green apple and then, when the apple was consumed and thoroughly enjoyed, pointed out that green apples were bad for children. The novel itself is unquestionably of the pulp variety, but what is interesting, is the Soviet reviewer's attitude toward it: "The author has poisoned his heroine with torturing thoughts and reflexes unnatural in a young girl. He has deprived her of the happy sense of Soviet reality, of the passionate urge to struggle for social ideals. . . . Literature's main purpose ought to be to create bright, attractive pictures of young people, youthful patriots who ardently strive to perform great feats with the object of enriching their country. . . . A novelist ought not to indulge in the description of misty or cloudy landscape; the Soviet countryside must be shown to be gay and sunny."

These observations sum up all that one can gather from a perusal of these dismal periodicals. No literature can be expected to produce anything of permanent value when its only objective, as ruled by the State, is to embody this or that governmental whim.

And by the way, where, oh, where is he, the arch-villain, our old friend the Baron von Something, alias civil engineer Schultz, who lurked with eyeglass and cigar behind the ranks of local wreckers in Soviet magazine stories up to September 1939?

41

Faint Rose, or the Life of an Artist
Who Lived in an Ivory Tower (Review, 1941)[*]

Some use marble or bronze—sheer weight versus the tide of time. I have heard of a lady who painted her sunsets on live spiderwebs. Others gloat over glass. Conder[1] chose silk: a certain quality of one's talent is perhaps naturally attracted by the quality of a certain stuff.

Still Conder seems to have been capable of something better than leaving posterity a faded little fan. His material perhaps was produced by too anemic larvae reared in chilly France, or his colors were not sound enough: for one cannot help thinking of the robust and radiant silks of the East, still fresh after centuries. Somebody has said about those trees in full blossom Conder so loved to paint—that his brush was made of a child's eyelashes. His diminutive pictures have always looked to me like the dimly iridescent memories of things that his limp genius was not strong enough to fix. But with all his limitations he was that tautological creature, a real artist: that is, he emphatically belonged to the world of Whistlers and had nothing to do with the knighted daubers of his time—or of all time.

It was in this decidedly pro-Conder mood that I tackled John Rothenstein's book *Life and Death of Conder* (Dutton, $5), skipping the introduction so as to come back to it later. The author's style is not particularly distinguished, with a slightly trivial note creeping in when he alludes to perfumed fingers or to what the French call fig leaf—for Conder's ultimate fate was to decorate the boudoirs of the rich—but although his pen is not exactly a phoenix quill he has produced a good

---

[*] V. Nabokov, "Faint Rose, or the Life of an Artist Who Lived in an Ivory Tower" (review of John Rothenstein, *The Life and Death of Conder* [New York: Dutton, 1941]), *New York Sun*, Jan. 21, 1941, 11.

biography by generously stuffing his narrative with the plums of rich documentation. The illustrations are intelligently selected and the printing is very fine.

IN AN IVORY TOWER

Conder's life may be said to resemble that of any temperamental artist who lodges in an ivory tower with a wine shop just around the corner; but let us not forget that hell is paved with glib generalizations: the unique feature defeats the would-be lumper: and Conder (1868–1909), that Englishman educated in Australia, seduced by France, reconquered by England, was certainly something quite special. Though his retina must have retained the initial vision of primrose girls in turned-up straw hats wandering through a park-like landscape under the pink glow of an Aurora Australis, what really mattered to him was Montmartre, the black puddle, the rusty rainpipe on the wall, the lump of sugar melting in the green liquor, Monet and Manet, and the almond trees along the rural Seine.

IN BOHEMIAN PARIS

Lank, indolent, sucking a cigarette, his limp hair falling over his temple, he shuffled his way into the bohemian heart of Paris, eager for its filth and fun; making friends, losing friends . . . well do I remember Dujardin,[2] a prosaic old man, telling me of those distant nights and how hard I found to imagine the speaker as he was then—top hat, eyeglass, black beard, red lips—robbing Conder of his mistress or chumming with Mallarmé. Poor Conder. The pallid germ was maddening his blood ever since a reckless affair in Sydney,[3] and what with his weakness for women and wine, the artist in him seems to have been most of the time a prisoner. But, as it happened to Swinburne, and as it did not happen to Verlaine, the last years of his life were soft and secure: his marriage proved a success, fame attended the fading of his talent and when the disease creeping up from behind proceeded to crush him, his end was more merciful than one might have been led to expect.

The Danger of Absinthe

Then I turned to the introduction. . . . I would have been hardly less surprised had Dr. Rothenstein as solemnly prefaced Conder's life by a medical paper on the dangers of absinthe. The impression conveyed by his very unfortunate warning is that he decided to find some excuse for the awful sin of devoting a whole book to a "pure artist" at a time when, as he meekly puts it, "the objective, the less personal elements in art are in the ascendant, and uncompromising individualism is liable to offend." Why on earth should we mind if it does offend? New methods in art or letters have always done that. Why must we take for granted that "the inmates of a workhouse" are so infected with the class inferiority complex that "a decoration by Conder would mock them"? The philistines of yore appear today merely in another dress—Communism or Fascism—though more powerful adversaries than the smug Victorians belong to the same breed as they, and the picture of, say, Soviet painters, are essentially of the type that graced the ghastly Royal Academy in Conder's time—colored photographs and sermons.

As a sneeze is always a sneeze, no matter the social position of the sneezer, so the intrinsic quality of art (which alone counts) does not change through the ages. The inspired caveman who pictured so beautifully an extinct species of deer, the Persian miniaturist, Leonardo, Picasso (I choose them at random) are closer kinsmen in time than the perfect citizens of a Perfect State may ever be in space, and if Conder does not quite survive, it is not because the world changes (or hosts and guests noisily change places), but merely because his art was too frail to compete with those of his prodigious contemporaries in France who went so much further than he along the same sun-dappled path under the same festive trees.

42

Interview with Beth Kulakofsky
for *Wellesley College News* (1941)[*]

On the Russo-German Pact
Because the Russian-German friendship had its roots as far back as the
Russian Revolution, there is little chance of its being dissolved in the
near future, even over the Ukraine. . . . Education in Germany and Russia is on the same stifled plane. The progress that has been made in the
last twenty years along cultural and economic lines is a natural development and would have taken place under any system of government. It
has recently been proved that the Russian worker has less purchasing
power today than he had under the tsar.

On Vermont, where he spent the summer of 1940
Looks like some parts of Siberia.[1]

[*] "Noted Novelist Confirms Sanctity of Russian-German Friendship," *Wellesley College News*,
March 21, 1941, 8. On the occasion of VN's three-week stint as visiting lecturer at Wellesley
College.

43

One Hundred Years of England in a Work Both Scholarly and Timely (Review, 1941)[*]

Pageant of England (1840–1940), by Arthur Bryant.
New York: Harper & Brothers, New York, 338 pages. $3.50.

The important thing about this sort of book is not so much what its author thinks, as the power he has of assimilating, selecting and conveying pertinent data. The reader skips the obvious generalization, relishes the illuminating detail and then does the thinking. Nor is a timely book necessarily a hastily written one and Mr. Bryant's brilliantly documented work certainly cannot be accused of sacrificing scholarly retrospection to the purposes of current politics. True, his literary style tends to lapse into the "iron horse" and "Shanks's pony" kind of stuff; and such refinements as the sudden definition: "England's leading comic journal," after numerous references to plain *Punch*, are old sins against crispness; but long-windedness and the ready-made phrase seem slight defects when one considers the very satisfying picture which the richly colored jigsaw bits of quotation and allusion gradually form under the author's able supervision.

Incontestably, the mellowest parts of this volume are the chapters devoted to the forties and the fifties. Mr. Bryant has finely illustrated the dual nature of nineteenth century England, the contrast between the nightmare filth of the old-fashioned factory town and the philoso-

[*] V. Nabokov, "One Hundred Years of England in a Work Both Scholarly and Timely" (review of Arthur Bryant, *Pageant of England* [New York: Harper & Brothers, 1941]), *New York Sun*, March 24, 1941, 32. Except for title, from corrected typescript in LCNA, box 8, folder 9.

phy of highly cultured men whose devotion to a creed of self-help and freedom allowed social injustice to be freely done. "The poor," as the author puts it, "were left to Vestries and Providence." A Morlock-like race of deformed beings, black vermin rather than men,[1] horribly toiled underground while independent scholars in secluded nooks read Plato with their feet on the fender, and "London hall-porters sat in vast hooded chairs with a footrest and a foaming tankard as witness of their masters' absence in the country."

Although a "dual nature" was a typical feature of other civilizations too, its British aspect was tinged with a special national temperament unknown in any other land. The comparative method is not used by the author, and indeed he could not very well have indulged in it without writing companion volumes describing the correspondent period in the history of other countries; but he might for instance have refrained from stating bluntly that "public opinion did not exist" in Russia in the days of the Crimean war.[2] Incidentally, his description of the siege of Sebastopol misses the rather subtle point that if the invaders were all heroes, there might be something to be said too for the besieged moujiks, who somehow held out for a year with the poorest of equipment.

The era of reforms and prosperity, the great exhibition in 1851 (with the trees of the park bursting out into a crop of eager urchins whom no policemen could dislodge), the development of the railway, Disraeli, colonial expansion and finally the First Great War, are intelligently and generously illustrated by contemporary observations in picture, prose and verse, though the colors get a little blurred toward the end and the figures of Britain's great men acquire a more symbolic aspect the nearer we get to modern times, which is a common optical illusion in Clio's Wonderland, as Mr. Bryant might have said. On the whole, his work, without condoning the many blunders committed by various Governments in England, stresses the wonderful capacity of the British to make up for lost time and lost opportunities in the last split second before disaster. An inborn sense of freedom has always been the main quality of that lovable nation and when one thinks of the moods and methods of some other European powers, one is somehow inclined to forgive Kipling his "sahibitions" and Rhodes his clay feet. "We are the first race in the world and the more of the world we inhabit the better it is for the human race"—this contention which, if seriously meant, would be merely ridiculous in the mouth of a German and pathetic in that of other Europeans, may be irritating but not wholly incongruous when voiced by the Anglo-Saxon, and criticism of such a contention can be only based on the curious aversion of other races to forfeit their dignity by accepting the idea of alien supremacy, involving as it does a nation's professional pride (just as an artist may not mind being informed that his neighbor is a better businessman than he, but will be incensed if told that the other fellow has a finer sense of color). The progeny of those to whom injustice was done in the past may become a source of national weakness and division; an England that is a good country for the healthy and successful but a fearful one for the clumsy and weak, may not be exactly perfect; the kindliness of British mastery in her colonies may be questioned; but the fact remains that others have done worse, and worse faults of officialdom may be abundantly discovered elsewhere. On the roads from Mons to the Marne River, in the agony of Somme and Passchendaele, on Dunkirk beach, and in the roaring starlight above the Channel, the national character of the British proved more important than the best laws devised by the best men; and (reverting to current politics) one cannot help applying to our times, that doggerel quoted by Mr. Bryant, the salutation addressed by *Punch* to the United States in the middle of last century (when even France had fallen a willing prey to despotism): "Oh Jonathan! Dear Jonathan! A wretched world we see; there's scarce a freeman in it now excepting you and me."

On the Occasion of M. Zheleznov's Review, *Novo Russkoe Slovo* (Letter to the Editor, 1941)[*]

in reference to its performance by a group of first-rate
émigré actors in New York in Nineteen-Forties[†]

Letter to the Editorial Office

Regarding M. Zheleznov's Review

Dear Sir, Mr. Editor,

In accordance with the good custom of the Russian press, I kindly request that you print the following:

"Sirin," notes Mr. Zheleznov with reference to my play *The Event* (*Novoe russkoe slovo*, April 6), "is settling old scores with a writer clearly belonging to our emigration and known to us all. The caricature succeeded brilliantly. . . . Dalmatov understood who Sirin had in mind."[1]

These words are not only unseemly but meaningless, too. There would have been a shadow of meaning in them had they referred to the staging of *The Event* in Paris, where the director, without any intention or knowledge of mine, added such a twist to Pyotr Nikolaevich that the Parisian audience discerned in him the manner of an actual person. But here, in New York, nothing in Dalmatov's excellent acting suggested or could have suggested a mimed connection with any prototype at all. So what's going on? What exactly did Dalmatov "understand," or, rather,

[*] V. Sirin, "Po povodu retzenzii M. Zheleznova," *Novoe russkoe slovo*, April 11, 1941.
[†] VN's later manuscript note in a copy in LCNA, folder 7, item 1.

what did the reviewer "understand" on his and my behalf? With whom am I settling what "old scores," in Mr. Zheleznov's facile expression?

By making my perplexity public, I am only trying to cut off a flight of presuppositions as mysterious as they are absurd. At the same time, I am battling the tempting thought that Mr. Zheleznov is simply one of my carefree characters and resides in the very townlet where my farce takes place.

Please be assured of my utmost respect.

V. Sirin

45

[Shakespeare, the Professors, and the People] (Review, 1941?)*

Shakespeare and Democracy, by Alwin Thaler.
The University of Tennessee Press, 1941. $2.50.

Shakespeare's Audience, by Alfred Harbage.
Columbia University Press. 1941. $2.25.

It is a pity that by far the flimsiest essay in Prof. Thaler's book should have been placed foremost to provide a title for the whole volume. That this kind of thing may be thought necessary in the present season to justify the appearance of a scholarly work is to be deplored. And nothing is sadder than to see a most admirable word used for this purpose.

To anyone who enjoys or studies a poet without bothering about his capacity to teach or ability to carry a message, it is quite a little revelation to discover that a curious quarrel has been going on between two types of Shakespeareans, the warm-blooded kind that uses the present tense to assert that Shakespeare rises to the height of our modern concept of democracy, and the cold-blooded kind that uses the past tense to retort that Shakespeare's social and political thinking belonged exclusively to his own Tudor England. In discussing this controversy Professor Thaler tends to reduce it to the question of whether Shakespeare was a Whig or a Tory and suggests a compromise grounded on the local occurrence of conservatives with good liberal instincts. That Shakespeare was no anti-Semite is plainly disclosed by Shylock's apologia "Hath not a Jew

* From corrected typescript (LCNA, box 8, folder 9) of untitled and unlocated review, with VN's later note "NY Sun?" Published in *New York Sun*, 1941[?].

eyes?"; that he had socialistic inclinations is shown by Gloucester referring to "the superfluous and lust-dieted man"; and that he could peep
through the arras of ages at a nightshirted figure counting the sheep
of the world in the darkness of Berchtesgaden[1] is implied by "uneasy lies
the head." Just as smoothly anything else might be proved by appropriate quotations. The gnostic value of the combination Shakespeare and
Democracy is exactly similar to that of "Shakespeare and Aristocracy"
or "Shakespeare and Vivisection" or "Shakespeare and *unser* Shakespeare,"[2] whether in the last case the lessee be a chubbily sentimental
Goethe, a muddled metaphysician of the old German school or a heavy
heil-Hitlerite of the new one. Except when the study of Shakespeare's
text is an adventurous quest scientifically conducted by those who know
the delights of Q1 and Q2 and F1, the interest of the reader is apt to
shift from Shakespeare to the character of this or that commentator
applying his own philosophy to more or less misread plays. Thus one
finds oneself more fascinated by what according to Prof. Thaler Walt
Whitman thought of Shakespeare (if that can be called thinking) than
by the futile problem of whether Shakespeare was or was not what
Whitman thought him to be.

The rest of the essays in the book are much more to the point. Professor Thaler brilliantly refutes the view held apparently by less keen-
witted students that no conscious art is perceptible in Shakespeare's
work, a view derived from the notion that art is something apart from
(and less than) the merits of a book. At a time when authentic art is pro-
claimed an esoteric crime, an antisocial sin to be branded by the familiar
accusation of flaunting one's weakness for Proust (or whoever happens
to be the black beast of the mass-minded critic) while the healthy crowd
of average readers is clamoring to be taught, led and saved, one is very
grateful to Professor Thaler for indirectly disposing of the myth that
Shakespeare being "above art" may be safely accepted as a reading
pabulum by those who like their writers raw. In another chapter the
author examines the hypothesis that certain hints and gaps point to lost
scenes in the texture of *Macbeth* and arrives to the conclusion supported
by similar cases of refraction of sense in other Shakespearean plays,
that those scenes were never written. Further on a study attempting
to trace the "original Malvolio," although containing a delightfully
documented description of the supposed prototype, is less satisfying:

we know so few of the people that Shakespeare may have known, and what we know of them is really so little, and the inventiveness of genius complicates so prodigiously the business of reversing the process of literary transmutation, that most researches of that kind, no matter how convincingly they disclose the explorer's acumen, must necessarily remain mere gossamer and gossip. Shakespeare himself, if confronted by Professor Thaler's plausible guess, a guess that might even have been made by Shakespeare's contemporaries, would very likely reply that he had had quite another person in view or had evolved Malvolio out of perfectly anonymous impressions. The human mind is so built that the acquisition of precise knowledge in the present seems to be facilitated by the fact of the limitless past being limited (always in the present) by its documentary remains; but the nearest approach to the truth at the likeliest point within these limits may really prove to be a distance of many dim miles if we apply to the past the complex aspect of our sensorial and spatial present. Incidentally, the evidence of Sir Thomas Browne having read Shakespeare seems to be founded as far as I can make out from Prof. Thaler's present inquiry (or perhaps one ought to go back to his *Shakespeare Silences*[3] for further information?) on Browne mentioning "The tale of Oberon" which Prof. Thaler takes to be an allusion to *A Midsummer Night's Dream*; but might one not suggest that "The tale of Oberon" was popular in England in the latter half of the sixteenth century in Bourchier's translation from the French?[4]

Although here and there a prying reader may espy a few mixed metaphors, such as "these two were not songbirds of a feather . . . but criticism makes strange bedfellows" (which conveys a quaint picture of a nightingale and a thrush neatly tucked up in one big bed) these essays are clearly and concisely written. They do not form a deliberately planned whole but afford some pleasant rambles along the footnote-bordered paths all around the "Shakespear Tombe in Stratford."

Until its social message begins to bulge the second book provides the reader with some interesting facts concerning the Elizabethan theater. "The evidence for habitual riotousness in Shakespeare's audience"—writes Professor Harbage—"becomes tenuous upon examination"—and considering the type of person who in those days was anxious to condemn the theater by heaping upon it solemnly stereotypic accusations ("scurrilous behavior," as three consecutive Lord-

Mayors of London put it) it is reasonable to think that on the whole this audience was brighter than its critics. Equally acceptable are the author's comments on the fallacy of regarding the Elizabethans as "galvanic creatures . . . furious in hate and love . . . sensuous and sensual . . ." Finally, there is something to be said for Prof. Harbage's inclination to idealize the groundlings, a tribe that has apparently died out nowadays much to Prof. Harbage's regret. I admit that it might be an invigorating experience for a modern dramatist to turn his back upon the unruffled rows and featureless faces of modern playgoers and suddenly find himself addressing the Globe seething with those unfortunately extinct spectators, enthusiastic tinkers, pewterers and fellmongers, bright-eyed button-makers, cropped-haired apprentices, red-faced bookbinders and "pincht needie" creatures such as ditchers all spending the price of a quart of small beer—one Elizabethan penny or thirty-one Rooseveltan cents—to see Will Shakespeare stalk in as the Ghost. That is, I imagine, the general picture that Prof. Harbage's account tries to convey. He is somehow less anxious to have us see the gentry in the 2d gallery, merchants and lawyers, and the young gallants and the old lords, and the Spanish Ambassador in the 3d orchestra seats. Why?

While he is dealing with the price of tickets his book is, I repeat, readable; it is his colorful generalizations that are all wrong. If, as he stoutly maintains, "a glimpse into the collective mind of the audience" is "equal to what a glimpse into Shakespeare's world would be" then it must be sorrowfully admitted that the remarkable capacity of an audience to generate Shakespeares has singularly dwindled with time. Prof. Harbage proves by judicious calculations that prices at the Globe fitted the purse of London and were truly popular. "The price inflation at the private theatres begat no second Shakespeare." The average daily attendance was about three thousand at all four theaters in Shakespeare's day; so, knowing the exact number of playhouses and playgoers and the ticket prices in this country today, it might be easy to calculate how many thousands of times more difficult it is for a modern audience to exude a great dramatist. Any attempt on a writer's part to take the opposite course and create his own audience is tabooed by the gist of Prof. Harbage's book.

With all due respect to Prof. Harbage's humane attitude toward a long deceased community and his spirited attempt to save it from biased accusations, I believe that he is quite unfair in regard to Shakespeare's art. In his last chapter he roundly rebukes W. W. Greg for arguing (in 1916)[5] that Shakespeare wrote at least two meanings into *Hamlet,* one for the bulk of the audience, the other for the "humaner" minds. He violently misses the essential point—namely that Dr. Greg's inspired hypothesis regarding the dumb-show and Prof. Dover Wilson's equally inspired explanation of that scene[6] both belong to an order of thinking that might make any Shakespeare proud of writing for Wilsons and Gregs. He has a sly dig at the learned Edward Topsell, who (in 1607) "expressed his contempt for the ignorant . . . but earnestly believed in the existence of the unicorn"—though the dig somewhat miscarries as Prof. Harbage fails to realize that the reference was to the Indian rhinoceros. He is under the naïve delusion that "the caviary for the general" merely turns out to be a bombastic play. In a word Prof. Harbage is all for the million, against the judicious few.

But would Shakespeare be really pleased with Prof. Harbage's notion of him? I doubt it. Hamlet's quibbling (to take an instance from Dover Wilson's *What Happens in Hamlet*) with its telescopic duplication and triplication of sense did not bother the groundlings because there was enough action in the play to keep them spellbound: the nimblest-witted apprentice boy took the quibbles as the gushing nonsense that a madman might be supposed to utter; but the very existence of these inner landscapes of the mind in Shakespeare's greatest play "proves that he could count upon a section of the audience . . . capable of apprehending any subtlety he cared to put them to and moreover armed like Hamlet himself with tables to set down matters they could not at once understand or wished especially to remember" (Dover Wilson). By all means have a cake for the general, but cram it with plums for the judicious—this seems to have been—whether Prof. Harbage likes it or not—Shakespeare's method.

In order to show the greatness of the London cockney of 1601 Prof. Harbage proceeds to describe in glowing terms the brains of a grocer and his family at a Shakespeare play. I am afraid that he completely confuses the issue. The point is not that the grocer, his wife and their young apprentice could or could not understand what the lord, his wife and their young son could not or could; the point is that not every grocer and not every lord could appreciate Hamlet at its worth, and naturally Shakespeare (as every honest writer) wrote with more pleasure for the more judicious of the lot. The question of the comparative percentage of perception among the groundlings and the nobles is hardly important but possibly it is not unreasonable to suppose that most of the students or inns-of-court men in the 2d seats might have been more likely to apprehend what most of the cordwainers in the 1d seats must have missed.

As to Prof. Harbage's concept of an Elizabethan audience (in itself a vague and debatable entirety) as a composite William Shakespeare, this reminds one of the fashion (formally adopted by some scholars) of explaining the personality of Hamlet in terms of an ideal and conceptual Hamlet, the composite hero of all five "versions." Unfortunately for Prof. Harbage's contention (look at the audience and you will see Will) we do possess a tangible sample of what an Elizabethan audience—at its worst—was capable to do in the way of "creating" Shakespeare's *Hamlet*. This "glimpse into Shakespeare's world" is the maimed and botched First Quarto.

46

Sickle, Hammer and Gun (Review, 1941?)[*]

The Guillotine at Work, by G. P. Maximoff.
Chicago: The Chicago Section of the Alexander Berkman Fund,
624 pages. $3.50.

The seven years of Lenin's regime cost Russia from 8 to 10 million lives; it took Stalin ten years to add another 10 million; thus, according to Mr. Maximoff's "very conservative estimate," between 1917 and 1934 there perished about 20 million people, some being tortured and shot, others dying in prisons, others again falling in the Civil War, with famine and epidemics eagerly participating. The appearance of this tragic and terse book is especially welcome because it may help to dispose of the wistful myth that Lenin was any better than his successor. The remarkably vicious and dishonest methods of Vladimir Ilyitch[1] are examined here with scholarly precision, and although a staunch communist might argue that in revolution splendid ends justify the meanest of means, nothing can justify—in Mr. Maximoff's proletarian opinion—the way Ilyitch bamboozled the Russian peasantry. This, rather pathetically, is set down to Lenin's belonging by birth to the Russian gentry.

A political creed based on some pet dream of mankind (and without the impetus of such dreams this world would soon cease to turn) is rather like the glib advertisement of a product which cannot be criticized until it has been tested; with this difference, however, that in politics no money is refunded in case you are not satisfied with

[*] V. Nabokov, "Sickle, Hammer and Gun," *New York Sun* [?], 1941[?]. Maximoff's *Guillotine at Work* was published in 1940, and VN's address on the corrected typescript, LCNA, box 8, folder 9, is 35 West 8[7]th Street, New York, where he lived from Sept. 22, 1940, to May 26, 1941.

the results. Mr. Maximoff, it would seem, happens to be one of those people to whom the notion of human misery is so utterly revolting that they will plunge into any adventure that holds the faintest chance of improving the world; after which they go and denounce Lenin's Elixir because, whatever its ingredients, it has resulted in bringing more pain into the world than it was supposed to allay. A noble passion for justice may excuse many delusions; it is the sneaky, clammy-handed, humorless keepers of Utopian books that make the most ferocious killers. The party to which Mr. Maximoff belongs accepted the Bolsheviks without any misgivings except "fractional" ones. He claims now that this party was cheated out of existence by Bolshevik liars and blackguards. The implication that everything would have been all right if Kropotkinism had triumphed over Leninism from the start discloses the kind of unconscious optimism which man, perhaps fortunately, will never forsake.

Theoretically speaking, and barring such things as the old-fashioned café-bomb, black flags and sundry emblems of death, there is something rather attractive about your true Anarchist, especially when his high-spirited condemnation of all shackles is compared to the dreadful smugness of Communism. But once a program is fixed and tactics established, and an ism has chosen its hiss, the freest dreamer unconsciously accepts certain limits which are the interests of his party, and not the wider ones of humanity. That is why Mr. Maximoff's book, although essentially honest, has its awkward limitations. His coy predilection for a cutthroat chieftain called Makhno (who, with his army of brigands, romped over South Russia, getting in the way of the Reds and Whites) just because he happened to term himself an Anarchist, affects the author's statistics, as he fails to take into account the thousands who died in Makhno's lusty pogroms. This, however, is the only serious flaw in the book. The general impression that the author is totally unconcerned about what the regime he condemns did to people holding less extreme political views than his own is not really so bad as it seems. Indeed, a certain type of reader who is apt to view any criticism directed at the Soviet Union as prompted by class hatred, malicious misinterpretation and the fury of a bourgeois deprived of his cigar and top hat, will be less reluctant to believe an author who limits himself to a narrowly proletarian point of view.

On the other hand, the more dispassionate student of Russian affairs comparing this book with other critical works, will note the mosaic way in which a difficult truth is built. Practically, all Russian classes, groups and parties that have their representatives abroad, from the Bolshevik's meek, bespectacled brother, the Menshevik, through different shades of Liberalism, pink, salmon and flesh-colored; down to various Counts de Popoff balalaiking in Hollywood dives, could tell a similar woeful tale about people of their particular set; and Mr. Maximoff's shortcomings are in a way less irritating than those of most other émigré publications.

What is really important is that Mr. Maximoff's book is an intelligent historical survey, a careful classification of the varieties of physical pain so thoroughly inflicted since 1917 upon the very enduring bodies of millions of men and women in silent Russia, while the rest of the world was having, on the whole, rather an easy time.

47

Mr. Williams' Shakespeare (Review, 1941)[*]

Mr. Shakespeare of the Globe, by Frayne Williams.
New York: E. P. Dutton and Company, 396 pages. $5.

The biographical part of this book will not disappoint the imaginary not-too-bright giant for whom blurbs are fattened and human interest lavishly spread. Surely, there must be something very attractive in the illusion Mr. Frayne Williams tries hard to keep up, namely, that environment can be made to influence a poet once it is neatly deduced from his works. "No poet," he says, "can be comprehended without estimating his attitude toward marriage." How very true! Let us peruse the sonnets Bluebeard composed. Let us listen to the giggles and slamming doors in the dormitories of time where mighty footsteps echo. Let us believe Mr. Williams when he asserts that Shakespeare "in his mother's description of her family and friends was later to find much that would help him in the depiction of gentle womanhood." The method by which the author reaches this happy conclusion is very simple: first he suggests that Shakespeare made Volumnia out of his mother, then the process is reversed and Mary Arden is described as a Roman matron. No wonder it all fits so well.

We are also asked to take for granted "young Shakespeare's bewilderment when he learned that he, a somewhat carefree youth [I like the "somewhat"], was about to become a father." Similarly, automatic imagination working on "country girl" and easily turning red apples into ruddy cheeks makes Anne Hathaway a "sturdy country girl in good health"—though surely she might have been lean and hysteri-

[*] Vladimir Nabokov, "Mr. Williams' Shakespeare" (review of Frayne Williams, *Mr. Shakespeare of the Globe* [New York: Dutton, 1941]), *New Republic*, May 19, 1941, 702.

cal, just as one meets now and then pale-faced butchers and forgetful elephants. "Whatever her limitations were," says the author, "it must not be forgotten that she directly or inversely ["inversely" is safer] helped to mold the genius of William Shakespeare." And when her son died "by infection's hand," Anne "stood beside the grave with her successful husband"—though strictly speaking this was not quite the right moment for him to feel successful ("blue-eyed, gray-haired So-and-So's headless corpse," as I read somewhere the other day). Finally, it is interesting to learn that "it takes two to make a conversation and the same number to make love"—which fact, together with the second-best bed ("the most intimate monument of her life"), is about all we and the voluble author really know concerning that particular marriage.

Perseverance, however, will take the reader through to that other part where Mr. Williams discusses Shakespeare discoveries and the staging of his plays. Here the style improves considerably and the author turns out to be an intelligent critic. He is especially good in his account of the mutilation Shakespeare suffered and suffers still at hands of actors and showmen: the powdered perversions of the eighteenth century and the purple violations of the nineteenth; the accumulation of dead theatrical tradition; and the horrors of our own time: stunt performances, the weird orgies of stage electricians, the step-step-step-and-platform complex, mystical backgrounds, open-air foolery, the criminal cutting of the best bits, the reshuffling of scenes and the platitudes of sociological suggestion.

I was disappointed not to find in *Mr. Shakespeare of the Globe* something which the pun in the title seemed to promise—a survey of his influence in other countries. Voltaire's version of *Hamlet, King Lear* as staged in Tsarevokokshaisk[1] and certain solemn researches of German scholars might afford more genuine fun and human interest than Shakespeare's filial affection or the hounding of masked W.H. and a disheveled brunette through the trimmed hedges of the Sonnets.

48

The Art of Translation, *New Republic*
(Letter to the Editor, 1941)[*]

SIR: I am sorry that a poor memory led me to make a "friend" of that child; but Mr. Nash is quite wrong in assuming that by correcting my quotation he has baudelairized the Russian version: that little joy-ride goes on undisturbed.

[*] Vladimir Nabokov, "The Art of Translation," *New Republic*, Sept. 22, 1941, 375, responding to E. W. Nash's letter on the same page, which had commented on VN's essay "The Art of Translation" in the Aug. 4 edition as containing "a beautiful example of the Art of Misquotation. He refers to a line from *'L'Invitation au Voyage'* as *'Mon amie, ma soeur, connais-tu la douceur. . . .'* Poor Baudelaire! The Russian translator didn't do so badly."

49

The Innocence of Hilaire Belloc
(Review, 1941)[*]

The Silence of the Sea and Other Essays, by Hilaire Belloc.
New York: Sheed & Ward, 253 pages. $2.50.

"Innocence is a gem, a hidden treasure, rarely to be brought to light," writes Mr. Belloc in the last of the forty-eight diminutive essays collected together in this volume. The gem may be a little dim at times, with a milky suffusion which is not always opalescent, but on the whole Mr. Belloc's book does convey a pleasing impression of your mild scholar's candor. His style, at its best, can be aptly compared to that mullion window he describes which has the "oblong light surmounted by a square" and where "the height of the light is the diagonal of the square above." To be sure, the satisfying fullness of perfect proportion is a great quality in all arts; but is there not something to be said, too, for the brilliant break, the shattered sentence, the breathtaking swerve, the move of the Knight? Mr. Belloc's pieces are all Bishops and Rooks, no doubt; many of his mental connections are far too obvious; here and there, a platitude in Sunday clothes gracefully greets the reader.

Some of these essays (such as the one "On the Underdog" or the one "On Hats") are much too easy to write. When the author requests "lucidity" of prose and sadly observes that nowadays "we have got tired of drawing things as they really are," he is airing a popular view which hardly ought to appeal to a writer's sense of truth; for where and in

[*] Title from VN manuscript, LCNA, box 10; V. Nabokov, "Belloc Essays—Mild but Pleasant" (review of Hilaire Belloc, *The Silence of the Seas and Other Essays* [New York: Sheed & Ward, 1940]), *New York Times Book Review*, Nov. 23, 1941, 26.

what age have things been drawn as they "really are"? Again, when Mr. Belloc seeks to express the idea of Permanence by referring at length to "a man plowing his field" (while cities become ruins and poppies), the regrettable permanence of a stale image (which neither these my poppies, nor those of Renan can save) tempts one to object that it is never the same man.

The trouble with Mr. Belloc is that he attempts to be trivial and remote simultaneously, making as it were a slide-preparation of the obvious and then peering at it through a telescope. The result is that queer distortion an instance of which can be discovered (with a little care) in the following verbal mess: ". . . if a young man write two love letters and put them into the wrong envelopes, the recipients will as likely as not each take his own missive to be intended for him or herself."

Mr. Belloc is at his best (as I have already hinted) when picking the plums out of Clio's cake (which she both eats and has, doesn't she?) or when (I apologize for all these parentheses, but Mr. Belloc's style is contagious) the poet in him makes much of few words. Consider this, for example: ". . . a full-rigged sailing ship that glory of England . . . that tower of canvas, many storied and alive, leaning, urging through foam." *Caressez la phrase: elle vous sourira*[1]—as a more cynical writer remarked. And speaking of smiles, I fail to chuckle when Mr. Belloc's eye twinkles: his humor is tame, his jokes ecclesiastical; still I should like to think that he is slyly indulging (at last) in some authentic fun when he solemnly suggests that "a despotism guided by high taste may rescue societies of other political types from artistic chaos." Or is he not? If he is being serious, oh, how one shudders to think of a country ruled by Mr. Belloc's candidate, the perfect critic with the noble mind who would blandly but ruthlessly enforce the laws of "beauty and majesty" upon tremulous hacks, schoolchildren, disgusted geniuses (and have his own tragedies performed and applauded in the colossal theater designed by himself)! No, I am sure it is mere leg-pulling, so let us by all means retain our "artistic chaos" where every book, good or bad, has its place and its right to live—the pulp romance, and the Wind, and the Bell, and Anna Livia Plurabelle,[2] and Mr. Belloc's quiet little essays.

50

Style (Lecture Fragment, 1941?)[*]

A writer knows that there are no objective words for describing an objective world. Neither of the two exist. You may reduce subject and style to their simplest combination and still not arrive at forming a standard sentence containing the truth and only the truth—that is, a truth that you cannot demolish or deepen. Naturally if in this simplifying process you pass a certain limit, you merely lapse into tautology, as for instance "wet water," where you extract and display a certain character which at the same time remains contained in the drawer of the noun, which reminds me of that local small-town museum where I was shown the skull of the local bandit when he was a child and his skull when he was a man. Wet water is mere nonsense,—but as soon as you try to make it into a sentence, adding the least you can do as the verb "is," then you are making this statement with a definite purpose, say, teaching a child the idea of quality for what it is worth or else transcending tautology by actual experience: for instance: water is wet only if you are not completely in it. A naked Malay groping for pearl-oysters at the bottom of the sea cannot be called and cannot feel "wet" and so water is not always wet and there was no tautology in the initial sentence. This shows that as soon as you touch, no matter how slightly, the simplest word-thought, it wriggles; it is already alive, it is yours. "The water is cold" is already a platform for a breathtaking leap into the unknown. If you leave it at that, it looks objective enough, with no personal style or personal idea; but just because it lacks any definite spirit and application it does not contain a single grain of meaning. You have to say *what* water you mean and instantly your world, your style of thought, comes

[*] "Style," draft lecture notes, corrected holograph, LCNA box 10, folder 17. Apparently by summer 1941, for VN's creative-writing class at Stanford.

into being. You are criticizing a bath in a French boarding house, but on the other hand you may be looking at a picture and explaining why you feel that the artist has not quite rendered the temper of that tropical bay: the water is *cold*. Now all the implications and applications that you unavoidably have to make, when taking, as we have been doing, an idea of almost absolute simplicity, this implication and application and all the other imps and apples of your fancy form around it and infuse into it your personal style. It is also obvious that so-called form [and content] are *one*. An egg is an egg whether you eat it or not. The intonation of "the water is cold," when speaking of your bath, is different from the intonation of the very same words when you are referring to a picture in exactly the same proportion as the differences between the two subjects; indeed, it *is* the difference. Intonation and the position of your main idea in the sentence are the essential characters of style. Choice of words does not mean style, any more than the proverbial mixture of delicious ingredients makes a girl. A good method, if one's memory is docile, is to read a couple of pages of some good writer and then try to write down at once as many of his word combinations as can be remembered. A little practice will show that even if the exact words cannot be remembered the lilt, the intonation of the survivors and the extras, the general pattern of those wrong words in the right places—and the very feeling you have of this or that being wrong—will tell you a great deal about the author's personal style.

You should also notice the counterpoint of style, the relationship between the arrangement of words in a sentence, of sentences in what Flaubert called "le mouvement" (which may or may not correspond to a paragraph) and the arrangement of such mouvements in the chapter if there are any chapters. The correspondence between these arrangements will be found to reveal a personal element of style.

There can be no personal style of writing without a personal vision of the world. The mere fact that you see or feel a certain association between two details of life, which escapes other people, will naturally correspond to a personal association of words. The deeper your power of discovery, the keener you feel the novelty of the world around you, the more Eve you are and the less serpent, the firmer you refuse to have your world limited by the association of things in terms of usefulness or habit,—the more individual your prose will be. A ready-made world unavoidably leads to the ready-made word, or worse still to the ready-made intonation, for in certain associations the stalest expression, the most hackneyed word may suddenly glow with new life or with a life it once had.

To acquire true style is impossible without having creative genius, and more people have it than is generally thought. Most children have it, many young people, very few men of settled habits and conventional tastes. On the other hand many a person who can at a moment's notice produce a triolet or hash any given subject into rhyme, or is praised by his or her friends for writing such perfectly lovely letters, is generally much more hopelessly removed from ever becoming a creative writer, than the one who emphatically denies any literary knack, but will experience that authentic, that unmistakable shiver of creative response when getting to the passage where King Lear recalls the names of Goneril's pet dogs.

An uncle of mine, a sporting gentleman of the old school, having returned from his first visit to Venice, was asked how he had liked it; Well, he answered, the beer was dreadful. This is already a phenomenon of style, and something far more poetic in the personal creative sense of poetry than many a retrospective swoon full of gondoliers.

As the preliminary mental process of artistic development requires first the complete dislocation of the given world and then a re-creation of it through the connection of hitherto unconnected parts, and as this process exactly corresponds to the process involved in actual literary composition—for I repeat style of vision and style of writing are really one and the same thing—as it is so, we must pay special attention to the verbal dislocations and verbal associations contained in a writer's creative prose. The dislocations refer to new strange-looking positions and intonations of words so that the reader who likes his fiction comfortable is annoyed and even appalled by finding all the objects displaced and some of them gone, but a more curious mind will soon discover that there is a definite order in the system of these gaps and odd perches—and this order is a characteristic of the author's individual style. Likewise the verbal associations, the comparisons, the metaphors and other dragon-like creatures whose labels have got rather mixed up since the days of solemn rhetoricians, may impress one as tomfoolery or lunacy as did for instance that beautiful word-connection in Gogol: the sky was the shade of that kind of cloth which is used for the uniform of soldiers, those good helpful and necessary fellows, whose only fault is a fondness for liquor. What had the liquor to do with the sky? queried the critics. Everything, for this was Gogol's unique and harmonious world.

I have spoken of intonation. There is also rhythm, which is another thing—and perhaps the least telling, as it is often connected—especially in the case of quite first-rate, but not super-class writers—with the general rhythm of prose in the period they live.

So to sum up: there is no impersonal style or impersonal world; the most primitive sentence comes to life the moment you handle it in your personal way. Water is not always wet, two plus two does *not* always make four and when water is turned into wine, the artist wants to know *what* sort of water, *what* kind of wine,—and this is meant very seriously.

51

The Creative Writer (Essay, 1941)[*]

The creative work of the mind is based upon a happy agreement between the rational and the irrational. By rational I do not mean the linear logic of pedestrian thought; and by irrational I do not mean the vulgar vortex of more or less neolithic instincts. In fact the natural coalition between that lower form of rationality and those clumsily masked instincts wages the main war against the creative mind and its perfect blend of the purest essence of reason with the deepest spirit of dreams. My present purpose is to hurl the invader back, and then to examine how the mind works in the hard-earned security of its own world.

At times of special political stress earnest people are apt to try and discover the exact whereabouts of a writer in relation to the national or universal community, and writers themselves begin to worry and wonder about their duties and rights. There is a lot to be said for mingling now and then with the crowd, and he must be a pretty fatuous author who renounces the treasures of observation, humor and pity which may be professionally obtained through closer contact with his fellow men. Likewise it may be a good cure for puzzled second-raters, groping for what they hope are morbid themes, to charm themselves back into the sweet normality of their little hometowns or to converse in apostrophic dialect with husky farmers and lumbermen. But taken all in all, I should still recommend, not as a writer's prison, but merely

[*] VN, in the 1941–42 academic year a visiting lecturer in comparative literature at Wellesley College, gave "The Creative Writer" as a talk, presented on Dec. 6, 1941, at the New English Modern Language Association, Simmons College, Boston; it was published in the *NEMLA Bulletin* 4, no. 1 (n.s.) (Jan. 1942), 21–29. Although familiar from its later version, "The Art of Literature and Commonsense," in *Lectures on Literature*, ed. Fredson Bowers (New York: Harcourt Brace Jovanovich/Bruccoli Clark, 1980), that version was missing two pages on p. 377, as its text admits. This version includes the overlooked pages.

as a fixed address, the much abused ivory tower, provided of course it has a telephone and an elevator just in case one might like to dash down to buy the evening paper or have a friend come up for a game of chess, the latter being somehow suggested by the form and texture of one's carved abode. It is thus a pleasant and cool place with a grand circular view and plenty of books, and at least one spare bedroom, and lots of useful gadgets. But before building for oneself an ivory tower one must take the unavoidable trouble of killing quite a few elephants. The fine specimen I intend to bag for the benefit of those who might like to see how it is done happens to be a rather incredible cross between an elephant and a horse. His name is—commonsense.

In the fall of 1811, Noah Webster, working steadily through the c's, defined commonsense as "good sound ordinary sense . . . free from emotional bias or intellectual subtlety . . . horse sense." This is rather a flattering view of the creature though perhaps it would be safer to assume that when I say commonsense I really mean false commonsense or at least commonsense in quotation marks. The biography of commonsense makes nasty reading. Commonsense has trampled down many a gentle genius whose eyes had delighted in a premature moonbeam of some rarer truth; commonsense has back-kicked dirt at the loveliest of queer paintings because a blue tree seemed madness to its well-meaning hoof; commonsense has prompted ugly but strong nations to crush their fair but frail neighbors the moment a gap in history offered a chance that it would have been ridiculous not to exploit. Commonsense is fundamentally immoral, for the natural morals of mankind are as irrational as the magic rites that they evolved since the immemorial dimness of time. Commonsense at its worst is sense made common, and so everything is comfortably cheapened by its touch. Commonsense is square, whereas all the most essential visions and values of life are beautifully round, as round as the universe or the eyes of a child at its first circus show.

Anybody whose mind is proud enough not to breed true to the smug *sapiens* species secretly carries a bomb at the back of his brain; and so I suggest, just for the fun of the thing, taking that private bomb and carefully dropping it upon the model city of commonsense. In the brilliant light of the ensuing explosion many curious things will appear; our rarer senses will supplant for a brief spell the dominant vulgarian that squeezes with fat hairy thighs Sinbad's neck in the catch-as-catch-can match between the adopted self and the inner one. I am triumphantly mixing my metaphors because that is exactly what they are intended for when they follow the course of their secret connections—which from a writer's point of view is the first positive result of the defeat of commonsense.

The second result is that the irrational belief in the goodness of man (to which those farcical and fraudulent characters called Facts are so solemnly opposed) becomes something much more than the wobbly basis of idealistic philosophies. It becomes a solid and iridescent truth, as far removed from its pale ghost lurking under the back stairs of commonsense, as a real gem in the palm of one's hand is removed from, say, the stone Optalmius, which, wrapped in a laurel leaf, rendered a person invisible, according to the bland sages of yore. This means that goodness becomes a central and tangible part of one's world, which world at first sight seems hard to identify with the modern one of newspaper editors and other bright pessimists, who will tell you that it is, mildly speaking, illogical to applaud the supremacy of good at a time when something called Hitler is trying to turn the globe into five million square miles of blondness and boots. And they may add that it is one thing to beam at one's private universe in the snuggest nook of an unshelled country and quite another to try and keep sane among crashing buildings in the roaring and whining night. But within the emphatically and unshakably illogical world which I am advertising, as a home for the spirit, Messerschmidts are unreal not because they are conveniently remote in physical space from the reality of a reading lamp and the solidity of a fountain pen but because I cannot imagine (and that is saying a good deal) such circumstances as might impinge upon the lovely and lovable world which quietly persists, whereas I can very well imagine that my fellow dreamers, thousands of whom roam the earth, keep to these same irrational standards during the darkest and most dazzling hours of physical danger, pain, dust, death.

What exactly do those irrational standards mean? They mean the supremacy of the detail over the general, of the part that is more alive than the whole, of the little thing which a man observes and greets with a friendly nod of the spirit while the crowd around him is being driven by some common impulse to some common goal. I take my hat off to the hero who dashes into a burning house and saves his neighbor's child; but I shake his hand if he has risked squandering a precious five seconds to find and save, together with the child, its favorite toy. I remember a cartoon depicting a chimney sweep falling from the roof of a tall building and noticing on the way that a signboard had one word spelled wrong and wondering in his headlong flight why nobody had thought of correcting it. In a sense we all are crashing to death from the top story of our birth to the flat stones of the churchyard and wondering with an immortal Alice in Wonderland at the patterns of the passing wall. This capacity to wonder at trifles no matter the imminent peril, these asides of the spirit, these footnotes in the volume of life are the highest forms of consciousness, and it is in this childishly speculative state of mind, so distant from commonsense and its logic, that we know the world to be good.

In this divinely absurd world of the mind mathematical symbols do not thrive. Their interplay no matter how subtly it works, no matter how dutifully it mimics the convolutions of our dreams, and the quantums of our mental associations, can never really express that which is utterly foreign to their nature, considering that the main delight of the creative mind is the sway accorded to a seemingly incongruous detail over a seemingly dominant generalization. When commonsense is ejected together with its calculating machine, numbers cease to trouble the mind. Statistics pluck up their skirts and sweep out in a huff. Two and two no longer make four, because it is no longer necessary for them to make four. If they had done so in the artificial logical world which we have left, it had been merely a matter of habit: two and two used to make four in the same way as guests invited to dinner expect to make an even number. But I invite my numbers to an impromptu picnic and then nobody minds whether two and two make five or five minus some quaint fraction. Man at a certain stage of his development invented arithmetics for the purely practical purpose of obtaining some kind of human order in a world which he knew to be ruled by gods whom he could not prevent from playing havoc with his sums whenever they felt so inclined. He accepted that inevitable indeterminism which they now and then introduced, called it magic, and calmly proceeded to count the skins he had bartered by chalking bars on the wall of his cave. The gods might intrude, but he at least was resolved to follow a system that he had invented for the express purpose of following it. Then, as the thousands of centuries trickled by, and the gods retired on a more or less adequate pension, and human calculations grew more and more acrobatic, mathematics transcended their initial condition and became as it were a natural part of the world to which originally they had been merely applied. Instead of having numbers based on certain phenomena that they happened to fit because we ourselves happened to fit into the pattern we apprehended, the whole world gradually turned out to be based on numbers, and nobody seems to have been surprised at the queer fact of the outer network becoming an inner skeleton. Indeed, by digging a little deeper somewhere on the Galapagos islands or in New Guinea a lucky geologist may one day discover, as his spade rings against metal, the solid barrel hoop of the Equator. There is a species of butterfly on the hindwing of which a large eyespot imitates a drop of liquid with such uncanny perfection that a line which crosses the wing is slightly displaced at the exact stretch where it passes through—or better say under—the spot: this part of the line seems shifted by refraction, as it would if a real globular drop had fallen there and we were looking through it at the pattern of the wing. In the light of the strange metamorphosis undergone by exact science from objective to subjective, what can prevent us from supposing that one day a real drop had fallen and had somehow been phylogenetically retained as a spot? But perhaps the funniest consequence of our extravagant belief in the organic being of mathematics was demonstrated some years ago when an enterprising and ingenious astronomer thought of attracting the attention of the inhabitants of Mars, if any, by having huge lines of light several miles long form some simple geometrical demonstration, the idea being that if they could perceive that we knew when our triangles behaved, and when they did not, the Martians would jump at the conclusion that it might be possible to establish contact with those oh so intelligent Tellurians.

At this point commonsense sneaks back and says in a hoarse whisper that whether I like it or not one planet plus another does form two planets and a hundred dollars is more than fifty. If I retort that the other planet may just as well turn out to be a double one for all we know, or that a thing called inflation has been known to make a hundred less than ten in the course of one night, commonsense will accuse me of substituting the concrete for the abstract. But this again is one of the essential phenomena in the kind of world I am inviting you to inspect.

This world I said was good—and "goodness" is something that is irrationally concrete. From the commonsensical point of view the "goodness," say, of some food is just as abstract as its "badness," both being qualities that cannot be perceived by sane judgment as tangible and complete objects. But when we perform that necessary mental twist which is like learning to swim or to make the ball break in tennis, we realize that "goodness" is something round and creamy, and beautifully flushed, something in a clean apron with warm bare arms that have nursed and comforted us, something in a word just as real as the bread or the fruit to which the advertisement alludes; and the best advertisements are composed by sly people who know how to touch off the rockets of individual imaginations, which knowledge is the commonsense of trade using the instruments of irrational perception for its own perfectly rational ends.

Now "badness" is a stranger to our inner world; it eludes our grasp; it is like picking out of our bathwater a hair visible only as a beady shadow at the bottom of the tub; "badness" is in fact the lack of something rather than a noxious presence and thus being abstract and bodiless it occupies no real space in our inner world. Criminals are usually people lacking imagination, for its development even on the poor lines of commonsense would have prevented them from doing evil by disclosing to their mental eye a woodcut depicting handcuffs; and creative imagination in its turn would have led them to seek an outlet in fiction and make the characters in their books do more thoroughly what they might themselves have bungled in real life. Lacking real imagination, they content themselves with such halfwitted banalities as seeing themselves gloriously driving into Los Angeles in that swell stolen car with that swell golden girl who helped to butcher its owner. True, this may become art when the writer's pen connects the necessary currents, but, in itself, crime is the very triumph of triteness, and the more successful it is, the more idiotic it looks. I never could admit that a writer's job was to improve the morals of his country, and point out lofty ideals from the tremendous height of a soapbox and administer first aid by dashing off second-rate books. The writer's pulpit is dangerously close to the pulp romance, and what reviewers call a strong novel is generally a precarious heap of platitudes or a sand castle on a populated beach, and there are few things sadder than to see its muddy moat dissolve when the holiday makers are gone and the cold mousy waves are nibbling at the solitary sands. There is however one improvement that quite unwittingly a real writer does bring to the world around him. Things that commonsense would dismiss as pointless trifles or grotesque exaggerations in an irrelevant direction are used by the creative mind in such a fashion as to make iniquity absurd. The turning of the villain into a buffoon is not a set purpose with your authentic writer; crime is a sorry farce no matter whether the stressing of this may help the community or not; it generally does, but is not the author's direct purpose or duty. The twinkle in the author's eye as he notes the imbecile drooping of a murderer's underlip, or watches the stumpy forefinger of a professional tyrant exploring a profitable nostril in the solitude of his sumptuous bedroom, this twinkle is what punishes your man more surely than the rope on the local chestnut tree or the pistol of a tiptoeing conspirator. And inversely, there is nothing dictators hate so much as that unassailable, eternally elusive, eternally provoking gleam. One of the main reasons why the very great and very gallant Russian poet Gumilev was put to death by Lenin's ruffians twenty years ago was that during the whole ordeal, in the prosecutor's dim office, in the torture house, in the winding corridors that led to the truck, in the truck that took him to the place of execution and at that place itself, full of the shuffling feet of the clumsy and gloomy shooting squad, the poet kept smiling.

That human life is but a first installment of the serial soul, and that one's individual secret is not lost in the process of earthly dissolution, becomes something more than an optimistic conjecture, and even more than a matter of religious faith, when we remember that only commonsense rules immortality out. A creative writer, creative in the particular sense I am attempting to convey, cannot help feeling that in his rejecting the world of the matter-of-fact, in his taking sides with the irrational, the illogical, the inexplicable and the fundamentally good, he is performing something similar in a rudimentary way to what the spirit may be expected to perform, when the time comes, on a vaster and more satisfactory scale.

Time and space, the colors of the seasons, the movements of muscles and minds, all these are for writers of genius, as far as we can guess, not traditional notions which may be borrowed from the circulating library of public truth but a series of unique surprises which they have learned to express in their own unique way. To minor authors is left the ornamentation of the commonplace: these do not bother about any re-creation of the world; they merely try to squeeze the best they can out of a given order of things; and the various combinations they are able to produce in these set limits may be quite amusing in a mild ephemeral way, for many minor readers, I understand, like to recognize their own ideas in a pleasing disguise. But the real writer, the fellow who sends planes spinning and models a man asleep and eagerly tampers with his rib, that kind of writer has no given values at his disposal; he must cre-ate them himself. The art of writing is a very futile business if it does not imply first of all the art of seeing the world as the potentiality of fiction. The material of this world may be real enough (as far as reality goes), but it does not exist at all as an accepted entirety: it is chaos, and to this chaos the author says "go!" allowing the world to flicker and fuse. It is now recombined in its very atoms—not merely in its visible and superficial parts. The writer is the first man to map it and to name the natural objects it contains. Those berries there are edible. That speckled creature that bolted across my path may be tamed. That lake between those trees will be called Lake Opal or perhaps Dishwater Lake.

In other words the creative process consists as it were of two stages: a complete dislocation or dissociation of things, and their association in terms of a new harmony. The first stage presupposes the capacity of the artist to make any object depart from its traditional series,—seeing for instance a mailbox utterly apart from the idea of posting letters, or the face of a person one knows in a new way quite unrelated to one's knowledge of him. Children possess something of that capacity—at least the good dreamy kind of child does, the child that indulges in the exquisite game of fondling a most ordinary word such as "chair" until gradually it loses all contact with the object; its sense peels off, and what subsists in the mind is the core of the word, something plumper and more alive than any known chair and colored perhaps a kind of pale leathery blue if moreover the child is endowed with the mental luxury of colored hearing. Again, many observant people will remember simi-lar experiences of "disconnection" as happening in the praedormitum state or when actually dreaming. We all know those brilliant epigrams we make in our sleep but which prove utter nonsense upon awakening, just as those limpid jewels that gleam at the bottom of sea pools turn into humble pebbles when fished out. Perhaps the sensation which approaches most closely the artistic process of shunting the sense of an object is when we are one-quarter awake, that split second of turning cat-like in the air before falling on the four feet of our diurnal wits, during which instant the combination of details we see, the pattern of wallpaper, the light effect on a blind, an angle of something peeping over an angle of something else, are totally severed from the idea of bedroom, window, books on a nighttable, and the world is as strange as if we had been camping on a lunar volcano slope or under the cloudy skies of gray Venus.

Commonsense will interrupt me at this point to remark that a further intensification of such fancies may lead to stark madness. But this is only true when the morbid exaggeration of such fancies is not allied to a creative artist's cool and deliberate work. A madman is reluctant to look at himself in a mirror because the face he sees is not his own: his personality is beheaded; that of the artist is increased. Madness is a disease of the commonsense, genius is the greatest sanity of the spirit—and Lombroso[1] when attempting to find their affinities got into a bad muddle by not realizing the anatomic differences between obsession and inspiration, between a bat and a bird, a dead twig and a twig-like insect. Lunatics are lunatics just because they have thoroughly and recklessly dismembered a familiar world but have not the power—or have lost the power—to create a new one as harmonious as the old. The artist on the other hand disconnects what he chooses and while doing so he is aware that something in him is aware of the final result. When he examines his completed masterpiece he perceives that whatever unconscious cerebration had been involved in the creative plunge this final result is the outcome of a definite plan which had been contained in the initial shock, as the future development of a live creature is said to be contained in the genes of its germ cell.

The passage from the dissociative stage to the associative one is thus marked by a kind of spiritual thrill which in English is very loosely termed "inspiration." A passing boy whistles a tune at the exact moment that you notice the reflection of a branch in a puddle which in its turn, and simultaneously, recalls a combination of damp green leaves and

excited birds in some old garden and the old friend, long dead, suddenly
steps out of the past, smiling and closing his dripping umbrella. The
whole thing lasts one radiant second and the motion of impressions and
images is so swift that you cannot check the exact laws which attend
their recognition, formation and fusion—why this pool and not any
pool, why this sound and not another—and how exactly are all those
parts correlated; it is like a jigsaw puzzle that instantly comes together
in your brain with the brain itself unable to observe how and why the
pieces fit, and you experience a shuddering sensation of wild magic, of
some inner resurrection, as if a dead man were revived by a sparkling
drug which has been rapidly mixed in your presence. This feeling is
at the base of what is called inspiration—a state of affairs that commonsense must condemn. For commonsense will point out that life on
earth, from the barnacle to the goose, and from the humblest bug to the
loveliest woman, arose from a colloidal carbonaceous slime activated by
ferments while the earth was obligingly cooling down. Blood may well
be the Silurian sea in our veins, and we are all ready to accept evolution
at least as a modal formula. Professor Pavlov's bell-hopping mice and
Dr. Griffith's rotating rats[2] may please practical minds and Rhumbler's
artificial amoeba[3] can make a very cute pet. But again it is one thing to
try and find the links and the steps of life and it is quite another to try
and understand what life and the phenomenon of inspiration really are.

   In the example I chose—tune, leaves, rain—a comparatively simple
form of thrill is implied. Many people who are not necessarily writers
are familiar with such experiences, others simply do not bother to note
them. In my example memory played an essential though unconscious
part and everything depended upon the perfect fusion of the past and
the present. The inspiration of genius adds a third ingredient: it is the
past and the present and the future (your book) that come together in a
sudden flash; thus the entire circle of time is perceived, which is another
way of saying that time ceases to exist. It is a combined sensation of having the whole universe entering you and of yourself wholly dissolving in
the universe surrounding you. It is the prison wall of the ego suddenly
crumbling away with the non-ego rushing in from the outside to save
the prisoner—who is already dancing in the open.

   The Russian language, which otherwise is comparatively poor in
abstract terms, supplies definitions for two types or stages of inspiration,

vostorg and *vdokhnovania*,[4] which can be paraphrased as "rapture" and "recapture." The difference between them is mainly of a climatic kind, the first being hot and brief, the second cool and sustained. The kind alluded to up to now is the pure flame of *vostorg*, initial rapture, which has no conscious purpose in view but which is all-important in linking the breaking up of the old world with the building up of the new one. When the time is ripe and the writer settles down to the actual composing of his book, he will rely on the second, serene and steady kind of inspiration, *vdokhnovania*, the trusted mate who helps to recapture and reconstruct the world.

The force and originality involved in the primary spasm of inspiration is directly proportional to the worth of the book the author will write. At the bottom of the scale a very mild kind of thrill can be experienced by a minor writer noticing, say, the inner connection between a smoking factory chimney, a stunted lilac bush in the yard and a pale-faced child; but the combination is so simple, the triple symbol so obvious, the bridge between the images so well worn by the feet of literary pilgrims and by cartloads of standard ideas, and the world deduced so very like the average one, that the work of fiction set into motion will be necessarily of modest worth. On the other hand I would not like to suggest that the initial urge with great writers is always the product of something seen or heard or smelled or tasted or touched during a long-haired art-for-artist's aimless rambles. Although to develop in one's self the art of forming sudden harmonious patterns out of widely separate threads is never to be despised, and although, as in Marcel Proust's case, the actual idea of a novel may spring from such actual sensations as the melting of a biscuit on the tongue or the roughness of a pavement underfoot, it would be rash to conclude that the creation of all future novels ought to be based on a kind of sublimated, to use a term of alchemy, physical experience. The initial urge may disclose as many aspects as there are temperaments and talents; it may be the accumulated series of several practically unconscious shocks or it may be an inspired combination of several abstract ideas without a definite physical background. But in one way or another the process may still be reduced to the most natural form of creative thrill—a sudden live image constructed in a flash out of heterogeneous units which are apprehended all at once in a stellar explosion of the mind.

When the writer settles down to his reconstructive work, creative experience tells him what to avoid, at certain moments of blindness which overcome now and then even the greatest, when the warty fat goblins of convention or the slick imps of the genus called "gap fillers" attempt to crawl up the legs of his desk. Fiery *vostorg* accomplished his task and *vdokhnovania* puts on her glasses. The pages are still blank, but there is a miraculous feeling of the words all being there, written in invisible ink and clamoring to become visible. You might if you chose develop any part of the picture, for the idea of sequence does not really exist as far as the author is concerned. Sequence arises only because words have to be written one after the other on consecutive pages, just as the reader's mind must have time to go through the book, at least the first time he reads it. Time and sequence cannot exist in the author's mind because no time element and no space element had ruled the initial vision. If the mind were constructed on optical lines and if a book could be read in the same way as a painting is taken in by the eye, that is without the bother of working from left to right and without the absurdity of linear beginnings and ends, this would be the ideal way of appreciating a novel, for thus the author saw it at the moment of its conception.

So now he is ready to write it. He is fully equipped. His fountain pen is comfortably full, the house is quiet, the cigarettes and the matches are together, the night is young . . . and we shall leave him in this pleasurable situation, and gently steal out, and close the door, and firmly push out of the house as we go the monster of grim commonsense that is lumbering up the steps to whine that the book is not for the general public, that the book will never never—And right then just before it blurts out the word s, e, double l, false commonsense must be shot dead.

52

[On Democracy]
(Essay, 1942)*

When a certain scientist in a certain country after a certain civic upheaval was asked officially how he regarded the new regime, his answer was, "with surprise." To a normal human being it is a surprise to discover that one's mind is something that can and must be nationalized and rationed by the government, and this is about all that can be said about modern dictatorships. In themselves they are much too ugly and dull and unappetizing to provoke anything more than contempt. But another kind of surprise comes when we try to define what we mean exactly by a *normal state* of affairs. The best definition turns out to be "democracy" and we are as astonished as Molière's Monsieur Jourdain was when he found out that he was speaking in prose.

The splendid paradox of democracy is that, while stress is laid on the rule of all and equality of common rights, it is the individual that derives from it his special and uncommon benefit. Ethically, the members of a democracy are equals; spiritually, each has the right to be as different from his neighbors as he pleases; and taken all in all, it is not perhaps an organization or a government or a community that we have really in mind when we say "democracy" but the subtle balance between the boundless privileges of every individual and the strictly equal rights of all men.

Life is a state of harmony—and that is why I think that the spirit of democracy is the most natural human condition. Here lie the dif-

---

* VN's contribution to a panel discussion on Feb. 6, 1942, at Wellesley College organized by the college's Emergency Service Committee in the wake of the American entry into World War II. Published with other contributions as "What Faith Means to a Resisting People: Panel Arranged by the Emergency Service Committee, Dorothy Sells, Chairman, Presiding," *Wellesley Magazine*, April 1942, 211–14; VN on 212.

ficulties experienced by those who try to express democracy in banners and catchwords when opposing the banners and catchwords of hideous political creeds. Because democracy is not really a political phenomenon—no wonder its well-meaning defenders encounter awkward difficulties when trying to meet the enemy on its own level. A German racial creed may be utterly vile and despicable, but *politically* it works perfectly and the best one can do in opposing it *politically* would be to shriek rather helplessly that this or that democratic regime is politically perfect too; but in doing so we degrade our democratic condition by trying to use terms intelligible to barbarous mentalities.

Democracy in its inner sense is not politics, or party-regulation, or things like that. A Russian democrat of the old days, and an American or an English one, despite the differences in forms of government in their respective countries, could meet with perfect ease on a common and natural basis—which basis is so familiar to democrats that it almost escapes definition.

Democracy is humanity at its best, not because we happen to think that a republic is better than a king and a king is better than nothing and nothing is better than a dictator, but because it is the natural condition of every man ever since the human mind became conscious not only of the world but of itself. Morally, democracy is invincible. Physically, that side will win which has the better guns. Of faith and pride, both sides have plenty. That *our* faith and *our* pride are of a totally different order cannot concern an enemy who believes in shedding blood and is proud of its own. Hyenas believe in dead bodies,—it is useless to talk to them of *life*,—and a snowstorm of propaganda leaflets over Germany is not quite as efficient as a little real snow in Russia!

53

Lecture on Leonardo da Vinci (1942)[*]

It is Leonardo da Vinci's art that takes him beyond the versatile amateurs.

But his science notebooks are overrated: Leonardo jotted down as much from medieval scholars as he did of his own observations and reflections.
The notebooks are a cross section of Leonardo's brain at work. . . . For the great artist, anatomy was princely.

[Leonardo's painting represented] a search for harmony, controlled movement, a remnant of the medieval burlesque, and a unity of genius.

The Last Supper
[The reality of the figures] transcends the reality of common life . . . a more robust reality.

La Gioconda
Though the yellow is seasick and the blue is impersonal, the painting still ranks as a masterpiece because of the lady's intangible smile.

Leda and the Swan
A splendid, delightful hoax.

Harmony is the only true greatness; Leonardo's personality was a blend of humanity's choicest ingredients.

---

[*] Unsigned, "Mr. Nabokov Ranks Art of Da Vinci Far Above His Science Notebooks," *Wellesley College News*, Feb. 26, 1942, p. 5. Report of a talk to Wellesley College's Circolo Italiano, in Wellesley's Recreation Building, Feb. 23, 1942.

54

Interview with Kathleen Lucas
for Wellesley College News (1942)[*]

On artists and art
There is no such thing as art. . . . There are artists, but they are individuals with different forms of expression.

Explaining that we confuse the result with the source, Mr. Nabokov gave the example of those who excavated in the cave region of France and Spain. They found beautiful drawings of bison and mammoths, and they labeled the drawings Prehistoric Art.
Prehistoric Art!—that's Mr. Boubou![1]

Against the "demon of classification"
Take the beetles, for instance. . . . In London there was a scientist writing a book on beetles, and when it was finished with every beetle in the world classified, he took it to the publishers'. But on the way to the publishers' a little black beetle crossed his path that he had never seen before, that didn't fit into any classification! He quickly put out his foot, squashed the beetle, grinding it into the sidewalk so that it existed no longer. This is the danger of classification.

Still against classification
Leonardo's *Leda and the Swan* is pure Picasso.

---

* "Nabokov Condemns Classification; Says No Art Exists, Only Artists," *Wellesley College News*, March 5, 1942, 5. VN was interviewed after his appointment as lecturer in Russian language at Wellesley College.

Art in Europe

Art in Europe today . . . is Party Art. You are not an artist—you are a Nazi Painter, or a Fascist Painter. Perhaps the classifying demons three hundred years from now will look back on today as the great Communist period of painting!

Mr. Nabokov has no thought that interpretive art will die out; he laughed at that idea.

Art is in its infancy!

Art lets us see

Last summer I was watching a brook, with pebbles at the bottom and water spiders shooting across the water. All of a sudden I saw Mickey Mouse at the bottom of the creek, with his big club feet and silly grin; but would I ever . . . have seen Mickey Mouse before Walt Disney created him!

The great tragedy of modern art . . . is that

an artist cannot look at an airplane and see anything but a plane.

Pointing to one of Dmitri Nabokov's drawings

Perhaps that is closer to what we are looking for—it does not look so much like a plane, but it has the spirit. . . .

55

In Memory of Iosif Hessen
(Obituary Essay, 1943)[*]

In my mind Iosif Vladimirovich's past, tied to my late father's past, was tied by a second, live, knot, to my present: I simultaneously saw I.V. in the fabled distance of Party meetings,[1] in historical perspective, where my childhood narrowed like a reversed cone of lines, and in human reality, with a glass of tea and biscuits, in the warmth of a world accessible to me. That I grew up to be friends with him is a magical anachronism;[2] I was proud of our friendship; the cathetus of its reality extended deep into my soul, the long hypotenuse mysteriously connected me with the courageous and pure worlds of *Pravo*[3] and *Rech'*,[4] once surrounding my heedless infancy. The Russian Berlin of the 1920s was nothing more than a furnished room, rented out by a rude and rank-smelling German woman (the foul sweat of that unfortunate people is unforgettable), but I.V. was also in this room, and, by avoiding the natives, we managed to extract a peculiar charm from this or that combination of furnishings and lighting. My youth arrived just in time for I.V.'s second youth, and we set off jovially, side by side.

He was my first reader. Long before my first books began to be brought out by his publishing house he would allow me, with paternalistic connivance, to feed *Rul'* with my unripe poetry.[5] The blue hues of Berlin's twilights, the tent made by the corner chestnut tree, faint lightheadedness, poverty, being in love, the mandarin tinge of a prematurely lit neon sign, and the animal yearning for a still-fresh Russia—all this was dragged in iambic form to the editorial office, where I.V. would bring the page up close to his face, as though he was latching on to what

[*] V. Nabokov-Sirin, "Pamyati I. V. Gessena," *Novoe russkoe slovo*, March 31, 1943, 2.

was written from its hem, from the bottom up, with a parabolic movement of his eye, after which he would look at me with a half-sarcastic benevolence, lightly shaking the page, but he would say only: "Hmm, hmm . . . ," and, without hurrying, add it to his publication material.

Indifferent to readers' reviews, I cherished the exception that I was accustomed to make for I.V.'s opinion. The complete candor of his judgments, sometimes so dreadfully cutting an author's vanity into quarters, lent a special significance to his slightest praise. I will forever be able to hear the bronze and booming force with which he would pronounce, over a book's corpse, "How could he write this—it's unfathomable!," with a terrible stress on "could" and "fath." For him, as for me, Pushkin alone was above human criticism; how well he knew his tragic, languid, mysterious poetry, familiar to most only from tear-off calendars and four operas.

The adventures and transformations of human nature constantly fascinated him, no matter whether we talked about a fictional hero, the Bolsheviks, or a mutual friend. He could simultaneously be engrossed in the political machinations of a hefty dictator and the question whether Hamlet's madness was feigned. He was living proof of the fact that a genuine person is a person interested in everything, including what interests others. Telling him anything was an extraordinary delight, since his engagement as an interlocutor, his very sharp mind, and the phenomenal appetite with which he consumed your rather unripe fruits transformed any trifle into an epic phenomenon. His curiosity was so pure it seemed almost childlike. Human characters or changes in the weather would become, in his energetic appraisal, extraordinary, unique: "I can't remember such a spring," he would say, and spread his hands and shrug in amazement.

I was delighted by the union in him of his Russian Europeanness merging so harmoniously with his membership in that most inspired tribe.[6] I infinitely respected his physical and moral courage; hundreds of times in my life I experienced his touching, angular, kindness. His weak eyesight and hearing in conjunction with his talented absentmindedness served him as purveyors of his own humor. With what glee he would tell me about the time he was visited by the actress Polevitskaya, and, wishing to please her, carefully took down and handed her a photograph of the singer Plevitskaya, with the words: "Look, I have your portrait hanging on my wall."[7] I feel that I, too, might be offering up a portrait of someone else when I speak of I.V., for a strange shortsightedness overpowers the soul after the death of someone one loves, and all sorts of empty trivialities pop up instead of the quintessence of his character.

I.V. once confessed to me that in his youth he had been seduced by Hegel's fallacious triad.[8] I think of the dialectic of fate. In the spring of 1940, before I left for here, I bade farewell to I.V. on a black Parisian street, trying to quell the painful thought that he was very old and not planning to come to America, which meant I would never see him again. So when I heard the news, here in Boston, that by a miracle he had arrived in New York, bigger than life (as he had always seemed to me), keen to get to work, bubbling over with his own and others' news, I hastened to give the lie to my premonition. Various circumstances forced me to postpone our meeting until April. In the meantime, the miracle of his arrival turned out to be only an antithesis, and now the syllogism is complete.[9]

56

Interview for *The Last Word* (1943)[*]

On Wellesley
My definition of Wellesley would be "Looks and Books."

On the students' attentiveness
I am sure I should laugh hearing myself lecture, but they don't.

He believes that the girls here have "been educated to listen closely," *so closely, in fact, that the lecturer can actually* "feel in contact with his audience."
The European university is concerned with the intellect, but not with the behavior of its students. Here, the college is as much concerned with the happiness of the individual as with the culture of the community.

Among the other things which Mr. Nabokov does not *like . . . are advertisements which express the idea that material acquisitions will bring complete happiness, cotton wool, oysters, Germans, and anything to do with mailing letters. Mailing letters always makes Mr. Nabokov feel morbid, because, to him,* this is the death of a letter. You kill it by posting it.

Neither does he like people who have no sense of humor.
For me, all people are divided into two groups—those who laugh, and those who smile. I like the ones that laugh, because laughter proves that a person is fundamentally good and real.

---

[*] "Vladimir Nabokov—A Profile," *The Last Word* [Wellesley College], April 7, 1943, 19–21. Interviewer unknown.

On Wellesley girls' obliviousness to the natural beauty around them
They have forgotten the touch of Mother Earth. In this respect Wellesley girls remind me of birds of paradise. For when the first birds of paradise were sent to Europe to the great naturalist, Linnaeus, the scientist described them as "birds without feet."

Mr. Nabokov urges us to be happy in such lovely surroundings, for he comments,
Misfortune is a good school, but happiness is the best university.

57

Profile by Katherine Reese
for *We* (1943)[*]

Nabokov teaching his Wellesley Russian language class

"Do you know the Russian word for 'nice'? No? Surely we learned it last time."

Whatever the word is, no matter how obscure, he is always sure we learned it last time.

"Then I shall tell you. It's m-ee-la. Lovely word, meela. Beautiful word." . . .

After reading the simple, English sentences in dramatic, dashing tone, he follows them with remarks in an undertone, such as,

"How am I supposed to know 'Where is the book?'"

Later he announces,

"And now we come to the saddest story ever told, 'She is here. He is there." . . .

He asks us to read aloud in Russian—"Aloud" proves to be three brave souls muttering under their breath in a confused jumble. After the sentence has fallen, mutilated, he sighs rapturously,

"So good to hear Russian spoken again! I am practically back in Moscow." . . .

"I have now something very sad to tell you. We have, in Russian, what we call the instrumental case, and it has different endings that one must memorize. But," *he adds cheerfully and soothingly,* "after you have learned those, you will know practically all there is to know about Russian."

---

[*] "Alias V. Sirin: A Sketch About Wellesley's Russian Author," *We* [Wellesley College] 1, no. 2 (Dec. 1943), 5–7.

He says that in the Midwest when he is hiking along looking for specimens, every car that goes by screeches to a stop and asks him if he wants a ride.

"Obviously all they want to know is what the devil I am doing with a butterfly net! And in Arizona," *he goes on,* "a horse, a total stranger, followed me for five miles. Then in New Mexico I was nearly arrested because I painted a farmer's trees with sugar to attract a certain type of moth."

When asked if the people in Europe acted any differently, he replied, "Oh, they are much politer. The peasants pay no attention to me when I pass. But if I look back, I always see them, staring after me rooted to the spot. Old men with hoes balanced on their shoulders, and little children with their fingers in their mouths, wide-eyed and motionless. Really amusing—very amusing."

He has a habit of repeating the last phrase of sentences. Words fascinate him and he cannot bear to part with them after one utterance. Once he heard someone say that since he had no flashlight, he should have to "stumble and bumble" *along in the dark. He chanted* "stumble and bumble" *over and over, delighted with the new sound. He listens carefully to our American slang and snaps at an unfamiliar term. If he likes it, the reward is* "Very good. Yes. Very good."

58

Cabbage Soup and Caviar (Review, 1944)[*]

A Treasury of Russian Life and Humor, edited, with an introduction,
by John Cournos. New York: Coward-McCann Inc., 706 pages. $3.75.

A Treasury of Russian Literature, selected and edited,
with a foreword and biographical and critical notes,
by Bernard Gilbert Guerney. New York: Vanguard Press,
1,072 pages. $3.95.

Some fifty writers are represented in Mr. Cournos' anthology and
some thirty in Mr. Guerney's. Except that the latter goes much farther
back into the past while the former includes a much greater number
of contemporary authors, both volumes cover much the same ground.
Both contain Gogol's "Overcoat" and his "Inspector General"; Pushkin's "Queen of Spades"; Lermontov's ballad about Kalashnikov, the
amateur pugilist; and Bunin's "Gentleman from San Francisco." Both
have Sologub—that very minor writer for whom England and America
show such an unaccountable predilection. Both open with the rather
too obvious prose poem by Turgenev concerning the greatness of the
Russian language. Both republish some of Baring's excellent translations of Russian lyrics. Here the similarity ends.

A good example of Mr. Cournos' powers of interpretation is
afforded by his explanation that Blok wrote "The Scythians" because
he was angry "when British and French troops were sent to intervene

---

[*] Vladimir Nabokov, "Cabbage Soup and Caviar" (Review of John Cournos, ed., *A Treasury of
Russian Life and Humor* [New York: Coward McCann, 1943], and Bernard Gilbert Guerney,
ed., *A Treasury of Russian Literature* [New York: Vanguard, 1943]), *New Republic*, Jan. 17, 1944,
92–93.

on behalf of the Whites." A glance at Blok's diary would have revealed to Mr. Cournos that the poem was prompted by the Allies' refusal to sign peace with Germany as urged by the Soviets in the days of Brest-Litovsk. Blok warns the Allies that if this plea, "the last call to a bright fraternal feast on the part of a barbaric lyre," is not heeded, gigantic, slant-eyed Russia will be through with the West. Mr. Cournos misses the point completely and mistranslates the penultimate stanza (and the one before) in a most astounding manner, making utter nonsense of the text. Thus Mr. Cournos:

> We shall close our ranks like the savage Hun, ghoul-like, rifle the pockets of corpses, burn down towns, drive human hordes into churches and roast the flesh of our white brothers.

And Blok:

> We shall not budge when the fierce Hun begins to rummage in the pockets of corpses and to burn towns and herd horses into churches and to roast the flesh of his white brothers.

The style of Mr Cournos' introduction agrees with the quality of translations in the volume. The conventional, dull, inexact versions by Constance Garnett are supposed to be samples of Gogol and Turgenev. The chunks of Dostoevsky are of the same cardboard quality. I do not know who is responsible for the "translation" of Gogol's "Overcoat," but really one wonders what on earth is the use of printing or reprinting this abominable version, which flaunts more omissions and blunders than poor Akaki Akakyevich's old cloak had holes.

The number of contemporary second-class and third-class writers welcomed by Mr. Cournos greatly exceeds the necessity for their existence. I was particularly impressed by one gem. It is a story of a certain Alexander Poliakov, which Mr. Cournos introduces with the cry "How closely akin to life is Russian realism!" The story is about a dog which Russian soldiers take prisoner:

> "Well, let's give him a name" said someone. From all sides came suggestions: "Fascist," "Gangster," "Adolf," "Hitler," "Goebbels,"

and so forth. "None of these will do, boys," Dormidontov interrupted his friends. His eyes flashed gayly as he drawled in a mock reproachful tone: "Comrades, is it really proper to give such a name to a dog? Why insult an animal?" His words were drowned out in a loud burst of laughter [realism! humor!]. "Then what name shall we give him?" insisted the tankmen. "Well," said Dormidontov, "we took the dog along with other German war materials. He's one of our trophies. Let's call him Trophy" [paragraph]. This suggestion was enthusiastically accepted [paragraph]. Several months passed [period]. Trophy became inseparable from the battalion. He quickly grew accustomed to his new name [I cannot stop quoting]. He was particularly attached to Dormidontov and when the jolly driver was away with his group, Trophy visibly missed him. All the tankmen became fond of the big pointer. They especially . . .

No, this is not a parody, this is a "true story" (*teste* Mr. Cournos), but it is curious how often stark realism and "simplicity" are synonymous with the tritest and most artificial literary conventionalities imaginable. The plot is so easy to deduce that it hardly needs to he hinted at. "The bold and intelligent pointer made three more trips with ammunition." As a matter of fact the bold and intelligent pointer had made—oh, many, many, more trips than that in his steady course from magazine to magazine, in all countries, through all wars. Innumerable times, tamed by innumerable lady writers and fireside correspondents, has the "intelligent animal bounded forward as though he understood clearly what was wanted of him." Mark you: "as though." Soviet literature, being human, never despised the oldest bourgeois clichés (the *avant-garde* touch being of course automatically supplied by political enlightenment), but I doubt whether the kindest Soviet critic would approve of this trash.

Compared with the translations in Mr. Cournos' volume, those by Guerney seem close to perfection. The two great qualities of his work are: a rich, pliant vocabulary and a gallant determination to render the original in full. One feels he loves tricky passages for the pleasure derived from the English quadrature of a Russian circle. The ingenuity of his verbal devices is so brilliant that at times the result seems a trifle too elegant, not to say precious (which on the whole is only welcome after the drabness one is accustomed to in these matters). Thus his rendering of Gogol's "Overcoat," although admirable in many respects (it is of course incomparably better than all previous attempts), does not quite convey the chaotic grammar, the splutter, the mumble, the nightmare logic (*e.g.*, that "old mother" which crops up in the description of the hero's birth) and the other irrational values of the prodigious story.

Mr. Guerney has also tackled "The Twelve." This is a bumpy poem—but then the bulk of Blok's writing is a heterogeneous mixture of violas and vulgarity. He was a superb poet with a muddled mind. Something somber in him and fundamentally reactionary (remindful sometimes of Dostoevsky's political articles), a murky vista with a bonfire of books at the end, led him away from his genius as soon as he started to think. Authentic communists were quite right in not taking him seriously. His "Twelve" is a failure, and no wonder its strangely irrelevant end made one Soviet critic remark: "It was hardly worthwhile climbing our mountain to cap it (*nakhlobuchit'*) with a medieval shrine." Guerney's version of it is not on the level of his prose translations, and certain passages are quite incorrectly rendered. The long-haired passerby who bewails the betrayal of Russia is meant to represent the liberal-minded, second-rate, widely read writer of the general prerevolution period, such as, say, Korolenko or Chirikov, and not at all "some writing gent paid a penny a line," as Mr. Guerney has it.

Again, although exquisitely worded, the translation of the celebrated "Lay of the Host of Igor" (presumed to have been composed by an unknown minstrel of unique genius at the end of the twelfth century) is not free from certain slips. Instead of the smooth, lovely Persian miniature that Guerney makes of it, one would have preferred a really scholarly presentation of the thing, fattened on copious footnotes and enlivened by a thorough discussion of the various readings and obscurities, which have been the distress and delight of Russian commentators. Even if it be accepted that in one mysterious passage the reference is to a squirrel a-running all over a tree, still this animal is not the impossible "flying squirrel" which Mr. Guerney sends "soaring away" "over a tree's bark." I also question a couple of other zoological details: the "tawny" wolf, whose coat is of a different color in the original text, and the "linnet," which is genetically quite distinct from the bird mentioned therein. But it would be ungrateful to pick out flaws in this or the other translations by Mr. Guerney. This seems to be the first Russian anthology ever published that does not affect one with the feeling of intense irritation produced by the omissions, the blunders, the flat, execrable English of more or less well-meaning hacks.

59

On Learning Russian
(Essay, 1945)*

There are two main methods of learning a language—Russian, in the present case: pick-up and dig-up. For the first, the requirements are a good ear and Russian surroundings. After a year or two of this a person may be able to speak the idiom with perfect although illusory fluency (the illusion being produced by a subtle blend of clichés and solecisms), but will not be able to read or write it.

The second method has less brilliancy and abandon, but is incomparably safer. Based as it is on a diligent study of the anatomy of the language, i.e., on grammar, it gradually gets into your system if your system can stand it, which, normally, it should. In fact, my pet theory is that English-speaking people are born linguists, most of whom, unfortunately, do not use their gift, while, on the other hand, Russians have no real aptitude for languages but brazenly pick them up under the false impression that all foreign tongues are simpler than Russian.

Before helping the born linguist to work his stumbling way through the intricacies of Russian grammar, I usually point out that what is going to bother him most, are the following two facts: First, that Russian vowels are pronounced in a way totally different from English ones, but in several cases are not dissimilar from, say, French vowels (at this point, I try to find out who among my students knows French but this

---

* "On Learning Russian," *The Wellesley Magazine*, April 1945, 191–92. A note heads the article: "The College offers this year, for the first time, a six hour course in elementary Russian, open to all undergraduates. An intermediate course is planned for next year, open by permission of the instructor. Mr. Nabokov, who teaches this course, came to Wellesley in 1941–42 as visiting lecturer in Comparative Literature." The byline of the main article reads "Vladimir Nabokov, Lecturer in Russian." He had been teaching elementary Russian since 1942 on a year-by-year basis, but only now had it become an established part of the college schedule.

does not help much since the French learned at school is comfortably pronounced the English way). A Russian vowel is an orange, an English vowel is a lemon. When you speak Russian your mouth ought to distend laterally at the corners, vowels being expressed by a horizontal line from cheek to cheek, rather than by a vertical one from chin to nose as in English. You can, and should, speak Russian with a permanent broad smile, which is a very difficult feat in English, where the mouth forms a proximo-distad directed oval to say O. Compress its poles, inflate its sides and you get the Russian equivalent. I strictly avoid the humorous touch when dealing with my classes, but suchlike explanations, which are merely meant to stress the anatomical differences between the two languages, oddly enough provoke a ripple of laughter, when all I ask for is a bland smile of the Cheshire cat type.

The other fact I immediately stress is that Russian is an inflectional language, which means that words undergo grammatical change of endings according to person, number, tense and case. "*Ahfrika*"[1] (the Russian for Africa) becomes for instance "*v* (in) *Ahfrike*" in the locative case: *ya zhivu v Ahfrike* meaning "I live in Africa."

These transformations (which may be compared to replacing the last coach of a train by a diner or a caboose, or eliminating it altogether, or adding another car, or to be frank, losing the better part of the train in a dark tunnel of uncertain location) are simple in themselves, but being numerous, must be learned with great perseverance so as to avoid constant accidents all along the line. The first course of Russian is really the study of these inflections and of prefixes (changeable locomotives), and however exasperating the unpredictable quality of Russian grammar may seem, the thing must be seen through. The conjuror's patter of the Berlitz School is not, in my opinion, a good introduction to the Russian language, and generally speaking I must admit to feeling a great deal of disgust for any leveling or oversimplification. Brains must work the hard way or else lose their calling and rank. The loaves of knowledge do not come nicely sliced. All you get is a stone-strewn field to plow on an exhilarating morning. Incidentally and apart from totalitarian regimes, the most despicable invention of our times is Basic English.

The investigation of grammatical phenomena should be accompanied from the very start by attempts to turn English sentences of "my aunt has a hat" type into Russian. The images evoked by such sentences

are unlovely but they must be endured for the sake of the grammatical point they loyally raise. I prefer to wait a little before having my
students memorize lists of useful words, although I expect them to
remember those they handle in their exercises. Anatomy must precede
systematics, and the importance of studying the behavior of a word
is greater than that of learning to say in Russian "goodbye" or "good
morning." I should like the student to *enjoy* the twists and turns of my
Russian eels, to enter into the spirit of the game and watch words at play
with a true naturalist's detachment rather than with a collector's greed.

The highest peak of Russian grammar is reached when the student
gets used to the transformations in sense which verbs undergo owing
to a change in the prefix. Most verbs moreover have reciprocal and
reflexive forms ending in *"sa"* and there again the addition of this *"sa"*
may give a perfectly new twist to the meaning of a verb already changed
by the prefix. *Govoritz*[2] for instance means to speak, *pogovoritz* to have a
talk, *dogovoritz* to say all one has to say, *ugovoritz* to persuade, *podgovoritz*
to instigate, *prigovoritz* to condemn, *peregovoritz* to talk something over,
rasgovoritz to draw somebody out, *sgovoritz* to bring people together and
vozgovoritz to launch upon an oration; but with other prefixes the verb
may have at least two meanings in each case, so that *vygovoritz* means
to pronounce, but also to stipulate, *progovoritz* to utter or to speak away
for a given amount of time, *zagovoritz* to start speaking or to overwhelm
one's interlocutor with words, *nagovoritz* to accumulate a number of
(nice, nasty) remarks, or to make a gramophone record, *ogovoritz* to
denounce, or to make some reservation when settling some matter, and
finally *otgovoritz* is either to dissuade or to rattle off a speech. Of these
fifteen prefix-modified forms of *govoritz* (producing as we have seen
twenty-one different shades of meaning) ten have moreover reciprocal
or reflexive forms, which not only may deviate in an unexpected direction from the meaning produced by the same prefix, but may also have
more meanings than one. Thus the reciprocal *dogovoritza* means to
reach an agreement, *ugovoritza* to decide upon some course of action,
sgovoritza simply to make an agreement, *razgovoritza* to enter into a
conversation, *nagozvoritza* to talk one's fill and *zagovoritza* to prolong
the conversation unduly (in all these cases of course the action is shared
with somebody else, hence the term "reciprocal"). On the other hand
the reflexive *dogovoritza* means to speak ("by one's self" in this and in

the rest of the following forms) until one has reached a certain, often nonsensical, point, *zagovoritza* to lose one's self utterly in the maze of one's speech, *podgovoritza* to ingratiate oneself, *razgovoritza* to become talkative if not actually garrulous, *progovoritza* to blurt out something that one would not have liked to tell, *otgovoritza* to find an excuse, *ogovoritza* either to make certain, purely verbal, reservations or to make a slip in speaking, and finally *vozgovoritza* does not mean anything at all.

This kaleidoscopic performance on the part of verbs is, I repeat, the most bothersome aspect of Russian grammar, and only when the student ceases to be flustered by it, then, and only then, he is safe. The difficulty for people who would have liked to have automatic mnemonic rules is obvious, but the good student will treat the most annoying Russian word with sympathy and help it to uncoil itself when it overdoes its playful contortions.

The first course in Russian takes us from the uncle's house to that circus of verbs. Exercises in grammar are accompanied by a good deal of reading of simple digestible stuff correlated with previously acquired rules and especially composed to illustrate them. I have found the story of an English couple, Peter and Mary, written by Elisaveta Fen for students of Russian, eminently suitable. A general though necessarily halting and bashful conversation in Russian should gradually become part of the lesson, while the second course will see Pushkin and Chekhov (plays, short stories) replace Miss Fen.

60

Profile by Sylvia Crane
for *Wellesley College News* (1945)[*]

"Anything can make a story," *said Mr. Vladimir Nabokov, gently shaking the foundations of English Composition 207 (Free Writing) at a meeting of all sections of that course Tuesday evening, April 17, at the Recreation Building. . . .*

"I get an idea," *said Mr. Nabokov*, "and I live with it for a long time, perhaps a month. After that time, I simply have to record the words on paper." *An uneasy titter rippled about the room.* "You mean you just sit down and—" *an unbelieving student began.*

"No," *interrupted Mr. Nabokov*. "I never sit. I lie in bed. Sitting up I am useless—I cannot think to write."

"But what do you do about putting the story together?" ventured another student. "How about conflict, for instance? You can't write a story without conflict." "Conflict!" *thundered Mr. Nabokov scornfully, and the class thundered back with appreciative applause. . . .*

The class was still not quite sure how Mr. Nabokov managed to find ideas so easily. "But it is simple," *he said. He gestured toward a lamp.* "For instance, look at that lamp. What is the first thought that comes into your mind?" *"Oatmeal," replied a nearby listener.* "Fine, fine," *he said.* "At one time in your life, you probably ate too much oatmeal. There is a story."

[*] "'Anything Makes a Story' Insists Mr. Nabokov, in Comp 207," *Wellesley College News*, April 26, 1945, 5. VN was guest speaker in Wellesley's Composition 207 class.

61

The Place of Russian Studies in the Curriculum (Essay, 1948)*

Whenever I am asked about the place of Russian in the curriculum of an American university, I recall three elderly and highly respectable American ladies I met as a boy at a European resort before the First World War. They had traveled around the world and were familiar with the customs of various exotic tribes. They would have felt at home in any Western European country or in any inhabited part of the Tropics, but they had carefully omitted from their traveling ventures all parts of Russia, both European and Asiatic. When Mother casually suggested that they go on their next trip to St. Petersburg, the ladies expressed utter horror and one of them finally declared that under no circumstances would they go to any such place from where they might be suddenly deported to Siberia. Now, this particular fear, which may or may not have become real under the present political regime in Russia, was certainly wildly absurd before 1917. The same ladies were not quite sure whether a Russian language existed. They were under the impression that French was the spoken language in Russia, with perhaps some Asiatic dialects.

All this has changed in recent years, and it is a good and important change. It is good and important for American students to study the Russian language, literature, history and philosophy, not only because in the present-day world all nations have become close neighbors, glaring at each other across fences (with the pumpkins of nationalism ripening in the late sun), but even more so because the study of Russian language and literature is a unique and exquisite experience holding in store for

* "The Place of Russian Studies in the Curriculum," *Wellesley Magazine*, Feb. 1948, 179–80.

the careful student endless enjoyment together with a most precious widening of spiritual and intellectual horizons.

There are two main reasons why a person may want to study a foreign language: he may want to speak it for some practical purpose— business, travel, politics—or he may want to tackle a famous master- piece in the original, and be able to win the confidence of his dictionary when requesting the latter's assistance. In an attempt to imagine the state of mind of an American wanting to study the Russian language, I see these two motives in a kind of seesaw arrangement. One of them is sure to pull the other down. In other words, it is rather a choice between the applied and the pure than their profitable combination.

I shall make my meaning still clearer if I say that the present interest in things Russian is fairly remote from the direct desire to probe the artistic subtleties of *Dead Souls* or *Anna Karenin*. We want to understand Russians because we feel friendly toward them or because we fear them. We are considerably more eager to find out what Stalin thinks of war than to know what Tolstoy thought of it. We are driven to buy Russian grammars by the pathetic vision of a "better understanding between nations" and not by the spirit of verbal adventure. Few are the gentle scholars who take advantage of the present vogue of Russian studies to learn Russian for the sole purpose of enjoying Russian.

I am not criticizing this state of affairs. That the practical side of learning has come to the fore, may be a normal phenomenon. I am just mentioning it because it is a fact from which I shall presently draw certain conclusions. And again, when I say "practical," I say it without irony, although one doubts sometimes that learning a language may help to bring together a freedom-loving well-meaning people and a nation which for thirty years has been under a totalitarian regime.

But no matter: whether one hopes to make a friend or whether one wishes to know a language sufficiently well to understand the whisper behind one's back, the threat, the sneer, the secret message,—there still remains the problem of learning the language. We now have two courses of Russian language here at Wellesley, with three weekly hours of instruction each. A student cannot major in Russian,—the time devoted to the study of the language would, of course, be quite insuf- ficient for this,—but there is a one-year course of Russian Literature in translation, elected by most of those students who have taken the two other courses, together with some sixty-odd other students, all of them Juniors or Seniors, who have not had any Russian at all. This is, of course, a compromise, since, logically, there ought to be a two-year course of Russian Literature in Russian after two years of intensive study of the language.

As I said, each of the two classes has three meetings a week. As far as my experience goes—and perhaps I have been exceptionally lucky—only one student out of ten has sufficient linguistic talent and perseverance to be able to speak and understand speech after two years of such leisurely training, proceeding from scratch. This percentage is really more than one could have expected, since three hours a week is not enough for the average student to master a difficult new language. When beginning this course, she encounters peculiar obstacles: an unfamiliar alphabet; ten vowels, nine of which are somewhat difficult and one extremely difficult to pronounce correctly; unpredictable stress accents; a most intricate grammar; and a vocabulary with no *point de repère*[1] in the way of familiar roots. Now, three hours a week of this kind of thing is inadequate unless they are supplemented by as many hours of practice. It seems to me that every lesson of grammar and translation should be at once followed by an hour of Russian conversation. This would equally help those who would like to obtain a practical knowledge of spoken Russian and those who would like to study Russian literature in Russian. It is my conviction that my successor next year[2] would be able to attain much more satisfactory results if the program of Russian studies were expanded.

Between 1820 and 1920 Russia produced one of the greatest literatures we know. A remarkably small part of its treasures exist in an adequate English translation—a fact probably due to the scarcity of gifted translators than to any other reason. However, I also submit that in practically no other language do literary masterpieces so much depend on the integration of an individual style with individually colored contents, as is the case in Russian. And this is one reason why it appears to me so important that educated Americans appropriate these riches and integrate them in their own spiritual endowment, thus contributing to the spiritual enrichment of the whole nation. The very development of the Russian language, on the other hand, rich in peculiarities unknown to Germanic and Romance languages, offers a further field rich in discoveries which, sometimes unnoticed by the student, allow him to find shortcuts for his thought, new vistas for his imagination. Then again: there is a certain unique quality about Russian literature, a quality of truth not rubbed in, of imagination controlled by dignified truthfulness, which has had an ennobling influence on the world literatures, but which, to be fully understood and appraised, calls for a knowledge of the workings of the Russian creative mind (or I would prefer to say, workings of a creative mind in Russian), which, in turn, calls for a sound knowledge of the language.

62

Thomas Mann, "The Railway Accident"
(Lecture, 1950)*

The little book before me is called *Nocturnes*. The author is Thomas Mann. Nobody in his right mind would use the word *Nocturnes* for a title but let that pass. The title page goes on to state "with lithographs by so-and-so" and "published in N.Y.C. by Equinox Press, in the year 1934." All very stylish. Very stylish and very abominable lithographs—lisping little pictures.[1] "The edition consists of a thousand copies signed by the author." This copy is numbered 861. Mr. Mann's appended signature is a little wobbly, after the 860 copies already signed. Say—five seconds—thousand by five—five thousand seconds—five thousand divided by sixty—about an hour and a half—say *two hours solid signing of copies*. The modest translator[2] is not mentioned.

The middle story is quite a famous Mann story—it's called "The Railway Accident."[3] The German text is roughly contemporaneous with Kafka's *Metamorphosis*.[4]

It begins in a rather coy fashion, which of course is a very commonplace approach.

"Tell you [a] story? But I don't know any. Well, yes, after all, here is something I might tell." (The grace of an elephant.)

This heavily flippant, ponderously bantering style is sustained throughout. The narrator is traveling first class from Munich to deliver a lecture in Dresden. As his train is about to leave, he contemplates

* Unpublished lecture notes, holograph and typescript draft, "[Cornell lecture notes] Introduction to Literature 311," VNA Berg, for VN's Literature 311–312 (Masterpieces of European Fiction) class at Cornell, presumably prepared for its first iteration, in 1950–51, and apparently designed to contrast with the work of the course's other author writing in German, Franz Kafka, and his *Metamorphosis*. The notes are rough, with scribbled words, misspellings, words and punctuation omitted; errors have been silently corrected where the intention is clear. It seems likely that VN may have used this section of a lecture only once, if at all, since there is no evidence of careful or later revision.

The little book before me is called Nocturnes. *The author is* by Thomas Mann. Nobody in his right mind would use the word Nocturnes for a title but let that pass. The title page goes on to state — with lithographs by so and so, *and* "published in N.Y.C. by so an Equinox Press, in the year 1934. all very stylish. *this glows at six admirable lithographs — any eight's little pictures.* On the last page we find the following: "*these three stories published under the title of Nocturnes no a twenn* are to published ok" — the edition consists of a thousand copies signed by the author." This copy is numbered 861. Mr Mann's appended signature is a little wobbly. *soft* after the 860 copies already signed. Say — five seconds — *thousand by five* 1000. five thousand seconds. five thousand divided by sixty *two* — about an hour and a half — say two hours solid signing of copies. *The modest translator's name is not mentioned.*

The middle story is quite a famous Mann story — it is called The Railway accident. The german text *was written* is *roughly* contemporaneous with Kafka's *about the work in that Metamorphosis*

It begins *rather coyly* in a rather coy fashion, which of course is *redicuous* a very commonplace approach.

" Tell you story? But I don't know any. *Oh* Well, yes, after all, here is something I might tell. ' (the grace of an elephant)

This heavily flippant, ponderously bantering style is sustained throughout. The narrator is *readily* first class *for* to deliver a lecture *Dresden* in *Munich*. As the train is about to leave, he contemplates the station platform from the window & identifies his trunk with his manuscript being carted towards the baggage car.

There " thought I " no need to worry, it is in good hands. Look at that *big* station guard with the *leaky* belt and the *sergeant* *mighty* moustache)

Lecture notes for a brief denunciation of Thomas Mann's story "The Railway Accident," apparently designed as a contrast—how *not* to write fiction—before tackling Kafka's *Metamorphosis*, the first time Nabokov taught his Masterpieces of European Fiction class at Cornell, 1950–51 the station platform from the window and identifies his trunk with his manuscript being carted toward the baggage car.

"'There,' thought I, 'no need to worry, it is in good hands. Look at that big station guard with the leather belt and the military moustache, watch him rebuking that old woman in the threadbare black cape—by golly, she almost got into a second-class carriage, when her place is third class.'"[5] See the idea? This is *sociological sarcasm*.

There is some more obvious stuff about this heavyweight station guard, representative of King Wilhelm's government—but that is sufficient for our purpose.

Another person is introduced: A man strolling up and down the platform wearing spats and a monocle. Aha! Aristocrat. Spats, eyeglass. Ha. With a handsome bulldog on a leash. He struts, his gaze is cold. He does not apologize when he bumps into people. Big bad aristocrat. He takes his dog into the sleeping car, which is against the rules. *The first point is made:*

little old woman not allowed even into a second-class carriage
High class dog of a high class nob *allowed* to enter

Magnificently deep and original, isn't it?

The train starts, the beds are not yet made apparently, presently the sleeping car attendant asks for the spatted gentleman's tickets. "I heard," says the narrator, "the gentleman's immediate burst of rage. 'What do you want,' he roared. 'Leave me alone, you swine.' He said swine. It was a lovely epithet (the narrator is being very sarcastic)—and then the ticket flew out of the compartment into the attendant's face. He picked it up with both hands [not a very natural thing to do—but it is needed in order to show his humility] and though a corner of his cardboard ticket had hit him in the eye, which was watering, through his tears he saluted and clicked his heels."[6] [Oh, the pity of it!]

Before we get to the accident let us check what we have had so far.

You will notice what is so completely inartistic: the characters are only there to represent this or that general idea. The easy and obvious—and therefore false—is everywhere preferred to the difficult and personal. Easy does it: want a pathetic type? four ingredients: woman, old, small, poor: there you are. Want a proud aristocrat—*Bitte sehr*—monocle, spats, mustaches, dog. Under the flag of this so-called realism the most preposterous actions take place. Tickets are sent flying into conductors' faces, and—but let us go on:

The train is derailed. The forward coaches are smashed up. Many of the compartments are telescoped. There is a good deal of wreckage under which children are buried. *But no lives are lost.* Mann, being a bad writer, does not see the accident: He just uses ready-made phrases to describe it. He is concerned with the moral of the accident and not with the authentic vision of it. The first-class sleeper is intact of course, but in spite of this, its occupants, women with bare arms and shoulders, stand wringing their hands. Just imagine that vision.

The spatted gent throws himself upon a case on the wall of the corridor, where an ax and saw are kept for emergencies, and breaks the glass with his bare fist. Through the broken glass he tries to pull out the tools but fails, and leaves the car.

Now comes the point of the story.

"Finally we were all stowed higgledy-piggledy into a special train. I had my first-class ticket—my journey being paid for—but it availed me nothing,—my carriage was as crowded as the others. But just as I found a little nook, who do I see opposite to me, huddled in the corner. [*Who indeed?*] My hero, the gentleman with the spats and vocabulary of a cavalry officer. His dog had been taken away from him and now sat howling in a gloomy prison just behind the engine (the last thing that would happen in an emergency). He sits there, the aristocrat, with a sour smile, resigning himself to the crazy situation.

"And now who gets in, supported by two firemen. A wee little old grandmother in a tattered black cape, the very same who in Munich almost got into a second-class carriage and now she is traveling first class."[7] Ah, what symbolism. How very realistic and profound. What humor. The story ends:

"Well, that was the railway accident I went through. I suppose it had to happen once; but whatever mathematics may say, I feel that I now have every chance of escaping another." Very funny. And that's that.

I would like you to ponder the difference between the seemingly fantastic but inwardly authentic world of Kafka, an artist of genius—and this kind of thing, where everything is built on the bog of platitudes, of average and therefore false and dead ideas, a phony world where—now comes my delightful discovery: a man who puts his fist through broken glass hasn't a single scratch to show.

63

Interview with Harvey Breit
for *New York Times Book Review* (1951)*

*Would you care to talk a bit about [*Conclusive Evidence*]?*
It is a memoir . . . and true. There is a good deal of selection in it, of course. What interested me is the thematic lines of my life that resemble fiction. The memoir became the meeting point of an impersonal art form and a very personal life story.

Is there any precedent for the memoir that is to some extent manipulated or constructed as a novel?
There isn't any precedent that I know of. It is a literary approach to my own past. There is some precedent for it in the novel, in Proust, say, but not in the memoir. With me, it is a kind of composition. I am a composer of chess problems. Nobody . . . has yet solved the chess problem in *Conclusive Evidence*.

What about a professional, a Reuben Fine,[1] *a Reshevsky,*[2] *or someone like that?*
I'm waiting for one to come along.

Are you going to go on with the memoir?
"I am perfectly happy here," *Mr. Nabokov replied, and for a moment his interlocutor didn't realize it was a reply.* "I am happiest here," *he said.*

* "Talk with Mr. Nabokov," *New York Times Book Review*, July 1, 1951, 17. Interview, May 28, 1951, for launch of *Conclusive Evidence* (later retitled *Speak, Memory*), which had been attracting attention in its serial publication, mostly in *The New Yorker*, since early 1948.

What was your first novel?
It was named *Laughter in the Dark*.[3] I wrote it in Russian and translated it into English myself. That was in 1938. It was a kind of thriller, but it was the only book that brought me in a little money now and then. It's not particularly good. It's a little crude. I think the double writing makes it somewhat peculiar.

Is there a precedent for that?
It irritates me a little when people compare me to Conrad. I am not at all displeased in a literary way: that isn't what I mean. The point is Conrad had never been a Polish writer, he started right in as an English writer. I had had a number of books in Russian before I wrote in English. My books were completely banned in Russia and circulated among the Russian émigrés only. There were millions of them.

When did you first come here?
In 1940, on a French boat, which was sunk on the way back. My first impression was wonderful. I got in on the very right angle, on the right chink: I had some boxing gloves on the top of a bag and the two custom officials took them out and began sparring. I got in a taxi and gave the driver a $100 bill and said give me $10 because the meter is $90. Of course, it was 90c. The driver said, if I could break a hundred I wouldn't be driving a cab. And he gave me the money back. . . . I went to Stanford then and had an excellent time teaching.

But what about your English?
It was my first language. I remember my mother taking a Russian book for children and translating it into English.

Wasn't that unusual?
No, not in certain circles in Russia.

Are you reading young American writers?
I haven't much time. I am in the past. My teaching course is from Jane Austen to James Joyce. But once in a while someone sends me a novel. What surprises me is the good bits in a bad novel even. In Europe, when a novel is bad it is bad totally. But I am a great reader, especially

of the critics. No, I wouldn't want to say which critics please me most and which least. I don't want to get mixed up in *that*.

Do you find in the American critics the vitality that is supposed to be there?
Vitality? Oh, I think there is, I think there is. I think there are fine critics in America.

64

News Feature Interview with Malcolm D. Rivkin
for *Harvard Crimson* (1952)[*]

"All this is just a reporter's story," *Nabokov said.* "It came to the paper after passing through several sources, none of whom was a naturalist."

Nabokov, who will teach Humanities 2 this term, continued, "The news article itself is also fiction, not fact. One type of fiction has been created by a reporter, and the other type has been created by Melville."

Nabokov said that it was always dangerous to try and relate real life and real facts to fiction, and that there was no connection with a real white whale and the one in the novel.

"The white whale has been created by Melville, as the whale has been created by God or by genes. Facts should not interfere with interpretation—let's keep them separate."

"The story of Moby Dick will stand as the Castle Elsinore stands, unchanged—and with no relation to the building that tourists call Elsinore," *he concluded.*

[*] "Recent Capture of White Whale Fails to Mar Melville's Meaning," *Harvard Crimson*, Feb. 5, 1952. Occasion: capture of a white whale off the coast of Peru; VN was about to teach "Humanities 2: Novel" at Harvard.

65

Salutations
(Seventieth Birthday Congratulations
for Mark Aldanov, 1956)[*]

I don't know how my dear friend, M. A. Aldanov,[1] regards the Russian newspaper tradition of celebrating anniversaries in print; most likely with good-natured irony. Nevertheless, I would like to take the opportunity of his being today the victim of such a celebration[2] by expressing my wish that he should write *more* beautiful, intelligent books. This reminds me very vividly: day turning to evening in émigré Berlin, I am around twenty, the light above the staircase comes on, my father comes in with an expression of tender appetite, carrying the latest novelty: *St. Helena: Little Island.*[3]

---

[*] V. Nabokov-Sirin, "Ot V. Nabokova-Sirina" ("From V. Nabokov-Sirin"), *Novoe russkoe slovo*, Nov. 4, 1956, in column "Privetstviya" ("Salutations").

66

Interview with Natalia Shakhovskaya
for Voice of America (1958)[*]

Thank you for finding the time for this interview; I know how busy you are with your writing and teaching. I think I should start by settling one question: will I be interviewing the Russian writer Vladimir Sirin, or the famous American writer Vladimir Nabokov?

Don't be disconcerted by the presence of this "combined team." Nabokov is here, of course, as is Sirin, and more. On the whole, the American Nabokov continues the Russian Sirin's work. Even though, from 1940 onward, I began to write novels only in English and sign them "Nabokov," my "Sirin" pseudonym still flashes here and there as an appendage to my surname under my Russian works—poems, articles.

Your translation of Lermontov's Hero of Our Time *has just come out in America. On the book's cover it states that your son helped you with the translation.*

Yes, part of the translation was done by my son, Dmitri, who recently graduated from Harvard and is fluent in both languages.

[*] "The American Nabokov Carries On the Work of Sirin," *Golos Ameriki* (*Voice of America*), radio broadcast, May 14, 1958. Typed transcript in LCNA, corrected in VN's hand, of radio interview by Natalia Shakhovskhoy, "Interv'yu radiostantsii 'Golos Ameriki,'" ed. Maxim Shrayer, *Druzhba narodov* 11 (2000), 194–96. Occasion: VN's success with *Pnin*, nominated for a National Book Award; the imminent publication of the American edition of *Lolita*, much anticipated after the French banning of the 1955 Paris edition of the novel; and the completion and submission of his *Eugene Onegin* translation and commentary. VN had known Shakhovskoy, now a lecturer in Russian at Barnard College, New York, for thirty years, from her former marriage to his cousin Nicolas. When he and his family had arrived in the United States, they stayed the first few days in her New York apartment.

So is your son planning on following in your footsteps and becoming a writer? (*Laughs.*) No. He's only twenty-four, he has an excellent velvety bass, and plans to be an opera singer. But that doesn't stop him from helping me. He just finished the index for my commentary to *Eugene Onegin.*

In fact, I wanted to ask you about your translation of Pushkin's Onegin. *Is it a translation in verse?*
Eugene Onegin has been translated numerous times in verse, into English, into German. But all of these translations are approximations, and, besides, they're teeming with unbelievable mistakes. At first I, too, thought that, with the help of some sort of magic manipulations, I could after all manage to convey not just the content of every stanza but also the whole constellation, the whole Ursa Major, of its rhymes. But even if the poet-alchemist managed to keep both the sequence of rhymes and the exact meaning of the text, the miracle would be useless, since the English conception of rhyme does not correspond to the Russian.

So how did you resolve this problem?
To translate *Onegin,* and not retell it in bad English rhymes, the translation has to be exact, interlinear, literal, and for this exactitude I was happy to sacrifice everything—"smoothness," elegance, idiomatic clarity, the number of feet in a line and the rhyme. The one thing I kept was the iambic meter, for it soon became clear that this condition, this small rhythmic constriction, turns out to be no hindrance at all but, rather, its opposite, serves as an indispensable screw for fastening the literal meaning. The commentary, explaining *Onegin's* content and the form, gradually grew into a volume of more than a thousand pages, which will be published together with the translation of the main text and all variants known to me from published drafts. It was a lot of work; I was engrossed in it for eight years.

How do you manage to combine your creative work with your university teaching?
The terms of my employment at Cornell University are exceptionally favorable in that respect. I give six or seven lectures in a week. One course offers an overview of Russian literature from *The Song of Igor's Campaign* to Alexander Blok; another course analyzes some wonderful

works of European literature from the nineteenth and twentieth centuries. In this course, I analyze novels like *Madame Bovary*, *Anna Karenin*, Proust's *In Search of Lost Time*, and James Joyce's *Ulysses*. My students in a special seminar study Russian poets in the original.

Vladimir Vladimirovich, let's now turn to what you've been writing in America.
I'd prefer to talk about my last two novels, *Pnin* and *Lolita*. *Pnin* came out last year in the United States and in England. Since then it has been translated, or is being translated, into French, Spanish, German, Swedish, Danish, and Dutch. Pnin is an émigré with a bronzed bald head and a tender, touching soul. Wholly imbued with all the best in Russian culture, he is lost in an alien environment, between three pine trees on the mowed lawn of American life. *Lolita* came out in English in August this year, published by Putnam. It's my favorite book. The story of a poor, charming girl . . . It is now being translated into six European languages. A Japanese publishing house has also been in touch. I've yet to receive any inquiries from a Soviet publisher.

Interview in *New York Post* (1958)[*]

Nabokov, distinguished writer, professor, critic, entomologist, is convinced "only fools" *would find* Lolita *obscene. . . .*

Contrary to best-selling traditions, the erotica taper off sharply in the second half, which leads Nabokov to believe "there's no danger of the book being pursued for its immorality." *. . .*

Nabokov . . . predicted:

"Those who keep looking for spicy bits will not find them. They will not be able to read the book through—they will get bored too soon. The only thing that might be attractive is the diary H.H. keeps. And then, who would be attracted by a 12-year-old girl?" . . .

"If a few elderly gentlemen read it in that spirit, that's surely their business."

Nabokov expounded this theory at a Harvard Club cocktail party. He was accompanied by his wife, Vera, a slender, fair-skinned, white-haired woman in no way reminiscent of Lolita. One guest commented that this was reassuring.

"Yes," said Mrs. Nabokov, smiling. "It's the main reason why I'm here."

Her husband chuckled.

"I toyed with the idea of borrowing a 'Lolita' "—*he held out a hand at waist-height*—"from one of my friends for this occasion."

. . . he has never heard of Peyton Place.[1]

"What is it?" *he inquired.* "A novel." "Who wrote it?"

---

[*] "*Lolita* Obscene? Not to Its Author," *New York Post*, Aug. 6, 1958, 10. Author unknown. For the impending first American publication of *Lolita*, Aug. 18, 1958. The first edition of the novel, in English but published in Paris, had been banned in France in late 1956, unbanned in Jan. 1958, and banned again, under another law, in July 1958.

Interview with Martha MacGregor
for *New York Post* (1958)[*]

"I'm very proud that America has not brought charges. It's wonderful, it's wonderful."

The author himself says of the charge of pornography: "Foolish." *And of conflicting theories on the meaning of* Lolita: "Just a story, a fairy tale, as all stories are." . . .

"I read English before I read Russian. I spoke English with my mother and my nurse—with my brother, I remember, I always spoke French. That was typical. The children would speak one language together and another language at table and another with their father and mother. Sometimes as many as four languages would be spoken.

"After I started going to school, at 11, my tutor stayed on and would tutor me at night for the next day. You learned a great deal that way.

"And we had wonderful courses in French literature. The French governess would read to us three hours a day—the English governess, too. We had all the English magazines and some of the American ones—*Little Folks* and *St. Nicholas*.

"I started reading Turgenev and Tolstoy when I was very small. My wife read *Anna Karenina* at 6. Her nurse said, 'Come, come, I'll tell that to you in my own words.'

"Even then she knew to beware of condensations," *Nabokov added, laughing.*

"I started writing Russian verse very early—when I was 13—and published a little book of verse when I was 15."

[*] "The Author of Lolita—An Unhurried View," *New York Post Weekend Magazine*, Aug. 17, 1958, M10. Published on the eve of the first American publication of *Lolita*, Aug. 18, 1958, a day on which many American newspapers reviewed the novel.

Lolita *was written in English, but Nabokov insists that he could have done better in Russian.* "It's simply that my knowledge of Russian is infinitely greater than my knowledge of English." ...

"What do you think of the Angry Young Men?" I asked Nabokov.

"What are *they?*"

"What do you think of the Beat Generation?"

This drew fire—an outburst in the passionate Russian manner.

"I don't like anything that becomes a movement, a school! I don't like labels, clubs. I don't like groups!

"It just doesn't mean anything to me if you say symbolists or classicists. It doesn't mean anything and that's what I teach my classes. I teach them books, not authors. Not groups or labels.

"Exist—exist—existen—" *Nabokov's lips pucker humorously as he made an amusing pretense at being unable to pronounce "existentialism."*

"I'm bored by the word itself! I read something Sartre wrote. I didn't know what he was talking about."

. . .

"Freudian voodoo!" *Nabokov replied vehemently.* "That's my *bête noire.* I think he has been one of the most pernicious influences on literature, children and schools. It's a medieval mind dealing in medieval symbols. The initial witch doctor and all the little witch doctors. The rather complicated question on which I will write later. A craze that's passing ...

"No interest whatsoever in politics or people with a capital P. I make my own people, my own politics, and my own gods—if any." ...

[On Lolita*]* "The book has no message. I'm no messenger boy. A book has to stand on its own two feet or fly on its own two wings, or four."

69

Interview with Paul O'Neil
for *Life* (1958)[*]

On the Russian émigré experience
No matter what country you were in, it was the same. You saw only Russians and the real people of the country simply seemed like scenery.

On being a tennis coach in Germany
It ruined my serve.

On what his science gave him
[An indescribable] sense of power, of triumph over nature.

On Lolita *as a new turn from Russia to America*
Humbert Humbert is a salad of genes, but he has no Russian genes.

On Hemingway
A writer for boys.

On Thomas Mann
A small writer who did big stories badly.

On Thomas Wolfe
Mediocrity!

[*] "*Lolita* and the Lepidopterist: Author Nabokov Is Awed by Sensation He Created," *Life International*, April 13, 1959, 63–69. VN was interviewed by O'Neil on Sept. 5 and 6, 1958 ("I spent two delightful days with Paul O'Neil, who pumped me very delicately with great skill and acumen," VN to Walter Minton, Sept. 9, 1958, VNA Berg), before Carl Mydans came to photograph him for the magazine on Sept. 13. The interview did not appear until seven months later, and not in the American but only in the international edition.

What lies behind Humbert Humbert's name?
Humbug.

On Humbert
A complicated European with backgrounds gleaming through backgrounds.

On what he felt in composing Lolita
The excitement and pleasure of creating my own world.

On the heroine of The Enchanter, *the original of* Lolita
[Only a] shadow—not a real person.

On television
That horrible instrument.

On how he feels when Mrs. Nabokov parks him under a tree to write
Comfortable, pleasantly enclosed, and shut off from the world.

On Olympia Press's accepting Lolita
Books are like children. . . . After you go to all the trouble of raising them you want to see them married. Perhaps this wasn't the happiest marriage for *Lolita*, but it was something. It at least offered me the chance of seeing my work in print and having it between covers for my bookshelf. . . . It sold more copies in the first few weeks, than all my other books put together. . . . What shall I do with the money? Perhaps I could buy a soccer team.

On filming Lolita
It was perfectly all right for me to imagine a 12-year-old Lolita. . . . She existed inside my head. But to make a real 12-year-old girl play such a part in public would be sinful and immoral, and I will never consent to it.

70

Interview with Gladys Kessler
for *Cornell Daily Sun* (1958)*

"Any work of art is above censorship. But censorship of course depends on what you call a book. A book, a novel above all, is a work of art and must be above all restrictions."

Professor Nabokov is a man of very firm opinions in regard to the place of the artist in society and his obligations to it and his reader. "The artist has no obligations to the reader," *he emphasized.* "If no communication exists between writer and reader then it is either the fault of the reader or it is the work of a poor writer who has no claim to the title of an artist."

"The artist survives and transcends time and place. Above all, I have been trying to root this idea of the artist as a product of his culture out of my classes. I am not influenced by my environment, nor by time nor society. And neither is the true writer." . . .

. . . "people may take symbolism from *Lolita,* but I put none in. If people take it out, so much the better for them," *he concluded.*

"But seriously," *he continued,* "*Lolita* is to be enjoyed as a detached, intellectual exercise. No tears to be shed. You're supposed to enjoy it with your spinal emotions, with a little shiver when you end it." . . .

An ardent foe of modern group-oriented "practical" education, Nabokov pleaded for a return to classical methods, with the emphasis on the teaching of Latin and Greek and a renewed interest in natural history—"not applied natural history for a purpose, but to know the world as it is, to know what makes corn, not cornflakes."

---

* "Author of *Lolita* Airs Views on Censorship, Role of Artist," *Cornell Daily Sun,* Sept. 25, 1958. In his ten years at Cornell, Nabokov had never been interviewed by the campus newspaper until this report, in the first week of class, a month after the American publication of *Lolita.* Interview took place on Sept. 18, 1958.

On the university level, he considers the library "the heart and center-piece of any good institution." *To profit from this* "our students need more solitude and concentration and especially, more sleep. There are too many clubs, too many group activities. A university should be quieter; what many students could use is a nice padded cell."

Professor Nabokov loves to write in both Russian and English. Although he prefers Russian because it is his native tongue and he is most at home with it, Nabokov claims that English is "the richest language in the world. The spirit of the language is a harmonious one. It is wonderful for expressing abstractions and for coining the names of things. But of course my English is just an echo of my Russian."

Feature Story in *Newsweek* (1958)[*]

"I have received many, many letters about *Lolita*, and I think only three objected to it. Of course, there has been some talk in some of the papers about my 'dirty book' but I think this is mainly a convention. Louella Hopper[†] for example." . . .

Nabokov is, of course, pleased by the calm acceptance of his book at Ithaca. "I think that perhaps this is a sign of American sophistication," *he said. Well aware that the banning of the novel from the shelves of some public libraries will boost the sales of* Lolita *in bookstores, Nabokov thinks the bans are* "all to the good. My publisher is disappointed that there haven't been more."

Sipping brandy from a champagne glass, Nabokov turned the discussion to the motion picture which is to be made from his best seller (an estimated 120,000 copies to date). "I have no idea what they will do with it," *he said.* "Of course they will have to change the plot. Perhaps they will make Lolita a dwarfess. Or they will make her 16 and Humbert 26. I just don't know. It's difficult to translate a book into a movie."

Vera Nabokov . . . refilled his glass. "Tell them about the child," *she said.*

"Oh, yes. I am rather bitter about this. I am in favor of child-hood—in fact the very first book I ever did was a translation of *Alice in Wonderland* into Russian. Anyway, a few nights ago, on Goblin night, a little girl—she was 8 or 9 I think—came to the door for candy. And she was dressed up as Lolita, with a tennis racquet and a pony tail, and a sign reading l-o-l-i-t-a. I was shocked."

---

[*] "Ithaca and *Lolita*," *Newsweek*, Nov. 24, 1958, 114–15. Interviewer unknown; interview took place about Nov. 7, 1958.
[†] *Newsweek* note: "A typically Nabokovian name-twist actually referring to Hollywood columnist Louella Parsons, who had said: 'I must say I am not easily shocked; but *Lolita* made me feel I needed a bath.'"

Letter to the Editor,
Cornell Daily Sun (1958)[*]

To the Editor:

In the *Cornell Daily Sun* of Sept. 30, page 3, you report that according to Mr. Richard L. Leed of the Division of Modern Languages, "there is . . . a slight increase in the number of students taking advanced courses in Russian language and literature."

I must assume that Mr. Leed's statement was erroneously reported. I am the only instructor in this University to give courses in Russian literature and I must state that the facts are in direct contradiction to your report. The "advanced courses" offered in alternate years are Russian literature 315–316 and 317–318. They presuppose some knowledge of the Russian language. This is the second year in succession that neither of these courses could be given for lack of qualified applicants.

Prof. Vladimir Nabokov

[*] *Cornell Daily Sun*, Oct. 3, 1958.

73

"A G.S. Man," *Cornell Daily Sun*
(Letter to the Editor, 1958)[*]

To the Editor:

I wish to correct two misstatements in Mr. Metcalf's article "Learning the Russian Language" (*The Sun*, Oct. 15):

The "one genuine Russian literature course" (Russian 317) is not offered this term [not] because of "lack of interest" but because of lack of grammar. The three bright and intelligent candidates who enrolled in this course after a year of Morrill Hall could not pass a simple test I gave them—proving that they had not been taught the most elementary rules of Russian.

I am not on the staff of the language and linguistics department as implied by the last paragraph of Mr. Metcalf's article. My courses in Russian literature (315–16 and 317–18) are given under the jurisdiction of the Department of Romance Literature and my course in Russian literature (325–326) under that of the Division of Literature.

In other words I am strictly a Goldwin Smith man.[1]

Prof. Vladimir Nabokov

---

[*] Prof. Vladimir Nabokov, "A G.S. Man," Letter to the Editor, *Cornell Daily Sun*, Oct. 20, 1958.

74

Interview with Pierre Burton and Lionel Trilling for Canadian Broadcasting Corporation (1958)[*]

[From index card] Well, I'm not particularly interested in those foolish attacks. Some of them are very amusing. But I may say that most of the haters of *Lolita* in the U.S.A. are just common scolds and old philistines.

PB: What do you mean by a philistine, Mr. Nabokov?
[From index card] Users of covers and cozies, ready-made souls in plastic bags, negligible generalities.

. . .

LT: Yes, but it seems to be that all great love affairs are tragic and they all end in death as yours does and . . .
[Impromptu] I would put it this way. That if sex, you see, is the servant maid of art, love is the lady of that tower.

[*] *Close-Up*, Canadian Broadcasting Corporation (Ottawa), date of transmission unknown. Television interview, filmed Nov. 26, 1958, Rockefeller Center studios, New York City, about twelve minutes (video selections now on YouTube). Text from unpublished Dieter E. Zimmer transcript (see acknowledgments).

Interview with Edward E. Van Dyne
for *Elmira Telegram* (1958)[*]

Emitting a series of sonorous chuckles, Nabokov opened the door of a large, red brick house.

The scantly furnished interior had a transitory air which Nabokov quickly explained.
We are birds of passage. When someone goes on leave, we take over. We've never owned a home. . . .

Reactions of Lolita's *reviewers?*
Some simply haven't read the book or don't understand it. It is not obscene; it has none of the dirt of many so-called realistic modern novels.

"*Most critics have failed to stress the pathetic side,*" *said Mrs. Nabokov.* "*It's really a tragic story. Here, in the hands of this maniac is this poor girl—.*" "And a very ordinary girl—" *Nabokov put in.* . . .

Recently we've received some wonderful reviews from smaller newspapers, in Texas and places like that. We didn't expect them and it's gratifying. America has lived up to her liberal heritage in this.

Repercussions of Lolita *on his role at Cornell?*
Absolutely none. Both faculty and students have been extremely serious and intelligent in their approach. It has made me feel very warm inside.

---

[*] "What Hath *Lolita* Wrought? Ithaca Author Distressed by Some Reactions," *Elmira Telegram*, Dec. 14, 1958. Elmira is a city close to Ithaca.

Your response to Dr. Zhivago *and Pasternak's Nobel Prize?*
The political aspect does not interest me. Of course, I'm sure the Soviets are really pleased with the whole thing. They've attracted a lot of attention and they get the royalties.

However, my concern is with the artistic character of a novel. From this point of view, *Dr. Zhivago* is a sorry thing, full of clichés, clumsy, trivial and melodramatic.

Your immediate future?
Just now there is a great deal to be done. I'm controlling a French translation of *Lolita*. Some of my early novels, originally written in Russian, will be coming out. I'm applying for a sabbatical leave. We'll probably go to California next summer, then to Europe.

76

Interview with Thomas B. Turley
for *Niagara Falls Gazette* (1959)[*]

How have people reacted to Lolita?

America is the most mature country in the world now in this respect. Some of the reviews have been splendid. And there's a tremendous number of intelligent, artistic readers in this country. They are the type a writer imagines he would like to have read his book.

Is your book pornographic?

I feel rather bitterly on that point. My colleagues—other writers—use so many obscenities. Not a single obscene term is to be found in the book. I detest many of the mediocrities writing enormous novels nowadays and filling them with mural words.

Are you surprised at the attention?

After all my first novel, in 1924, was a best seller.[1] It is not as if I had suddenly been discovered.

Can you describe your teaching?

I have six hours of classes a week. When I first came to Cornell 10 years ago my classes sometimes used to run up to around 300 pupils. I guess they thought I'd be easy. Well, I fooled them. Now my largest class is about 150 pupils.

We analyze the essence of a novel. I want them to see how a writer continually builds up his story by packing in detail, detail, detail.

---

[*] "Author of *Lolita* Scoffs at Furore over His Novel," *Niagara Falls Gazette*, Jan. 11, 1959, 10B.

Do you closely follow Lolita's *fate?*

I feel obliged to keep up with the destiny of *Lolita*. After all, people stop me on the street and ask me to comment on opinions. So I have to know what is being said about me.

Lolita is an indictment of all the things it expresses. It is a pathetic book dealing with the plight of a child, a very ordinary little girl, caught up by a disgusting and cruel man. . . . But of all my books, I like it the best. The last bone always tastes best.

77

Interview with Alan Nordstrom
for *Ivy Magazine* (1959)*

Why did you compose Lolita *in a car?*
The only place in America with no noise and no draft.

On rejecting authors' father figures and personal philosophies in his teaching
You only know the author through his book. An artist is original. He first assimilates his experience and then re-creates and invents a world in his book.

On teaching methods
The ideal method of teaching is to pass out recorded lectures, which have been carefully and concisely prepared in the quiet of the teacher's study. With the present system the lecturer undermines his effect with hems and haws, while the student, perhaps, transcribes a name, a dash, and a date.

On art
The highest virtue of a writer, of any artist, is to stimulate in others an inward *thrill*.

What contemporaries do you value? Sartre? Faulkner?
They are not artists.

Salinger?
A great, wonderful writer—the best American novelist.

* "My Child *Lolita*," *Ivy Magazine* [New Haven], Feb. 1959, 28.

Pasternak?

Pasternak is a poet, not a prose writer. *Dr. Zhivago,* as a novel, is nowhere—though quite in line with the Soviet conservative literary style. It wanders like *Gone with the Wind* and is filled with all kinds of blunders and melodramatic situations. Compared to Pasternak, Mr. Steinbeck is a genius.

The role of the writer?

Literary expression must, first of all, be clear, even when treating obscurities; it must be a unique approach to what the artist feels. . . . This must be the constant quest of the writer.

78

Interview with Robert H. Boyle
for *Sports Illustrated* (1959)[*]

Showing Boyle the volume Colorado Butterflies
This butterfly which I discovered has nothing to do with nymphets. I
discovered it in the Grand Canyon in 1941. I know it occurs here, but
it is difficult to find. I hope to find it today. I'll be looking for it. It flies
in the speckled shade early in June, though there's another brood at the
end of the summer, so you came at the right time. . . . Another group
of butterflies I'm interested in are called Blues. This I discovered in
Telluride in southwest Colorado.

Showing Boyle Alexander Klots's A Field Guide to the Butterflies, *and the
sentence "The recent work of Nabokov has entirely rearranged the classification of this genus."*
The thrill of gaining information about certain structural mysteries in these butterflies is perhaps more pleasurable than any literary
achievement.

On Lycaeides melissa samuelis
I discovered it and named it *samuelis* after Samuel Scudder, probably
one of the greatest lepidopterists who ever lived. Karner is a little rail-

[*] "An Absence of Wood Nymphs," *Sports Illustrated*, Sept. 14, 1959, E5–E8, combined also
with Boyle's slightly expanded version, "An Absence of Wood Nymphs," in Robert H. Boyle,
At the Top of Their Game (New York: Winchester Press, 1983), 124–32; see also full version in
Nabokov's Butterflies. Sports Illustrated commissioned Boyle to write on VN and the element of
sport in butterfly hunting. Boyle spent June 1–2, 1959, on the hunt with VN in and around
Oak Creek Canyon, Arizona, and wrote up his time as a narrative—VN himself, as he stalks
butterflies, sometimes playing with the role of narrator. VN particularly wanted to find, catch,
and show the butterfly he had caught in 1941 in the Grand Canyon and named *Neonympha
dorothea*, now *Cyllopsis pertepida dorothea*, Nabokov's Wood Nymph.

way station between Schenectady and Albany. People go there on Sundays to picnic, shedding papers and beer cans. Among this, the butterfly.

Over breakfast
The Southwest is a wonderful place to collect. There's a mixture of arctic and subtropical fauna. A wonderful place to collect.

On a trail by Oak Creek Canyon
This Nabokov's Wood Nymph is represented by several subspecies, and there's one here. It is in this kind of country that my wood nymph occurs.

Pointing to a butterfly under a leaf and noting the white spots on the wings
Disruptive coloration. A bird comes and wonders for a second. Is it two bugs? Where is the head? Which side is which? In that split second the butterfly is gone. The second saves that individual and that species. You may call it a large Skipper.

After netting a butterfly
This is a checkered butterfly. There are countless subspecies. The way I kill is the European, or Continental, way. I press the thorax at a certain point like this. If you press the abdomen, it just oozes out. This is a beauty! Such a beautiful fresh specimen. *Melitaea anicia*. It's safe in the envelope until I can get to a laboratory and spread it.

Advice on technique
The thing is, when you hit the butterfly, turn the net at the same time to form a bag in which the butterfly is imprisoned.

On spotting, netting, and releasing a butterfly
A large male! I'm not going to kill it. A common species.

Noticing another butterfly
A dusky-wing Skipper. Common.

Noticing an Epargyreus clarus, *a silver-spotted Skipper*
I've seen that same individual on the same twig since I've been here.

There are lots of butterflies around, but this individual will chase the others from its perch.

Noticing a day-flying Peacock moth
In quest of a female. It only quiets down at certain hours of the day, I have found them asleep on flowers. Oh, this is wretched work. Where is my Wood Nymph? It's heartbreaking work. Wretched work, I've traveled thousands of miles to get a species I never got. We went to Fort Davis, Texas, but there was no Wood Nymph. Toad-like sheep with their razor-sharp teeth had eaten everything. Horrible!

After returning from rushing off the trail after a butterfly
There I did something I shouldn't have done. I went up there without looking for rattlesnakes, but I suppose God looks after entomologists as He does after drunkards.

Spotting another butterfly
Ah. Oh, that's an interesting thing! Oh, gosh, there it goes. A white Skipper mimicking a Cabbage butterfly belonging to a different family. Things are picking up. Still, they're not quite right. Where is my Wood Nymph? It is heartbreaking work. Wretched work.

After returning to the cabin for Véra, and when the car does not start
The car is nervous.

After noticing with delight the name Chipmunk Apartments
They have considerably improved all the motels across the country. No comparison with what they were in the early '40s, I shall never forget the motel-keeperess who said, when I complained that they didn't have hot water, "Was there any hot water on your grandmother's farm?"

Watching a swarm of butterflies around a puddle
These are all males and this is their pub. They suck moisture in the ground, in mountains, European mountains, where the mules have passed and pissed, it's like a flowery carpet. And it's always the males. Always the males.

On a butterfly sipping nectar from yellow asters
Here's a butterfly that's quite rare. You find it here and there in Arizona. *Lemonias zela*. I've collected quite a few. It will sit there all day. We could come back at four, and it would still be here. The form of its wings and its general manner are very mothlike. Quite interesting. But it is a real butterfly. It belongs to a tremendous family of South American butterflies, and they mimic all kinds of butterflies belonging to other families. Keeping up with the Smiths, you know.

Capturing another butterfly
Now here is something I really want. "One flick, one dart, and it was in his net." I'm not suggesting anything. A Checker, but it seems to be another form of the butterfly we took earlier. Quite interesting. I would like to take some more.

Missing a butterfly
Chort! I have been doing this since I was five or six, and I find myself using the same Russian swear words. *Chort* means the devil. It's a word I never use otherwise.

Catching another butterfly, backhanded
Haha! Haha! A prize! One of the best things I've taken so far. That's a darling. Wonderful! Ha, so unexpectedly. Haha. Look at it on this fern. What protective coloration. *Callophrys*. I'm not sure of the species. Isn't it lovely? You could travel hundreds of miles and not see one. Ha, what luck! That was so unexpected, and just as I was about to say there was nothing interesting here today. A female that has hibernated. That was very nice, very nice indeed. Quite exciting. That was one of those things that make coming here worthwhile. This will go to Cornell, this little green thing. The best way to put it is, "A green Hairstreak not readily identified in the field."

Netting two at once
I took two in one diabolical stroke of my net. A female Blue. A *Lygdamus* female Blue, one of the many species of Blue in which I am especially interested. This other, by freakish chance, is a male Blue of another species that was flying with it. That's adultery. Or a step toward adultery.

Working over a dry stream bed
Quite a number of little things have appeared today which I haven't
seen before. It's picking up. The next week will probably go much faster.
I give the Wood Nymph a week to be out. I may go to Jerome for my
Wood Nymph. It's a ghost town on the side of a mountain. I know of
several collectors who were there and brought back my butterfly a few
years ago.

Three at once
Three with one sweep of the net. This one is an Angle Wing. It has a
curiously formed letter C. It mimics a chink of light through a dead
leaf. Isn't that wonderful? Isn't that humorous?

After boxing the Anglewing
They won't lose any color. I saw an Indian moth, probably taken in the
middle of the eighteenth century, that had been presented to Catherine
the Great, and the color was still fresh. Some of the butterflies of Linnaeus, the first great naturalist, a Swede, are quite fresh. They are less
fragile, I suppose, than pickled human beings.

Heading back to Sedona
I lost two butterfly collections. One to the Bolsheviks, one to the Germans. I have another I gave to Cornell. I dream of stealing it back.

*After lunch, looking at the wind-swept buttes on the way to the next hunting
ground*
It looks like a giant chess game is being played around us.

Waiting in a supermarket as Véra shops
When I was younger I ate some butterflies in Vermont to see if they
were poisonous. I didn't see any difference between a Monarch butterfly
and a Viceroy. The taste of both was vile, but I had no ill effects. They
tasted like almonds and perhaps a green cheese combination. I ate them
raw. I held one in one hot little hand and one in the other. Will you eat
some with me tomorrow for breakfast?

Evening, showing Boyle his long article on the Nearctic members of the genus
Lycaeides Hübner

The most interesting part here was to find the structural differences between them in terms of the male organ. These are magnified thirty-four times. These are hooks which the male has to attach to the female. Because of the differences in the size of the hooks, all males cannot copulate with all females. Suddenly in Jackson Hole, I found a hook intermediate between the two. It has the form of the short-hooked species, but the length of the long-hooked species. It is almost impossible to classify, I named it *longinus*. This work took me several years and it undermined my health for quite a while. Before, I never wore glasses. This is my favorite work, I think I really did well there.

On Soviet awareness of his lepidopterological work: in an attack by Lubimov in the Literary Gazette

He said that I was starving in America, compelled to earn a precarious existence selling butterflies.

Next morning

We are going to Jerome, a ghost town. We are looking for my butterfly, the Wood Nymph, which should be out, I hope, on Mount Mingus.

On the way to Jerome

Butterflies help me in my writing. Very often when I go and there are no butterflies, I am thinking. I wrote most of *Lolita* this way. I wrote it in motels or parked cars.

Above Jerome

We're getting into oaks and pines. The greatest enemy of the lepidopterist is the juniper tree. Charming! Charming! Charming butterfly road!

An iris-covered meadow

I can't believe there won't be butterflies here. . . . I'm very much disappointed. *Rien. Rien.* Iris is not very attractive to butterflies anyway. It's rather ornamental, and that's it.

Nabokov starts narrating his lack of success

It was very sad. "And then I saw that strong man put his head on his forearms and sob like a woman." . . . This will be our last stop today. . . .

It is this kind of place that my nymph should be flying, but with the exception of three cows and a calf, there is nothing.

Sad . . . "His face was now a tear-stained mask."

Boyle captures a butterfly, and they head home
A winged cliché . . . What can I say? What is there to say? I am ashamed, for the butterflies. I apologize for the butterflies.

Interview with Lee Belser
for *Los Angeles Mirror News* (1959)[*]

The Library of Congress would like the Lolita *manuscript?*
But I really don't have it. I threw it away. I write in longhand on these
cards, and when I'm through with them I toss them away.

Can you report on Invitation to a Beheading?
My son is translating it now. It's a story about Russia in the year 3000.

What happened to your first, Russian, version of Lolita, The Enchanter?
It was never published, because I was never really satisfied with it.

Who should play Lolita in the Harris-Kubrick film?
It's completely out of my hands, but a child should play the role. I wish I
could turn back the clock on some of our better-known actresses. There
are several who could do a remarkably good job.

Did Lolita *have anything to do with personal experience?*
Lolita never existed. I merely invented her and I approached the subject, not as a social problem, but as an artistic one.

---

[*] "*Lolita* Strewn Across Nation, Author Reveals," *Los Angeles Mirror News*, July 31, 1959.
The Nabokovs had traveled from Oak Creek Canyon, Arizona, where they had spent much
of the summer, to Los Angeles, partly to meet with Stanley Kubrick, who had acquired the
film rights to *Lolita*.

Interview with Neil Hickey
for *Washington Post* (1959)[*]

Why did you write such a thing as Lolita?
What did I do? I'm no messenger boy. If the novel conveys some kind of moral, then God bless those who *find* it.

Is Lolita *pornographic?*
My definition of pornography is "a copulation of clichés" in which an author puts the reader on familiar ground and then makes a direct attempt at provoking the most basic response. This is not the case with *Lolita*.

Is there anything personal in your interest in little girls?
My knowledge of nymphets is purely scholarly, I assure you. . . . In fact I don't much care for little girls. I have a 25-year-old son, so I'm probably better qualified to write about little boys.

Are you worried about the filming of Lolita?
A motion picture has a life of its own. As to who should play the main roles, I'm not movie fan enough to say.

What about the American sex symbols—Marilyn Monroe and Jayne Mansfield? Do they represent sex for you?
Well, first of all, Miss Marilyn Monroe is one of the greatest comedy actresses of our time. She is simply superb. Miss Mansfield I've never seen. But the usual concept of the bosomy female does not represent

[*] "The Author of *Lolita*," *Washington Post and Times-Herald*, Oct. 4, 1959, AW 10.

sex from my point of view. Sexual appeal seems, to me, something far more subtle than that.

Should there be co-education at high school?
Young girls mature so much faster than boys. They become voluptuous and get into the habit of wearing tight woollen sweaters that make for enormous distraction. That just defeats the whole process of education.

81

Interview of Vladimir Nabokov
and Alain Robbe-Grillet with André Parinaud, Roger Nimier, and Paul Guimard for *Arts* (Paris) (1959)[*]

How did the idea of writing Lolita *come to you?*

I don't remember. I know that there was a certain problem I wanted to resolve, I wanted to find an economical and elegant solution, as in chess problems where there are certain rules that must be followed. It was a very difficult problem: I had to find the idea, the characters, the inspiration too, the little shiver. And as I explained at the end of my book, this little shiver came to me when I read somewhere, I think it was in *Paris-soir* in 1939, the story of a poor ape that had been given pencils, and this ape was in its cage and began to draw: and what it drew were the bars of its cage: the first thing the little prisoner drew. So it was the idea of a man imprisoned in his passion. That was perhaps the start. And I began to write this novella in Russian, and it didn't work out. There were little French girls who weren't French enough for me, because I didn't know little French girls. So I forgot the thing, and the idea came back to me in America.

---

[*] "Tandis que *Lolita* fait le tour du monde l'entomologiste Nabokov, l'agronome Robbe-Grillet échangent leur pions sur l'échiquier littéraire" ("While *Lolita* Travels Around the World, the Entomologist Nabokov and the Agronomist Robbe-Grillet Exchange Pawns on the Literary Chessboard"), *Arts* (Paris), October 28–Nov. 3, 1959, 4. VN had traveled to France, his first time in Europe since fleeing with his family in 1940, for the Oct. 23, 1959, launch of the French translation of *Lolita*. Asked whom he would like to meet most among French writers, he named only Raymond Queneau and Alain Robbe-Grillet, whose *In the Labyrinth* had just been published that month. Queneau was away, and although *Arts* had opposed Robbe-Grillet, they did bring the two writers together.

Several years later?
Yes, the gestation was rather long; it took me six or seven years, with gaps.

So you wanted to solve a kind of literary chess problem?
NABOKOV: Yes.
ROBBE-GRILLET: You already solved one in an old book. It was the story of the madman who threw himself out a window. There's an astonishing chess game in this book.
NABOKOV: That was *The Defense, La Course du fou.* It's a sort of pun, because the word *course* refers to the movements of the chess pieces, and *fou* . . .[1]
ROBBE-GRILLET: You play chess?
NABOKOV: Yes. I compose chess problems, which isn't the same thing as playing.

Were you expecting Lolita *to have this, let's say, in a sense, scandalous success?*
I wasn't thinking of scandal. I thought it would be hard to publish the book. There would be a certain number of copies printed for my friends, for scholars, but that's all; I had great difficulty in publishing it. It was published, finally, here in Paris, in 1955, by Olympia. And then several American [publishers] wanted to [publish] it[2] and I had only to choose my publisher, which is always very pleasant.

Do you read the reviews your book has inspired, and which have surprised and interested you most?
ROBBE-GRILLET: Another way of putting the question: all the reviews talk about the book by telling the story at length; no one has talked about how it is written.
NABOKOV: When you read a review, you don't read the part where they tell the story, you want to know what they think of it. And if that doesn't happen, then you forget it all, because, after all, the story has already been told better. But there have been very good reviews, which have talked very well about the book's romanticism. It's like you, in *Jealousy*. That's the finest love novel since Proust.
ROBBE-GRILLET: That hasn't been said very much. What happened for me was the opposite of the way it's been for you. In *Lolita*, in

France, people have looked most of all at the story. In my case, they didn't see that at all in *Jealousy*. They wrote only about the way it was written. But with *Lolita* they have noticed only the most obvious things—for example, that the character speaks at the same time using "he" or "I," and often in the same sentence, which gives a very curious effect of division. It's a fundamental theme all the same: cutting the character in two.

Could you work out a sort of geography of the reactions Lolita *has provoked around the world?*
That would be very interesting. In Japan, for instance, they brought out the book with a beautiful cover where you see the image of a young blonde woman with well-rounded breasts,[*] eyes slightly aslant. A sort of Lolita Monroe. The Japanese have some very curious ideas.

It came out also in South and Southeast Asia, in Turkey. There, they thought there was no need to make such a fuss over things so normal, so natural. That's another point of view.

In Sweden, the book got burned. I don't read Swedish, but any Russian can combine a little German with a little Russian and manage to decipher the Swedish; my wife took on the task, since we were surprised the book was so short. It was quite a small book, flat as a flea. It turns out that what they did was leave in only the more or less spicy scenes and get rid of all the rest. So, like de Sade, don't you think?

Each one of your books has the same concern: to solve a problem of literary chess.
NABOKOV: I think so. It's more or less conscious, and I think it's the same for Robbe-Grillet.
ROBBE-GRILLET: Always. And it's even amusing, because, usually, they reproach me for it. They talk about the form and the content.

In Lolita, *who's the most likable person for you?*
It's Lolita. It's with her that the good reader should become friends. American readers, generally, talk of her as an unbearable kid, but you pity her as you would pity any kid. There's something touching in her.

---

[*] In the *Newsweek* feature on VN, June 24, 1962, 47, he described this cover as showing "thunderously large breasts."

Does your hero or Lolita feel real passion?
We know very little of Lolita's passion, but it's my hero who feels at first this sensual passion, this storm of sensations, and then at the end, so to speak, human and divine love. My hero renounces this passion, but although she's no longer a nymphet, she is now the love of his life.

In the United States, are you completely on your own as a writer?
NABOKOV: Sometimes I feel echoes, little rather muted whiffs of Nabokov, but not much. Hard to say, but I've never set up a school.
ROBBE-GRILLET: Me, neither, you know!

When you write, do you write a great deal from your memory—which is said to be excellent?
NABOKOV: Yes, but only for certain things. My memory is very good for effects of light, for objects, for combinations of objects. . . . For example, a train stops in a station. I look out the window and I see there, on the platform, a little pebble, a cherry pit, a silver paper; I see these things so well in this combination that I think I will recall them forever. But not only does one forget this, but one forgets how one was looking at them. But what can one do to remember all that? You have to link it to something else.
ROBBE-GRILLET: You know Kafka's journal. The notes of a trip to Reichenberg where he notes only things of that kind? "I saw someone who had a glass in front of him and was leaning forward a little," or "There was a stone beside the door." He notes down only things of that kind. Very curious.
NABOKOV: It's when one wants to recall, anchor points. I think there are this kind of people, and another kind, who like "great ideas."

Which of your books do you like most?
There are three for me on the same level: *Lolita*; it's the best book I've written, I think. There's also a book called *The Gift*. And then there's *Invitation to a Beheading*. That's just appeared in English. I wrote it in Russian when I was thirty.

Do you write in a regular routine?
No.

You have no work regime?
No. I write in bed, I write on index cards.

Do you write in English and French?
In English. I've written only little things in French.

82

Interview with J.-F. Bergery
for *Arts* (Paris) (1959)[*]

On Paris
It seems to have become a permanent automobile showroom, with the Eiffel Tower or Sacré-Cœur as background. Not that I'm complaining much—I like cars—but why aren't they yellow anymore, like before the war? It's a pity. And, then, it doesn't smell like before. What has become of the smell of dead leaves? I imagine they treat the trees with pesticide and that kills the autumn odor, or God knows what. The three things I've rediscovered are the police stations (what a marvelous farce they play there), the Place de la Concorde, lit up at night, and the tepid air of the Métro.

On his new wealth
Now I don't need to earn a living, I have a girl called Lolita who earns it for me. In short I'm an old pimp and I have a girl who's on the game. . . . Oh, don't write that. . . . What do you think, Véra? All right, do as you like.

After summarizing his life
There you are. I'm sorry, I've never been a ragpicker, or a taxi driver, or even a dishwasher at Fouquet's.

---

[*] "Je n'ai plus besoin de gagner ma vie" ("I Don't Need to Earn a Living Anymore"), *Arts*, Oct. 28–Nov. 3, 1959, 4.

Interview with Jeanine Delpech
for *Nouvelles Littéraires* (1959)[*]

Why America?
I've made myself a very warm nest in this admirable country, whose immensity people always forget. On his last trip Graham Greene phoned me from New York to say he would be around in an hour. Since I live in the state of the same name, he couldn't believe that we were five hundred kilometers apart. Everything is so well organized there: department stores of culture. You have lowbrow readers, for whom only the sentimental side of a book counts; middlebrows, fond of ideas; and finally the highbrows, responsive to art.

Have you written other novels since Lolita*?*
No. I devoted seven years to a five-volume study of Pushkin, the first of our great writers. . . . Since Pushkin was fed by your eighteenth-century authors (to the point of plagiarism, conscious or not) I had to read a lot of them. I love André Chenier, whom Pushkin knew by heart. Diderot dazzles me, Sade bores me, Marivaux is only a journalist to me—like Stendhal and Balzac, for that matter.

Lolita
She came entirely out of my imagination. Critics, in general, find her odious; I pity her: an orphan, alone in life with a demanding forty-year-old. When I wrote about her last meeting with Humbert, I cried, like Flaubert at the death of *Madame Bovary*.

    "She cries every night, and the critics don't hear her sobs," said Mrs. *Nabokov.*

---

[*] "Nabokov sans *Lolita*" ("Nabokov Without *Lolita*"), *Nouvelles littéraires*, Oct. 29, 1959, 1–2.

Interview with Pierre Mazars
for *Le Figaro Littéraire* (1959)*

At the Hôtel Continental
It's here that I have my earliest memory of Paris. I'd come as an infant with my parents and I recall keeping myself entertained by spitting into this courtyard from my fourth-floor window.

Strolling in Paris
I saw the director of the Tuileries puppet show this morning, taking out from a very small box a heap of accessories, décors, and even a stall. It was like Proust's madeleine, from which a whole world emerges. What's struck me most in Paris (I haven't been back since 1940) is that the cars are darker in color. Where are the red and yellow taxis of old? The smell of the gasoline has changed, too. It's only in the public gardens that I find the same smells. The smells and the paths.[1]

The origin of Lolita
It was in 1939. September 3, I'm sure. I remember having seen a sensational photograph in a newspaper. At that time, I read *Le Figaro* and *Paris-soir* every day. In which of the two papers was it? I can still see where the photo was, on the left, inside the paper. It was the portrait of an ape. A chimpanzee or a little orangutan. Scientists had wanted to get it to draw, and the first drawing the ape made was of what it saw before itself: the bars of its cage. From there, I began to write a little story, the "prototype" of *Lolita*. I read it to two friends, one of them

---

* "À Paris, avec Vladimir Nabokov. Le Héros de *Lolita* a un sosie ... en fuite au Mexique avant d'avoir pu lire le livre" ("In Paris, with Vladimir Nabokov: The Hero of *Lolita* Has a Double ... Who Fled to Mexico Before He Could Read the Book"), *Le Figaro littéraire*, Oct. 31, 1959.

Mark Aldanov. And the other day my wife brought me the manuscript in triumph. She had found this first story, which will go, like the others, to the Library of Congress in Washington, the repository of all my papers, as they had requested of me, with an agreement not to make them available before 2000.

Yes, *Lolita* is the man attached to the barriers, the bars of his passions, and Lolita, the little nymphet struggling with him, is beauty. The idea of sex, to my sense, depends on beauty, contrary to what Freud thinks. Sexual charm is just a tiny detail in the beauty of the world.

Note that this should come out like a scent in my book. I detest theories, messages, imposed ideas, morals. Flaubert is my favorite author; Proust, too. One needs a certain detachment before life. A true artist is never engagé.

What difference have butterflies made to your life?
I learned German very young, from a big book on butterflies. At seven, I knew all the butterflies of Europe. And when I arrived in America, they offered me the post of curator of butterflies at Harvard, considered the greatest entomological museum in the world. I enjoyed describing new species, dissecting them to draw their organs. I found strange coincidences between the butterflies of South America and the butterflies of France. Structures repeated themselves; that gave me a very deep sense of evolution. For seven years, from 9:00 a.m. to 1:00 a.m., I worked on butterflies at Harvard.

Certainly, this exactitude I seek in butterflies, in my anatomical studies, can be found in my books. This links me with Robbe-Grillet. I appreciate his way of looking. Object and man, it's the same thing for the man. Each object is so charged with humanity. . . . Yes, and what I appreciate still more in this kind of book[2] is that there are no formulas, no general ideas, no bridges between the sentences.

Your forthcoming novel?
Invitation to a Beheading. The last days of a condemned man who talks to another prisoner. This prisoner is the executioner, who needs to get to know his victim before taking his life.

Yes, it's true, the hero of *Lolita* is also in prison. Odd, I hadn't made the connection. But, then, *Lolita* is, to say it again, a prison of feelings.

What does Mrs. Nabokov think of Lolita?

Oh, she read my book from the artistic point of view. Like something outside us . . . But I'm going to tell you a curious story that I haven't told anyone. Just after *Lolita* came out in America, the newspapers announced the arrest of a Russian. His house, near New York, had caught fire. To settle the insurance, the company rummaged in the debris and they found movies he had filmed with little girls and with other men. He was charged with corrupting minors, but he was released on bail. He left with his car and dog for Mexico; he fled and then hid. No one has ever seen him again.

He was a Russian who spoke English with a Russian accent. I saw his photo: a rather gloomy face, unpleasant but intelligent. My man exactly. And in my novel there's a fire at the end. No, he couldn't have read *Lolita*. The book had barely appeared when he was arrested.

Interview with John Wain
for *The Observer* (1959)[*]

Rejecting the suggestion that he found himself at home in America because, like Russia, it is huge
My America is quite small, academic America, and the wild mountains where I go hunting for butterflies. And my Russia is very small. A road here, a few trees there, a sky. It is a treasure chest to which one returns again and again.

On Trinity College
It was the perfect atmosphere within which to keep up my Russian.

On America
In Paris, I worked very hard to find myself a niche. I never really succeeded. But in America, I was at home immediately.

---

[*] "Small World of Vladimir Nabokov," *The Observer*, Nov. 1, 1959, 21. On VN's first visit to England since 1939, for the launch of the British *Lolita* on Nov. 6.

Interview with Jean Duvignaud
for *Les Lettres Nouvelles* (1959)[*]

On writers, life, and lives

The writer has to remain outside the ambience he suggests: not of his work itself, but of the life by which he must not let himself be caught. In short, he is like a God who would be everywhere and nowhere. The formula is Flaubert's. I have a very special love for Flaubert. . . . I'm well aware that in France there are the "Stendhalians" and the "Flaubertians"; I prefer Flaubert. In *The Real Life of Sebastian Knight* I wanted, of course, to satirize fictionalized biographies, those "unhappy lives of Rimbaud" and such twaddle. It's what allowed me to situate myself at a distance from my character. I am not my character. After all, when I write a novel, I myself invent myself. There's my character, the character who speaks, and sometimes two, three, four series of other levels. It's something like what happens in modern physics: I make the design of the world, and it's inscribed in a universe.

Sartre explains your distance from your characters in Despair *in terms of your uprootedness, your émigré status.*

I think he's wrong. I'm not rootless. Even if the Revolution hadn't happened in Russia, I would have lived in France or Italy. My family, which was politically liberal and cosmopolitan, had me live in an international climate where French and German took the same place as Russian. I am not, as Bunin was, a representative of traditional Russia. I feel much closer to Kafka, for example. And after all I am very close to French literature, and I'm not the first Russian writer to say that!

[*] "Nabokov: 'Quand j'écris je m'invente moi-même'" ("Nabokov: 'When I Write I Myself Invent Myself'"), *Les Lettres nouvelles*, Nov. 4, 1959, 24–25.

On Lolita

It's not at all a work of social satire, as some American critics have said. I wasn't born in America, and there are aspects of America I don't know at all, so I can't satirize it. I wouldn't dream of it. . . . I saw Lolita as a little American girl of the kind you meet there, but I've never known one! The critics haven't understood very well that *Lolita* is at heart a tender work, suffused with a certain kindness. In the end, Humbert realizes that he has destroyed Lolita's childhood, and that makes him suffer. It's a work of pity. . . . Humbert has confused morbid love and human love and he has remorse. So he understands why he is writing this book.

87

Interview with Anne Guérin
for *L'Express* (1959)[*]

In France, like everywhere for that matter, Lolita *has had a great success. Were you expecting it?*
When an author writes a book, he has a certain vision of this book. Success is part of that vision: If one writes a book, it's so that it will be published. If it's to be published, it's so that it will be read. And read well. In other words, so it can be successful. Success goes along with the book. It's an element of the book itself.

I must say that *Lolita* is my favorite book. Among the tens of novels I've written in Russian and in English, it's the one I like most. I told myself: there are many good readers around the world, it will be read. But I imagined it would appear in a limited edition, restricted, reserved for a few literati. I also thought it would be banned in the United States. Now, for it to be banned in England and Australia, that's normal. But that it should be approved in the United States and banned in France, there's a paradox!

What kind of success has Lolita *had in the United States?*
Artistic and philosophic. It hasn't been a *succès de scandale*. Strangely, Americans haven't thought of *Lolita* as a book that one shouldn't put into everyone's hands. The young read it just as they read anything else. Then they come to find me, students, high-schoolers, and say to me: "Here's a copy of *Lolita*. I'd like to give it to Father for Easter, to Mother for Christmas; can you sign it for me, Mr. Nabokov?" I didn't

[*] "Le Bon M. Nabokov. Le père de Lolita délaisse les nymphettes au profit de Pouchkine et de Robbe-Grillet" ("The Good Mr. Nabokov: *Lolita*'s Father Forsakes Nymphets for the Sake of Pushkin and Robbe-Grillet"), *L'Express*, Nov. 5, 1959, 32–33. Unsigned, but the interviewer is Anne Guérin.

sign copies, but it's the move that's interesting. Then Papa would read it and say nothing to me. On the contrary: religious groups have asked me to lecture on *Lolita*. I haven't done it. And I've received letters from readers around the world who have liked the book and discuss it subtly.

For many of your readers Lolita *appeared, so one hears, to be a shocking love story. Is that what you wanted?*
In *Lolita* there's something chock-full, replete, with harmony. I think a writer sees his book as a certain design he wants to reproduce, and I think I've reproduced this design rather well; the contours are there, the details, too. There was a moment when I said to myself: "There, that's it, I can't add anything." I may have then cut out a few pages here and there, a few *longueurs*. But the book is there. I worked hard on it, for years. I had other things to do: my university lectures at Cornell, a work on Pushkin that took me ten years (I was going to say a hundred). I wrote *Lolita* only during the vacations. My wife and I crisscrossed motel America, the whole of America. We hunted butterflies in the Rockies, and when it rained, when the weather was dull, if I wasn't tired, I'd settle down in our car parked near the motel cabin and write. I'd write a page, two pages, and if it was going well, I'd carry on.

You wrote in your car?
Yes, I write by hand on what we call "index cards." I write in pencil. My dream would be to have a pencil that always stayed sharp. This first draft I then write out in ink on ordinary paper. Then my wife types it up. I don't know how to type. I can't do anything with my hands. Not even drive a car.

Didn't you say you hunted butterflies?
Oh yes, indeed, that's the only thing! When I start to take a butterfly apart, to dismember it to examine under the microscope, that's when suddenly I develop very dexterous hands, tapering fingers, and I can do everything with my hands. But that's the only thing. Then once more I'm all thumbs.

Do you make many corrections in your books?
Always. That's why I write first in pencil: you can take an eraser and fix

mistakes. For me writing doesn't come in a continuous stream. I have a lot of trouble, a lot of difficulty.

Writing a letter, even a postcard, takes me hours. I don't know how it's done.

Why the name Lolita?
That began with Dolores. It's a very beautiful name, Dolores. A name with a long veil, a name with liquid eyes. The diminutive of Dolores is Lola, and the diminutive of Lola, Lolita.

You know where there's a Dolores? I've remembered just now: in *Monte-Cristo*. I read it when I was little.

Hasn't the theme of Lolita *been in your books for a long time already?*
So critics say. I have young girls here, three very young girls there, perhaps a little perverse. . . . I don't know. I'm going to publish a book of memoirs with Gallimard, there's a childhood love story there. I'm talking about a little girl I knew on the beach at Biarritz. I was ten, she nine. It was a perfectly Platonic love. Absurd to see the first Lolita there.

Was it you who invented the term "nymphet"?
Yes, it was me. There was "nymph" already. And Ronsard, who likes Latin diminutives, used "nymphet" in a sonnet. But not in the sense I've used it. For him, it was a pleasing nymph.

Yours isn't. You've been rather hard on Lolita.
Yes. But she's also a very touching character. Toward the end of the book, the reader and the author pity her, this poor child who has been sacrificed on the altar of motels. It's very sad. She's married with this poor lad, this Schiller, and at this moment, Humbert Humbert understands that he loves her and that this time it's real love. She's not pretty anymore, she's not graceful, she's going to have a baby, and it's now that he loves her. It's the great love scene. He says to her, "Leave your husband and come with me," and she doesn't understand. It's still his Lolita, and he loves her very tenderly. Not with this morbid passion. Then she dies. Already in the introduction I spoke of a Mrs. Schiller who died in a little settlement in Alaska, Gray Star. It's her, but since the reader doesn't know she is going to marry and be called Schiller, he doesn't understand. Yet it's already there: a "plant," as the Americans say.

Lolita is dead, since the book is published, and that was the stipulation.[1]
All this cost me tears of blood. All these little details. It's very difficult
to make a book which hangs together from end to end.

Are you writing something now?
Yes, a huge work, this project on Pushkin I told you about. Five volumes. It's just finished and in the hands of two publishers in New York,
Random House and Morning Press. Now I'm going to relax, chatting
a little with you, and then I'm going to write another book. A novel, I
think.

On what?
No, I can't tell you about it. If I start talking of these things, they die.
It's like metamorphosis: it won't happen if anyone is watching.

*Lolita's style has been much admired. Do you think that your knowing three
languages, Russian, French, and English, has made a difference?*
I like words. Yes, I know these three languages well, this troika, these
three horses I have always hooked up to my carriage. My first maid,
my nurse, was English. Then I had a French governess. All this time,
of course, I spoke Russian. Then seven or eight English governesses,
an English teacher, and then a Swiss teacher.

Is it indiscreet to ask you in what language you think?
Do we think in language? We think, rather, in images. That's the mistake Joyce made, it seems to me, the difficulty he couldn't completely
overcome. Toward the end of *Ulysses*, in *Finnegans Wake*, it's a flood
of words, without punctuation, trying to express inner language. But
people don't think like that. In words, yes, but also in ready-made formulas, in clichés. And then in images; the word dissolves in images, then
the image produces the next word.

*What difference in usage would you point out in these three languages, these
three instruments?*
Nuances. If you take *framboise* in French, for example, it's a scarlet color,
a very red color. In English, the word *raspberry* is rather dull, with perhaps a little brown or violet. A rather cold color. In Russian, it's a burst

of light, *malinovoe;* the word has associations of brilliance, of gaiety, of ringing bells. How can you translate that?

Humbert Humbert seems profoundly shocked by what's scandalous in his adventures. Whereas the author seems to keep a certain distance, to place himself ironically in relation to all the drama Humbert Humbert makes of his relations with Lolita. Isn't that true?
I don't take sides. It's his business. He dies from it. You could say, ultimately, there's the moral, the policeman's moral that arrives at the end of the book. But also . . . he has to die of it. If not, there would have been no book.

And more than that: Humbert Humbert wasn't lucky enough to find himself where he could have been. In a state like Texas or Mississippi, one can marry a girl of eleven. But that my character didn't know!

Why didn't you say so?
If I had, there'd have been no book!

Your own ideas about America: what are they?
It's the country where I've breathed most deeply.

Haven't you had to suffer from its materialism?
Not at all. It's like everywhere else, there are the angry, the interesting, the philistines, and honest folk. All societies are materialistic. They were even when people wrote with a goose quill and with powder to dry their ink.

Will you return to Russia?
No. Never. Not to Russia. Russia's finished. It's a dream I had. I invented Russia. It turned out very badly. It's over.

Do you read a lot?
Yes. Too much. Two or three books a day. And then I forget it all.

Do you read novels?
For this Pushkin project, I reread all of French literature to Chateaubriand and all of English literature to Byron. I read quickly, but that

took me some time. *La Nouvelle Héloïse,* for example. I read it in three days. It almost killed me, but I read it.

I also read the Abbé Prévost. *Manon Lescaut* is very fine. You were speaking of love stories: *Manon Lescaut* is one of those books which give you a shiver, you know? That shiver . . . A little violin note, long sobs.

Do you think love novels are still being written today?
There's Proust. . . .

I was talking about contemporaries.
I was twenty when Proust died. He's of my day. But take Robbe-Grillet's *Jealousy:* there's a very fine novel about love. One of the most poetic novels I know, which gives this little shiver we were talking about.

Really?
Yes, the finest love novel since Proust. But let's not talk about contemporaries; the poor things, they aren't dead.

Yes, we shouldn't kill them ahead of time. Do you like Gide?
Not much. There are very good things, *Les Caves du Vatican.* But in the long run, he's boring. He doesn't know life. He knows nothing of the world. His description of little Arabs is perhaps not too bad . . . a sort of preserved fruit. . . .

Do you go to the theater?
I know very well the theater of Scribe,[2] where one dusts the furniture in the first act. . . . And I loved the plays of Lenormand[3] when I was young. Are they still put on?

No.
All gone, gone. They were so lovely, so poetic. I don't often go to the theater. The last time was in 1932.

And films?
There's television. Seeing Hitchcock here or there, it comes to much the same, doesn't it?

Do you take an interest in the film they're going to make of your book?
I know there will be a very pretty Lolita, very well developed. But that's all.

What year did you leave Europe?
In 1940, on the *Champlain*. A charming boat—it sailed zigzag, to evade submarines, no doubt. That was its last voyage. It sank straight after. Pity.

What has changed in Europe over twenty years?
Cars. That's about all. And also there are more bathrooms.

88

Interview with David Holmes
for BBC Radio (1959)[*]

What does Lolita *mean to you?*
The book means to me just what I put into it. It has no special purpose; it has no special message.

If you had been able to foresee Lolita's *reception, would you have still written it?*
I don't think I ever thought what would happen to the book. I dimly surmised that there might be some trouble eventually in finding a publisher, but I also was quite prepared to its not being published at all. I thought that perhaps it might be published with a limited number of readers. But that's about all.

This wouldn't have made any difference to your going on with it?
No. I would have gone on; the book had to be written and I would have completed it. It really doesn't matter one way or another.

Did you intend it as a savage observation of American adolescence?
It was not my intention; it was not my purpose. The book contains, as far as I can see, no deliberate message, and it has no practical purpose, no aims, besides the delights of art. But [readers] of course are welcome to any interpretation they desire.

---

[*] BBC Radio Newsreel, "Interview with David Holmes," Nov. 5, 1959, on the eve of the first British publication of *Lolita*, Nov. 6, 1959. Typescript transcription of telephone interview to VN at Stafford Hotel, London, VNA Berg.

You weren't commenting on American society?
No, not at all. And of course there were those statistics, for instance, which this fictional character mentions in his foreword. I really haven't the vaguest idea if they mean anything in reality; that whole passage is invention—and the whole book is an invention, and in fact America is my invention.

The America in your book seems a very realistic place; one recognizes it.
Well, you recognize it after reading it, you see, after the book—I think that any serious work of fiction, work of art, if you put it this way, does after all perhaps influence people in seeing things a little differently, in seeing colors that they missed before—landscapes that they never really noticed—but I really leave all that to my readers.

When did you start learning English?
English was the fashionable language in the kind of Russian family to which I happen to belong. We had English nurses, English governesses, English tutors; and my first books—the books that were read to me—were English books. In the morning Miss Sheldon would read to me *Little Lord Fauntleroy;* in the afternoon Mademoiselle Miauton, [my French] governess would read to me *Les Misérables.* And of course I remember all the pictures in *Chums* or in the *Boys' Own Paper,* and later on there was my father's library, which was full of English and French books; and I just read and read and read.

English and Russian?
I think that in the long run the English and Russian languages would seem to me the richest languages on earth. Perhaps Russian somewhere, somewhere in me, provokes certain new English forms, and vice versa. My knowledge of English has been seen to influence my Russian even in the old days. This was continuously brought up, that I went to school in England, and that has somehow influenced my Russian style. So it is a kind of intertwining, interlinking influence between the two languages, between these two treasure houses. . . . I speak Russian at home, I speak Russian with my wife, I speak Russian with my son; and all the simple things of life are much easier said in Russian, at least I feel that, than in English. But otherwise I really couldn't say what

I think in English or in Russian, because I generally think in images anyway.

But you'll go on using English for writing?
Oh yes, I will use it for writing, and I may write something in Russian if I feel that way.

89

Interview with John Coleman
for *The Spectator* (1959)[*]

On his Russian fiction
My artificial but beautifully exact Russian world.

On his goal-keeping at Trinity College, Cambridge
I had the Mediterranean, *prima-donna* style, out of place in England.

On the U.S.A.
It's such a *receptive* country. *Lolita* went to four publishers who turned it down in horror—there had been all that fuss over Edmund Wilson's *Hecate County*[1]—then, of course, it came out in Paris in the Olympia Press edition. But it was able to be published in America finally, because critics of Trilling's caliber have helped to create the climate of opinion over there. You feel they really have some influence.

On dialogue
I have no ear for dialogue, you know. Yes, I managed the American rhythms in the end in *Lolita*, but it was exacting work. I'd be at sea if I had to do, oh, Dorsetshire farmers, or Londoners even, even harder—London is very difficult. The hardest of all for me now, of course, would be two *Soviet* farmers. Yes, the language has changed a great deal. It is Basic Russian now; provincial.

[*] "Nabokov," *Spectator*, Nov. 6, 1959, 619.

On influences
English writers who have moved my pen to the right or left? No one, really. I don't believe in movements. But, of course, I enormously admire Shakespeare, Keats—not Shelley, not Swinburne.

Favorite works?
The literary achievements that most satisfy me now are a paper I wrote on South American Blue Butterflies[2]—and *Lolita*.

90

———

Interview with John G. Hayman
for *The Twentieth Century* (1959)[*]

On criticism of Lolita *as pornography*
Just plain silly.

On the redeeming personal characters of writers he disliked
Galsworthy was a good *man*, I believe. . . . Gorki was a great *character*.

On his being untroubled by the supposed isolation of the American writer
I write for myself and hope for hundreds of little Nabokovs.

On generalizations about America
A little town in New England is so entirely different from a little town in Oregon. And a little town in one part of Oregon is so entirely different from a little town in another part.

On how he became an American writer
I read *Webster's Dictionary*, for one thing.

Objecting to the suggestion that his originality of expression depends on his nonnative ear
My Russian novels were just as far from the cliché.

On eighteenth-century writers: Richardson
A third-rate writer. Such frigidity . . . But there was Sterne. Sterne was a first-rate writer.

[*] "A Conversation with Vladimir Nabokov—with Digressions," *Twentieth Century*, Dec. 1959, 444–50. Based on an interview at Cornell earlier in 1959.

Objecting to the suggestion that in Lolita *he often preferred incomplete phrases to whole sentences*
I sometimes think one could best describe lightning in a long, elaborately built sentence. But one could also do it by using two words. Truth is what matters, isn't it?

Gorki once wrote: "The sea is laughing." But, then, Gorki was a bad writer. As Chekhov commented, the only thing you can say about the sea is: "The sea is big."

On reading for identification with characters
A low pleasure—one for minor readers (you see, there must be minor readers because there are minor writers) . . . [The good reader] takes pleasure in his aloofness and yet enjoys the shivers along the spine and the tears.

"Olympia Press," *New York Times Book Review* (Letter to the Editor, 1960)[*]

To the Editor

Mr. Popkin says that at the request of Monsieur Girodias, the first publisher of my *Lolita*, "I did some rewriting."[1] I wish to correct this absurd misstatement. The only alterations Girodias diffidently suggested concerned a few French phrases in the English text, such as *"bon,"* *"c'est moi,"* *"mais comment,"* etc., which he thought might just as well be translated into English, and this I agreed to do.

Vladimir Nabokov
Los Angeles, Calif.

[*] Letter to the Editor, *New York Times Book Review*, May 15, 1960, 20.

Interview with Paul Karolus
for *Neue Illustrierte* (1961)[*]

Have you read all that has been written on the book since its publication?
Not all, not every one of the countless banal comments that bear witness to the writer's incomprehension. You know as well as I that all
serious critics have praised my book. I'm delighted to say that the most
sensitive and subtle, most imaginative and substantive reviews have
appeared in Germany.

Could Lolita *be a dangerous, seductive influence on young readers? Does it
destroy a taboo?*
These are questions I don't like to answer, since basically they're no
concern of mine. If my book, which of course is not written for children,
nevertheless falls into their hands, they will surely soon set it down,
bored. And any grown men who for one reason or another are attracted
to adolescents will be influenced by *Lolita* neither for good nor for evil.
Every day things turn up in the press reporting dreadful sexual crimes
against the young. In detail and vividly expressed. Children and adults
read it. That was so before *Lolita* and will be no different in future.

Even answering such questions, which have nothing to do with my
book, is offensive. I am no moralist, and I hate any kind of literature
that wants to announce a message and makes ideological gestures. . . .
Besides, isn't it foolish to keep identifying an author with the creatures
of his imagination?

---

[*] "In London vor der Kamera: 'Das "anstößigste" Roman-Kind dieses Jahrhunderts'"
("Before the Camera in London: 'The "Most Offensive" Child-Novel of the Century'"), *Neue
Illustrierte*, Jan. 24, 1961, 11–12. Unsigned. Early publicity for the Kubrick film of *Lolita*, with
photographs of James Mason and Sue Lyon. Karolus interviewed VN in Nice on Jan. 14, 1961.

What will become of the film? Do you have influence over the filming, can you prevent commercial film interests from producing an insipid, slippery imitation that has nothing to do with your screenplay except the title?

I have confidence in Mr. Kubrick, to whom I recently sold the rights after I had a good and thorough talk with him. Kubrick is a serious person, and intelligent and artistically sensitive to boot. He called my screenplay, which makes no concessions of any kind to mass taste, one of the best ever written. He would be a stupid fool if he robbed himself, through concessions and crude simplifications, of the opportunity to make a great, artistically valuable film.

93

Interview with Anne Guérin
for *L'Express* (1961)[*]

On Nabokov as speaker
I can't speak. As a teacher, I would write out all my lectures. Without notes, I was lost. One day, I had to talk on Dostoevsky, whom I don't like.

What?
Whom I don't like. He's a journalist: he doesn't create, he hasn't the time. He writes, like Richardson and Rousseau (who inspired him), sentimental literature for young girls . . . but which also pleases young boys *(laughs)*.

So—I wanted to demolish Dostoevsky. But by mistake I had brought a lecture on Chekhov. So I mumbled, stammered, . . . and spoke on Chekhov.

Whom you like?
Oh yes! He, at least, doesn't secrete general ideas. I detest general ideas. And I've never in my life signed a petition or belonged to a club. Except tennis. And lepidopterists.

On revolution and police states
There was only one Russian revolution, which brought Kerensky to power. Communism, what has it given us? Well-organized police. But

[*] "Entretien, Nabokov: Il aime l'humour, le tennis et Proust. Il n'aime ni les communistes, ni Sade, ni Freud" ("Conversation, Vladimir Nabokov: He Likes Humor, Tennis and Proust. He Hates Communists, Sade, Freud"), *L'Express*, Jan. 26, 1961. Guérin visited the Nabokovs in Nice just before the publication of *Autres rivages*, the French translation of his autobiography.

the tsars were already doing this well. My father's servants were police agents. One of them, hiding behind a door, was exposed. He threw himself at my father's feet, sobbing.

And what did your father say?
"At least give him something to drink," or something like that.

In changing countries so often, have you changed yourself?
Ideas, no. Not even style. (I wrote correctly in several languages, even if, sometimes, the Slavic spirit rang out.) Dictionaries only. A single very difficult crossing: from Littré to Webster's.

Hasn't that mix of cultures altered your output?
Hardly. My Russian culture was already a mix of several others: French above all. No, I've had few masters, but I recognize certain affinities: with Proust, for example.

This title, Autres rivages . . .
. . . is the start of a Pushkin poem, romantic, in Lamartine's vein, where the poet sees again the lake of his youth. The original title of the autobiography is *Conclusive Evidence*. Not that it was conclusive. But those two "v"s pleased me.

Researching Lolita
I found an unfindable book on *The Measurements of Young Girls*. I couldn't after all undress one to measure around her hips.

What! You didn't know a Lolita?
When I wrote the book, Lolitas didn't even exist. (Now one sees them everywhere.) The interesting thing for me was obsession. (Besides, the case of Humbert, whom I also invented, has his place in the statistics that I consulted.) And then this almost scientific problem: how to handle his love?

You could have found something more normal.
Of course. It's interesting to ride a bike. But to do it without hands, without tires, without wheels, is still better, because more difficult.

Then would Lolita *be above all a satire?*
Not at all! It's a very tender book. An American Map of Tenderness. An America of my own, imaginary: a maquette.

Is Lolita *amoral?*
On the contrary. It has a very moral moral: don't harm children. Now, Humbert does. We might defend his feelings for Lolita, but not his perversity.

Sounds like the Church.
In this, nature is on the Church's side, alas! And Lolita, isn't she a victim and not a little slattern. . . . After all, haven't I indicated the evil of all this, in giving Lolita a stillborn child?

But the ending
. . . shows a purer Humbert, doesn't it? The good reader should have a little smarting at the corner of his eye when Humbert gives money to his Lolita, mature and with another.

Pornography?
Have you read the Marquis de Sade? The orgies? Things start with one person, then five, then fifty, then they invite the gardener! *(Enormous laugh.)* There's your pornography: quantity without quality. It's banal, it's not literature. The intention of art is always pure, always moral. . . . I hate the Marquis de Sade.

Psychoanalysis?
A disgusting racket. Psychoanalysis has something Bolshevik: internal police. And the symbols: those umbrellas, those staircases! Good for the Viennese, perhaps. But for an American of our time, who has no umbrella and uses only elevators? . . . Let's be serious: Freudianism is dangerous for art: symbols kill the thing, the individual dream. And sexuality! But this depends on art, not the other way around, you see: it's poetry that has refined love, over the centuries.

Poetry will soon be the focus of a Nabokov novel!
It will be much more difficult than *Lolita;* I have to explain a man's life in a poem, the best poem he's ever written . . . which I have to compose.

94

Interview with Janine Colombo
for *L'Information d'Israel* (1961)[*]

Yes, I'll go to Israel in February.

In a few weeks?
Impossible, you see, since I'm writing a new novel and that will still take me some time, two or three months, perhaps.

So you're coming to Israel—let's see, I'm counting—two, three—April? or May?
In February, I tell you. . . . In February or not at all, and I count on going, so it will be in February and only in February.

Why especially and only in February?
Because of the butterflies, my dear!

Butterflies?
Butterflies! And don't look at me with eyes as round as saucers; no, I'm not crazy! For me, you see, every country I see in terms of butterflies and shades of butterflies. I am a collector, and I know that one species of butterflies, butterflies with pastel hues, very rare, can be found on Jerusalem's hills in February. That's why I want to go there only in February.

---

[*] "Si Nabokov vient en Israel ce sera à cause des papillons de Jerusalem" ("If Nabokov Comes to Israel It Will Be for Jerusalem's Butterflies"), *L'Information d'Israel*, Feb. 3, 1961. Colombo interviewed him in his apartment on the Promenade des Anglais, Nice.

So you see a country in terms of butterflies. I didn't know of the existence of this species in the hills of Jerusalem, in February; since I'll be there then, and you've intrigued me, I'll go to see if I can find any.
And don't forget to tell me, unless you send me a few specimens with your newspaper.

On Sue Lyon

Why is Kubrick hiding his star? Simply because he's afraid people will write so much nonsense about this! That's it! In the book, the heroine is twelve; it was a little difficult to transpose a plausible story onto the screen with a little girl of twelve. So they chose a high-school girl of fifteen, who has just been filmed in the studio, like a worker putting in his day's shift, and she'll get back from there when she can to her place at school.

Do you know her? What do you think of her?
I don't know her and don't want to know her. I went to Hollywood especially to write the screenplay and the dialogue; but once the script was done, I hurried back to the Côte d'Azur, far from all that. But when I was in Hollywood, where the hopefuls were being cast, I saw the photos and remember saying to Kubrick, "Without a doubt, this is the one, in my opinion!" And that's whom he chose, after a decisive audition. No, I won't go to see the filming, I'll keep well away. Here I have peace and can get my new novel ready.

The name of your new novel?
What, give a name to the infant you're still carrying? Wait until it's born!

Do you have links with Israel?
Many very old and dear friends. That's why Israel is the only country where I'd like to give a lecture. I know *Lolita* is read there; it seems there are three or four translations, I think. I've been given Warhaftig's translation as a present; do you know it? I ask because certain translators, in certain languages, have taken, how shall I put this, liberties with the girl. *Lolita* as a book should be at the same time more chaste and more amusing.

95

Interview with Gershon Svet
for *Novoe Russkoe Slovo* (1961)[*]

Translating Eugene Onegin
All the translations of *Onegin* are riddled with errors, often monstrous ones. Even such a major literary scholar as the well-known Polish poet Julian Tuwim, Babette Deutsch, the German Wulf and others have translated Pushkin's text unfaithfully. The translation of *Onegin* into French by Turgenev and the famous singer Viardot is flawless.

Doctor Zhivago?
A mediocre melodrama with Trotskyist tendencies. It is an antiliberal work, undoubtedly pro-Bolshevik, even if anti-Stalinist. The book is badly written, very badly. Pasternak was never a good prose writer. He is, of course, a good poet. Not as great, of course, as Blok, but good.

Soviet literature?
Sholokhov's *And Quiet Flows the Don*? Third-rate. [My] favorite Soviet writers are Yuri Olesha, Mikhail Zoshchenko, Ilf and Petrov [and] among poets [Osip] Mandelshtam and [Ilya] Selvinsky. Soviet literature is philistine literature. This is typical of the literature of any country with an extreme political regime. Ilya Ehrenburg? He's a dazzling journalist and a big sinner. My late mother at one time would read and reread his long poem "A Prayer for Russia," which he wrote while his stance was still anticommunist.

---

[*] "Vstrecha s avtorom *Lolity*" ("A Meeting with the Author of *Lolita*"), *Novoe russkoe slovo*, Feb. 5, 1961, 8. Svet interviewed VN in Nice.

Alexei Tolstoy?

Peter the First and *Road to Calvary* are virtuosically written, but a sequence of chapters there is artificially accommodated to the "general line." Nonetheless, Tolstoy is without a doubt a major talent. Some of his stories are masterfully written.

96

Interview with Rosalie Macrae
for the *Daily Express* (1961)[*]

Ah, my American Lolitas. I do not find you here, my Lolita. You do not come to this Côte d'Azur. You here, you are post-Lolitas. You are Bardotists, not Lolitas. You are too aware. For you, Americana and Lolitaism is a cult. You are not the Lolitas I invented.

I never really knew any Lolitas, did I, darling? I do not think I have ever even talked to a schoolgirl of 12. I have a son of 26, and all my friends have sons. But I was aware that they were around.

And I know motels. I have always lived in them. We have never really had a home of our own.

In my book the American girls of *ce genre* met me more than halfway. Now Lolitas are everywhere. Look at St. Tropez: every girl tries to look like Lolita, my Lolita, but somehow never succeeds.

And yet there is something about the Riviera. Perhaps it comes from being here when I was a little Russian boy on holiday from St. Petersburg and looking at the fat chocolate-cream Riviera trains deluxe passing by.

Perhaps I come here because of the butterflies. I discovered a new butterfly here in 1939 up on the hills, and I still go out hoping to find a new one. But the butterflies now in this region are all friends. I remember I wrote a poem about discovering this butterfly.

Yes, it might be the butterflies, or the beautiful sea, or the fact that French is spoken here, and *ça j'adore*, and the changing tropical vegetation.

---

[*] "Nabokov, Butterflies and the Côte d'Azur," *Daily Express*, April 8, 1961. Macrae interviewed VN in Nice on April 6, 1961.

And it might be renting an apartment like this in a hideous yellow birthday cake Victorian villa which now looks beautiful beside the shelfed, white modern flats.

Here I am at ease. But mine is a different Côte d'Azur. I shun the world. I hate restaurants and cafés. When I eat, I go to the big hotel along the road. It is quiet, dignified, and somehow splendid.

I have come down here this time to write—about a man who composes 999 lines of a poem and dies before he reaches the thousandth line. It is after his death, a friend tries to analyze the poem, and involves his own life in doing so.

I allow myself no rest. And when I do try to give myself relaxing time the muse is fighting to get me started again.

I always write in English now. To write in Russian again would be like playing ordinary hockey after ice hockey. I need that American twang for experience.

When I knew you were coming I decided not to shave my head. I will probably do it tomorrow.

It is such a nice sensation. Look at my special bald-headed cap made of white linen.

I am never really happy without a head covering. In bed I always wear a nightcap.

The other day my son Dmitri—he is an opera singer, a wonderful *basso profundo* baritone—was setting off for winter sports and left his ski cap on the bed. The maid saw the cap, thought he was another of the mad Nabokovs, and shoved it under his pillow. The poor boy had to go skiing without it.

Interview with Claude Mercadie
for *Nice-Matin* (1961)[*]

On Lolita

It's my best book in my English vein. It took me seven years' work, from 1948 to 1955.... The subject was pure imagination. There was in this story a rapport between two very different beings. That's all.

On literary composition

Creation isn't a discipline. It's a state. There's neither place, nor time, nor surroundings. Often, I compose in my bath. I work just the same, morning or afternoon or night. Sometimes I write two books at once, or several pages at the same time belonging to different chapters. I always have on me my ruled index cards and a pencil. Once the machine gets going, I scribble on the pages I will sort out, that I'll use, I'll rearrange later....

The English author M. Imott, when he worked on a novel, stuck a piece of red paper on his forehead to let it be known he was not to be disturbed. One day, I stuck a postage stamp on me. But it was, how shall I put it, it was a farce. When I'm at work *(amused glance at his wife)*, it shows.

On catching a butterfly

I spent the day in the hills around Villeneuve-Loubet. Come and see what I caught.... Look: I managed to capture it at the foot of an arbutus after waiting four hours. It's marvelous.... It's a *Callophrys avis.* Careful, make sure you write it with a lower case. It's a very rare species, it's very important. I was very lucky.

---

[*] "Sur la promenade des Anglais Vladimir Nabokov la père de Lolita a planté sa tente de nomade" ("On the Promenade des Anglais Vladimir Nabokov, Lolita's Father, Has Planted His Nomad's Tent") *Nice-Matin,* April 13, 1961. Mercadie interviewed VN in Nice on April 8, 1961.

"Invitation to a Beheading," *Esquire* (Letter to the Editor, 1961)[*]

Helen Lawrenson's article, "The Man Who Scandalized the World," in your issue of August 1960, contains some absurd misstatements:

1. ". . . said Mrs. Nabokov calmly, '. . . when we were very poor in Paris I supported him by working as a milliner, and he has always been so grateful that he never gets angry at me.'"

My wife never worked as a milliner, nor in any other shop, and anyway could not have made that trite and silly remark.

2. Her father was not "the former owner of the largest and most important publishing house in Russia." He was an industrialist, and a jurist by education.

3. "In the opinion of some of his colleagues [on the Cornell University faculty] 'if the book had not been such a success, he would have been fired.'"

The book, published in 1955 by the Olympia Press of Paris, did not become "a success" until published by Putnam in 1958. There was ample time in which to fire me. Actually, however, during the years my book was banned in France, prohibited in England, and vilified by vulgarians, and up to 1959, when I deliberately and regretfully left Cornell, administration, faculty and students showed me nothing but sympathy, respect and understanding.

4. Finally, let me quote this incredible passage: "He . . . of course, feels that in the good old days of the Czar, 'a freedom-loving Russian

---

[*] Letter to the Editor, *Esquire*, June 1961, 10. Although the letter appeared under the title "Invitation to a Beheading," the header reflects not the subject of Lawrenson's article (*Esquire*, August 1960, 70–73), which was focused on *Lolita*, but Nabokov's then-latest novel available in English, *Invitation to a Beheading* (1934; trans. DN with VN, New York: Putnam, 1959)—which Lawrenson mentions only briefly—and the force of Nabokov's response to Lawrenson's article.

had more freedom than under Lenin,' without, however, specifying whether he meant freedom-loving aristocrats or freedom-loving serfs."

Irony, of course, is all right, but when starved by ignorance it chokes on its own tail; for surely any schoolgirl should know that no serfs existed in Russia since 1861, one year before the liberation of slaves in this country, and all lovers of freedom certainly realize that it was Lenin who restored serfdom in Russia.

I do not intend to continue though there are some other less piquant items I might list. None of these blunders was inevitable: all you had to do was send me your article to check the factual points before publishing it.

Vladimir Nabokov
Nice, France

99

Interview with Phyllis Meras
for *Providence Sunday Journal* (1962)[*]

All writers that are worth anything are humorists. I'm not P. G. Wodehouse. I'm not a funny man, but give me an example of a great writer who is not a humorist. The best tragedian is O'Neill. He is probably the worst writer. Dostoevsky's slapstick is wonderful, but in his tragedy he is a journalist.

Lolita *is satirical. Isn't it a humorous book?*
It's not humor. It's not a story. It's a poem.

    You really can't define humor, though. In Russian and in French there is no word for humor. In English, it has a kind of cozy sound, but there is a savage humor, too. Perhaps humor is simply seeing things in a singular, unique, extraordinary way. This almost always sounds funny to the average person.

    "When our son was very small," Mrs. Nabokov interjected, "they asked him in school, 'What does rain remind you of?' and he said 'It gives gooseskin to the puddles.' This is too unusual, the teacher said."

    Yes, the unusual is funny in itself. A man slips and falls down. It is the contrary of gravity in both senses—that's a great pun, by the way.

After noting that he generally writes more than one book at a time
Plots have a way of breeding—of living in sneaky little labs. Then they break out of their cocoons and I have to mop up the mess.

---

[*] "V. Nabokov Unresting," *Providence Sunday Journal*, May 13, 1962, W-24. Meras interviewed VN in Montreux on April 1, 1962, for the first appearance of *Pale Fire*, scheduled for May 28, 1962, in the United States.

When I was writing *Lolita* I was doing *Pnin* for *The New Yorker* at the same time. And then I was translating Pushkin's *Eugene Onegin* as well. It's Russia's most famous novel and it has never been adequately translated.

On his butterfly work

For seven years, you see, I was responsible for the butterflies at Harvard. I was practically curator there. There's a butterfly in every one of my novels. One of the first things I ever wrote in English was a paper on Lepidoptera I prepared at the age of 12. It wasn't published because a butterfly I described had been described by somebody else. But the paper itself was written in beautiful, precise English.

On the languages he writes in

It doesn't matter to me in what language I write, language is just another instrument. Except that, of course, English is the language with the richest literature. It breaks my heart to say it, but after English there comes a little gap. Then I would say Russian and French were on a par as far as literature is concerned. But English literature is huge— especially in its poets. English poetry is supreme.

Russian literature only got started in the 18th century, and then it had only a century and a half in which it could go before the Revolution occurred. Of course, during that period, it had such prose writers as Tolstoy—and, well—I don't think he has any peer in any other country. I think he's much greater than Proust or James Joyce, to take two other greats. But then in the 20th century in Russia, it all stopped.

I suppose there is still some goodish writing in Russia—Mandelshtam, who died in a concentration camp, was a wonderful poet, for example— but literature can't thrive where limits are set to human fantasy.

My books? They are absolutely banned in Russia. Every word of mine, after all, is filled with contempt for the police state.

When do I write? Whenever I feel like it. I write in shorthand— sometimes on a bench in the garden, or in the park, or in the car, or in bed. I always write in pencil on index cards. When the whole thing is one gray smudge of writing and erasing, I tear the whole thing up and make a fair copy. Then all the cards go to the Library of Congress, and they cannot be consulted for fifty years.

After Nabokov said he hadn't expected Lolita *to become a best seller*
And I didn't know that the first company that agreed to print it—that
was the Olympia Press in Paris—printed mostly pornography. I was a
little taken aback. But it happened that way because, after I could not
find a publisher in America, my agent said perhaps we could find an
English language publisher in Paris to do it.

100

Unidentified Interview (1962)[*]

On his butterfly passion

There's a butterfly in each one of my novels, you know. Someday I'd like to have a special institute for breeding a certain genus of butterflies. They're a North American kind, though, that live on special breeds of violets. I'd like to see them through their lives from the time they're caterpillars.

"And every now and then he wants to write a book about butterflies," Mrs. Nabokov interjected.

Among reasons for living in Switzerland

. . . for *Pale Fire*, I needed a little France and a little Switzerland. It's a book with a kind of European streak or strain in it.

It's a rather complicated book, and it's very difficult to say anything about it in a few words, but it's a combination of scholarly work, a poem, and a mystery thriller. The novel itself is the commentary to a poem of about 1,000 lines written by an Atlantic Seaboard poet; and the commentator is his colleague in an American university. There is also an imaginary kingdom called Zembla involved in the book, and that, of course, I had to create. That was the reason it was useful being in

---

[*] "Vladimir Nabokov Likes to Hunt Butterflies in Switzerland's Valais," in unidentified English newspaper, May 1962 [?]. The reporter sets the scene: "Vladimir Nabokov is getting impatient these days for summer to begin in earnest so that he can be off to hunt butterflies in the Valais"; *Pale Fire* seems not to have been published yet, and VN would be in New York on June 5, just after *Pale Fire*'s publication, for the launch of Kubrick's film of *Lolita*. From a clipping in the files of VN's younger friend and Harvard lepidopterological colleague, Charles Remington, without date, author, or source of publication. Some of the answers overlap with those Meras cites in the preceding interview, suggesting she conducted this interview, too. Remington had suggested the newspaper was perhaps the *Christian Science Monitor*, but the spellings and the language ("then went to the United States") indicate a British source.

Europe. I had to create Zembla out of the rejects of other countries—small countries, large countries—mostly northern countries.

I have a lot of index cards and files and I gradually collected certain details pertaining to various countries which hung together, zoological, geographical details. I've been doing that for two years.

Explaining his Eugene Onegin *project*
It's the most famous Russian novel. But it's never been adequately translated into English. It was written in the early 19th century. It all started because I wanted my students to have an adequate translation of it in class, and then my wife said, "Why don't you translate it?" and the Guggenheim people liked it. It's to be published by the Bollingen Press in four volumes. When did they say it would come out, darling?

"They promised it in 1963," Mrs. Nabokov said.

How do I write? I write whenever I feel like it. I write in longhand, on index cards—sometimes I do my writing on a bench in the garden; in the park; in a car. I always write in pencil with an eraser. When the whole thing is one gray smudge I tear it up and make a fair copy. All the cards go to the Library of Congress, and they cannot be consulted for 50 years.

For whom do I write? I write for the good reader. And you know, I have had some wonderful readers. Some of my readers have read my books better than I have written them. They're wonderful people. And it hasn't been just *Lolita* they've written about. Even more wrote about *Invitation to a Beheading.*

"My favorite letter," Mrs. Nabokov interjected, "was from a boy of 13 or 14 who gave a list of his questions."

And you saw he was a real reader. To be a real reader, you have to reread a book. The first time, a book is new. It may be strange. Actually, it is only the second reading that matters.

On languages and literatures
... The trouble with French literature has been that in the 18th century, for example, poetry was a beautiful dead fish. The general was substituted for the specific. It's a good point in logic to take the general

and not the specific, but for the writer, it meant you couldn't use the word "beetle," you had to say "insect."

It has always puzzled me, too, why Italy has not produced more first rate writing. I don't know why English has been so successful. Perhaps it's a luckier language. There are more words in it. The flexibility of the vocabulary is great.

101

Interview with Maurice Dolbier
for *New York Herald Tribune* (1962)*

On Pale Fire

I think it is a perfectly straightforward novel. The clearest revelation of personality is to be found in the creative work in which a given individual indulges. Here the poet is revealed by his poetry; the commentator by his commentary.

It is jollier than the others, and it is full of plums that I keep hoping somebody will find. For instance, the nasty commentator is not an ex–King of Zembla nor is he Professor Kinbote. He is Professor Botkin, or Botkine, a Russian and a madman. His commentary has a number of notes dealing with entomology, ornithology, and botany. The reviewers have said that I worked my favorite subjects into this novel. What they have not discovered is that Botkin knows nothing about them, and all his notes are frightfully erroneous.... No one has noted that my commentator committed suicide before completing the index to the book. The last entry has no numbered reference.... And even Mary McCarthy, who has discovered more in the book than most of its critics, had some difficulty in locating the source of its title, and made the mistake of searching for it in Shakespeare's *The Tempest*. It is from *Timon of Athens*. "The moon's an arrant thief, she snatches her pale fire from the sun."[1] I hope that pointing out these things will perhaps help the reader to enjoy my novel better.

---

* "Nabokov's Plums," *New York Herald Tribune*, June 17, 1962. The interview appears to have taken place in May 1962, before VN's trip to New York.

On Soviet writing
  Evgeni Evtushenko
I've seen his work. Quite second-rate. He's a good communist.

Soviet fiction
There are no good novels. Everything is either political or melodramatic, very tame and conservative in style, dealing in generalities, and with tired old characterizations that go back as far as Dickens. Even novels that supposedly represent tendencies that oppose the regime, and are smuggled out of Russia, are often smuggled with official connivance. Russian authorities today think they need a kind of loyal opposition. People outside keep trying to find in the work of youngish Soviet writers something that would reveal a certain thawing of the political ice block. But the thaw is very slight, indeed, and always controlled by the State.

How can there be any good or original writing in Russia when its writers can't know the West, can't know what freedom really means? Even the very few authors who do visit England and America see only what the tourist sees—the British Museum, Central Park, the Twist; nothing to change the picture they had already formed of us before they came. For some, their first whiff of freedom is when they see an American sprawled in a chair, feet outstretched, hands in pockets. But unfortunately they cannot recognize this as a form of liberty and democracy. They think it is not cultured. They say: "Americans don't know any better."

Are Soviet intellectuals familiar with your work?
Yes, they have read *Lolita*, but in a French edition. Really smuggled in, and I assure you, not by the publisher Gallimard with the sanction of de Gaulle.

102

Interview with Lewis Nichols
for *New York Times Book Review* (1962)[*]

Things he doesn't do
Drive a car, use a typewriter, play golf, listen to music, fish, dance, eat
oysters, get drunk, go to analysts.

Lolita *and* Pale Fire *will not please*
Philistines, vulgarians, champions of the social comment school of
fiction, Sovietophiles, homosexuals, symbol seekers and the kind of
solemn reader who dots every "i" with the author's head.

---

[*] "In and Out of Books," *New York Times Book Review*, June 24, 1962, 8. VN had prepared
answers for reporters meeting him when the *Queen Elizabeth* docked, on June 5, 1962.

103

Interview for *Newsweek* (1962)[*]

On himself
A person of no public appeal. I have never been drunk in my life, I never use schoolboy words of four letters, I have never worked in an office or in a coal mine. I have never belonged to any club or group. No creed or school has had an influence on me. My pleasures are the most intense known to man: butterfly hunting and writing.

On the ironies of Lolita*'s subject matter*
I rather dislike little girls, and I am not an expert in sexual aberrations. But publishers keep sending me only one kind of fiction: Novels truffled with obscenities and weird incidents.

His early response to the thought of filming Lolita
There is a child in it, and you would have to teach the child things no child should be taught.

After Kubrick raised the age of the actress playing Lolita to 14, and charmed him
I knew that if I did not write the script, somebody else would, and I also knew that at best the end product in such cases is less of a blend than a collision of interpretations.

He rises from bed to lectern
I can have ambulation of thoughts.

[*] "Lolita's Creator—Author Nabokov, a 'Cosmic Joker,'" *Newsweek*, June 25, 1962, 47–50. Interviewer unknown. The interview took place about mid-May, for the May 28 publication of *Pale Fire*, with VN as the subject of the magazine's cover illustration.

On writing on index cards
"I don't think I've ever written anything straight through from begin-ning to end," *Nabokov says, explaining that the card files make it easier to fill in what he calls* "the crossword-puzzle sections" *of a work.*

His audience
A writer writes for one or two perfect readers, his wife, perhaps, or a friend or two.

His Russian and his English
As a writer, I am better in Russian.

On the first impact of arriving in America
I knew I had come to a wild and wonderful land, and that Americans are a liberal people. You sense it right away in the manner in which they address each other, in the way they walk, and the way they put their hands in their pockets.

On humor
Humor is really a loss of balance—and appreciation of losing it. Also, it involves a fast and free association of values.

104

Interview for *Daily Colonist* (1962)*

On the Original of Lolita: A Screenplay
It all started with Hollywood asking me to work on the screenplay. I was hunting butterflies in Arizona at the time. The sum offered me was considerable, but the idea of tampering with my own work caused me only revulsion, so after weeks of meditation I turned the offer down.

Four months passed. In December 1959, we were at Lugano in one of those wet spells you get in Europe every so often. I had long since stopped thinking about the film, but one night I suddenly had an illumination, perhaps a little diabolical, but certainly very compelling. I had the feeling that I was watching a color film of *Lolita*, and very soon I perceived a way to do the script. That very week by sheer coincidence I received a cable from Hollywood asking me to reconsider my decision. I did.

I moved out to Hollywood in March 1960, and had no trouble projecting *Lolita* on my own mental screen, using a sound track of my own writing. The germ which produced the book was still alive in my mind.

On reading and identifying
When I teach I always advise my students never to identify with characters. I tell them to stand aloof, so that they may feel the intrinsic merit of the artist. If they must identify, let them do so not with characters but with art.

---

* "After a Series of Improbabilities . . . Meet Mr. Nabokov, Author of *Lolita*," *Daily Colonist* [Victoria, B.C.], *The Islander* (magazine section), July 15, 1962, 15. Unsigned. VN was present in New York for the premiere of the Kubrick *Lolita* film.

Was Pale Fire *difficult to write?*
It was maddening. The structure of the book was something new. First, I had to create a New England poet who was a follower of Robert Frost. Then I had to evoke some kind of inspiration to produce a good poem, and I hope I did.

105

Interview with Jacob Bronowski
for Associated Rediffusion Television (1962)[*]

Do you feel that your novels are larger than life?
I'm not sure this isn't an illusion. For me, life is not an independent, objective entity. Its image depends on the observer. And there are too many observers—coming and going, and turning away, and looking again, and shading their eyes again—too many changing observers and changing lights, too many of them to enable one to establish an average picture of life. If you find I see life larger than life, this implies only a difference between you and me—not between life and my vision of life. We all are the makers of reality, and there are as many makers of reality as there are men. The real unreality is the conventional and the common.

But in Lolita *you chose a rather grotesque and violent form of passion. Surely this is a deliberate choice, a dramatic sharpening and heightening so that the readers' experience of life becomes larger than life.*
I disagree. Life in the objective and neutral sense you give it does not really exist—so that one thing cannot be larger than another thing which does not exist.

---

[*] Notes for planned but aborted television interview for Associated Rediffusion, scheduled for Sept. 2, 1963, in London. Emended typescripts and correspondence with VN holograph additions and revisions, VNA Berg. VN replied in writing to Bronowski's questions on Aug. 5, 1962, and to a supplementary batch of questions on Aug. 16, but plans were canceled when DN was hospitalized on Aug. 20. Bronowski wrote to VN on Aug. 13 suggesting dropping some questions and focusing on what to him were the key themes he wished to sound. VN replied on Aug. 16: "I agree to leave out exchanges 4, 5, 8, 9 and 15, but I must retain Nos. 2 [*Lolita* as hopeless passion or social criticism], 10 [novel as universal and social or personal] and 13 [involvement of scientists versus artists in their work]. They are the basic ones on my side of the interview."

B. For example, I think that LOLITA is a novel about hopeless passion,
   and in that sense is everybody's experience. Do you think of it in
   that way or is LOLITA a work of social criticism?

N. LOLITA is the hopeless passion of a rather clumsy and disagreeable

   grown-up man for a specific little girl whose life he breaks. It is

   a specific case and not everybody's experience. As to social

   criticism, I don't give a hoot for it. I think social criticism in

   novels is at best a stylistic trick which is centuries old, and as

   tedious and stale as eighteenth-century comedy. Why write novels

   if one is a social critic? Write essays, dash off articles in

   political reviews.

Carbon copy of a question sent by Jacob Bronowski, answered by Nabokov, and typed out by Véra Nabokov or a secretary, for a 1962 television interview for Associated Rediffusion. Filming was canceled because of Dmitri Nabokov's hospitalization.

Do you think of Lolita *as a novel about hopeless passion or is it a work of social criticism?*

Lolita is the hopeless passion of a rather clumsy and disagreeable grown-up man for a specific little girl whose life he breaks. It is a specific case and not everybody's experience. As to social criticism, I don't give a hoot for it. I think social criticism in novels is at best a stylistic trick which is centuries old, and as tedious and stale as eighteenth-century comedy. Why write novels if one is a social critic? Write essays, dash off articles in political reviews.

The duel at the end of Lolita *between Humbert and Quilty seems to me inspired fantasy. Or do you intend the reader to take it seriously?*

I don't think I could name a single striking scene in a worthwhile work of fiction that can be taken seriously in that sense. Only the conventional and common is serious or better say—solemn. Another special aversion of mine is the epithet "sincere." How can a conjuror be serious or sincere—and a good artist is always a conjuror. To take some examples. Flaubert imposes a magnificent illusion on his readers when he describes Emma's escapades which in so-called "real life" would have set tongues wagging long before the author was ready to dispatch his lady. Consider the nightly meetings of Emma and her lover in the garden pavilion. Can a reader take seriously the fact that Charles Bovary, a healthy young husband, never once turns to his young wife in the middle of the night to find the better half of the bed empty. Or take some of those impossible eavesdropping scenes in Proust—for example, that little affair between Charlues and Jupin. Or in *Bleak House*, that stunning chapter in which the sinful and ginful old man is literally consumed by internal and external fire. Who cares if all this does not conform to serious average life? Down with the serious and sincere reader. After all, not all readers are children who ask if the story is true.

I don't think your two examples are alike. The escapades of Madame Bovary *are made more plausible than they would be in average life, yes. But the man in* Bleak House *who dies by spontaneous combustion is not just implausible—he is incredible, a creature of fantasy. This is what I think about the scene between Humbert and Quilty. We believe it because it relieves our pent-up feelings, but it is unbelievable.*

I think you are wrong. Art is always implausible since art is always deception; and the relief of pent-up feelings is generally the reaction of a very juvenile reader.

There is a strong visual sense in everything you write. Do you have a mainly visual imagination?

Let me put it this way: All the books I like—*Hamlet, Dead Souls, Madame Bovary, Bleak House, Anna Karenin, The Passionate Friends*, and a few others—have good eyes. And all the authors whom I find mediocre and tedious, such as Cervantes, Stendhal, Dostoevsky and *many* others, are dim-sighted or blind.

Did you enjoy turning Lolita *into a film?*

I did not turn it into a film. I only wrote the screenplay. This work took me six months. I composed the thing scene by scene, in a lovely green-and-blue Los Angeles canyon, in 1960. I hope to publish it someday.

It was great fun writing it.

What were the problems in making the novel into a film?

There were two problems involved—a general one and a specific one. The general problem is that of time. An ideal film should omit nothing, should follow the text phrase by phrase, and present visually every metaphor, every abstract thought. Even so, the result would be a stylistic compromise, a limitation of perception.

Do you think that the Film is as expressive as the Novel; will it take the place of the Novel?
What a bizarre thought! It is like saying that someday perhaps all novels will be published with illustrations. After all, you perceive a novel with your visionary mind, with your vibrant brain, and not with your physical eyes and ears. It would be rather disturbing for an author who, for instance, has taken great pains to build verbally a delicate, deliberately blurry image, to have some matter-of-fact chap with a camera come between him and his phrase.

This is not quite what I meant. The novel itself is quite a modern invention— the English novel is only 200 years old. Before that, writers told such stories in epic poems or in plays. Are we now coming to a time when creative minds find it more expressive to write directly in the visual imagery of the film?
I don't think I care; all I know is that *my* creative mind is concerned only with written words, and not with photographed things shot and killed by a camera.

Can you conceive yourself thinking of a new work as a script for a film directly, and not as a novel?
Certainly not.

Is the exile especially characteristic of this age?
No. There are as many exiles and ages as there are banished men or banned minds. The term "this age" means nothing to me.

It seems to me that you are interested in universal and social situations, but that you always see them in very personal terms. Do you think that this is the essence of the novel?
I'm afraid I'm not interested in social situations or problems. As a writer I am practically immune to social or moral ideas. Moreover *the* novel does not exist for me as a generic idea. But specifically a few novels do—among which are *Hamlet* and *Eugene Onegin*, both written in verse. For me, the idea of a book lies in its main structural theme, which is a

verbal thing, a stylistic phenomenon, just as one can speak of the idea of a musical composition or of a chess problem without any moral or social implications. Of course, there are some good readers who, among the more important matters, are interested in the social and moral ideas of a novel even if the author did not put them there; but alas, it is generally the bad reader whose lazy mind prefers the easy general idea to the difficult specific details of a work of art. This is why young simpletons all over the world love Dostoevsky—because it is so easy and fascinating to discuss mysticism and sin without reading him closely; and that is why my worst students (when I was a university professor) always preferred such second-rate fellows as Faulkner and Camus to any real artist.

For most of your life you have been a scientist. Do you think of your scientific work quite differently from your novels?
Though I have always hunted butterflies, I've been an active scientist—in the sense of probing certain taxonomic problems and publishing my findings—only for ten years or so—from about 1940 to about 1950. Otherwise I have always successfully combined butterfly hunting with my literary work. And generally speaking: I think there is a bond and a blend between art and science at suitable altitudes. Lowlands do not interest me. By science I do not mean those popular or unpopular technological gadgets that impress journalists. I mean natural science and pure mathematics.

You said at the beginning of this discussion that not all readers are children who ask if the story is true. Tell me how you think that science is true. Is the truth in a scientific theory more literal than in a work of art?
I did not say that science is truer than art. When a child demands truth it is the clamoring for a convention—not for truth but for an average fact that is held to be true. As to scientific theories, they are always the temporary gropings for truth of more or less gifted minds which gleam, fade, and are replaced by others. Both art and science are very subjective affairs.

Are you the same character when you are working with butterflies as when you are working on a novel?
No, not quite. In ordinary life, for example, I'm strictly right-handed, but when manipulating butterflies, I use my left hand more than my

right. I am also much more nervous, much gloomier and greedier when hunting them. I emit strange sounds, curses and entreaties. Finally, we should all remember that a lepidopterist reverts in a sense to the ancient ape-man who actually fed on butterflies and learned to distinguish the edible from the poisonous kinds.

Do you think that scientists are as deeply and personally involved in their work as the novelist is?
I think it all depends on what scientists or novelists you have in view. Darwin or Gauss were as deeply and rapturously involved in their work as Browning or Joyce. On the other hand, in both camps we have those crowds of imitators, those technicians and administrators and career boys who cannot really be called scientists and artists. They, of course, dismiss their work from their minds after office hours.

Is there something personal and revealing about your choice of butterflies as a subject of study?
No, they chose me, not I them. It all started on a cloudless day in my early boyhood—started as a passion and a spell, and a family tradition. There was a magic room in our country house with my father's collection—the old faded butterflies of his childhood, but precious to me beyond words—now almost a hundred years old, if they still exist. My mother taught me to spread my first swallowtail, my first hawk-moth. That enchantment has always remained with me. I have spoken of this much better in my memoir *Speak, Memory*.

Is there something personal and revealing about your choice of characters in your novels?
I suppose a novelist can't help giving his pet notions to his intelligent characters, and giving his stupid characters such notions as he holds in contempt. It has been noticed that most of the people in my books, the clever ones as well as the fools, are always sort of nasty or half nasty— anyway, much nastier than I am in ordinary life. But generally speaking I object to being looked for in my books. And there is a sign over all my books: Freudians, keep out! And in case they don't, I have laid a few little traps here and there.

106

Interview with Pierrette Blanc
for *Tribune de Lausanne* (1963)[*]

O, no, I'm not going out after butterflies this morning. It's too cold. I'm afraid of catching colds. . . . You could say that the season, in Switzerland, ends about August 15.

Have you found interesting species?
I'm happy to hear you say "species" and not "specimen," for specimens are only samples. I spent the month of June in the Valais, in the Rhone Valley, where I could pursue interesting inquiries. Flowers, which are the breeding plants, are abundant enough there. On the Simplon I saw things one doesn't find anywhere else.

My passion for butterflies was born sixty years ago, when I was only five. Russia is an enormous country that encompasses all sorts of species. In the steppes, on the high mountains, there are some that are very little known. A lot has been written about grasshoppers, because they risk being destroyed by harvests, but far too little on butterflies.

Do you have a nostalgia for your country of birth?
For certain landscapes, certain trails. But nostalgia is Chateaubriand, and that I don't experience. I have no wish to see Moscow as I might visit Belgrade or any other town. I think in fact I'll never go to Russia again. Factories don't interest me, and the only thing that attracts me is a little landscape near Petersburg, because it represents my childhood.

[*] "Vladimir Nabokov, auteur de *Lolita*: Je ne connais pas une seule petite fille" ("Vladimir Nabokov, Author of *Lolita*: I Don't Know a Single Little Girl"), *Tribune de Lausanne*, Sept. 1, 1963, 11. Blanc visited VN in early Aug., while he was staying at the Grand Hôtel, Les Diablerets, in Vaud Canton, in pursuit of butterflies.

What was the genesis of Lolita?
I thought you'd come to talk about butterflies?

Haven't I repeated often enough that I had no moral, political or ethical idea? I am an inventor, I'm interested only in the construction of the novel and only artistic creation counts for me.

But I assure you that nothing in this case is based on real facts. Besides, I don't know a single little girl, whether she be American, Russian, or French. Simone de Beauvoir wrote an essay on the Lolita syndrome that I don't agree with at all. I'd rather show you something that will interest you.

You're rather critical of American society in your novels.
But I adore America, it's my country. American universities are very fine. It's so easy to get rare works, even Russian editions that the USSR itself doesn't have. In Paris, just try to buy a book. . . .

What do you think of young Russian literature?
Evtushenko? He's a little Aragon. These aren't real artists, journalists at most. Dostoevsky? A journalist, like Balzac. I divide writers into journalist and poets. Camus is a third-rate novelist. Flaubert, a poet. Goethe, a very great poet; but Schiller is nothing.

What do you think of Switzerland?
It's perfect, but I don't like the cows much. They drive off the butterflies.

107

Interview with Henri Jaton
for Radio Suisse Romande (1963)[*]

Have you thought about a vocation as a writer since childhood, or did it happen by chance?

No, I think I was born like that, a precocious genius, a wunderkind. Besides, all children have genius, but circumstances often stifle them, and sometimes encourage them. I've been at work in literature since I was very small. I remember vividly that at age five in St. Petersburg, where I was born, I would tell myself stories in bed or while playing, all sorts of stories, mainly heroic adventures. There'd be a whole procession of images traipsing around me and through me. And then, at ten, I started writing poetry in English, in Russian, in French. I belong to the breed of prose writers who debut as poets, and who pass a long period of apprenticeship in writing poems before writing prose, a prose not poetic, but based on poetic disciplines, having so to speak the woof of poetry.

You learned French as a child?

Yes, at six, I think. I had a French governess who lived in our family from 1905 to World War I. She was a Swiss woman, from Vevey, Cécile Miauton.

Whom do you write for?

I must say, I have never been interested in commercial success; in other words, I've never sought to push my books. I've never written except for a single reader, Mr. Nabokov, for him alone. I have a vague

[*] Radio interview for Radio Suisse Romande, Lausanne, taped on Oct. 5, 1963. Emended typescript with VN manuscript revisions and additions, in French, VNA Berg.

impression that my first English books, written and published in the United States—books like *The Real Life of Sebastian Knight,* or the story of Professor Pnin—found readers here and there, for intellectual life in America has an incomparable intensity and variety, but I didn't pay much attention to this little plashing of gray glory. Then, when I published my *Lolita* (almost ten years ago), I was at first surprised by its success. To tell the truth, I sometimes think that people buy this book for reasons not artistic, but, how shall I put it, erotic, but all this doesn't concern me, although I'm very comfortable that this lovely child is made so much of.

What are you working on now?
My workshop is one for my translations and proofs—dismal games, to tell the truth. Writers of the past didn't know the miseries of the translation supervised by the author. People started translating me from Russian into German and French almost forty years ago, but now, over the last few years, the Tower of Babel babbles and burbles louder and louder.

And finally, as an extra treat, it's almost a year now that I've been working on the most difficult novel I have ever tried to write. I don't want to say more for the moment.

Letter to the Editor, *Russkaya Mysl'* (1963)[*]

It is with sadness that I learned of the passing of Princess A. L. Shak-hovskoy. She was a sweet and kind person. Alas, I had not seen her in over a quarter of a century and only once in all this time, when I was in California, did I speak to her on the telephone, to pass on the regards of her daughter, Natalia Alexeevna Nabokov, who has been a longtime friend to my wife and me.

I'm afraid I must ask you to print the following correction to the article published in her memory in *Russkaya mysl'* (no. 2048).[1] The article contains a phrase (supposedly said by me to Princess Shakhovs-koy) foisted on me by Mr. Berezov's imagination: "But what am I to do, Aunt, if American readers are only interested in such themes?"

I could not have said this, not only because I never called Princess Shakhovskoy "Aunt," or discussed *Lolita* with her, but, most important, because I consider *Lolita* my best book. Only buoyant blockheads who haven't actually read the work they're criticizing could explain away its composition as a vulgar calculation to please some vulgar taste. I doubt that Mr. Berezov was consciously trying to join their number.

Vladimir Nabokov

---

* Letter to the Editor, *Russkaya mysl'*, Oct. 8, 1963, 5.

Interview with M.V.
for *Journal de Montreux* (1964)[*]

Of all your books, which do you love most?
It's usually the latest. Therefore: *Pale Fire*. But it's also the one that took the most work, the one that let me approach closest to the first idea of its creation. *Lolita* is a child who has given me a lot of trouble. I don't love her any the less for that.

I invented her. She existed somewhere in the world, perhaps, but not in literature. Ever since my novel first appeared, she has started to live and be seen—for example, if you open the columns of American and Italian dictionaries, where she designates what she is: a girl prematurely depraved.

Do you think the film brought something to the written work?
Absolutely not. Film adaptation has necessarily simplified the vision and the idea of my book.

But I loved the film, which I've seen three or four times. James Mason and Sue Lyon play their roles well.

Montreux?
We enjoy Montreux very much, and we like its situation, the play of colors in every season, the houses stepping in tiers down to the lake. And then so many writers lived here, Byron, Rousseau, not to mention Casanova. . . .

From here I can have close contact with my publishers about translations that I have to supervise. Just one complaint: the dangerous and intolerable traffic on the cantonal highway.

[*] "L'Écrivain Nabokov aime Montreux et adore les papillons" ("The Writer Vladimir Nabokov Likes Montreux and Adores Butterflies"), *Journal de Montreux*, Jan. 23, 1964, 1–2.

What are your favorite occupations outside your work as a writer?
Entomology first of all. I hunt butterflies in summer, I classify them in my collections in winter. But also reading my favorite authors, as dear to my heart when they're French or English as when they're Russian: Flaubert, Ronsard, La Fontaine, Senancour (an author too little known who wrote, around 1830, in the *Journal* of his life, splendid descriptions of the Alps); among the moderns, Alain Robbe-Grillet, Joyce, without forgetting the finest poets in the world, the English, starting with Shakespeare. And of course Tolstoy, Chekhov, and Pushkin, whose life has been the focus of a large work of mine I've been preparing for years.

110

Interview with Douglas M. Davis
for *National Observer* (1964)*

Switzerland?

It is the most pleasant and poetical country in Europe. Gogol, Tolstoy, Byron, Dostoevsky walked here. Gogol wrote *Dead Souls* here. Dostoevsky found himself penniless here. Tolstoy caught a good case of venereal disease here. As I say, it is a poetical country.

America?

In 1935, my wife and I decided to go to America and live, since the language there was the language I wished to be near. We had a little boy, too, and I wanted him there. And people began to translate my books in America. So the practical was associated with the metaphysical.

What do you think of the United States after twenty years?

America is my home now. It is my country. The intellectual life suits me better there than any other country in the world. I have more friends there, more kindred souls than anywhere. I don't care for American food, mind you. Ice cream and milk are all right in their place. The American steak is a mistake, there's a pun for you.

But these are material things, not important, really. No, there is something about American life and people and universities which keeps me perfectly and completely happy.

The reception of Lolita*?*

What bothered me most was the belief that *Lolita* was a criticism of

---

* "On the Banks of Lake Leman—Mr. Nabokov Reflects on *Lolita* and *Onegin*," *National Observer,* June 29, 1964, 17. In Montreux, a week after the publication of VN's translation of and commentary to *Eugene Onegin.*

America. I think that's ridiculous. I don't see how anybody could find it in *Lolita*. I don't like people who see the book as an erotic phenomenon, either. Even more, I suppose, I don't like people who have not read *Lolita* and think it obscene.

I don't think *Lolita* is a religious book, but I do think it is a moral one. And I do think that Humbert Humbert in his last stage is a moral man because he realizes that he loves Lolita as any woman should be loved. But it is too late; he has destroyed her childhood. There is certainly this kind of morality in it.

Do you set out to mislead the reader?

I play with him, yes, but not as a cat with a mouse. I suppose there is a lot of shifting in my work, but that is natural to me. As one face or phase passes, another takes over. But there is no teasing. I am very honest, actually.

On Robert Frost

Not everything he wrote was good. There is lots of trash. But I believe that rather obvious little poem on the woods[1] is one of the greatest ever written.

On Ernest Hemingway

Hemingway did some wonderful things. But those long novels—*For Whom the Bell Tolls* and the rest—I think they are abominable. He was, after all, a short-story writer.

On William Faulkner

I am completely deaf to Faulkner. I do not understand what people see in him. He has been invented. Surely, he was not a real person.

Your three languages

At this point I write English better than the other two, and prefer it. I am appalled by the provincial inclinations and philistine thought of modern Russian.

On his Eugene Onegin

You have not asked about my labor of love. It is the great work of my life.

111

Interview with Horst Tappe
for *Die Welt* (1964)*

Why, when you're in Europe, do you live in Montreux in particular?
I've known it well from long ago. You know, Russians like to travel—my
wife, too, was in Montreux as a child—and we have now voted it, as it
were, our family meeting place. My son lives in Milan, which isn't far,
and we can see each other often. He graduated from Harvard and is
now studying singing in Milan. He has a wonderful bass voice. I myself
am completely unmusical, I have no ear for music.

What are you working on now?
A few very pleasant and interesting months past, I read from my own
work at Harvard and in New York. Now I'm writing here for my book
on European butterflies; in spring I'll go to London, to work more on
this in the British Museum; the book will come out in England.[1]

*How do you write? Before you start a new novel, what comes first: a character,
out of whose personality the plot arises, or the story?*
Neither. Never. Rather, colors, pictures, visions. That's also the reason
I don't begin with the beginning or end with the ending and above all
never proceed chronologically, if I'm writing a novel. I begin anywhere,
then carry on somewhere else, to set down a quite different image, and
end by filling in the holes.

---

* "Schmetterlinge und *Lolita*: Gespräch mit Vladimir Nabokov" ("Butterflies and *Lolita*:
Conversation with Vladimir Nabokov"), *Die Welt*, Aug. 25, 1966. Although this was published
in 1966, the biographical details in the interview clearly date it to the summer of 1964. The
photographer Tappe lived in Territet, on the eastern edge of Montreux, and had been pho-
tographing VN since 1962.

And why do you write?

Out of an inner need, a necessity. I have always written, as I have always been interested in butterflies. I was seven years old when I tried to translate the then very well-known children's book *The Headless Rider* into French and—just think—into alexandrines at that.

If you had to decide between your scientific and your literary work, what would you choose?

Both belong together; for me one without the other is unthinkable, they augment each other. The precision of poetry and the inspiration of science.

About Lolita . . .

Sometimes I get quite fed up with questions about *Lolita*, but, despite everything, it's my favorite book.

112

Interview with Guy de Belleval
for *Journal de Genève* (1965)[*]

Why Montreux?
Here, everything is calm, peaceful. And, then, for me, Switzerland remains the cultural center I'm at home in. You don't feel apart from the world. You can still work in it.

What's your schedule?
In the morning I get up around six. Until eleven I shut myself in my study to write. I'm not home to anyone. Before lunch I go for a short walk. As soon as the meal's over I go back to work. I stay at my texts until 5:00 or 6:00 p.m. Then I read the papers. At seven I have dinner. After, my wife and I play chess. It's rather rare for me to go to bed later than nine.

On his Eugene Onegin
I am particularly fond of Pushkin, who to me puts in concrete form the effect of French culture in Russia.

On the Lolita *screenplay and film*
I had a great time on this work, and for me my stay in Hollywood will remain an excellent memory.

It seemed to me at first that the film would be good. . . . Of course, I'm not entirely in agreement with what was screened, but I must admit I wasn't expecting much. I'd taken the risk.

I'm not like that French writer I like very much: Robbe-Grillet. He likes writing for the cinema. That I can't really understand.

[*] "Buvant du xérès chez monsieur Nabokov" ("Drinking Sherry chez Nabokov"), *Journal de Genève*, March 13, 1965, 4.

On French literature

My best friend is Gustave Flaubert. Of course, I'm still loyal to Marcel Proust, whom I loved passionately in my youth. I should say, too, that recently I read with sheer pleasure *Warrior's Rest* (*Le Repos du guerrier*) by Christiane Rochefort.

Home and travel

I feel at home in North America, especially in New York. So I spend my time between the U.S.A. and Switzerland. From time to time, I take a little trip to Milan to see my son, who sings at La Scala.

On Véra

She's my collaborator. We work with the most sweet and open affection. She types my texts, which isn't always easy, because I'm very demanding.

On Lolita

Lolita is no doubt the book that has given me the most joy, but this joy's more for the book itself than for me.

113

Interview with Gordon Ackerman
for *Weekly Tribune* (1966)*

On being an American in Europe
I have to hear conversations in American around me in order to nourish myself. Writers hear interior conversations, of course, but they require outside nourishment.

On Hollywood
We managed to avoid most of the cocktail parties, because every time I went to one I offended someone.

At the first one, I was introduced to John Wayne, and asked him, "Excuse me, but what kind of work do you do out here?"

Then at another party I was introduced to a lovely, dark-haired young woman to whom I spoke French. I told her she had a wonderful Parisian accent. "Parisian, hell!" she said. "It's Roman French." It turned out to be Gina.[1]

On Berlin and Paris
Those places are behind me. When you are finished with a place it no longer inspires you. I never liked Paris much, and I like it less now. It's too noisy and messy. We don't like nightlife and clubs.

---

* "Nabokov and the Innocent European," *Weekly Tribune* [Geneva, Switzerland], Jan. 28, 1966, p. 12.

114

Interview with Alberto Ongaro
for *L'Europeo* (1966)[*]

Has female emancipation killed love? Is Lolita a new model of woman? Are today's girls perhaps your daughters, Lolita's sisters?
Lolita's sisters, well, maybe. My daughters? I wouldn't say so. The relationship in any case seems pure chance. While writing *Lolita*, I did not think of any real live model. I did not know America, I did not know American girls or their psychology, or their way of life. *Lolita* is a spark of the imagination. If this spark has taken shape and has become a girl of flesh and blood—two girls, three, a hundred, millions—what have I to do with it? There's no need to pin a paternity suit on me. Yes, I know, they say that today's girls feed only on comics, are crazy about television and films, just like Lolita, they're cold in romantic relationships, they have no other interests than those suggested by so-called mass culture. But I repeat: the similarities are accidental, I did not mean to denounce or predict a change of mores.

*How, then, do you explain the "*Lolita *cult"? How do you explain all these girls who move, act, dress, and talk like Lolita?*
I wouldn't know. Perhaps it is a result of the way the popular press has distorted my poor Lo. It has come up with something that has absolutely nothing to do with the book or Lolita the character. *Lolita* is the story of a sad little girl in a very sad world. The "*Lolita* cult" is something completely different. No, I don't think *Lolita* has influenced

[*] "L'amore oggi: Visto dall'autore di *Lolita*" ("Love Today: How the Author of *Lolita* Sees It"), *L'Europeo*, June 23, 1966, 28–33. The comics writer, journalist, and novelist Ongaro interviewed VN in the garden of a hotel in Chianciano Terme, where he was staying for his summer butterfly hunt. The interview was probably conducted in English, a language usually well known among anti-fascist writers like Ongaro.

the way people behave. It can often happen that a reader finds in a novel implications an author did not think of. These are always things smuggled in without the author's knowledge. The only influence one could speak of is this: in America the name Lolita has disappeared from birth notices. Before, it was a fairly common name; now no parents would dare to call their own daughter Lolita. Now they give the name to dogs.

But Lolita *has a definite link with modern mores. Girls branch out more from the family, develop earlier psychologically and morally.* Lolita *was the first champion of the teenager and of adolescent sexuality.*
Yes, maybe. But we must not forget that adolescent erotic games have always been there. They aren't new, a discovery of this age, something peculiar to "our society." In other cultures this adolescent play is even encouraged by adults. I see nothing new in all this. Nor do I believe we can say, in general terms, that adolescent psychological and moral development comes earlier. Generalizations always seem dangerous to me. What teenagers? We need to be precise. Of course, if we go to London or New York and see all those girls with miniskirts, unruly hair, painted lips, and heavy eyeliner, their attitude can strike us with wonder. But if we go to Madrid or Boston the picture changes completely. Anyway, even if it didn't, even if the tidal wave of teenagers, in their sense of the term, were to reach the most unexpected places and fill not only Boston and Madrid but also, let's say, Terracina, or Tucson, Arizona, with rouged girls and long-haired youths, I do not believe that would mean different sexual behavior or a new way to see love.

But love has changed, according to sociologists, novels, and films: casual sex, infidelity, no sense of sexual jealousy. Sex has been emptied of feelings. Godard shows on his screens modern lovers as anonymous and absolutely two-dimensional.
I do not know the films of Godard. I know Fellini's *8½* and *La Strada*. I found them extraordinarily romantic, deeply touching. I agree with you all the same that literature and cinema deal with the problem of sex more frequently than they once did. In fact, you could say they deal with little else. And that in my opinion is the only perceptible change in this field. There is more openness, less shame, less shyness in discussing sexual facts. Even if the past has a rich erotic literature, contemporary literature is less prudish than in the past, with the exception of Russia,

which has never been freed from prudery. On the contrary. But for other Western literatures the fact is undeniable. The times seem to have changed. In Balzac, for example, there aren't explicit references to characters' erotic relationships, even if they were taken for granted. Now it comes up everywhere. Authors describe the physiological side of love in detail. But this is a fact about the history of literature and cinema rather than of mores. In short, it seems to me that sexual customs in civilized countries are always the same and that only the way of showing them has changed.

Haven't feelings been transformed in our time?
Not to my knowledge. You see, I don't think we have a reference point for talking about transformation. Talk of changes, of transformations, always implies a starting point, an ideal model from which the evolutionary process starts. We don't have this when we're talking of love. We know the mores of the Greeks and Romans, who calmly practiced homosexuality. Is this our model? I would say not. Persian or Arab mores? Still worse.

We have an idyllic, spiritual idea of love in the Middle Ages, but if we look at certain engravings of the time, we see the spiritual knights bathing nude with their ladies. So what, then, is the ideal model to compare our customs with? There is none. There is none, because love has always been the same. Love now is no different from in Catullus's day. You see, I think we need to research much more deeply in history than sociology does to determine whether there really has been a transformation.

But the nineteenth century was so different, so puritanical. Couldn't that be the reference point?
I think it's a commonplace to say that the nineteenth century was a puritanical age. To take just one example, adultery in the nineteenth century was a kind of sacred institution. The Paris feuilletons were full of adulteries in high society. And don't forget the married couples unfaithful to each other by mutual consent. And incest was very frequent, if not usual, in the Russian countryside and in the rest of Europe. In Pushkin's time unspeakable things went on. No, I do not believe that the nineteenth century was a particularly puritanical age. As I don't believe the eighteenth century was more libertine, or that the era in which we

live is particularly libertine. I do not believe such labels. They seem arbitrary and unfounded. In my view, forms of puritanism and freedom have coexisted simultaneously in every era.

But never as now: newspapers, cinema, billboards cannot do without sex. This is transforming us stealthily. The experts think it a serious threat to mankind.
The bombardment of images may be an innovation of our times. But that's only in terms of quantity. The visual depiction of the erotic has always been there. There was no dearth of paintings evoking love in the past. The examples are endless. All the painted Venuses, Leda and the Swan, Susanna and the Elders, to say nothing of the Pompeian frescoes, some of which, in this so-called libertine and shameless age, cannot be seen because they are considered too scandalous. Nowadays painting no longer depicts love. Now it's up to the cinema, television, and advertising. I do not know if the quantity of these images can affect sensibilities and transform them. I don't think so. Anyway, the phenomenon is not a transformation, but a transference. A transference to another means of expression.

A related phenomenon: the changing place of woman. Not man but woman leads the way. We are heading toward a form of matriarchy.
Not at all, not at all. The idea of matriarchy seems to me ridiculous. The sociologists must forgive me. Personally, I cannot be convinced that there are no biological differences between men and women. There are, and how. I don't believe the patriarchal structure of society has prevented women from developing in their own way. It is fashionable now to neglect biology and apply socioeconomic measures. But that's not enough. Reality is different. Even if it's a commonplace, the reality is that women are biologically weaker than men.

But you have treated the man-woman relationship differently: Lolita, despite everything, is much stronger than Humbert Humbert.
She's stronger only because Humbert Humbert loves her. That's all.

Do you think a love like that of Humbert Humbert and Lolita is still possible? A total abandonment to feeling?
Humbert Humbert is a villain and his case is no model. But if by this question you want to know if I believe people still fall in love and in the

same way as before, I will answer yes. You see, I have taught for a long time in universities. I know young people well, I have seen couples who loved each other, couples who broke up painfully, others who broke up painlessly, as always, as always. The young people I've known were no different in love from the way I was nor from how young people are today or will be like tomorrow. Love and sex, I repeat, are always the same.

Isn't it risky to say this? If man does not change now, how could he evolve? And it's not far from saying that man is always the same, regardless of historical context.
I do not believe that man exists, but men; and men are different from each other and the same in the essential elements that persist through time. And love is an essential element. Certainly there can be social, moral evolution, but not in love or in the feelings that can be always the same, the joys or sorrows that love can give.

But the general trend seems to be to take the pains of love less seriously. Love today seems to rest in an emotional vacuum.
I do not think this is a general trend, but a phenomenon that affects some milieux, milieux that perhaps have never taken love seriously. Certainly the bohemians of New York or London, artists living in Greenwich Village and Soho, are very casual in this regard. But their behavior is no different from that of bohemians of other eras. In other milieux, on the other hand, what has always happened continues to happen: people continue to suffer for love, to rejoice in the same way, to kill, and to kill themselves. No, I don't think we can speak of a general tendency to underplay love.

To derive an overall judgment of a phenomenon on the basis of its frequency can be superficial and presumptuous. You end up giving too much value to what is merely fashionable. And fashion is "a passing flu, an epidemic of ideas, an attack of banality that infects the herd." We cannot even speak of "our society," because we do not know its boundaries, and because it simultaneously presents contradictory and irreconcilable aspects. Society is an abstraction; only individuals exist.

115

Interview with Penelope Gilliatt
for *Vogue* (1966)[*]

Is the Queen pregnant? . . . When I saw her on television at the World Cup watching football she kept making this gesture.

He mimes smoothing a dress, and Gilliatt comments: "She always does that."
Oh, I see. A queenly movement. Permanently with child. With heir.

On the Montreux Palace
A lovely Edwardian heap.

On his body
I am six foot. I have very thin bones. The rest is flesh.
    (GILLIATT: *"He picked at his arm as if it were a jacket."*)

Gilliatt comments on Nabokov's "delicate and pure" French, which he regards as dated.
The slang goes back to Maupassant.

The Nabokovs are thinking of returning to America, to California for the climate, to the country for the language.
We were in Italy, but we don't want to live there. I don't speak Ital-

[*] "Nabokov," *Vogue*, Dec. 1966, 224–29, 279–81. Penelope Gilliatt visited VN at the Grand Hotel and Kurhaus, Bad Tarasp, in the Engadine, on Aug. 20, 1966, in advance of the publication of *Speak, Memory: An Autobiography Revisited* (copyrighted 1966, published Jan. 9, 1967). Gilliatt, a novelist, film critic, soon to become celebrated as the scenarist of the critically acclaimed film *Sunday, Bloody Sunday*, and married to the playwright John Osborne, drew all eyes when she arrived in a miniskirt, Véra reported to her friend Jane Rowohlt, wife of VN's German publisher, Heinrich Maria Ledig-Rowohlt.

ian. And the *scioperi* (strikes) . . . I don't much care for de Gaulle. I fear things will happen there when he dies. I would go to Spain, but I hate bullfights. Switzerland: lakes, charming people, stability. All my publishers pass through from one festival to another.

On his taking a spa bath in the basement of the Kurhaus
I discovered the secret of levitation. One puts the feet flat braced against the end of the bath and rises covered with bubbles like a fur. I felt like a bear. A memory of a former state.

When they order whiskey, rather early in the morning, Nabokov asks for a soda to go with his drink, which looks small.
Make the glass grow. The grass glow.

When Gilliatt sees Nabokov's notebooks of paper squared like mathematics books, she reflects, "The formal pattern that might distract most people obviously stimulates him. I could understand this: It must be a little like seeing figments in the black and white tiles in public lavatories."
Some of my best poems and chess problems have been composed in bathrooms looking at the floor.

They play anagrams, Gilliatt proposing "cart horse" (with "orchestra" as the solution), Nabokov offering "Her actors," while knowing the solution should be one word. The conversation moves to Nabokov's teaching.
I know Dublin exactly. I could draw a map of it. I know the Liffey like the Moskva. I have never been to Dublin but I know it as well as Moscow. Also, I have never been to Moscow.

Nabokov talks of his past with Véra, the possibility that they could have met in St. Petersburg, then:
Vera's coming down in a moment. She's lost something. A jacket. I think. When she loses things, it is always something very big.

He laughs at this, and then:
Vera has been doing "cart horse" as well. Eventually she suggested "horse-cart." She hadn't much hope.

On modern novels
The avant-garde French novels that I've read don't stir my artistic
appetite. Only here and there. Even Shaw can do that.

Genet?
An interesting fairyland with good measurements.

Ostrovsky?
[He has] a streak of poetry that he unfortunately put down because he
was so intent on writing about the merchant class.

On the Russian translation of Lolita, *about to be published in New York*
To be smuggled in,[1] dropped by parachute, floating down on the blurb.

On hospitals
In Massachusetts once I was ill with food poisoning. I was being
wheeled along a corridor. They left the trolley by a bookcase and I drew
out a big medical dictionary and in the ward I drew the curtains around
myself and read. It wasn't allowed because it looked as if I were dying.
They took the book away. In hospitals there is still something of the
eighteenth-century madhouse.

Pasternak?
Doctor Zhivago is false, melodramatic, badly written. It is false to history
and false to art. The people are dummies. That awful girl is absurd. It
reminds me very much of novels written by Russians, of, I am ashamed
to say, the gentler sex. Pasternak is not a bad poet. But in *Zhivago* he
is vulgar. Simple. If you take his beautiful metaphors there is nothing behind them. Even in his poems: what is that line, Véra? "To be a
woman is a big step." It is ridiculous.

   This kind of thing recurs. Very typical of poems written in the Soviet
era. A person of Zhivago's class and his set, he wouldn't stand in the
snow and read about the Bolshevist regime and feel a tremendous glow.
There was a *liberal* revolution at that time. Kerensky. If Kerensky had
had more luck—but he was a liberal, you see, and he couldn't just clap
the Bolsheviks into jail. It was not done. He was a very average man,
I should say. The kind of person you might find in the Cabinet of any

democratic country. He spoke very well, with his hand in his bosom like Napoleon, because it had almost been broken by handshakes.

Yet people like Edmund Wilson and Isaiah Berlin, they have to love *Zhivago* to prove that good writing can come out of Soviet Russia. They ignore that it is really a *bad book*. There are some absolutely ridiculous scenes. Scenes of eavesdropping for instance. You know about eavesdropping. If it is not brought in as parody it is almost philistine. It is the mark of the amateur in literature. And that marvelous scene where he had to get rid of the little girl to let the characters make love, and he sends her out skating. In *Siberia*. To keep warm they give her her mother's *scarf*. And then she sleeps deeply in a hut while there is all this going on. Obviously Pasternak just didn't know what to do with her. He's like Galsworthy. Galsworthy in one of his novels gave a character a cane and a dog and simply didn't know how to get rid of them.

And the metaphors. Unattached comparisons. Suppose I were to say "as passionately adored and insulted as a barometer in a mountain hotel" *(he said, looking out at the rain)*, it would be a beautiful metaphor. But who is it about? The image is top-heavy. There is nothing to attach it to. And there is a pseudo-religious strain in the book which almost shocks me. *Zhivago* is so feminine that I sometimes wonder if it might have been partly written by Pasternak's mistress.

As a translator of Shakespeare he is very poor. He is considered great only by people who don't know Russian. An example. *(His wife helped him to remember a line of a Pasternak translation.)* What he has turned it into in Russian is this: "all covered with grease and keeps wiping the pig-iron." You see. It is ridiculous. What would be the original?

GILLIATT: *"Greasy Joan doth keel the pot?"*[2]

Yes. "Keeps wiping the pig-iron"!

Pasternak himself has been very much *helped* by translation. Sometimes when you translate a cliché—you know, a cloud has a silver lining—it can sound like Milton because it is in another language.

VÉRA: *"Isn't that what happened to Pushkin?"*

He had translated the French writers of his day. The small coin of drawing-room poets and the slightly larger coin of Racine. In Russian it became breathtaking.

Out driving with Véra, while Nabokov jibes about the sheer drops where she has sometimes chosen to turn
Sometimes my son wishes I wouldn't joke so much.

After a long wait for a waitress "who had seemed not to have heard the order," he says peacefully:
I can tell by the nape of her neck that the cakes are coming.

Gilliatt asks him whether Lolita would have turned into a boy if his own real child had been a girl.
Oh, yes. If I had had a daughter Humbert Humbert would have been a pederast.

On the origin of Lolita
I had written a short story with the same idea as *Lolita*. The man's name there is Arthur. They travel through France. I never published it. The little girl wasn't alive. She hardly spoke. Little by little[3] I managed to give her some semblance of reality. I was on my way to the incinerator one day with half the manuscript to burn it, and Véra said wait a minute. And I came back meekly.

 "I don't remember that. Did I?" said Mrs. Nabokov.

 What was most difficult was putting myself. . . . I am a normal man, you see. I traveled in school buses to listen to the talk of schoolgirls. I went to school on the pretext of placing our daughter. We have no daughter. For Lolita I took one arm of a little girl who used to come to see Dmitri, one kneecap of another.

Nabokov's translation of Alice's Adventures in Wonderland?
I always call him Lewis Carroll Carroll, because he was the first Humbert Humbert. Have you seen those photographs of him with little girls? He would make arrangements with aunts and mothers to take the children out. He was never caught, except by one girl who wrote about him when she was much older.

Lolita *again*
was a great pleasure to write, but it was also very painful. I had to read so many case histories.

116

Interview with Dieter E. Zimmer
for Norddeutscher Rundfunk (1966)[*]

From 1922 to 1937, I believe, judging from the way you describe Germany and Germans in your early books, your impressions became more and more sinister. In your book on Gogol, written toward the end of the last world war, you said that what you term poshlost'—*bad taste, triviality, smugness, kitsch—forms an essential part of the German national spirit, and also that one would like to see Germany destroyed to the last beer mug and forget-me-not. Have you had any reason to change your opinion?*

I am not overfond of my flippant little book on Gogol, written hastily more than twenty years ago, but the particular passage you mention is not quite as flippant as it seems when quoted out of context. Let me restore the beginning of the paragraph: "To exaggerate the worthlessness of a country at the awkward moment when one is at war with it and would like to see it destroyed to the last beer mug and the last forget-me-not means walking dangerously close to that abyss of *poshlost'* which yawns so universally at times of revolution or war." After all, the Japanese also yearned for the destruction of America down to the last peanut and the last pinup. In that chapter I speak of the *amo et odi*[1] emotions with which Russia as a nation viewed Germany as a nation. My personal attitude toward Germany is more complicated than that. Two facts should be taken into account: First, that I lived and wrote in Germany during precisely those years when not only my own impressions

[*] "Despot in meiner Welt" ("Despot in My World"), Norddeutscher Rundfunk (Hamburg) television interview, broadcast Oct. 21, 1966, 3rd Program, "Aus Kunst und Wissenschaft." Typescript questions in English, Dieter Zilligen (and Dieter E. Zimmer) sent to Véra Nabokov, Sept. 30, 1966, VN index-card typescript answers in English, dated Oct. 5, 1966, VNA Berg, the day of filming in Montreux; published in feuilleton, *Die Zeit*, Nov. 1, 1966, 9; collected in Dieter E. Zimmer, ed., *Eigensinnige Ansichten*, vol. 21 of VN, *Gesammelte Werke* (Reinbek bei Hamburg: Rowohlt, 2004). Dieter Zimmer had already become VN's main translator into German, and had compiled the first comprehensive bibliography of his writings.

but also those of my German friends, and in fact history itself, became, as you put it, "more and more sinister," until the cruel kitsch they and I loathed developed into a regime which for sheer sinister vulgarity is only matched by the Russia of the Soviet era. This is one thing to be noted; the other is that on my paternal grandmother's side I can trace my ancestry back not only to Baltic barons but to a famous composer in Saxony and to a distinguished book publisher in Königsberg, and way back to an obscure church organist at Plauen, near Warenbrück, in the sixteenth century, and no doubt to many an amateur *Schmetterlingfän-ger*[2] who may have had beer mugs on his shelf and forget-me-nots in his album. I would like to add that, in the light of what looks in retrospect as a dismissal of German culture in a bitter footnote, I feel some embarrassment when confronted today with a third fact—namely, that in the postwar era German critics have understood and appreciated my books with unusual subtlety and artistry.

Have you been to Germany since the war?
I have not been to Germany since I left it in 1937.

Do you intend ever to go there again?
No, I shall never go there again, just as I shall never go back to Russia.

And why not?
As long as I am still alive there may be brutes still alive who have tortured and murdered the helpless and the innocent. How can I know the abyss in the past of my coeval—the good-natured stranger whose hand I happen to clasp?

What have you done to wield the English language to your purpose?
Although the actual switch from one vocabulary to another was agony, I should explain that I had known English since infancy, and had learned to spell English before I could write Russian.

Do you miss your native Russian idiom?
Of course, I miss Russian. On the other hand, Russian is the language I speak with my wife and son, and as late as 1960 I was still able to compose Russian poetry.

Is it true that you are translating Lolita *into Russian, though for the time being there is no chance of having it published in Russia?*

I completed my Russian translation of *Lolita* about a year ago. It was not easy to find a Russian typist, and when I did, she took a long time typing it. It will soon be published in New York by Phaedra and smuggled to Russia, I hope. My Russian may be somewhat rusty, but only in comparison with my own Russian of, say, thirty years ago. My main object in setting myself that difficult task was to thwart the hack who might have mutilated *Lolita* in a future Russian version. Apart from a number of inner creative difficulties—problems of style and tone—I had to cope with the foreign flavor of the book. I had great trouble translating technical terms, names of everyday items in America, referring to automobiles, motels, clothes. Per contra, I did not find it too difficult to render the wordplay and the literary allusions, many of which had to be reinvented.

You are now an American citizen, but for some years you have been living in Swiss hotels. Do you prefer Europe after all? Why?

I live in Europe for certain family reasons. I have chosen Switzerland because it is an especially charming and comfortable country. There are fascinating butterflies in the mountains. Collecting in the Simplon region or the Grisons is a marvelous pleasure, and some of those renowned localities—Pontresina, Zermatt, Laquinthal, the Rhone Valley—are classical haunts that still yield unexpected discoveries despite the generations of English and German collectors who roamed there in the past.

Do you want to go back to America and to teaching again?

America is my real home, and I shall return to live there in a year or two. I am not sure if I shall teach there, but I shall probably want to live near a university library.

Would you ever want to settle down someplace?

Yes, my wife and I imagine very clearly the quiet sunny spot in America where we would like to settle down. But I also intend to collect butterflies in Peru or Iran before I pupate.

Have you ever wondered what sort of writer you would have become if the revolution had not driven you out of Russia?

It is an amusing vision. But even so I would not have stayed at home much. We should remember that, unless forcibly restrained by the government, practically all Russian writers traveled abroad frequently and extensively, especially to Switzerland, Germany, France, and Italy. The hazy blue lake view I admire from my window today was admired by Zhukovsky, Karamzin, Tyutchev, Gogol, Tolstoy, many others. Had the revolution not happened the way it happened, I would have enjoyed a landed gentleman's leisure, no doubt, but I also think that my entomological occupations would have been more engrossing and energetic and that I would have gone on long collecting trips to Asia. I would have had a private museum, and a large library comfortably housed.

What books would you have written if you had been allowed to lead a nice and safe and quiet life in a peaceful Russia?

I am quite sure that my books would have displeased the same kind of people that they irritate nowadays, and I cannot imagine the Russian government that would have fully approved of them. Certainly, in questions of censorship, America is the most comfortable country for a writer to live in.

You had written eleven novels and many stories and poems when Lolita *appeared in 1955, suddenly establishing your worldwide reputation. Did you expect this attention?*

Frankly, I seldom examine the illusion of my reputation and success. When writing *Lolita*, which took me half a dozen years, I did not bother to think of my work as receiving or not receiving attention. Indifference to adverse criticism may not be exactly a form of modesty but it is good for one's health. I dimly envisaged a very limited and obscure sale. I allowed the possibility of a fourth good reader joining eventually our little group: my wife, my son, and me. I did not exclude a complete understanding on the part of the entire reading planet. But that is as far as I probed *Lolita*'s future.

You do not care, I believe, to be put into one line with various other taboo-breakers in literature. When writing Lolita *it was not your intention to extend the area of the permissible or to accomplish any social function of this sort—or was it?*

I am not concerned with taboos or taboo breaking. I write what I like and some like what I write—that about sums it up.

Where would you draw the line between straight political or sociological literature and your own type of work?

I leave this unprofitable task entirely in the hands of such critics as are more excited by politics and sociology than I am.

What makes literature worthwhile?

Talent, inspiration, invention, and the mysterious gift of seeing beyond the horizon of things and through the texture of things just a little further than do the users of things.

You are today known not only as a writer, you are also an entomologist, a lepidopterist of renown. Do you see any connection between your butterflies and your words?

Let us not exaggerate: actual publication of scientific papers is limited in my case to one hectic decade, roughly from 1940 to 1950, when I tackled relatively narrow problems in lepidopterology.

Do the two occupations afford you some similar form of contentment?

I confess that my passion for entomological research, in the field, in the laboratory, in the library, is even more pleasurable than the study and practice of literature—which is saying a good deal. In that decade I have reworked the classification of various groups of butterflies, have described and figured several new species and subspecies. My names for the microscopic organs that I have been the first to see and portray have safely found their way into biological lexicons. The tactile delights of precise delineation, the silent paradise of the camera lucida, and the precision of poetry in taxonomic description represent the artistic side of the thrill which the accumulation of new knowledge—knowledge useless to the layman—gave me in the course of that occupation.

How do you go about planning and writing a novel?

There is no special planning. The novel is engendered in one flush of conception. The next stage, however, is often a physically exhausting one. In my twenties and early thirties, in furnished rooms in Berlin (Motzstrasse, Passauerstrasse, Leopoldstrasse, Nestorstrasse, and other streets where I lived in those days), I used to write dipping pen in ink and using a new nib every other day in exercise books, crossing out, inserting, striking out again, crumpling the page, rewriting it three or four times, then copying out everything in a different ink and a neater hand, then recopying it with new corrections, and finally dictating it to my wife, who has typed out all my stuff. I'm a slow writer, a snail carrying its house at the rate of two hundred pages of final copy per year. In those days and nights I generally followed the order of chapters when writing a novel, but even so, from the very first, I relied heavily on mental composition, constructing whole paragraphs in my head as I walked in the streets or sat in my bath or lay in bed. In the late thirties I switched to another, physically more practical method: that of writing with an eraser-capped pencil on index cards. Since I always have at the very start a curiously clear preview of the entire novel before me, I find cards especially convenient when not following the logical sequence of chapters but preparing passages at any point and filling in the gaps in no special order.

The whole book is in your mind before you begin?
I don't wish to get mixed up with Plato, whom I do not care for, but I do think that in this case it is true that the entire book, before it is actually on paper, seems to be ready ideally in some other, now transparent, now dimming, dimension, and my job is to take down as much of it as I can make out, and as precisely as humanly possible.

What exactly is ready: the outline, scenes and pictures, even verbal formulations?
Oh, everything. The greatest happiness in composing is when I feel that I cannot understand, without presupposing an already existing creation, how or why that image or structural move, or the exact formulation of a phrase, has just come to me.

Does a book take a different turn than you expected?
I have never had that experience. Novelists who have must be very minor or insane. No, the design of the book is fixed in my imagination, and every character follows the course I imagined for him. There is no parliament, no representatives of the people in an artist's imagination. I

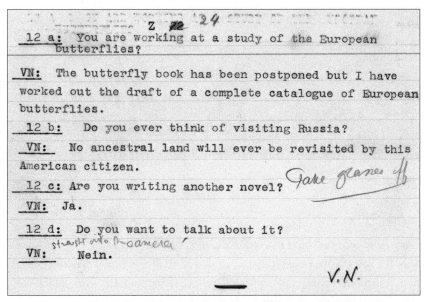

Typed index-card questions, by Dieter E. Zimmer, and answers by Nabokov for a 1966 television interview for Norddeutscher Rundfunk. Nabokov stages the dramatic and comic ending, his last two answers suddenly switching from English to German, opening up the prospect of a dramatic revelation only to close it down with his final word.

am the perfect despot in that private world insofar as I alone am responsible for its stability and its truth. Whether I reproduce it as fully and faithfully as I would wish, is another question. Some of my old works reveal dismal blurrings and blanks.

You are working on a comprehensive study of the European butterflies?
The butterfly book has been postponed, but I have worked out the draft of a complete catalogue of European butterflies.

Do you ever think of visiting Russia?
No ancestral land will ever be revisited by this American citizen.

Are you writing another novel? [VN note to himself: Take glasses off]
Ja.

Do you want to talk about it? [VN note to himself: Straight into the camera]
Nein.

Interview with Pat Garian
for German *Harper's Bazaar* (1967)*

How long have you been interested in entomological research?
Oh, let me think, I was eleven, no, I was twelve when I wrote my first article on butterflies. In English. I sent it to a specialist journal in London, but it was never published. *(Laughs)* Fortunately.

Do you speak German?
I know a little German. I've never really learned it, because I was afraid I'd lose my Russian. But my grandmother was a Baltic German. Do you know how Balts speak? *(He concentrates for a minute and then gives a perfect parody of the long-drawn-out expression of his grandmother:)* "Aber bittä scheen mit doppelten Tiieren . . ."[1]

* "Vladimir Nabokov," *Harper's Bazaar (Deutsche Ausgabe)*, March 1967, 42–43. In German.

Interview with Drago Arsenijevic
for *La Tribune de Genève* (1967)[*]

On Montreux

It's a town I love dearly, and for many reasons: it's beautiful, welcoming, and good to work in, and in fact the action of a part of my new book takes place in this area. My wife and I love walking. The arrangement of the flowers along the path from Territet to Clarens is the work of an artist. I like thinking of all the English and Russian poets and prose writers who went walking here, leaving the imprint of their imagination on the scenery after having drawn on it themselves. But let me add that it would be very sad if this delightful area began to be spoiled. It's perhaps useless to protest against the noise in our narrow streets, but really the trucks—immense, double, triple, sometimes transporting a whole forest or a landslide, these grotesque and dangerous monsters—there needs to be (it's my nerves talking) a special tunnel made for them under the road or the lake. And, besides, people drive too fast through the town, far faster than through American towns, where there are more policemen, inexorable judges of speed.

Something else: I was speaking of this to Henri Jaton on Radio Romande, four years ago. It's the question of milk. Oh, it's not the quality that's at issue, it's always excellent. But why isn't it sold anymore in bottles, but in cartons of a more or less pyramid shape? That's perhaps very good as a masterpiece of abstract art, this sharp-pointed breast, this female pharaoh's mammary. But, to handle this rickety contraption with

---

[*] "Vladimir Nabokov n'aime pas qu'on l'appelle 'le père de Lolita'" ("Vladimir Nabokov Does Not Like Being Called 'Lolita's Father'"), *La Tribune de Genève*, suppl., *Tribune Arts/ Jeunes*, Oct. 25, 1967, 1. Emended typescript with VN's manuscript corrections, Sept. 23, 1967, VNA Berg.

a multisided surface and a secret elasticity, one should live in a world
of four or five dimensions, a space on an inclined plane. I'm told that
bottles are difficult to wash, but they've been washed for centuries, since
we've been mammals.

On the local birdlife

I especially like the choughs which come for the winter from the high
mountains. *Coracia graculus* in Latin, Alpine Chough in English, *alpiy-
skaya klushitsa* in Russian. With their black plumage and their pointed
yellow beaks, they resemble a croaking and comical cross between a
crow and a blackbird. At dawn I hear their wet whistles on the hotel's
balconies. On sunny days, they execute magnificent maneuvers, aerial
acrobatics in the grand style. Then, at sunset, they pass like a whirlwind
of crows to swoop down, for the night, on the poplars on the shore.

It's in the cold season, too, that the lake tribe is very visible. My
favorite creature there is the biggest of the three or four grebes, the
crested grebe, *khokhlataya chomga* in Russian. I like to see a couple of
these birds face one another like two closed parentheses, shaking their
fine bronzed tufts with a jerk like a dog tormented by a freakish collar.
There's nothing more amusing in the aquatic line than the way a grebe
begins to sink, affecting a certain sad dignity, before diving, suddenly,
in a quick agile somersault, showing its fish-glossy belly. I also like the
common coot, which Montreusiens misname the *poule d'eau* (moorhen),
its cousin. Its head shake when it swims is as funny as the white flanks
of the black duck, called tufted duck, which swims carrying under its
arms one of those long flat cartons they sell ties in.

I'm fairly indifferent to our *rieuses* [black-headed gulls], which wear
black masks for the annual ball, and whose droppings are their thanks
for the alms they're given. And I detest the yellow plush on the dirty
neck of our mute and unpleasant swan, which carries one of its rubber
feet across its back when it glides on the water with a perfectly classic
banality.

On his Russian fiction

My Russian novels published in Berlin or Paris circulated only among
émigré readers, and the success I enjoyed was international only insofar
as my readers were scattered in every country of the world—including

some clandestine and courageous readers in the depths of Russia, where a few copies of my books have sneaked in.

On sales
I confess I wasn't interested in commercial success, that's to say, I have never sought to push my books, although I am enchanted to be well paid.

On his new book
It's almost five years that I have been working on the most arduous and audacious novel I have ever attempted: *Ada or Ardor*.

119

Interview with Pierre Dommergues
for *Les Langues Modernes* (1967–68)[*]

On Nabokov's image, in his autobiography, of his life as a colored three-stage spiral: the thesis, his Russian years; the antithesis, his émigré years; the synthesis, his American years

First of all, forgive me if I express myself slowly in French. I know three languages fairly well—English, Russian, and French—but I speak them all with difficulty and cautiously. François Condorcet, who shouldn't be confused with Charles, said, "An honest man should know only one language, his own." That poor man knew thirty-four! But never mind. You ask about my multicolored spiral. This description of my personal triad is a stylistic effect, a paragraph composed with care but with little meaning outside the book into which I put it and where it has to remain to live.

What was the place of French literature in your adolescence?

Several Russian authors of the nineteenth century belonging to the privileged class, from Pushkin to Tolstoy, underwent the profound influence of French literature and culture, which their French tutors crammed them with. Others, like Gogol and Chekhov, never learned French, but nevertheless you find in them secondary currents transmitted by imitations and translations from French to Russian. On the other hand, English was less in fashion than French: neither Pushkin nor Tolstoy knew it well. All of Shakespeare, all of Walter Scott, all of Byron, all of Richardson was read in flat French paraphrases. I'm more fortunate,

[*] "Entretien avec Vladimir Nabokov" ("Conversation with Vladimir Nabokov"), *Les Langues modernes* 62, no. 1 (Jan.–Feb. 1968), 92–100. Conducted in Nov. 1967 or earlier; part of the interview was published in *Le Monde* on Nov. 22, 1967.

since from my tender infancy I had not only a French governess but also several English governesses. At twelve, I had read Shakespeare's tragedies in the original, as I had the prose of Flaubert and the poetry of Rimbaud. No surprise that some of my Russian readers accuse me, not without indignation or even disgust, of being too Western in my writing. These same imbeciles think that I devote myself to butterflies, to entomology, out of snobbery. I am a tricolor Russian, an American brought up in England, a St. Petersburger with a Parisian burr in Russian but who, in French, rolls my "R"s in the Russian manner.

In your Lolita *afterword, you write that it took you forty years to invent Russian and Western Europe and that now you had to invent America. What was the process of this invention, what were the American ingredients?*
This has nothing to do with what is called "realism." What is called "realism" seems to me to be a certain average of impressions perceived by an average brain, an apparatus which by the way doesn't exist outside statistics. There's nothing more abstract and fuzzy than so-called realism. . . . The word "reality" is the most dangerous there is. . . . The reality of art? It's an artificial reality, a created reality, which remains reality only in the novel. I don't believe that there's an objective reality. But the combinations that the artist invents give or should give the reader the feeling not of average reality, but of a new reality distinctive to the work. The world of its invention remains the secret of its creator. The inscription over the door of my workshop said "No entry" when I was working on *Lolita*. Today this door is wide open, but the workshop is dismantled, the workers are gone, the tools vanished, a little golden dust floats in a slanting ray of light, that's all.

You have been an American citizen since 1945. What is your connection with America?
Yes, I admit it, I adore America. It's the only country I have been in where I'm perfectly happy, where I'm right at home. . . . I don't know why. But I've met people there, I've lived in an atmosphere which corresponded perfectly to what I consider the benign, the happy life for a writer. But it's not only the intellectuals, but the man who takes my suitcase—in fact everybody, people of all classes, of all races. . . . I feel a sensation of warmth and pride when I show my green American pass-

port at the borders of Europe. The gross criticism of America shocks me deeply. I am for an antisegregationist policy. In foreign policy, I am firmly on the government's side. And when I'm unsure, I choose the method of choosing the political line least favorable to the Reds and the Russells.[1]

How does your stay in Montreux fit into this colored spiral of three times?
For several years now, we have been living in Montreux. My life there is very regular, but full of action. I can give you an idea of my day. I get up early, about 7:00 a.m., swallow a glass of fruit juice, put on my monastic bathrobe, and go to the lectern to write. Victor Hugo and Flaubert also wrote standing up, believing—wrongly, it seems—that the thunderbolt of a stroke hits the vertical writer more rarely than in any other position. After an hour or two of work, I eat a very modest breakfast, a bowl of cornflakes, a cup of coffee without sugar, and my wife reads me my mail, often amusing, always voluminous—after which I get back to my desk. About eleven, I shave and have my bath. We often lunch in town. At two, work resumes, but generally I leave the lectern in the afternoon to settle down with my index cards in an armchair. We have dinner at seven. I go to bed at nine and fall asleep at once, like a child. At midnight, I wake up in a state of infernal twitchiness in a desert of insomnia, and then the dramatic dilemma starts: to take or not to take a sleeping pill. As you see, it's a very agitated life.

In summer it's quieter. My wife and I travel in search of butterflies. I love mountains, in Switzerland, in Italy, and in the south of France. I like to stay a thousand meters up and climb to two thousand meters to hunt alpine butterflies. I know few things more delightful than to go out early in the morning with my hunting net and to climb in the chairlift toward a cloudless sky, all the while watching under me, off to the side, the shadow of the aerial chair with my seated silhouette, the shadow of my net in my fist, gliding along the slope, undulating under the alders, still climbing, slender, supple, rejuvenated and stylized by the effect of the projection, climbing gracefully in an almost mythological ascension. The return isn't so pretty, because the sun has changed position, and you can see the shade stunted, you can see two big knees, everything is changed. The perspective of the net is changed, so I don't look any longer.

Your aversion to "ideologies" and "-isms" is well known. But isn't there a dif-
ference between "idea" and ideology? Isn't there a recognition, even if ironic,
of the idea in your sarcasm?

Let's take specific examples. What can be more lugubrious than the
political novel, the sociological novel—for example, by people like
Émile Zola. It's unreadable, the propaganda novel. Most American
writers today are of great interest to the historian, but hardly from the
literary point of view. Most of them are of stupefying mediocrity. I don't
want to malign my contemporaries; I'm saying this under the mask of
anonymity. Current events, fashion, grand feelings don't make great
books. Nevertheless, I maintain that the percentage of, say, a dozen
good writers among these forty mortals[2] surpasses the lamentably low
level one finds today in England or in France.

What part does perception play in your work? And could you say more about
what you mean by "colored hearing"?

Children very often have this capacity to see and hear letters as shades
of color. Sometimes infinitely subtle shades. But when a child says
this at school or at home, he's given a smack or told he's stupid. That
a "B" can be red, or a "C" black, means nothing, so don't think about
it anymore—and the sensation vanishes and it's gone forever. When
I spoke of these things to my mother, she told me: "I have that, too."
"So tell me, what's your A like?" "It's black, or blackish, it's a little like
ebony." "Mine is reddish. . . ." The "N" is a neutral color, a whitish color,
with a little gray perhaps. If I had a brush, I could do this in colors. That
would be interesting, a painting of my auditory colors.[3]

Your novels are peopled by spies and the spied-on; most of your characters in
fact are one or the other or both. Do you see a link between the artist and the
voyeur, the artist and the spy?

I don't like this term "voyeur," which has too much sexual resonance,
even if it's the ample and profound title of one of the finest novels of
our time.[4] As for my spying characters, yes, they spy. What can I do
about it? They're made like that, I made them like that. The only link
between the artist and the spy, it seems to me, is that both observe
things and people and know the importance of detail: detail, that's
everything.

What's the link between memory and imagination?
I think memory and imagination belong to the same rather mysterious world of human thought. It seems to me that someone without much imagination also has a poor memory. The child who imagines nothing while playing in the corridors of a castle will remember the castle only very vaguely. There is something in the imagination that connects to memory, and vice versa. Memory could be said to be a sort of imagination concentrated on a certain point. . . . When you remember a thing, you never remember the thing itself, you remember the relation, the association of the thing with something else. And it's the imagination that makes this link between things.

What connection do you see between chess and the work of art?
There's no connection between literature and the game of chess. But there's certainly a connection between the art of literature and the art of chess problems. Problems and games are two different things. It's not easy to speak of these two things, because not everybody, not even all chess players, can appreciate the difference between the game of chess, which is journalism, and the chess problem, which is poetry.

The link between the composition of a chess problem and that of a novel lies in the originality of the combinations and the economy of their realization.

It's a magnificent, complex, and sterile art, akin to the ordinary form of the game only to the extent, for example, that a juggler, in inventing the interlacings of a new sleight-of-hand trick, draws on something in the properties of a sphere. In fact, most chess players, masters and amateurs, take only a moderate interest in these refined enigmas, purely invented and requiring great specialization, and although they appreciate a problem with a trap inside, they would be absolutely disconcerted if they were asked to compose one.

In common there are themes, stratagems, ambushes, sacrifices, pinning and unpinning, and all sorts of maneuvers, but combined in a certain way. Because it's the combination of the different themes that makes a problem. Deceit pushed to the point of diabolism. In this sense, I think one can find a certain parallelism between the chess problem and the problem of literary compositions.

And on the level of characters' strategies?
No, that's something else. This is becoming allegory. One thinks of those chess figurines.

Is your treatment of time and space linked to the handling of pawns on the chessboard?
There is no time on the chessboard. Time replaced by a bottomless space . . .

The knight jumps a square. But if, for example, it is at one side of the chessboard, then one wonders why it can't jump from the other side, in the space beyond the chessboard. I have myself thought up problems which incorporate the possibility of a knight who flies off and then who comes back from that space.

Is chess strategy visual?
When a chess problem comes into my mind I don't see the chessboard, I don't see squares as they are, I see perhaps little abysses, not holes, but different tensions, positive, negative. It's not a question of form. It seems to me that in literary art there's no privileged form, at the compositional level. One could speak of a spiral, of a certain structure, but these are metaphors.

In terms of form, it would be, rather, "anything goes," everything works, doesn't it, all is allowed. I always have an interesting combination, complicated and with a certain form, but not each part of the combination.

*Don't you find that the English title of your memoirs (*Speak, Memory*) is more revealing than the French?*
Autres rivages (*Other Shores*) is also the Russian form of the title—because I've also done the book in Russian—and it's a phrase of Pushkin that talks of other shades, other waves.

But I think that *Autres rivages* works quite well. There was a third title, *Conclusive Evidence*, which I like because there are two "V"s, my "V" and that of my wife, Véra, juxtaposed there, but no one understood that.

What is the link between the work and the reader?
I see it every morning when I shave. The only true reader, the best
reader, the model reader, is the author of the book. It is true that sometimes the author knows people, friends who—he knows—are going to
understand his book, people for whom it's worth the trouble of writing.
I know perhaps a dozen, thirteen people who read my books almost as
well as I do. But note that if these charming readers didn't exist, I would
still write all the same in full confidence, with utter good cheer, because
I can always easily invent as many readers as I want.

*French readers are fascinated by the use of language in your work. Is a preoc-
cupation with language essential to you?*
I let words play. I allow them to gambol with each other. Some of my
characters have fun catching a phrase unawares, because one could
define a pun as two words caught *in flagrante*. The inversion of syllables
charms and excites my characters more than me. The English are more
devoted to puns than Americans. I often see in the literary supplements
of London newspapers punning titles that an American publisher would
find disgustingly vulgar.

*Doesn't the fact of moving from one language to another predispose a writer
to linguistic exploration? I'm thinking of Conrad and Beckett in particular.*
I don't accept this comparison that you have introduced. I haven't read
the plays of Samuel Beckett—I think he has written plays, hasn't he?—
but I've been shown recently two or three little poems he has written
in French—and it's bad Verlaine, completely banal and false. The case
of Conrad is perhaps more interesting. He worked hard on a language
he didn't know. I think he spoke French better than English when he
started writing. But I detest his books, his books say nothing to me.
When I was a child I would read them, because they are books for
children, they swarm with clichés, it's unendingly romantic, the style,
the structure in French is that of Pierre Loti.

*Isn't there a comic "character" in your work? I think of Charlie Chaplin,
and the scene in* Pnin *where the old émigré, unable to get used to the modern
world, suddenly falls in love with a washing machine. He puts a tennis shoe
in the machine, from which it comes out as if this had happened in a Charlie
Chaplin film.*

Pnin has absolutely nothing Chaplinesque. A movie agent must have invented this. Chaplin is as good as Laurel and Hardy or Buster Keaton. But in terms of ideas, his genre has absolutely nothing to do with the comic art of literature, which is infinitely more complex than the art of the most refined clown.

Perhaps it's right to say that I am very aware of the comic side of politics. Dictators are the buffoons of history. Mao, Nasser, Hitler, the bearded Cuban whose name escapes me, the melancholic Kosygin, the formulaic style of Lenin's writings, all that is as grotesque as those staged triumphs and those fools paid to applaud. Politics perhaps isn't my forte, but I am practiced in the science of destiny. I can therefore predict that one fine day Russia and China, united in evil, will try to invade the West, and that once again America will save Europe by freeing France, and in that sense one could really cry out: Long live free France!

Monsieur Nabokov, you are becoming a propagandist. Can you say, to conclude, why you write?
It's a hard question to reply to. But I think I write to amuse myself. Pushkin liked to say, "One writes for oneself and publishes to earn a living." That's my situation. The aesthetic bliss I speak of in *Lolita* I could have found elsewhere. I see myself, for example, as a painter. I see myself very clearly inventing landscapes, combining mirages and mirrors. On the other hand, I think sometimes how sweet it would be to be an entomologist, an obscure museum conservator somewhere in America, five or six hundred dollars a month, impassioned discoveries, scientific quarrels, the radiant silence at the bottom of the microscope.

120

Interview with Alden Whitman
for *New York Times* (1969)[*]

You will be seventy in a few days. How will you celebrate your birthday?
Yes, April 23, Shakespeare's birthday and mine. On the eve of that day my wife and I shall, I trust, have set out aboard an Italian liner for New York from Genoa. We shall stand on the deck and toast with champagne the glittering *grálitsa*—a beautiful Russian word for the ripply reflection of a celestial body setting or rising over a vast expanse of water. [*Crossed out in VN's manuscript, with note:* "Trip cancelled."]

Although you have written two "autobiographies," you seem not to be very revealing of your private self. Indeed, Ivan Bunin, I believe, once said to you, "You will die in dreadful pain and complete isolation." He had reference, I am told, to a widespread impression that you have never been too close to anybody. Why have you considered your private self out of place?
One is often tempted to ask an opulent-looking stranger how much money he has in the bank; but he mumbles evasively. It is quite true that acquaintances do not know the exact contents of my private self's secret safe. The very few friends who do will not talk. Bunin was not a close friend of mine.

[*] Part published in "Nabokov, Nearing 70, Describes his 'New Girl,'" *New York Times*, April 19, 1969, 20. Emended typescript with VN's manuscript corrections, April 1969, VNA Berg. Anticipating VN's impending seventieth birthday, April 23, 1969, and the publication of *Ada*, May 5, 1969, Whitman sent questions which VN received on March 28. VN had a "merry" interview with Whitman on April 16, and was disappointed that "only two or three of my answers" were retained in *The New York Times* (*SO*, 131). He therefore published some of the omitted answers in *Strong Opinions* in 1973.

You have written under several pseudonyms. What is the significance of this?
Using various pseudonyms is quite in the tradition of Russian literature
since the beginning of last century. In fact, it might be curious to compare the number of entries in the encyclopedia of Russian pen names
past and present, with a list of American ones. My father's first name
was also Vladimir, and I did not wish to embarrass him by signing my
elegies with the same name. My main pseudonym, Sirin, thrived from
1920 to 1940, that is up to the date of what was to me the American
Revelation. Occasionally I used the little silk mask of an additional pen
name in order to deceive this or that captious critic—with most gratifying results ("At last a great writer!" cried my favorite Zoilus, the late
Georgiy Adamovich, in 1939).

Your new book?
I have no doubt that my new girl will be seen as a literary littermate
of *Lolita*.

    Ada is a leisurely, ample old-fashioned family chronicle some 600
pages long. A childhood romance between closely related Van Veen and
Ada Veen in an unspoiled part of New England develops into a lifelong
obsession with tragic interludes, reckless trysts and a rapturous end in
the 10th decade of their cosmopolitan existence.

    The noble and wealthy Veen clan—it's an Irish name—includes
bizarre parents and a pathetically charming half-sister, Lucette Veen.
This clan blends Irish and Russian blood. This is not uncommon in
the world of the novel, in which some accident in space-time allows
remnants of Russia to sprawl happily over most of Canada under our
Stars and Stripes, leaving Europe to the Union Jack and Tartary to her
dreary mysteries behind a golden curtain.

    The crucial chapter in *Ada* is the penultimate part of the book,
entirely concerned with an exploration—a scholarly exploration—of
the texture of time mainly by means of metaphors. The two leading
characters die. Indeed, they die away to a built-in blurb with a sort of
perdendosi effect . . . a musical term meaning to get lost, to die off.

And what about Lolita? *How do you view it?*
With unalterable tenderness. She was horribly distasteful to imagine,
and beautifully difficult to make. I shall never forget her. Though I was

careful to have French-born Humbert start his story with a lesson of pronunciation, English-speaking people, I note, pronounce her name incorrectly. Each "l" in it should be a delicate dental Latin caress—not a fat British or American snail curling up and clinging to the palate. I remember the pure shock of delight when I heard my old friend the Spanish poet, Jorge Guillén, pronounce: Lolita. Pity old Humbert was not there to share the thrill.

Why have you chosen, in many stories, to create characters preoccupied with their pasts, often touched off by a death?
My creatures are not more preoccupied with the past than any other novelist's creatures. Most of mine (I say most because, for instance, the man in *Invitation to a Beheading* triumphantly transcends the scaffold) must die someday one way or another. Generally speaking, the immortality of a fictional character admits of two interpretations, e.g. he is a non-mortal young rabbi; and he represents a deathless old myth.

Protest movements?
My protest against protesters in America and elsewhere is that the greatest conformists and philistines are young people, especially hippies and their group beards and their group protests. For me they are squares. I think all young people are conservatives—even if they are revolutionaries. It is the ripe man who knows what a revolution is—who changes things. You have to know the world before you can change it.

Have you read Portnoy's Complaint?
It is a ridiculous book. It has no literary worth whatever. It is so obvious and not at all funny—a ridiculous book.

Your next novel?
I see a kind of pre-dawn gleam in the gloaming.

121

Interview with Roberto Tabozzi
for *Panorama* (1969)[*]

A definite autobiographical factor comes out in all your works (Lolita, The Gift, Pnin). *Is this factor also present in* Ada?
The only autobiographical feature in *Lolita* is a bunch of motels having some resemblance to those my wife and I stayed at in the forties and fifties during the several summers we spent, when covering fifty thousand miles of America, in hunting butterflies. There is no such factor in *Ada* save maybe the rearing of interesting caterpillars that I conducted in my boyhood very assiduously and successfully.

What is your opinion of the hippies and the student revolts?
I feel nothing but contemptuous pity for the illiterate drug-dazed hoodlums I have happened to observe, but I do not assume that all hippies are violent cretins. Many of them are young conformists following an American fad, and some are intelligent political agents disguised as students.

Have you read Marcuse?
I have seen excerpts. I wonder if anywhere—perhaps in some African or Asiatic tongue—"Marcuse" is a diminutive of "Marx." Perhaps the youngest Marx Brother. What I read was intolerably trivial.

---

[*] "Lo Zar Nabokov" ("The Tsar Nabokov"), *Panorama*, Nov. 6, 1969, 50–56. Emended typescript with VN manuscript corrections, in English, VNA Berg. *Ada* was translated very rapidly into Italian and was about to be published in Nov. 1969 by VN's regular publisher there, Mondadori. Tabozzi visited Montreux with the Mondadori publicist on Oct. 16.

Do you place much importance on what literary critics say about your works?
I feel touched when a reader likes what I like in a book—not necessarily my own book. Per contra, adverse criticism is so often the outcome of mental infirmity or a display of sullen malice, or both, that I tend to disregard accusations, which may not be altogether unjust.

The film rights have been sold for Ada. *Will you help in the filming?*
Oh, I intend to be fantastically cooperative in the shooting of *Ada*. Otherwise, all I want from the cinema is compensation in hard currency.

Can you give me your own judgment on yourself, from a critical and "humanitarian" point of view?
Mr. Nabokov, a European American or American European, is a modest, humble, handsome, sincere, amiable person. *Lolita* is not his only good book. His weight in kilograms has been, for the last ten years, 85 in July, 89 in December. He is seventy years old but looks fifty-six in the morning and sixty-five after dinner.

Are you writing a new book?
Yes, I have begun a new novel. It is still in its cradle. It cannot speak yet but can smile already most winningly.

Do you think that having money—a lot of money—changes a writer's ideas and way of thinking?
The feeling is not exactly new. I have only recouped a small part of the money I lost in 1917. I would have got back more if the taxes that all Americans have to pay were not so huge. Moreover—speaking of those rather superficial emotions—I have never been really hard up since 1940, when I migrated to America, where various rewarding lectureships were immediately available to me, so that the *Lolita* boom in 1958 did not come as too great a shock. Does money change a writer's ideas? No, apparently not in my case. Witness the organic continuity of my compositions.

122

Interview with Gaetano Tumiati
for *La Stampa* (1969)*

How can you reconcile the sense of perfect harmony that you experience when you are alone in a forest among the trees, in contact with nature, with the "micro-aggression" and the scientific pedantry of the entomologist who doesn't limit himself to looking at the butterflies, but kills, collects, and classifies them? First of all, let me say to you that to enjoy a thing you have to see and know the thing. A man who walks alone, as you say, "in a forest among the trees" will not see a single butterfly (there is too much shade) if I, who do know them, do not point out to him the moth whose wing pattern blends with the arabesques of the bark to which it clings. I do not know how one can call the knowledge of natural objects or the vocabulary of nature "pedantry." Is it the relative smallness of an insect that makes entomology seem comic to the layman? For, on the other hand, everyone can distinguish a cat from a lion or a leopard, and no one finds catalogues of rare books ridiculous. Not only do we collect butterflies, but we also examine under the microscope their minuscule organs, whose form serves to classify the animal more surely than the colors of its wings. And, believe me, the emotion of recognizing in an alpine meadow the butterfly which one knows to be different from another and whose special behavior one observes—this emotion is a feeling whose science side and art side join in an apex of sharp pleasure unknown to the man who goes for a walk under trees he cannot even name.

---

* "Signor Nabokov, un'altra Lolita?" ("Mr. Nabokov, Another Lolita?"), *La stampa*, Oct. 30, 1969, 3. Typescript, questions in Italian and French, with typescript of VN's answers, in French, VNA Berg. VN's Italian publisher, Mondadori, had repeatedly importuned him to come to Milan for the publication of the Italian translation of *Ada*. An alternative was set up: a number of journalists and the academic Marina Bulgherini visited him in Montreux on Oct. 30, 1969. He had sent the answers to their written questions by Oct. 24.

Can you tell me why, speaking of Vyra,[1] *you give a sense of languishing for a paradise lost, and at the same time you have chosen to live in some hotel? And why have you chosen to spend most of your life in Switzerland?*

I don't doubt that the visa application I made on Monday would produce a veritable sensation among the Soviets and that on Wednesday I would have been received with open arms in Moscow. The first little chill would come when I replied I don't care a fig for Moscow (where I have never been) any more than for Peking or Liverpool. And why? Old churches and palaces bore me, and I would not recognize the sites of my youth near Leningrad. My memory is the best guardian of my past. I would have refused, with my usual arrogance, to visit museums and factories, and two days later the U.S. ambassador would be making unheard-of and perhaps vain efforts to extricate me from the Soviet dungeons.

If, hypothetically, you hadn't emigrated and had stayed in Russia, surviving the country's upheavals, do you think you would also have written something? (I don't say published, just written.) And would your eventual works have had some analogy with those of today?

The answer is simple: I left Russia in 1919 because otherwise my whole family, including me, would have faced the firing squad of the Bolsheviks who had just invaded Crimea, where my father was minister of justice, member of a regional Cabinet, the last refuge of Russian liberalism. Your hypothesis contains far too many secondary suppositions for me to be able to imagine surviving in the situation of an Olesha or a Bulgakov.[2]

123

Interview with Claudio Gorlier
for *Corriere della Sera* (1969)[*]

Is your Russian origin an asset or a liability?
My most precious possession is my Russian language. In a sense I inherited my own self.

Do you not find Switzerland dull? Does your choice of Switzerland imply a rejection of America?
I find nothing more tedious than the political passions in less fortunate countries than Switzerland. There is peace and justice here. I confess I prefer one honest Swiss merchant to a dozen mediocre poets in any country. A street in a Swiss town is just as noisy as a street in Boston or Baghdad. There is nothing more anonymous and leveling than poverty. As to my residence in Switzerland, my choice is prompted not only by the absence of political turmoil but also by family considerations. . . . I think of America with nostalgic love and hope to go back there as soon as I can muster sufficient energy. I am a very sluggish person and get easily accustomed to this or that comfortable nook.

Why do you engage in so much wordplay?
The wordplay that so dazzles my critics is merely a handful of confetti scattered on a threshold.

[*] "La scherma di Nabokov" ("Nabokov's Fencing"), *Corriere della sera*, Oct. 30, 1969, 12. Typescripts, in English, VNA Berg. Conducted on same day as the Tumiati interview, above.

Does the sociologese of most contemporary fiction in America disturb you?
I have never understood why a story about, say, a generalized family of winegrowers, or a sociologically slanted novel about a factory worker, should be supposed to produce a greater impression of reality and be of more interest than the life story of, say, an obscure botanist. All individual milieux and realities are limited: it is not only an artistic, but also an organic principle.

124

Interview with Constanzo Costantini
for *Il Messagero* (1969)*

Why the extraordinary success of Lolita, *when you had been publishing novels since 1926?*
I don't know if you have noticed, but there are in *Lolita* several passages that suggest—how shall I put it?—a love affair between an adult and a child. Well, sometimes I wonder if those passages do not lure a certain type of reader, who is morbidly attracted by what he thinks are erotic images, into reading at least half of the novel. I realize the idea is rather extravagant; yet maybe something of the kind happened to my poor, innocent little book—which is still banned in some countries!

What are the best and most successful works in literature?
Homer, Horace, the New Testament, Dante, Shakespeare, Chateaubriand, Pushkin, Flaubert, Joyce, one or two others.

Do you care for literary critics?
On the whole I am indifferent to what critics think of my books—perhaps because nobody can think so tenderly of them as I do.

What do you think about the so-called crisis of the novel? Is it, in your opinion, a real crisis?
Frankly, I don't know what "the novel" means. A few books that I like, generally classified as "novels," including my own, do not seem to undergo any crisis. I think that "crisis" is something invented by third-rate novelists who cannot keep up with second-rate ones.

---

* "Per Nabokov non esiste crisi del romanzo" ("For Nabokov, There Is No Crisis of the Novel"), *Il messagero*, Nov. 2, 1969, 3. Typescript questions and answers, in English, VNA Berg. On same occasion as the two preceding interviews.

*You were born in St. Petersburg. What do you think about the literary and
political situation of the USSR today?*
I do not believe that basically very much has changed in the course
of the last fifty years. Same misery, drabness, deceit, torture, captivity.

*You lived for many years in the United States. Do you think that all creative
and imaginative work is destined to disappear or to survive in America's
technological society?*
The American way of life is not more technological than that of any
Western European country. In fact, I have heard and denounced more
transistors (instruments of infernal torture!) in a small Italian resort
than in New York or Los Angeles. On the other hand, the ameliora-
tion of living conditions owing to various gadgets has certainly given
American writers more time than formerly to write in comfort.

Which are the writers you have been influenced or inspired by?
I cannot think of any writer who has influenced me. This solitude does
not irk me, but it irritates a certain type of critic who likes to link up
writers in chains of parallel passages and literary schools.

Which are your favorite contemporary writers?
Shakespeare.

We said "contemporary."
Always Shakespeare.

And which Italian writers do you like most?
I know only three languages, Russian, English and French, and hardly
ever read translations. In any period of, say, twenty-five years, there
is a very small number of absolutely first-rate living novelists, three
or four, with that *je ne sais quoi* about them which designates them as
certain to survive.

On D'Annunzio
I read him as a young man, I liked "The Rain in the Pine Forest";[1] I
never knew a man whose head so surprisingly resembled an egg as that
of D'Annunzio.... I read little, and almost nothing of modern litera-

ture. I read a D'Annunzio book in a French translation, but I do not know if the translation was good or bad. So I can't express an opinion.

What do you think about the great theoreticians and writers of eroticism, start-ing with Bataille? Do you think there is a philosophy of eroticism?
I know nothing about those theories. All I can say is that since art appeals to the senses, an erotic strain in it presents nothing unusual. And another thing of which I am sure is that it is absurd to look for erotic symbols everywhere, in all kinds of objects, leathern helmets, galoshes, umbrellas, etc.

Interview with Nantas Salvalaggio
for *Il Giorno* (1969)[*]

How do you respond to critics who reproach your bravura style?
Critics who are by nature moralists, good, fragile men, full of self-pity
and pity for mankind, should not touch my books. The people I invite
to my feasts must have stomachs as strong as wineskins, and not ask
for a glass of Beaujolais when I offer them a barrel of Château Latour
d'Ivoire.

What do you ask of your translators?
I demand total fidelity: A translator should know the tongue from which
he translates as precisely as the tongue into which he translates. His
vocabulary in one tongue should be the mirror image of his vocabulary
in the other.

What is the wordplay in the title of your new novel?
The *gioco di parole* in the title of my new novel, *Ada or Ardor: A Family Chronicle*, is purely utilitarian, being meant to suggest to English-speaking readers how my girl's name was pronounced by her relatives
in the book. In modern Anglo-American pronunciation the first syllable
rhymes with "aid" or "maid." I want it to be pronounced in the Russian,
Italian and German manner.

---

[*] "Incontro in Svizzera con Vladimir Nabokov: La nuova droga del padre di Lolita" ("Meeting with Vladimir Nabokov in Switzerland: Lolita's Father's New Drug"), *Il giorno*, Nov. 3, 1969, 3. Typescript questions and answers, in English, VNA Berg. On the same occasion as the three preceding interviews.

Interview with Marina Bulgherini
for *American Literature* (1969)[*]

The subtitle of Ada, *"A Family Chronicle," implies a conventional evaluation of time and history, which is, however, denied throughout the whole book. Why the subtitle?*
I suppose I found something pleasantly nostalgic in the contrast between that old-fashioned subtitle and the fantastic world of my book.

How would you explain your recurrent aesthetic use of adolescents as characters in your work and of adolescent eroticism as a theme?
Caravaggio liked fruit and leaves in his pictures, Baudelaire liked young elephants; every artist has his own ornamental detail or watermark.

You have sometimes underlined your idea of literature as gamesmanship, as the art of creating riddles. What is the specific role of the riddler-novelist in our time and society?
I know very little about our time and society. I lead a very retired life. When I want people I paint them on the wall of my cave.

[*] If published, details unknown. Typescript questions and answers, in English, VNA Berg. On the same occasion as preceding four interviews.

Interview with Nurit Beretzky
for *Ma'ariv* (Tel Aviv) (1970)[*]

Do you still feel in Exile?
Art is exile. I felt an exile when I was a child in Russia among other children. I kept goal on the soccer field, and all goalkeepers are exiles.

Does being a refugee mean being rootless?
Rootlessness is less important than a confirmed refugee's capacity to branch and blossom in a complete—and very pleasant—void.

In which language do you think, count, and dream?
I do not think in any language, I think in images, with some brief verbal surfacing of a utilitarian sort in any of the three tongues that I know, such as "damn those trucks" or "*espèce de crétin*." I dream and count mostly in Russian.

How far do you get involved with your characters while writing? Do you think of them after the book has been published?
I suspect that the Almighty's interest in Adam and Eve was neither very sincere nor very enduring, despite the success, on the whole, of a really marvelous job. I, too, am completely detached from my characters, while making them and after making them.

---

[*] "Sicha im 'avi Lolita'" ("A Conversation with 'the father of Lolita'"), *Ma'ariv*, Feb. 13, 1970, 60. Typescript questions and answers, in English, VNA Berg; questions sent on Jan. 5, 1970, answered on Jan. 9, interview conducted on Jan. 19.

How do you want your books to be read? Do you think about your reactions?
I cannot expect any reader to know any of my books as well as I do, but if his mind cannot retain at least a certain percentage of specific details then he is a bad reader, that's all.

What is boring for you? What is most amusing for you?
Let me tell you instead what I hate:

Background music, canned music, piped-in music, portable music, next-room music, inflicted music of any kind.

Primitivism in art: "abstract" daubs, symbolic bleak little plays, junk sculpture, "avant-garde" verse, and other crude banalities.

Clubs, unions, fraternities, etc. (in the course of these last twenty-five years I must have turned down some twenty offers of glamorous membership).

Oppression. I am ready to accept any regime—Socialistic, Royalistic, Janitorial—provided mind and body are free.

The touch of satin. Circuses—especially animal acts and robust ladies hanging by their teeth in the air. The four doctors: Dr. Freud, Dr. Schweitzer, Dr. Zhivago and Dr. Castro.

Causes, demonstrations, processions.

"Concise" dictionaries, "abridged" manuals. Journalistic clichés: "the moment of truth," for example, or the execrable "dialogue."

Stupid, inimical things: The spectacles case that gets lost; the clothes hanger that topples down in the closet; the wrong pocket. Folding an umbrella, not finding its secret button. Uncut pages, knots in shoelaces. The prickly aura of one's face after skipping one's morning shave. Babies in trains. The act of falling asleep.

What do you think of the situation in the Middle East?
There exist several subjects in which I have expert knowledge: certain groups of butterflies, Pushkin, the art of chess problems, translation from and into English, Russian, and French, wordplay, novelism, insomnia, and immortality. But among these subjects, politics is not represented. I can only reply to your question about the Near East in a very amateur way: I fervently favor total friendship between America and Israel and am emotionally inclined to take Israel's side in all political matters.

128

Interview with Hanspeter Riklin (1970)[*]

Could you tell us what you know about a new book before you start writing?
They used to say of a bad writer, of a smearer of paper, that he put
"white on black." But in a subtler sense that's just what I do, when a
book of which I still have only an abstract sense (although I know it
exists already as an unexplored mountain or an undescribed flower
exists somewhere) appears to me like a dark space that I lighten up here
and there to reveal the design that's there.

*Do you create first your heroes, who then live in a certain context, or do you
work on a whole that then gives rise to the characters?*
In the totalitarian state of art as I conceive it, all my heroes are perfectly
equal among themselves, and besides they have no more artistic importance than the objects and the animals surrounding them. The nuance
of a wave interests me as much as the girl drowning in it.

Do you do research for your books? What sort of documentation do you use?
That depends on the book. *Lolita,* for example, required a lot of
research—from books, of course—on the physical and psychological
development of American schoolgirls. I like precise detail and rare
information. For *Pale Fire,* I drew a few handfuls of old jewels from
Scandinavian folklore. For *Ada,* I studied orchids. It's always exact
knowledge that attracts me, and not the general idea or philosophism
in fashion.

---

[*] For "Swiss newspapers," but no publication details known. Typescript questions and answers,
in French, VNA Berg, and Diary, VNA Berg. VN dated his answers to Riklin's questions Jan. 5,
1970, and met Riklin for the interview on Jan. 25.

Can you tell us what the finished book represents for you in relation to the initial project?

I ask myself first of all if the reflection remains faithful to the ray; if I have indeed followed the contour of the initial vision. The correspondence seems very indifferent in my first works; but in my last three or four novels I keep closer to the ideal, and in opening *Pale Fire* or *Ada* I feel a shiver of tenderness one would have to be very foolish or very honest to admit.

How does a day of work unfold for Monsieur Nabokov when he works on a new novel?

I swallow a fruit juice at 6:00 a.m., shave, and, standing at my old lectern, write until 10:30. Then I take my bath. Over lunch, my wife and I watch our favorite program on television (Jacques Martin and his little Danièle[1]). Then I return to the lectern or have a little siesta. It can be that I work until dinner, but never later than 7:00 p.m.

Do readers, the audience of your books, have a face for you? Is this audience present in some sense for you as you write?

The face is only mine. In other words, the circle of my good readers is very small. Their attention touches me. Flat and peevish criticism leaves me indifferent.

Why do you live in Switzerland?

I love mountains. I love the butterflies of the Valais and the Grisons. I love the Swiss air, as many Russian writers, by the way, have loved it: Karamzin, who got down from his Berlin coach to kiss "the soil of freedom"; Zhukovsky, who translated into fine Russian verse an English tourist's rather mediocre "Prisoner of Chillon"; Gogol, who at Clarens only detested the poor little lizards he would thwack with his walking stick; Tolstoy, finally, who courted the hotel maids, as he reports, with certain regrets, in his private journal.

Do you take part in social and political life? From what point of view? How do you keep yourself informed?

I do not. I have never in my life signed a declaration or belonged to an organization. I think I am the least *"engagé"* man in "our time." I'm not even sure that "our time" means something.

What do you think of the young who almost everywhere are breaking freer and freer from traditional and institutional life and trying hard to find new or "different" ways of life?

I think that the young who almost everywhere imitate American youth are everywhere what they have always been. Far from breaking free of traditional life, the young you mention show a comic conformism in forming groups, essentially petit-bourgeois in their hatred of real freedom of spirit—which in fact is nourished by concrete and hard-won knowledge and not by Chinese commonplaces.[2]

What do you think of efforts to enlarge the field of our sensibility and experience? What do you think of drugs?

Drugs are as degrading as drunkenness. The hallucinations that they arouse ruin health while remaining at the level of the hypnagogic kaleidoscope too well known to the healthy but overworked brain, or of these insipid mirages of mystical neurosis that go back to the Middle Ages. One must be very stupid to follow a fashion which only those whose task is to destroy the mental resistance of still-free nations could approve.

Could you tell us what in your opinion is the meaning of an artist's work for himself and for his public?

For me? Pleasure. For my best readers? Pleasure, again. For the average reader? A painful suspicion that perhaps literature isn't what he thought it was.

129

Interview with Andrew Field
for His Biography (1970)[*]

*Was there vodka on the table at Vyra? When were you first taught to, or
allowed to, drink?*

Vodka appeared only on the hors d'oeuvres side table, and hors d'oeuvres
appeared only when there were guests. There was always claret and port
wine on the dining table, and a furtive boy would find some way to take
a forbidden sip of one or the other. A typical dinner menu would start
with a Russian soup or a French potage, invariably accompanied by
hot *pirozhki*, fish would follow (trout, sole or zander), the meat course
might consist of beefsteak or veal, or chicken or game (such as hazel
hen or duck), and then there would be ice cream or a soufflé or stewed
fruit. My father (a nonsmoker but a great lover of good wine) frowned
on my smoking and drinking even at fifteen, but my mother was more
lenient. See *Ada*, chapter 38, for other gastronomic items shared by
Ardis and Vyra.

*Who are the Valentina Shulgin and the "E.L." to whom many of your pre-
revolutionary poems are dedicated?*

My relations with V.Sh. lasted exactly one year, from the end of summer
1915 to the end of summer 1916. After that began an extravagant series
of lesser romances up to the early 1920s. Of these the only more or less
serious and lengthy one began around Christmas 1916, when I met E.L.

[*] Unpublished; emended typescript with VN's manuscript annotations, VNA Berg. Field had
asked if he could undertake VN's biography, and VN, pleased by much in Field's *Nabokov:
His Life in Art* (1967), especially the consideration of his Russian and English works together,
and Field's high rating of his novels, agreed. Field sent the questions on June 12, 1970; VN
returned the answers on Aug. 24. See Andrew Field, *Nabokov: His Life in Part* (New York:
Viking, 1977) and *VN: The Life and Art of Vladimir Nabokov* (New York: Crown, 1986).

at a winter resort (Imatra) in Finland, and continued intermittently till late autumn 1917. I saw her again in 1919–20, in London. I remember spending a weekend with her and her uncle at his villa in Margate (when I took my first, and penultimate, airplane ride). Eva Lubrzhinski (she insisted on the "r") was a Polish young lady of fashion, very cosmopolitan and learned (she had studied chemistry under Mme. Curie in Paris and in her uncle's laboratory in Manchester). She later married a Cambridge college mate of mine, the son of an English architect (Lutyens). Eventually they separated. My publisher, Weidenfeld, curiously enough, was minister of finances in the first Israeli Cabinet presided by Eva's uncle (her mother's brother) Chaim Weizmann.

On Valentina Shulgin. Elena [Sikorski][1] recalls seeing the two of you "walking in the fields" from a coach. Does this feed your memory in any way? She had a sister. What do you recall of her? Did you visit in the Shulgin house or cottage or whatever it was?

The "Tamara" of *Speak, Memory* (as well as the "Mashenka" of *Mary*) was Valentina (diminutive Valyusya, diminished again to Lyusia) Evgenievna Shul'gin (born in 1900). Her mother, whom I never met but of whose corpulence and caprices Valentina spoke in detail, with engaging irony, was called Taisia Nikanorovna (Thais, daughter of Nicander; Shakespeare has a "Thaisa" in *Pericles*). The lady's husband managed the large Poltava estate of an opulent landowner, and lived apart from his family; he was seldom mentioned by his daughter. She had three or four sisters (of whom I knew the eldest, Natalia, a seventeen-year-old beauty, very like Valentina but taller and slimmer, and Anastasia, a fourteen-year-old neutral blonde), and a brother of eighteen, Vadim, who by 1916 had finished the Officers School and early in 1917 was wounded in Galitsia in the course of a cavalry charge. It so happened that he was the first member of the family I met, namely in early summer 1915, prior to the events described in my two books: he called or wrote to inquire if I would take part in a soccer team he was forming and would my people grant the use of one of our meadows for a friendly match with the Siverski eleven. I rode over with my tutor on horseback to the dacha the Shulgins rented near the Rozhdestvenski Church and talked to Vadim (transmitting to him the permission but declining to participate in the game). Valentina still unknown and unseen sat high in an apple tree looking down through the branches.

My sister's scant recollections are corroborated by a passage in
Speak, Memory, but it was a convertible automobile, not a coach.
The Shulgins' winter quarters were a flat (perhaps belonging to
some relative—I can't find the address in your *Ves' Petrograd*[2]) on the
Sergievskaya, a handsome residential street abutting at the Tavriches-
kiy Sad[3] where usually I would be waiting for her. I know practically
nothing about her existence after I had *otryahnul nezhniÿ prah Rossii*[4]
in the spring of 1919. I think she married a Ukrainian doctor, and
I think they lived in the Caucasus. Please note that the information
about her is absolutely confidential and should not be used for further
investigations.

Samuil Rozov?
Samuil Izrailevich Rozov (now an architect in Jaffa), my best friend at
school, was a small delicate lad with handsome features and the heart
of a lion. I remember the astounded stare of our worst bully, who stood
like a cliff when R. attacked him with his little fists. He was first in
my form, and generously helped everybody with tutorial elucidations,
especially in mathematics. He and I discussed Chekhov, and poetry
and Sionism. I saw him again forty-five years later: he came to see me
at Zermatt and we went for a long walk with my wife, my sister (who
had just arrived from Geneva), her dog (Appenzeller, now no more)
and a German photographer (who had also arrived on that same day
of artistic coincidences).[5] A steady drizzle hampered butterfly hunting
but the gray light seemed to be just right for pictures. R. said he did
not know what amazed him more, the quantities of wildflowers (he had
not seen any Northern ones since boyhood) or the amount of film Herr
Tappe was wasting by clicking his camera every few seconds. One of
his pictures, the one in the gnomish hood on *Pale Fire* and elsewhere,
amply repaid all those clicks and remained a memento of that day, that
rain, those wet flowers.

*You have a poem (written 10.18) which is written "v otvet na pis'mo N. Sh"
("in answer to a letter from N.Sh"). Who is this?*
I wrote this to Nikolay Shustov—another of my school chums (the one
I mention visiting me in the butterfly chapter of *Speak, Memory*), whose
letter from St. Petersburg had miraculously reached me in the Crimea.
A couple of years later, in London, I got another letter from him, this

time from Finland: he had enlisted in General Yudenich's army. He was a very gentle, pathetic boy with a bizarre squint and a bad stammer. Coarse schoolmates harassed him with requests for brandy in idiotic allusion to Shustov's Cognac (no connection).

You have a poem (7.1.19) which has the notation "na smert' Sh. i K." ("on the death of Sh. and K."). Kindly identify.
Shingaryov and Kokoshkin, members of my father's political party, his close friends (I well remember both), heroic idealists and pure souls, who were murdered in their hospital beds by Lenin's police (late 1919—I am not sure of the exact date, and do not recall whether it happened in St. Petersburg or Moscow—probably the former).

Your sister remembers a childhood masquerade in which you were dressed as a toreador. Can you recall anything about this?
The party was a children's ball around 1911 at the house of an acquaintance, Princess Kudashev. My brother went as Pierrot and I wore a vest of purple velvet with a cummerbund of sky-blue silk made by our house seamstress. She was not a particularly attractive girl, but two or three years later I remember discussing the possibilities of her seduction with Yurik.[6] He went down a long corridor to take a connoisseur's glimpse at her in her distant room and came back shaking his head.

I have a newspaper report of a commemorative speech that you gave about Sasha Chorny in 1932. Do you have the speech? Can you remember the general gist of what you said? Or could you perhaps simply tell me something about your relations with Chorny?
He was small, had fine features, a swarthy skin, a round head, short graying black hair. He was a dear man and a good poet—and might have become an even better one had he lived to continue the new, serious trend of poetry that he switched to (from humor and satire) after the revolution.

> *Tsvetut tsveti, tomyas', shumyat derev'ya.*
> *Poka u nas ne vïkololi glaz,*
> *Mï, zabïvaya gor'kie kochev'ya,*
> *V lad'e mechtï uteshimsya ne raz*

I quote from memory the last stanza of a short poem, published in *Zhar ptitsa*, circa 1920. Here is an adequate translation (with the two last lines transposed):

> The blossoms bloom, the restless trees keep rustling;
> And while our eyes have not been gouged out yet,
> In Fancy's bark not seldom finding solace,
> Our bitter nomad camps we shall forget.

I do not recall my commemorative speech of 1932, but surely I must have mentioned in it Aleksandr Glikman's[7] kindness to my wretched young verse.

I am told that you first registered to study entomology at Trinity, but switched. Reasons? Who was your initial tutor?
Zoology, not entomology. After dissecting fish for one term I told my college tutor C. E. Harrison that it was interfering with my verse writing and could I please switch to Russian and French. I have never taken any courses in entomology, a fact that surprised my MCZ[8] colleagues at Harvard.

May I please have Nikolai Nabokov's address?
I think N. is teaching at Aspen. I would not believe one word he says about me. He makes up stories about people and keeps retelling them until the anecdote rots in the stew of its own variations. Then he forgets it.

Can you recollect any of your conversations with [Graham] Greene at your Lolita *party in London? Also, you had lunch with him once?*
Yes, Véra and I had lunch with him—it was our only meeting, and nothing of it remains in my memory—except a vague feeling of amusement gradually dawning upon me as we talked that he had apparently gathered from a passage in *Lolita* (about a kind Canadian priest) that I too was a Catholic convert and now realized his awful mistake.

Can you tell me anything about your stays at Chamonix? Was this the area where you nearly bought a house a year or two ago?
We never stayed at Chamonix. We have a small bit of land at Les Diablerets, Vaud. We have inspected many houses in the Vaud, the Valais, the

Tessin and elsewhere. The whole thing is a bore. I am perfectly happy in our shabby little flat here. The abstract dream of a château in a park can neither live up to remembered reality, nor adjust itself to such problems as that of collecting phantom furniture and faceless servants.

Can you recall in any detail your conversation with Marilyn Monroe?
There was no conversation. I saw her at a big party given by Zelnick.[9] She was gloriously pretty, all bosom and rose, and remained separately sitting and holding hands with a French fellow called Montand (stage name).

Can you tell me something about your friend W. T. M. Forbes, who died last year?
When I knew him in the Forties and early Fifties he was a corpulent, carp-shaped, white-whiskered eccentric, with a pink complexion that gradually deepened to a frightening carmine as he pottered about, wearing several layers of wool, in his overheated laboratory among the glass trays with spread butterflies, volumes of entomological journals, remnants of a messy snack, and an accumulation of mystery paperbacks, of which he was inordinately fond. He was not a talented scientist but a learned and opinionated one with a prodigious memory for butterfly names and localities, and although taxonomic discussions with him gradually turned into a droning monologue which swept over all the obstacles one tried to put in its way, it was fun talking to him about Lepidoptera. Unfortunately, he much preferred to propound his views (in the same monotonous uncontrollable flow of words, his eyes moving as if watching tennis) about more worldly matters such as politics, genetics, "Niggers and Hebrews," comic strips, his sister's books and the history of the music hall in America. Being culturally *nicht stubenrein,*[10] he was never invited to our small parties in Ithaca, but I saw a lot of him in the museums (my own collections generally ended up in the MCZ, Harvard, or the Comstock Hall, Cornell, where he also worked). And I confess that sometimes, upon seeing his pink pate within its crown of white fluff bent over a distant desk, I would try to slip into my corner as quietly as possible. I am sorry to say that the above is part of my *Speak on, Memory,* and cannot be quoted yet.

The Kerby-Millers? Sylvia Berkman?
The Kerby-Millers, a heroic pair, were close friends of ours. She was my staunch champion and backer at Wellesley College, where philistine infiltration caused the authorities to question my "constantly insulting in class the literary achievements of our allies, such as Sholokhov." The last time I saw him, in 1964, Charles K-M was desperately ill with the Parkinson disease. Miss Sylvia Berkman is another good friend. Her short stories were much admired in the Fifties and deserved that praise. She checked my grammar in the stories I sold to the *Atlantic*.

You rented May Sarton's house in 1952. Do you have anything to tell me of your conversations with Miss Sarton?
The house came with a cat, an amiable animal that we re-christened Tomski. When showing us over the house before leaving for Europe, May Sarton advised us, in connection with a side window of her upstairs study which gave on a convenient elm limb, to keep the casement open, since sometimes the cat used that issue at night "when desperate." Another cat, a Siamese with a milky stare rented with the Sharps' house in Ithaca, proved a more difficult pet.

Is there much of your brother Sergei's personality in the story "Orache"? His shyness, etc. Could you comment on the name-day parties you attended during your childhood?
It is partly autobiographical and partly invented. I was not thinking of S. when composing it. The festive chocolate in the linden avenue comes at the end of a chapter in *Speak, Memory*, and the festive picnics are depicted in *Ada* (with some incrustations, of course). Here is a list of summer fêtes at Vyra, Old Style calendar: namesday, two Elenas, May 21; namesday, three Sergeys, June 5; birthday, my father's, July 8; namesday, Olga, July 11; namesday, two Vladimirs, July 15; birthday, mother's, August 17. There were also fêtes at Batovo and Druzhnoselie.

What do you remember of the popular singer Miss Jan-Rouban?
Vladimir Pohl, a small frail bald-headed man with a goatee, had become a health faddist after a severe bout with tuberculosis. In consequence of various forms of physical training, some of them vaguely Oriental, he had developed a giant's stamina, and my father and I had difficulty in

keeping up with him along the steep trails of the Crimean mountains. He died in his nineties, only a few years ago. His wife, niece of Ivan Petrunkevich (whose second wife was by a first marriage the mother of the Sophia Panin, on whose estate they and we lived in 1918), sang at concerts under the name of Jan-Ruban. She was not a "popular" singer at all (I suspect Plevitskaya emitted a muffled note at the back of your mind), but on the contrary a very sophisticated *kamernaya pevitsa*[11] for whom I translated a lot of Heine for her Schumann recitals in Yalta.

Interview with Christopher Givan
for *Los Angeles Times* (1970)[*]

On being asked how he would teach a creative writing class, as Givan was about to do, and after beginning to answer that he believed creative writing couldn't be taught, that either one had talent or not

The great thing, which can, I suppose, be taught, is to avoid the cliché of one's time. At all cost, never, never use, for example, the word "dialogue," absolutely never. I would have them write their memoirs, first thing. Write about some incident in the past and this would show right away who had a knack for writing and who didn't. In reading their papers you could tell by who began "I was born in Ohio and I have two sisters" and who began a little differently, with a twist—you could be on the lookout for something unusual.

. . . they should write down conversations they had or overheard. That is an important thing, to be able to remember and reproduce—accurately—conversations. And *(smiling)* they could learn what a dentist does—learn about different professions. That's very old-fashioned. Flaubert's idea. Learn the little secrets of a trade, of the different professions, so that they can write about them.

---

[*] "Cocktails with Nabokov: 'The Thing Is to Avoid the Cliché of Your Time,'" *Los Angeles Times*, Aug. 7, 1977, sec. IV, pp. 1–2. Givan called on VN at the Montreux Palace one Saturday in the summer of 1970, but did not publish his write-up until the month after VN's death.

Interview with Alan Levy
for *New York Times Magazine* (1970–71)[*]

Quoting from Nabokov's afterword to Lolita, *which amends a critic's description of the novel as "the record of my love affair with the romantic novel. The substitution 'English language' for 'romantic novel' would make this elegant formula more correct," Levy asks Nabokov to elaborate on the nature of this love affair and its recent course.*

It is now a kind of second marriage, I bald and benevolent, she, difficult but still chic, and much courted. Metaphors apart, I feel a certain hardening of my vocabulary, with London's modish phrases and New England slang no longer oxygenating the bloodstream of my style. In a sense, the same thing occurred in regard to my Russian after several years of expatriation in Berlin and Paris.

Can you pinpoint or generalize when you think in English now and when you think in Russian?

Unless one actually recollects or devises sentences, spoken or written, one thinks in images, not in languages (and this is why Bloom's mental soliloquy is a stylized exaggeration, a delightful kind of delirium). If I am asked, "Do you remember that conversation we had the other day?," it comes back to me in a shapeless flash. The blur may be flavored with French, or tinged with Russian, or soaked in American—that depends

---

* "Understanding Vladimir Nabokov: A Red Leaf Is a Red Autumn Leaf, Not a Deflowered Nymphet," *New York Times Magazine*, Oct. 31, 1971, 20–22, 24, 28, 32, 36, 38, 40–41. Emended typescript with VN's manuscript corrections, VNA Berg. Levy came from Prague to visit VN in Montreux on Oct. 5, 1970, and Feb. 26, 1971; VN sent him a batch of answers on April 28, 1971; Levy joined VN on a butterfly excursion late in the summer of 1971. VN was not at all happy with the amount of informal chat featured in the article; after VN's death, Levy included even more in his book *Vladimir Nabokov: The Velvet Butterfly* (Sag Harbor, NY: Permanent Press, 1984).

solely on the tongue in which the conversation had been conducted—
and a phrase I wish to recall or cannot help recalling may stand out with
full verbal precision; but that is all. The same occurs if I say to myself,
"I know that I shall tell Ivan Ivanovich" (who happens to be a profound
monolinguist) or "I know what old François (another unfortunate) will
reply." To put it in a coconut shell, the actual words (both mine and his)
are framed by the lips of the mind if there is intent on retroanalysis but
the choice of language itself has no psychological significance; and of
course an imagined tower or tree stands speechless.

On Prague and advice to an exile
I cannot match your specific questions with a nonspecific answer.
Prague means little to me, a bleak bridge across a bleak river, rain,
the wet gargoyles of some place of worship, a local lepidopterist in an
entomological laboratory, growling (in 1923), "Our Germans are bad
enough, but our Jews are worse." And the supper *à la fourchette*, to which
Kramarzh,[1] married to a White Russian, invited White Russians, and
my sister Elena poking casually at an untouched dish and remarking,
"Oh it's not cream, it's some sort of *chaud-froid*," and being at once swept
aside, fork in hand, by a pack of hungry convives.

*On the rumor in Montreux, especially among tradesmen, that Véra is VN's
ghostwriter*
The charm of that rumor is enhanced by the fact that what most
Montreusiens seem to know of my work, or of its shadow, is the film
Lolita (shown in Switzerland half a dozen years ago). My wife reads my
stuff only after I have completed the fair copy in longhand on lined
index cards which I fill out while standing at my lectern or lolling in the
garden. I am an uncommunicative toiler, and in the case of the longer
novels my patient first reader awaits the unknown book with serenity
for years and years. Formerly, that is before we could afford secretar-
ies, she used to type all my works and correspondence. She continues
to read, very carefully, typescripts and proofs, correcting my grotesque
misspellings and sometimes querying an obscure or repetitious word.
She also types my Russian letters. It may very well be that the observant
and intelligent people who bring me fruit and wine, or come to repair
radiators and radios, jump to wrong conclusions because they never see
me sitting at a desk, let alone typing.

"*Nabokov . . . loves to tell you something which isn't true and have you believe it; but even more he loves to tell you something which is true and make you think he is lying.*" (Celebrity Register, *ed. Cleveland Amory, 1963.) Do you subscribe to this analysis?*

I do not possess that Register, and do not know who said that, but whoever did (here comes a bit of palmistry) is a touchy and basically naïve person who writes good English, likes to generalize, and constantly misconstrues another's motives in specific cases of human behavior.[2] I have as many faults as the crest of a mountain chain but deceiving the naïve is not one of them.

On Morris Bishop's claim that at Cornell the only newspaper Nabokov read was Father Divine's periodical

My old friend Morris Bishop is a great stylist and he has brought up the "Father Divine's periodical" on a wave of style. I don't think I ever read it.

Nowadays, in Switzerland, I dip into quite a number of periodicals: the *Herald Tribune*, the *National Review*, *The New York Review of Books*, *Time*, *Newsweek*, the *Saturday Review*, *The New Yorker*, *Playboy*, *Esquire*, *Encounter*, *The Listener*, *The Spectator*, the *New Statesman*, *Punch*, the London Sunday papers and so forth.

We talked the last time about the Manson case, but I never did find out why and how it fascinates you or why it made you wish for once to be a journalist.

I have a taste for case histories and it would have interested me greatly to look for one spark of remorse in that moronic monster and his moronic beast girls. I would also have been interested to find out more about the cretins who "admire" those brutes.

As one American to another, where do you stand on Vietnam?

All I know is that I would not like S. Vietnam to turn into Sovietnam, and that blunders do not win wars.

On the butterflies of 1970

It's been a wonderful summer for butterflies. Generally, their emergences are staggered. But this year, May and June were such bad months that the butterflies just waited—and then they all came out together!

On the questions a woman in Prague has been posing Levy for her Czech translation of Lolita

Tell her that "ululate" is not a dirty word, "Lull" is a boy's name; at least the only person I knew named Lull was a boy. "Matted eyelash" means just that—not a pubic hair—and a "red autumn leaf" is a red autumn leaf, not a deflowered nymphet.

On Walter Minton (unnamed in the article) of Putnam's, Nabokov's and Levy's former publisher

He's a rather astute man with a coarse streak right down the middle and—do you know?—I think it's his coarse part that kept me with him for so long. Each time I visited his city, he would take me home for dinner and—every single time—he would tell me, as we crossed his threshold, "This is the house *Lolita* built." Well, I've wrecked some lives in my time, but I also like to think that at least I made a house.

On Véra

Véra was a pale blonde when I met her but it didn't take me long to turn her hair white.

On his Russian translation of Lolita

. . . not because I wanted tourists to smuggle it in, but because I was more afraid some Moscow hack would do a translation and—well, for example, there's no such term as "blue jeans" in the Russian language.

On Alfred Appel, Jr.[3]

. . . my pedant. A pedant straight out of *Pale Fire*. Every writer should have such a pedant. He was a student of mine at Cornell and later he married a girl I'd taught at another time, and I understand that I was their first shared passion.

On journalists and fans

Every Englishman, no matter what his title or credentials, turns out to be a journalist of some sort, but I enjoy talking with them. The Americans I seem to meet are often out to get more than they're here to give, so I tend to be wary. Not long ago, there was someone with an American name who kept leaving vague messages for me all over Montreux.

I started leaving messages, too, that I was unavailable. Then I got one more message—a slip of paper that said, "F—— you."

Well, this was so much more explicit than the others that I asked the desk what kind of person had left this message. And the desk said, "That wasn't a person, sir, that was two rather wild-looking American girls." This intrigued me even more, so I looked at the slip of paper again. And there I found something at the end of the message which I hadn't noticed on my first reading, a question mark!

On Véra's comment that the furniture in their suite was a joke
Except for my marvelous wooden lectern . . . The hotel found the lectern somewhere and gave it to us soon after we moved in. It was used by Flaubert once. . . . It's very old and very shaky, but it's not broken. *(Véra notes a crack in the wood connecting two legs.)* Let's just say that the legs are the weakest part. Looking at it, I can only guess that some Early American child came over to Europe and set about systematically kicking it to pieces.

While stalking butterflies around Grangettes, near Montreux, looking for the Purple Emperor
. . . its beautiful violet sheen . . . If you turn it this way and that way the shimmer changes. It used to fly here until they asphalted this road. Now it's getting scarcer and scarcer. I saw one the other day up in Caux— but I couldn't look at it closer because it was flying higher and higher in such a hurry. Ahhhh! *(Catches a butterfly.)* A brimstone, not uncommon . . . This was supposed to be the first butterfly ever noticed: hence the name "butterfly." Another version has it that the name was derived from *flutter by*—making it all a Spoonerism!

After Levy congratulates VN on the swoop of his butterfly net
I'm glad you appreciated that. . . . It's not easy to take a flying butterfly— because it dodges. The best way is to wait for it to settle on a flower—or on damp earth, it's quite easy to take.

On a Gray-Veined White he has caught
So pale! . . . A very common butterfly that gradually grades into an Alpine form . . . If you go up certain hills and mountains for about eigh-

teen hundred meters you'll find a peculiarly beautiful gray-yellowish version of this—but, all along the way up, you'll encounter intermediate forms. This one and that one fly differently and have different caterpillars, but you can see the changes as you go.[4]

On the hazards of butterfly hunting, including vipers

Their bites are not fatal—unless you're ill or old or very young. . . . I have walked among rattlesnakes. Yes, in Arizona, when I was writing the screenplay for *Lolita*. We would take my index cards in the morning and go out collecting and writing until lunch. And one day, I remember killing an immense rattler that was just lying in wait for us when we came out toward the road. I was the first to hear its hysterical rattlings. Véra almost stepped on it, but I held her back. Then I picked up a piece of lead piping and smashed the thing. A moment later, I saw its female slither away. Véra called me "St. George" for quite a while after that!

More butterfly talk and action

The dimmer the place, the better the butterfly . . . This one I will take. A lovely intergrade between the common Veined White and its cousin Bryony White.[5] Could you ever hear me explaining that subtlety to the ranger?

The butterfly in the Band-Aid box

An *old* Band-Aid box *(laughing)*. That envelope will hold the butterfly until I want to spread it. In there I can keep my butterflies for years and years, hundreds of years. When I am ready, I have only to relax them between wet towels and leave them overnight—and the next day pin them. . . . Oh, didn't you see me pinching it under the net? That killed it, though sometimes I have to repinch them. When Véra's with me, she keeps an eagle eye on them. She hates to see half-dead butterflies.

Homage to Franz Hellens
(Birthday Tribute, 1971)*

At the beginning of 1936 Madame Malévitch-Malevsky[1] organized a reading for me in Brussels and introduced me to several of her friends, Belgian prose writers and poets. That's how I had the joy of meeting that great writer Franz Hellens. I have not seen him again in the course of these thirty-four years, but I have never lost my admiration for his talent. His books follow me on my many pilgrimages. I have enormous admiration for *Oeil-de-Dieu*[2] and I adore *La Femme partagée*.[3]

I shake his hand warmly from afar.

---

* "Hommage à Franz Hellens," in *Franz Hellens: Recueil d'études, de souvenirs et témoignages offert à l'écrivain à l'occasion de son 90e anniversaire*, ed. Raphaël de Smedt (Brussels: André de Rache, 1971), 253. Franz Hellens (1881–1972), Belgian novelist, poet, and critic, wrote in French. In a 1970 interview with Alfred Appel, Jr., VN mused: "All novelists of any worth are psychological novelists, I guess. Speaking of precursors of the New Novel, there is Franz Hellens, a Belgian, who is very important. Do you know him? (Appel: No, I don't. When was he active, in which period did he write?) The post-Baudelaire period. (Appel: Could you be more specific?) Hellens was a tall, lean, quiet, very dignified man of whom I saw a good deal in Belgium in the middle thirties when I was reading my own stuff in lecture halls for large émigré audiences. *La femme partagée* (1929), a novel, I like particularly, and there are three or four other books that stand out among the many that Hellens wrote. I tried to get someone in the States to publish him—Laughlin, perhaps—but nothing came of it. Hellens would get excellent reviews, was beloved in Belgium, and what friends he had in Paris tried to brighten and broaden his reputation. It is a shame that he is read less than that awful Monsieur Camus and even more awful Monsieur Sartre" (*SO*, 174–75). Despite VN's endorsement and his suggestion to a publisher (not James Laughlin of New Directions, who might have been a better bet, but Walter Minton of Putnam's), Hellens's only book to be translated into English is *Memoirs from Elsinore*.

Interview with Paul Sufrin
for Swiss Broadcast (1971)*

You've written Pnin; *how soon will you sit down to write* Vnin?
I presume you refer to an American continuation of my autobiography, a kind of *Speak on, Memory*. Yes, it would be rather fun to describe my academic experience—at Wellesley, Cornell, Harvard, and elsewhere. But that peach is still as hard as wood in my mind. It is curious that the sensation of duration—and this has nothing to do with Bergson or Proust—the sensation of duration in regard to the distant past is both stronger and smoother than the recollection of time apprehended more recently. My childhood, my youth automatically fall into an artistic pattern, but my rather recent thirty years in America form an irregular patchwork with all sorts of gaps in my memory and with lumps of raw matter. In other words, if the distant past is highly organized poetry, the recent past is nothing but rough topical prose.

---

* For Swiss Broadcast, European and Overseas Service. Emended typescript with VN's manu-script revisions, in English, VNA Berg. On Sept. 8, 1971, Sufrin came to Montreux to record his interview with VN, who had prepared his answers by Sept. 5. VN published some of the exchange in *SO* (interview 18), but not the question and answer given here.

Interview with Stephen Jan Parker (1971)[*]

What do you consider your top three stories?
The leading troika is represented by "Ozero, oblako, bashnya" ("Cloud, Castle, Lake"), "The Vane Sisters" and "Vesna v Fialte" ("Spring in Fialta"). They express exactly what I intended and do so with the greatest prismatic glamour my art is capable of.

In your lectures at Cornell you spoke of the novelist as being part entertainer, teacher and enchanter.
I spoke of a Generalized Novelist. My own novels and stories lack the didactic element and do not aim particularly at entertaining the reader; and some of my plots and worlds are held together by magic alone.

Should we see the short story as a genre distinct from the novel?
Many widespread species of Lepidoptera produce small, but not necessarily stunted, races above timberline. In relation to the typical novel the short story represents a small Alpine, or Polar, form. It looks different but is conspecific with the novel and is linked to it by intermediate clines.

What to you is an exemplary story? In our conversation, for example, you praised Zamiatin's "Peshchera" ("The Cave") and Olesha's "Vishnevaia kostochka" ("The Cherry Pit").
An "exemplary" short story (such as "Dama s sobachkoy" ["The Lady with the Little Dog"], "Metamorphosis" ["Die Verwandlung"], "Vesna

[*] "Vladimir Nabokov and the Short Story," *Russian Literature Triquarterly* 24 (1991), 68–72. Typescript and manuscript, VNA Berg. Parker, a former student of VN's at Cornell, by then an academic Slavist, and one of the first to write a Ph.D. thesis on VN, was working on a project on VN as short-story writer. He stayed with VN from April 19 to 21, 1971, then sent questions by mail. VN sent his answers on Oct. 22, 1971.

v Fialte" ["Spring in Fialta"] and those you mention) is physically a slim book and biologically a diminutive novel.

Is your process of composing stories different from that of composing novels?
My short stories are produced in exactly the same way as my novels. The latter take a longer time, that's all. On the average a story of ten pages takes me a fortnight to compose, a novel of 200 pages about one year.

What do you think of the modern experimental story?
I have never quite understood the term "experimental." The other day I bought a collection of modern "experimental" stories: and all of them—though written in staccato rhythms, with dirty words and fine ideas—were utterly banal and stale.

Although critics seem to agree parody is important in your work, there seems little parody in your Russian short stories, with some notable exceptions, perhaps because parody may be more effective and better sustained in longer prose writings than in a short story.
Yes, that's right. But, then, I'm not sure that "parody" is such a central character in *all* my novels. For instance *Pale Fire* is a very direct, realistic tale.

Have you stopped writing stories?
I am often tempted to compose a short story. Now and then a very complete image of one flashes before me, quivers for a moment, and is firmly dismissed. I wish to conserve my energy for ampler tasks; old age is cautious and thrifty.

Are the challenges and pleasures of short-story writing different?
No, the same pangs, the same pleasures.

Field states (Nabokov: His Life in Art, p.115) that "Pis'mo v Rossia" ("A Letter That Never Reached Russia") "was announced as a chapter from a novel with the rather unNabokovian title Happiness." *Would you care to verify this?*
Quite right. I planned an epistolary novel. I don't recall what happened in it or to it.

Would you care to comment on any or all of these writers you referred to, and mention any stories by them which you admire?
1 Pushkin 2 Gogol 3 Leskov 4 Chekhov 5 Ilf & Petrov 6 Zoshchenko 7 Zamiatin 8 Bunin 9 Andreev 10 Poe 11 Hawthorne 12 Hemingway 13 Salinger.
1. "Pistol Shot." 2. "The Carrick" ("Shinel'"). 3. ? 4. "Dama s sobachkoy" ("The Lady with the Little Dog"). 5 & 6. No special favorites. 7. "Peshchera" ("The Cave"). 8. "Lyogkovoe dïkhanie" ("Light Breathing"). 9. The one about the happy jailbird.[1] 10. A pleasant blur. 11. Same 12. "The Killers." 13. Etc. no comment re the quick.

What are your current literary plans?
The correcting of the French translation of *Ada* has confused my schedule. I hope to finish the new novel sometime next year. My collection of nonfiction will include mainly interviews, reviews, rejoinders, letters and various odds and ends. I have not yet reread my old lectures but I know that I will not reprint my *Bleak House, Ulysses* and *Mansfield Park* lectures.

Interview with Kurt Hoffman and Jochen Richter
for Bayerischer Rundfunk (1971–72)*

On his butterfly passion
It is odd but I have never quite made up my mind how much the various elements of sport, science and nameless delight combine in the soul of a butterfly collector.

On childhood
I had the happiest childhood imaginable.

On Peter I
Never call him Peter the Great, I always call him Peter the First.

On Dmitri
Very frank with me—he tells me his innermost thoughts. . . . I'm very proud of him and we're wonderful friends.

On remaining in Montreux
A sort of inverted Old World nostalgia.

---

* "Vom Gewebe der Zeit: Vladimir Nabokov erzählt" ("Vladimir Nabokov Talks About the Texture of Time"), interview for Bayerischer Rundfunk, München TV, Bayern III (coproduced with BBC, CBC, ORF, RM Produktion, and Schweizerische Radio- und Fernsehgesellschaft), broadcast May 26, 1972, and July 7, 1977. Videotape, Dieter E. Zimmer collection. Hoffmann visited VN in Montreux on Sept. 14 and 15, 1971, and again, for filming (questions and answers in English), from Oct. 10 to 17.

136

Interview for *New York Times* (1972)[*]

Quite right. . . . He [Bobby Fischer] can't be subject to the clicks and flashes of those machines above him. It's like a tennis player having tennis balls flung at him.

[*] "For Bobby Fischer, the Nabokov Defense," *New York Times*, July 21, 1972, 32 (item discovered by Shun'ichiro Akikusa). Interviewer unknown. American Bobby Fischer was challenging Russian Boris Spassky for the world chess championship in Reykjavik, Iceland. The first game took place on July 11, 1972; the last was adjourned on Aug. 31, before Spassky resigned. World interest was unusually high in the contest, which would become known as "The Match of the Century," not least because of Fischer's vocal anti-Sovietism and his unusual demands, among which was his objection to the use of television cameras. VN, as author of *The Defense*, was phoned for a comment on this demand.

Interview with Seth Goldschlager
for *Newsweek* (1972)[*]

Could one accurately describe the structure of Transparent Things *as a Moebius strip of time and form?*
One could, metaphorically—if one first defined "form": is it matter? is it space?

Could one view the book as the definitive dissection of the tea-moistened madeleine? (Or does this question crumble?)[1]
The question falls apart, limply and soggily, like a tea-soaked petit-beurre biscuit.

Transparent Things *illuminates in suspension the moment of death, the form of that instant of crossover of time zones; can readers of your future work expect another examination of that moment?*
I wonder how long it will take critics to see the main point of *Transparent Things*. I will not divulge it. It was completely missed, for example, by Michael Wood (*The N.Y. Review*, Nov. 16), otherwise a subtle reviewer.

Do you think the media of film and television provide the raw materials for creating artistic works?
The only material for creating artistic works, on canvas or paper, is provided by self-enchantment, which is another term for individual imagination.

[*] Intended for *Newsweek* but not published. Emended typescript with VN's manuscript corrections, VNA Berg. VN wrote out his replies on Nov. 4, 1972, and had them typed up on Nov. 6. Planned for the publication of *Transparent Things*, which first appeared in *Esquire* in Dec. 1972 and then in book form (McGraw-Hill) the same month.

Is it possible to reproduce the artistry of a novel in the form of cinema or would that necessarily require the transformation implicit in an attempt to transfer a work of literature onto canvas?

A completely faithful cinema reproduction of a novel would mean filming one after another all its printed pages turned by an invisible hand at the rate of a three-minute pause each soundlessly and without any vignettes for the benefit of those too lazy to open a tangible book.

Is there a valid definition of obscenity or is that term a meaningless one that should vanish?

I call a novel obscene if it fulfills the following three conditions: 1. it is indecent, 2. it is talentless, and 3. it is boring. I consider, therefore, that the term "obscenity" is a useful one, separating as it does lewd, dull mediocrity from, say, entertaining erotic art.

When and if you reread your past published work are you tempted to rewrite or to re-edit? Would you yield to such a feeling?

No English novels of mine need any revamping. Of the nine Russian novels . . .[2]

B. F. Skinner has recently drawn from behaviorism the message that man's freedom and dignity are self-destructive myths that call for some form of new authority over "freedom of will." Would you care to comment on this Skinner message?

I am utterly ignorant of B. F. Skinner's writings and cannot perceive any logical link between objective liberty and subjective dignity.

It appears as if the current leaders of the United States and those of the USSR are finding rapprochement on a comfortable and increasingly mutually profitable position. Does this surprise you? Is it a trend which can continue?

Economic convenience comes and goes. What does not and will never change is the blessed abyss between our free country (our free thought, our free oddities) and the Bolshevist Police State. An American tourist, gaping at some corny old church in Russia, may not be conscious of the abyss; but the Bolshevist visitor to the U.S.A. is glumly aware of it every moment.

138

Interview with Claude Jannoud
for *Le Figaro Littéraire* (1972)[*]

On the near-uniqueness of writing great literary works in two languages
The case you mention isn't "almost" unique: it simply is unique. One might unearth at a pinch in the recesses of world literature authors who began their careers writing ten or so books in one language and who, after forty, wrote ten or so in another, but I do not know a writer whose successive sequences in one and the other language are of the same importance. I hasten to add that Joseph Conrad was never a writer in Polish.

Why Switzerland?
I live in Switzerland for family reasons. They have no interest for your readers. I love Switzerland, but each spring I feel heartrending nostalgia for America, my preferred homeland. Over the last ten years I have seen it again only twice. Travel by boat takes a long time, and I detest planes. All the same, I bank on offering myself a good slice of California sun next year.

Who was your audience in France before the war?
Most of my literary audience in Europe in the interwar years consisted of Russian émigré intellectuals. Apart from my royalties, which around 1935 brought me enough to live on (given the great number of journals and reviews in Russian in Berlin, Paris, Prague, etc.), there was the money I earned reading my poems and prose to the Russian

---

[*] "Vladimir Nabokov, le plus américain des écrivains russes" ("Vladimir Nabokov, the Most American of Russian Writers"), *Le Figaro littéraire*, Jan. 13, 1973, 13, 16. VN finished the replies on Nov. 22, 1972, and had them typed by Nov. 28, when he met Jannoud in Montreux.

audience. In the thirties I had very pleasant relations with a few French writers—Supervielle, Paulhan, the writers of the *Nouvelle revue française* and *Mesures* group.

Have you remained a Russian writer in spirit and do you feel yourself a cosmopolitan writer?
My first novels, published between 1925 and 1940 by Russian-language publishers in Berlin and Paris, were often accused by émigré reviewers of being too cosmopolitan, just as, when I was a schoolboy, my teachers found that I used French or English terms too often in my Russian exercises. The Slavic spirit isn't my forte. I know Russian in depth, and I recall each little path, each little oriole flute-whistle in the park of my childhood, but that's all. At the cost of breaking the hearts of my Russian readers, I declare proudly that I am an American writer. Besides, my Russian work has been translated into English by my son and myself, but of all my English novels, only *Lolita* has appeared in a Russian translation (which took me a good year of work). This book (like all my others) is banned in Russia, but copies sneak in there all the time.

Is there something of Bobby Fischer in Luzhin?
I don't see any resemblance between Fischer and my Luzhin, a flabby, gentle, gloomy, and touching man. Up to the age of fifty I was a very good player, but what always particularly interested me was the composition of chess problems.

What of the Kubrick film of Lolita, *in which you had a hand?*
It's true that I wrote the screenplay. It's true, too, that Kubrick used only three-quarters of it, changing all sorts of details that I had combined so well. His film is excellent, with marvelous actors, but it isn't my nymphet at all.

Your conception of the novel?
I have no conception of the novel. I venture to say even that the "novel" as a general idea does not exist. I detest general ideas. For me, *Madame Bovary* is so different from *Sentimental Education,* and both are so different from the inept *Charterhouse of Parma* or the insipid *The Stranger,* that the phrase "the novels of Flaubert, Stendhal, and Camus" means

nothing to me. I find *The Voyeur, Jealousy,* and *In the Labyrinth* infinitely superior to all I have read in the way of French "novels" for thirty years, but I must add that the theories advanced by my friend Robbe-Grillet leave me completely indifferent.

The translations of your books?
I know enough of three languages, Russian, English, and French, to control every detail of the translations of my books. I insist that the translation be faithful, without the least sin of omission or commission. I ask that the objects and aspects of my landscape remain recognizable and that I am not tossed an *"ombre pourpre"* when I write "purple shade," *"ombre violette"* in French. I'm always ready to take care of everything tricky or needing special knowledge.

I am responsible for the glints of verse incrusted in my prose, for so-called untranslatable wordplays, for the velvet of this metaphor, for the cadence of that phrase, and for all the precise botanical, ornithological, and entomological terms that irritate the bad reader of my novels. The only thing that the translator must absolutely know thoroughly is the language in which my text is written; and yet I affirm with more sorrow than astonishment that the most celebrated translators from English into French are at ease only when they deal with clichés. Anything original leads them astray.

Your new novel?
The title of the novel, which has just appeared in America, is *Transparent Things*. An incorporeal being, the soul of a novelist who has just died of a liver disease, evokes the difficulty that phantoms have in perceiving our world, of resting on the level of our present, without sinking into the past through the transparency of human things. It's a very funny novel. But it isn't for everybody.

Your critical work, especially on Pushkin, is not well known in France.
I don't understand why some French scholar doesn't translate *Eugene Onegin* into faithful prose, with the commentaries and explanations I provide in the course of my four-volume work in English. What's this new indifference of the French reader to really important works?

139

Interview with Mati Laansoo
for Canadian Broadcasting Corporation (1973)[*]

How do you regard the Nobel Prize for Literature? The people who have seriously read your works realize that you are indisputably the greatest living author in the world. Given that, how do you explain the lamentable omission of your works by the Nobel Prize Committee? Is it a matter of geographic boundaries and ideological differences?

Your first question is so precisely and pleasantly phrased that I feel embarrassed by the display of vagueness with which I must formulate my reply. Now and then, in the course of the last three or four decades, I have caught myself idly reflecting on the attractive resemblance between the beginning of the name of that famous prize, and the beginning of my own name: N.O.B., N.A.B., what a delightful recurrence of letters! Alliteration, however, is a deceptive relationship. Its magic cannot hope to establish the fortunate link between laurel and brow. On the other hand I do feel that as a writer I am not inferior to say, Rabindranath Tagore (Nineteen Thirteen) or Grazia Deledda (Nineteen Twenty-Six); but, then, of course, quite a number of uncrowned authors must exist, at this very moment, nursing the same forlorn feeling. In response to the conjecture at the end of your question I can only affirm my conviction that honest judges should not be prejudiced by my geopolitical situation—that of a non-progressive American hailing from a nonexistent Russia. The situation may look somewhat bizarre; it would be absurd to call it hopeless. After all, let us not forget that

---

[*] Radio broadcast, Canadian Broadcasting Corporation, Jan. 29, 1974. Holograph draft and typed transcript, VNA Berg. Published in *Vladimir Nabokov Research Newsletter* 10 (Spring 1983), 39–48. "Took four days to write 10 answers (= 20 minutes)," VN noted in his diary on March 20, 1973.

another Russian in much the same position as I did get the prize. His name is no doubt on your lips. I am referring of course to Ivan Bunin (Nineteen Thirty-Three).

One often hears the word "responsibility"! How do you hold yourself responsible to the children as an "elder," in the anthropological sense?
I'm afraid that the little I know about anthropology as a science is limited to its taxonomic aspect dealing with the classification of various subspecies of *Homo sapiens* and with the problems relating to the skulls of ancestral forms of the creature. Otherwise I find the subject of popular or applied "anthropology" tedious and even repulsive. The noun "elder," within that frame of reference, conjures up for me the image of a shaggy hermit all beads and beard with a more or less prehistoric cast of rugged features and a cave of sorts in the background. Tribal generalizations mean nothing to me. I prefer to use the term "responsibility," in its proper sense, linked with moral tradition, with principles of decency and personal honor deliberately passed from father to son. I can also speak of responsibility in the capacity of any educator of the profession of literature, which I taught for some twenty years in America. Here I was on my own, founding my own tradition, following my own taste, creating my own artistic values and trying to impress my approach to art upon the minds of my students—or at least some of my students. I am responsible for having taught those best children of my time a method of appreciation based on the artistic and scholarly impact of literary fiction, but I never was directly concerned with the general ideas that they might derive from this or that great novel or the question how they would apply its more or less obvious ideas to their own life. That was the duty and choice of their actual, not metaphorical, elders.

Having read your brief treatise on "Inspiration" in the Saturday Review of the Arts,[1] *I wonder, outside your art, what tumbles your grimace from irritation to pain?*
The list of things, big and small, that I find utterly hateful is a long one. Pet hates are generally more banal than loves. Let me limit myself to a few obvious samples. Cruelty comes at the top, then dirt, drugs, nuisance by noise, coat hangers of wire, modish words (such as "charisma" or "hopefully"), quick quack art, breaking a fingernail with no scissors

in sight, mislaying my spectacle case, finding that the current issue of my favorite weekly is suddenly devoted to Children's Books.

At what portals has the burglar of laughter broken and entered into your edifice?

Oh, laughter is not a burglar at all. Good old laughter is a permanent lodger in every house I construct. He is in fact the built-in roomer. He has the right to keep a mermaid in the bathtub. He is responsible for consigning Freud and Marx to the garbage can and destroying quite a few dictators. He drives some of my silliest critics mad with helpless rage. To extend your metaphors, which I seem to be doing all the time—my books would be dreary and dingy edifices indeed had that little fellow not been around.

Why do the Swiss make such good mercenaries and watches?

I am the last person to be consulted on the subject of watches. I am apprehensive of watches, as some people are of a coiled snake—and how abnormal it is to carry a watch twisted around your wrist or keep one in your waistcoat pocket like a spare heart! Despite my terror of them I love expensive watches—I shall always remember a very flat, thin, golden one of Swiss make that I had as a foppish boy sixty years ago, it lay on the palm of my hand like a pool of cold dew; yet watches detest me, I never had one that was not fast or slow, and it takes at least a fortnight to have a Swiss watch repaired in the place where it was bought; and most terrible of all are the fake clocks of clock makers' shop signs, which are set at a motionless and meaningless quarter to three to show how appealingly they can spread their hands.

The eggheads' endeavor involving the pressure cooker blasted to the moon has hatched such rewards for mankind as Teflon, the five-year flashlight battery and the pocket mini-computer. How might the artist have hoped to improve on these dubious returns?

The undescribable excitement and delight of reaching a celestial body, of palpating its pebbles, of sifting its dust, of seeing things and shadows of things never seen before—these are the emotions of unique importance to a certain uniquely important variety of man. We are speaking of divine thrills, aren't we, not of comic-strip gadgets. Who cares for the practical benefits derived from the exploration of space! I shall not mind if more and more trillions of dollars are spent on visits to the moon or Mars. I would only recommend that our jaunty and fearless space sportsmen be accompanied by a few men of acute imagination, true scientists of Darwin's type, an artistic genius or two—even some gray octopus of a poet who might lose his mind in the process of gaining a new world, but what does it matter, it is the ecstasy that counts.

Why did Fischer beat Spassky?
Apart from the fact that Fischer showed himself to be the better player, there are psychological complications to be reckoned with. Fischer when he played that match was the free champion of a free country with no whims barred and no fear of retribution for a fatal blunder. Wretched Spassky, on the other hand, always had a couple of stone-faced agents dogging him on an island with no escape or hiding place. He felt the presence and the pressure of the Soviet police state all the time—and one wonders would Fischer have won had the roles been reversed and the eyes of those grim annotators followed *his* every move with the same governmental threat. The farcical little scene of the wife being flown over from Russia was I thought especially gruesome but also rather hilarious as a desperate hygienic measure revealing the peculiar animal stupidity that is in a way a redeeming feature of the most elaborate dictatorship.

A Canadian artist has intimated that time is the thing that stops everything happening at once, and space is the thing that stops it happening all in the same place. Could you comment on this?
That's very neatly put. But it is only an aphorism, only a flourish of wonderful wit. It suggests the way a timepiece and a piece of space work in relation to each other, but it tells us nothing of the texture of time or the substance of space. When composing my chapter about Time in *Ada*, I concluded—and I am still leaning upon the gate of that conclusion—I concluded that Time has nothing to do with Space, and is not a "dimension" in the sense that Space is a dimension. Thought, for example, in order to breed properly, needs the broth of Time, no matter how scanty, but does not require Space. Yet even when we speak about a "little" time or a "long" time we are not actually referring to

size, and what we measure is not Time itself or the distance between two tangible points of Time (as we measure Space), but a stretch of our own existence between two recollections in a medium which our mind cannot really grasp. Everything in the nature of life is impossible to understand but some things are less possible to understand than others, and Time is among the most slippery ones.

Is there anything that interests you about your audience, or, how would you interview your interviewer?

In the first flush of my so-called fame, just before World War II, around, say, 1938 in Paris, where my last novel written in Russian started to run in an émigré magazine, I used to visualize my audience, with tender irony, as a group of my Russian émigré fans, each with one of my books held in his hands like a hymnal, all this in the rather subdued light of a back room in a café. Ten years later, in my American transposition, the room of my fancy had grown as large as a comfortable auditorium. Still later, more and more people had to stand for want of seats. Then, in the sixties, after the appearance of *Lolita*, several new halls had to be built, both in the New World and in the Old. I have readers now not only in Brazil and Israel, but in the Soviet Union, where factually my works are banned and every ghostly smuggler is equal to a hundred legitimate readers elsewhere. What interests me, or better say moves me, in regard to my present audience, is that a figment of my fancy, not much more solid than an invented castle or cloud in one of my stories, has become an actual event. I am a shy, retiring person, I feel stupidly confused to have my book provoke such attention and ask so much of my readers, whose eyesight in some cases is not too good (as their nice letters, with stamps enclosed, tell me) and whose fathers or children happen to be hospitalized with some terrible terminal illness which a simple auto-graph from me would certainly cure. "Dear Vladimir Nabokov," some say, "excuse me for using a page of my exercise book, but teacher has assigned all your books—and I am only a high-school kid"—all this in the handwriting of an old professional collector of autographs. I am an old collector too, but of butterflies, not autographs, and it is my entomological hunts in Canada that come to my mind as my voice is being projected onto Canadian air. One of my favorite spots remains a ravine smothered in flowers, near Fernie, three miles east of Elko, British Columbia, where on a summer day in 1958 I collected specimens of a very local little blue butterfly (*Lycaeides idas ferniensis*) which I badly wanted for the Cornell University Museum. Your curiosity about audiences has produced as you see quite a bit of digressive response, so let me now have your tenth and last question.

How does you wife, Véra Nabokov, puzzle you?
I am puzzled by many things about her: by her inability to keep figures and dates in her head, by the disorder on her desk, by her gift of tracking down a needed item that is the more precious the more complicated the search in the maze. I marvel at the way she can quote by heart old Russian sayings and ditties—sometimes quite new to me after almost half a century of shared life. I find fascinating the accuracy with which she picks out the best book in the batch that publishers send me every month or so with their compliments and hopes. I am filled with wonder every time that my random thoughts or actual sentence is simultaneously voiced by her in those flashes of domestic telepathy whose mystery is only enhanced by their frequency. And I also find enigmatic the stroke of miraculous intuition that makes her find the right words of consolation to give me when something awful, such as a misprint somehow left uncorrected by me in a recent novel, causes me to plunge into a torrent of Russian despair.

140

Interview with Roberto Cantini
for *Epoca* (1973)[*]

What are your current projects as a writer and your interests as a reader? And your pastimes and hobbies?

I'm writing a new novel. I read what comes to hand. My greatest enjoyment is lepidoptery. I'm back from Cortina d'Ampezzo, an enchanting valley, where I had a very successful hunt. Another, more recent, hobby is genealogy, appropriate to a robust old age. I learned with pleasure that I have a burning drop of Italian blood: one of my direct ancestors is none other than Can Grande della Scala, Lord of Verona, who welcomed Dante in exile: his coat of arms (two big dogs gracefully holding a staircase) adorns the Decameron.

What do you accept and what do you reject of today's civilization?

Modern Western civilization is incomparably more refined, more humane, more artistic in its literature than its counterparts in Russia and in China today. All that I expect from the state—from the servant of the state—is individual freedom. I hate and despise any form of cruelty.

Which of your characters do you like most?

Lolita, Pnin, and the father of the protagonist in *The Gift*—in that order.

* "Nabokov tra i cigni de Montreux" ("Nabokov Among the Swans of Montreux"), *Epoca*, Oct. 7, 1973, 104–12.

141

Interview with George Feifer
for *Sunday Telegraph Magazine* (1974)[*]

You have said that you think like a genius, write like a distinguished author, and speak like a child. Can you confirm the implication that your writing is unequal to your thought?

What I really meant and could not quite express was that I think not in words but in images, swimming colors, in shaded shapes—a type of cogitation that used to be termed "cold delirium" (*holodnyy bred*) by psychiatrists in old Russia. The feeling of power that I experience in my inmost self, among the delights of an abnormal mind, fades away when I speak or write. You are free to contradict me but I maintain that my English is a timid unreliable witness to the marvelous and some-

[*] "Nabokov," *Sunday Telegraph Magazine*, Nov. 14, 1976, 40–46. Typescript questions, typescript draft article with VN's manuscript corrections, correspondence, VNA Berg. An interview had been proposed in Feb. 1974, but was delayed to appear around the time of the English edition of *Look at the Harlequins!* Feifer sent his questions on Aug. 14, 1974; VN finalized his answers for Feifer's visit to Montreux on Aug. 25. VN was upset by many of Feifer's details in the accompanying story, which he felt violated his conditions and his privacy, and after a telegram to Danny Halperin, editor of the *Sunday Telegraph Magazine*, on Nov. 12, followed up with a detailed letter the next day asking that they be corrected or removed: "Unfortunately I find Mr. Feifer's contribution to the prepared dialogue extremely disappointing. Not only does his tone show that he has not read my novels but his comments contain—besides a few pardonable errors of fact—several passages that may seem piquant to the interviewer but are absolutely intolerable to the interviewee. I have jotted down below the gross gaffes that should be struck out. The report on my relations with Solzhenitsyn is factually wrong and morally crude. I am on good personal terms with him, am indifferent to his politics, and do not want Feifer to purse my lips for me as he does on p. 13. The arch allusions to the 'scholar,' who is no other than Andrew Field, must also go; the situation regarding him has become complicated and nasty and I wish to be circumspect. I did call Stravinsky an old idiot but I had carefully warned Feifer to avoid reporting that kind of irresponsible chitchat. Other more innocent errors of taste or truth, listed below, are attributable to the interviewer's complete ignorance of this author's type of mind and manner." The *Sunday Telegraph* eventually published the interview with VN's deletions and corrections; the *Saturday Review* published Feifer's account as he had written it ("Vladimir Nabokov: An Interview," *Saturday Review*, Nov. 27, 1976, 20–26) and with slightly fuller versions of some VN answers, incorporated here.

times monstrous images I try to describe. How more fortunate Joseph Conrad, who deals in conceptual platitudes with a stale style matching perfectly his beautiful popular thought!

Why do we see so little of you in England? Are the memories and images of your Cambridge residence in 1919–1922 in any way responsible for our deprivation?

No, not at all. In fact so many secret ties, which it would be mawkish to discuss, linked me with England before and after my university years that I made a great effort in 1938 (two years before migrating to the States) to obtain an academic job in your country. As a Nansen-passport holder I had a hideous time squeezing a visa out of the British consul in Paris, and when I overstayed it he attempted to reprimand me. A business visit to Cambridge proved a dismal flop (the person I spoke to kept wondering *why* did I think I could teach Russian literature), and when I decided to accept a lectureship in West Riding I discovered that the position had just been canceled. Nothing is lost, however: English readers have not been deprived of this American's books, a great consolation, especially as I prefer "lift" to "elevator" and "shop" to "store."

What surprises you in life?

Its complete unreality; the marvel of consciousness—that sudden window swinging open on a sunlit landscape amidst the night of non-being; the mind's hopeless inability to cope with its own essence and sense.

You have said that no creed or school has had any influence on you whatsoever and that you have no social purpose, no moral message. What is the source of your immunity?

Mainly, an innate passion for independence; partly, my having realized very early in life that commitment to a particular cause disguises bad art and corrupts the good artist. I am running out of nutshells.

Is there a person, place, or situation that haunts you, in the sense that you have not used it to your own satisfaction in your work?

A strange streak of kindness in my nature prevents me from depicting in a contemplated memoir (*Speak on, Memory*) many burlesque characters I have filed away in the last three decades. As to "places and situations" that "haunt" one, as you neatly put it, there exists in my mind a long series of trails, valleys, mountain slopes, rocky debris, bewitching little peat bogs associated with certain difficult butterflies that I longed to see alive, and saw at last, in natural motion or at rest, among the plants of their exiguous breeding places. Yet what can I do with that heavenly stuff as a writer? I am certainly not afraid to bore readers with nature notes worked into a memoir or story. I am afraid to trim my science to size or—what is much the same—not to take full advantage of my art in speaking of "scientific" details.

What role has sport played in your life; what role does it play now?
At one stage or another of my ancient reveries I have been H. L. Doherty (the younger of the two brothers), or some precursor of Gordon Banks. Many times did I save England—or still better some small obscure country—on the playing fields of boyish fancy while going on with the writing of no less imaginary novels under some dazzling pseudonym. The urge I have always had to enjoy and multiply the properties of a sphere—catching it, kicking it, spinning it—may be seen by a solemn symbolist as a craving to dominate the terrestrial globe; but that leaves out, in my case, the sting of sheer pleasure, the healthy physical thrill inherent in a perfectly executed stroke. In modest reality I never won prizes in sports, but played strong effortless tennis well into my sixties, when an accidental interruption grew into a permanent quit. As to football, I kept goal as late as 1936 for a Russian émigré eleven in Berlin, in games with incredibly rough young Germans—factory teams and the like.

Igor Stravinsky was long no less reluctant than you are to visit Russia yet, like Marc Chagall, was profoundly moved when he did. Might remnants of the stimulus to their creativity survive in Russia to be perceived by sensitivities such as theirs—and yours?
I am unfamiliar with the music of Stravinsky and indifferent to the paintings of Shagal (correct transliteration). Besides, since they did revisit Moscow (where I have never been) they were evidently less reluctant to return than I. Stimulus, indeed! Churches and tenements. Corn, sweet corn. Another drop of vodochka, dear Vladimir Vladimch! I can assure you that my shudder is final.

References to "asses," "anonymous clowns," and persons who move their lips while reading abound in your comments to interviewers. Most of these "hacks" (i.e., almost everyone) appear to be less imaginative than yourself. How much is your self-confessed good nature, gayness, warmth, and sweet temper dependent on isolating yourself from the likes of me?

You have rather mixed up things in your question. I have nothing against the likes of you. I was referring to the asses and geese among reviewers, not interviewers. Even so, I may have been a bit brusque. Lately I have prepared a kind of descending scale to grade critics from A-plus to D-minus. You will see that I am concerned exclusively with the amount of information that the reviewer possesses in regard to my works. It goes something like this:

A+ The reviewer of my new book who has read and reread all my previous novels. (He may have developed in the process, or been unable to surmount, a vague repulsion toward them but that is beside the point and does not affect his grade.)

Plain A. Has read almost all my books (this is perhaps over-generous but the descent will be rapid).

B–. Knows everything except *The Gift, Pale Fire,* and *Ada.* Promises to catch up with his reading. Had family worries, etc.

C. Is an ardent admirer of *Laughter in the Dark* (my frailest book) and remembers something about mushrooms in an anthology years ago. That is all he has read. Admiration does not increase marks. Sorry.

D. Thinks he has seen a film based on one of my books.

D–. Has never opened my new book—the one he is writing about— relying entirely on the opinion of a friend who reads fast but prefers yarns about miners and samurai. Spells my name with three o's.

Nothing bores you more, you have said, than the literature of social intent. Is Solzhenitsyn's purpose—the healing of Russia through literature— uncongenial to you?

Gulag is an important historical work, not fiction. I was speaking of fiction-coated tracts (Dreiser, Upton Lewis, numerous earnest young writers of today).

In your recent experience, has pollution affected the life and existence of butterflies?

Pollution itself is a lesser enemy of butterfly life than, say, climatic changes. One sees Skippers and Blues relish rich black filth near country garages and camping grounds. In the case of very local species whose numbers are not kept up by wide-wandering impregnated females, the destruction of an uncommon food plant by some idiot vineyardist can of course wipe out a habitat. But nature is hardy and certain delicate semitransparent little larvae are known to have outmaneuvered the most modern pesticides. It is wonderful to pick out in the crazy quilt of an agricultural area as seen from an airplane the number of green holes where a lovely insect can safely breed. The gloomiest lepidopterist perks up when he thinks that butterflies have survived millenniums of reckless farming, overgrazing and deforestation.

What do you want to do most in the next two years?

Hunt butterflies, especially certain Whites, in the mountains of Iran and in the Middle Atlas. Quietly take up tennis again. Have three new suits made in London. Revisit certain landscapes and libraries in America. Find a harder and darker pencil.

You have been quoted as saying that biography can produce no keener likeness of its subjects than macabre dolls. Are you making any provisions to enable your biographers to make their mistakes?

The biographer is apt to become a macabre doll himself if he does not accept, meekly and gratefully, to comply with all the desires and indications of his still-robust subject—or those of wise lawyers and hawk-eyed heirs. If the subject is dead and unprotected, a century or so should be allowed to elapse before his diaries can be published and chuckled over. In this connection I see that the reviewer of an unauthorized biography of T. S. Eliot believes that "a famous man dead or alive is fair game." Such a pronouncement coming from a usually sensitive and sober critic strikes me as revolting. The facts in my *Speak, Memory* and *Strong Opinions* as well as a collection of special notes should prevent a vicious mediocrity from distorting my life, my truth, my anecdotes.

142

Interview with Helga Chudacoff
for *Die Welt* (1974)*

April 17, 1974

Dear Miss Chudacoff,

I thank you for sending me the list of your questions for an interview in the *Welt des Buches*. You say that "in some instances" similar questions had been set before. That is an understatement. I am directing you back to *Strong Opinions*, and listing the pages therein which you might consult for the German translation of my answers. For me to reword them would be a dreadful duplication of labor. Of course, all the quotations should be copyrighted in the name of McGraw-Hill.

I would be glad to meet you, but I would not like to disappoint you: only such answers as are given here or fished out of *Strong Opinions* may be attributed to me. Direct impressions would be necessarily meager. I must reserve the right to approve the German text.

Do you draw from your own experience or is it all fantasy?
Both.

Some of your characters are pretty cruel,
(NB: many others are saints or artists)

---

* "Schmetterlinge sind wie Menschen" ("Butterflies Are Like People"), *Die Welt*, Sept. 26, 1974, *Welt des Buches*, p. III. Emended typescripts with VN's manuscript corrections and correspondence, VNA Berg. Intended to coincide with the publication of the German translation of *Ada*. After nine months of letters and phone calls, VN met Chudacoff at the Hotel Mont-Cervin, Zermatt, where he was hunting butterflies, on June 20, 1974. VN added corrections to an English version of her typescript in Oct. 1974.

bordering on the perverse perhaps—do you get rid of your own monsters by writing about them like many artists in your and other fields do?
No.

And why do you object to Freud so strongly?
For the same reason that I object to kitsch and astrology. See pp. 23–24, 115–16 (NB).

You were quoted as stating that you loathed Van Veen.[1] What do you hate most about him?
The demonic strain in him.

Do you think Ada *is especially hard to translate because of your play with sounds and words?*
That is one of the difficulties.

How do you feel about other Russian writers, for instance Alexander Solzhenitsyn? Now since he is safe maybe you care to comment, which you did not want to before.
Omit.

And why is the only German you describe in Speak, Memory *somebody who takes a delight in watching executions?*
I also describe some of my German ancestors.

Do you still work as a lepidopterist?
Yes.

And have you finished your book on butterflies in art?
No. See pp. 135–36, 168–69, 190–91 (NB), 199–201.

Did you accomplish everything you set out to accomplish in life or do you have some regrets?
I have no regrets (see pp. 106–7, though), and have not yet finished milking my mind.

May 15, 1974

Dear Miss Chudacoff,

We shall probably spend part of the summer in Zermatt. I shall be glad to talk to you sometime during the summer but not on a butterfly hike, I cannot imagine what interest there could be for you in seeing me between the rain and the butterfly on a muddy mountain trail. There is nobody more gloomy, silent, and edgy than a lepidopterist in the pursuit of his task.

Here are the answers to your 25 new questions:

What gives you more satisfaction, the actual hunting and finding of a butterfly or the scientific evaluation afterward?
See *Strong Opinions.*

Have you noticed any changes or sicknesses in butterflies due to air pollution, poisoning of streams and other environmental factors?
None.

Where will you go butterfly hunting this year? Do you have a favorite spot you visit again and again?
No.

Do you ever exchange butterflies with specimens of other lepidopterists?
No.

You said (p. 191) that your American butterfly collections are in American museums. How big is your European collection by now?
About 5000 papered specimens.

In your latest published book Transparent Things *you look at a butterfly through the eyes of somebody who does not like them. The animal actually appears to be "particularly gross." How do you feel about the butterfly as a living animal—do you sometimes just watch and enjoy it or do you approach it purely from a scientific point of view?*
See *Strong Opinions.*

Will this novel—published in 1972 *in the U.S.A.—be translated into German in the near future?*
Hope so.

Reading this slim volume, one has the feeling death is present throughout this story. . . . What does death mean to you?
Nothing.

One of your characters in Transparent Things *says: "It is generally assumed that if man were to establish the fact of survival after death, he would also solve, or be on the way to solving, the riddle of Being." What exactly was meant by survival after death? Do you mean physical survival or survival of spirit or soul? And do you believe in a life after death?*
No comment.

You have often described your insomnia problems. Do you help yourself occasionally—like Hugh Person—by playing several games of tennis in your fantasy as means to go to sleep?
No comment.

Although you prefer to live in the splendor of a Grand Hotel, you are very good at describing dismal third-rate hotels, the Ascot in Transparent Things *being the last one in a long row. When did you ever stay in such dreary, melancholy places—or did you ever?*
Often.

Film people came to see you and you indicated your willingness to write or help write a screenplay of Ada *(p. 125). Yet a movie was never made of your novel (at least not to my knowledge). Are there still plans for a film and why were movie plans abandoned then?*
No plans.

Where is the setting of your just-finished novel Look at the Harlequins!*?*
Five countries.

How long did you work on the new book and how many index cards did you fill?
About 15 months. 800 cards.

What are your plans for the next few months? Do you plan another novel? Or will you start your new memoir Speak on, Memory *(p. 198)?*
No comment.

Have you been back to the U.S.A. lately and have you noticed any changes?
No comment.

How would you describe the difference between American and European mentality?
What is "European"?

What do you think of the so-called Senior Citizen settlements that are so popular for people over 65 in the U.S.A.?
Nothing.

Next year you shall be married 50 years. In these times of quick marriage and easy divorce there are opinions of all shades about marriage: from a good chance of survival to hopelessly outdated. How do you see the future of this institution for today's young people?
Don't care.

You recently received one of America's most distinguished literary prizes: the National Medal for Literature. Are you as indifferent toward praise as you are toward criticism (Speak Memory, German edition, *p. 176)?*
It depends.

Did you have a chance to see the German TV production of your novel Invitation to a Beheading? *If you did—what did you think of the production, the acting and most importantly of the adaptation of your novel for television?*
I was told it was excellent. I never saw it.

Are you interested in the theater in neighboring Lausanne and Geneva? In perhaps working on a play (you wrote seven plays, p. 89) or just plain theatergoing?
No interest.

If there is a gray sky hanging over the Lake of Geneva, does this affect your mood, your work? Is there any type of day that you prefer to work by in Montreux?
No.

Why do you make it so difficult for your interviewer?
Interviewing is a difficult art.

The man Vladimir Nabokov and the writer VN do not have to harmonize, but they must have something to do with each other. Why do you separate the man and the writer so strongly?
I, the man, am a deeply moral, exquisitely kind, old-fashioned and rather stupid person. I, the writer, am different in every respect. It is the writer who answers your last and best question.

From oral exchanges:
    Your daily routine in Zermatt
I have breakfast at 7:30. A quarter to eight I saunter out of the hotel with my net, choosing one of the four or five possible trails. Depending on the weather, my hike can last three hours or five. On the average I walk 15 kilometers a day. Quite often, later in the season, I use a cable car. By the way, the chairlift is a beautiful invention, you just glide along. Once in Italy I used a chairlift with music—and not only music, but Puccini and *La Traviata*. Often I spend two or three hours on the same meadow waiting for a certain *Falter*. Then perhaps I would find a friendly little *Stube* where I would have a drink. When it rains, however, a lepidopterist has to have even more patience. Butterflies keep quiet for some time after the rain. This morning it was cloudless, the sun was shining after yesterday's rain, and nevertheless they did not come out until ten o'clock.

Does the aesthete in you sometimes prevent the scientist Nabokov from killing a butterfly because it happens to be especially beautiful?
Not because it is beautiful. All butterflies are beautiful and ugly at the same time—like human beings. I let it go if it is old and frayed, or if I

don't need it for my collection. I hate to kill a butterfly which is useless to me. It is an unpleasant feeling—you pinch it automatically and you feel guilty afterward.

On being an enthusiastic American
I don't even know who Mr. Watergate is.

143

Interview with Peter Zeindler
for Swiss Television (1974)[*]

Why do you live in a hotel?
A large first-rate hotel is a fertile and civilized island. My surroundings are neutral, I am comfortable; that is the purpose of the exercise.

What influences you, what gives you pleasure?
Nothing has ever influenced me overmuch. I'm a self-contained organism. But I must confess that for sheer physical well-being a summer day spent hunting butterflies in the Valais, the Ticino, or the Grisons, is only comparable to the delights of Colorado, Montana, Utah.

What do you think of Switzerland's greatest writer, Rousseau?
As a novelist, as a man imagining men, Rousseau was mediocre. But there are great passages in his *Confessions*—passages that my governess, Mlle Miauton, from Vevey, would skip in confusion, but I easily discovered those bits when rummaging in my father's library—a pale little boy of ten with darker eyes and thicker hair than today.

What Swiss authors do you like?
I am sure that if my reading were wider—less specialized and less trivial—I would have come across many talented Swiss authors.

[*] For Schweizer Fernsehen (Zürich), "Perspektiven 58: Russen in der Schweiz," interview by Peter Zeindler, directed by Bernhard Safarik, broadcast Oct. 10, 1974. Holograph draft of answers, in English, VNA Berg. Part of a series on Russians in Switzerland that also featured Alexander Solzhenitsyn and Viktor Nekrasov. VN was filmed on Sept. 25 or 26, 1974.

3. Nothing has ever influenced me overmuch. I'm a self contained organism. But I must confess that for sheer physical well-being a summer day spent hunting butterflies in the Valais, the Ticino, or the Grisons, is only comparable to the delights of Colorado, Montana, Utah.

4. As a novelist, as a man imagining men, Rousseau was mediocre. But there are great passages in his Confessions — passages that my governess, Mlle Miauton from Vevey, would skip in confusion, but I easily discovered those bits when rummaging in my father's library — a pale little boy of ten with darker eyes and thicker hair than to-day.

Fair copies in pencil on index cards of answers to questions by Peter Zeindler for Swiss television (Schweizer Fernsehen, Zurich), 1974. Nabokov would happily introduce local references for his immediate audiences.

What Russian authors do you like?

My Russian favorites of an earlier era are Pushkin, Tolstoy, Chekhov. I will not discuss my contemporaries since my rule is never to speak of living writers in public. As a matter of fact I would not speak of my living readers, either, though there are some real geniuses among them. And quite a few asses.

Do you feel isolated in Switzerland?
All artists, *alle Dichter,* are lonely at a certain level of art. One mountain peak is far removed from another. A congress of original artists is a contradiction in terms. The average authors come together and form pen clubs, or typewriter clubs, et cetera. I think that if there had been no emigrations, or if I were born in Boston instead of St. Petersburg, the lamp above my desk would have shed the same light as now.

Do you plan to translate the work of any other writers?
No, but I intend publishing a revised edition of my *Eugene Onegin* with a still closer translation than ten years ago. I would dearly love to translate another classic, Griboedov's *Woe from Wit,* if I were younger. Much of that kind of labor is nocturnal, a system of nightly agonies destroying the mind.

144

Interview with Dieter Zimmer
for Hessischer Rundfunk (1974)[*]

You have defined yourself as a very moral writer. Your literary fame, however, has been established by what has been regarded as a highly immoral novel—about an elderly gentleman loving a girl named Lolita. In Ada, *incest is added to child-love. I believe you will want to do away with this apparent contradiction?*

If an author's moralistic intent can be seen as his personal shadow passing through his fiction, mixing with the flora and fauna of the book, then my books are shadowless. I do not preach, and I do not take part in the pastimes of my characters. The morality of my works lies in the art of my works. If their art is good, so are their morals. I realize, of course, that when a novel contains criminal scenes some readers experience an intolerable itch of trying to puzzle out if the author commits similar acts in his spare time. Curiosity is one of the most banal human traits but not everybody is as fortunate as Bluebeard's last wife. In this connection I can recall a Dutch critic's conjecturing a few years ago that I castigate Freud out of fear that Freudians might find in my fiction "symbols" divulging secrets of my private life. An interesting idea.

Why is Ada *set on a slanted reflection of earth called Antiterra, not on earth itself?*

The timetable of Terra differs from that of Antiterra. Some events come earlier, others later, others again do not come at all; and what's more

[*] "Titel, Thesen, Temperamente" ("Titles, Theses, Temperaments"), Hessischer Rundfunk (Frankfurt), television broadcast, Oct. 3, 1974. Manuscript index cards, emended typescript with VN's manuscript corrections, in English, VNA Berg. For the German publication of *Ada*. Questions sent Sept. 9, 1974, answers ready for day of filming in Montreux, Sept. 29, 1974. VN also read a paragraph from the end of pt. 2, chap. 8 of *Ada*, p. 409 in the first edition.

the fate of this or that Empire on the other planet does not conform to our schedule. *What* is there so strange after all for a novelist to set up a world unlike the so-called "real" one? The Venice and Denmark of Shakespeare are fantastic realms made to fit his fantastic heroes and their even more fantastic attendants.

Why did you make the beginning so difficult for the reader—with all those ghostlike appearances and disappearances of ancestors?
Genealogical matters occupy less than two pages in the beginning of the book and are preceded by a perfectly clear family tree. I know exactly what scares and irritates the reader: it is the fact that the exotic Russian names in those first pages are impossible for him to pronounce and since so many unfortunate people move their lips when reading, they cannot help stumbling over "Prince Zemski, Governor of Bras d'Or," etc.

Ada *abounds in puns, in allusions, in wordplay of all sorts, forcing the reader to suspect anagrams or the like in every line. . . . Would you care to say whether this is just exuberant verbal imagination, or whether your way of treating language has another meaning.*
This is greatly exaggerated. If you count the pages with no wordplay, with not a single anagram or pun, you will see that the number of such pages is vastly superior to the number of those where a firework of words celebrates an especially important scene.

In your works there is a definite clair-obscur: *there are characters you are fond of, others which you loathe as morons or rogues. Your strong opinions on what you detest in life and in literature have earned you the reputation of being harsh and cold. Would you admit there is such a dualism? How do you explain it? Wouldn't you say that dismissing most of mankind as innately vulgar, stupid and cruel means condemning everything to stay as it is?*
Your words reflect a grave misconception. How can an artist be said to "dismiss most of mankind as vulgar, stupid and cruel"? When mankind does not inhabit his novels, which are populated by purely imaginary, invented beings whose fate is quite unconnected with that of "humanity" in the ordinary sense of the word? I also object to your accusation of my making my characters either completely good or completely bad.

Lolita is a pathetic child and not only a depraved nymphet. Ada herself is a combination of a marvelous mind, tender emotions, animality and heartlessness.

Do you see yourself as old-fashioned or a modern writer?
An "old-fashioned" author may mean an author who uses stock situations, ready-made types and verbal clichés. It can also mean a writer who is above fashions and is, in fact, a jolly good writer, like, say, Sterne, or Flaubert, or Kafka. I dislike those vague schoolman terms and thus could not say, without a lot of marginal remarks, if anyone in his right mind is able to define me as either "old-fashioned" or "modern." The term "modern," which I suppose shades into "modernistic" and "avant-garde" in all arts, is the last refuge of ambitious mediocrity. In a similar sense the sheep of our cities, illiterate young people drifting through life, tend to join the most "extreme" political groups and hasten to take part in protest marches. No, let us leave "modernism" out of real literature.

145

Interview with Gerald Clarke
for *Esquire* (1974)*

My dear fellow, I am *gorged* with questions. . . . I admire people who can speak and it all comes out in well-ordered, beautifully rounded sentences. I cannot do that. I can't speak that way. I am an idiot in conversation.

What are you working on now, or preparing to write?
At the moment I'm basking in the afterglow of a novel I have just completed, *Look at the Harlequins!* (do not drop the exclamation mark). This stage of retrospective sunbathing is a very short, very private affair, unconnected with any awareness of impending publication, etc. It includes a mental rereading of the thing in spectral script. My next task is a meticulous checking of the French translation of *Ada*—a huge bedraggled tome typed on anemic paper. The preparation of an interview for the German TV and the examining of an English translation of yet another collection of my old Russian stories will fill up the intervals between the next chapters of Fayard's adventures with *Ada*. And after that, or still somewhere in between, I shall go on accumulating the bones and flints of a new novel—a rather paleontological kind of research in reverse, so to speak. According to some of my criticasters, the unfortunate readers of my books have to look up words like "paleontological."

---

* "Checking In with Vladimir Nabokov," *Esquire*, July 1975, 67–69, 131, 133. Emended typescript with VN's manuscript corrections, VNA Berg. Typescript answers prepared for Clarke for Sept. 17, 1974, the day he visited VN in Montreux; additional oral exchanges edited by VN and returned on Oct. 28, 1974.

Could you describe a typical day in the life of VN? Do you have any habits or devices that get you started writing, like sharpening pencils or filling pens?
Friends would sigh and foes grind their teeth if I relisted for the hundredth time my daily habits to an innocent interviewer. It is all in my *Strong Opinions*, you know. All I care to repeat is that the first sentence of the day is composed in my morning bath.

Which modern writers do you read for pleasure? Are there any living writers you particularly admire? Or particularly dislike?
I find morbidly fascinating the leisurely letters in which English authors of a former age praise at length contemporaneous writers (mostly their correspondents) or revile in detail writers belonging to other so-called "groups" or "schools" of the time. And mind you, those epistolarians' professional output was a tomb-slab-thick novel per year. My personal letters are rare and brief. Though anything but a prolix novelist, I fear squandering the energy reserved for my novels. On the other hand, I am happy to report that my library of modern literature, which is housed in an attic kindly allotted to me by the hotel, is growing steadily owing to contributions from publishers. A great number of those volumes are ephemeral—you know the type—romances all slaughter and semen or collections of essays by pretentious hacks—but when I think of the care that went into every detail of the jacket, into this or that pathetic little touch of the printer's art, I feel disinclined to ridicule the dream between the covers.

Your life has been divided into geographic segments—Europe, America, and now Europe again—yet you are an American citizen. Do you still consider yourself American? Do you think that your writing has an American accent?
I have spent nineteen years in Russia, three in England, sixteen in Germany, four in France, twenty in America, thirteen in Switzerland. Of these the longest time segment is the American one. I am American.

Someone has described you, with some admiration, as "a brilliant monster."
Would you care to comment? Do you feel very monstrous?
I guess you've invented that "someone" but it is a plausible invention. One of the definitions that my dictionary gives under "monster" is "a person of unnatural excellence." Of course, I'm aware of my unnatural excellence. I am aware of it, however, only in certain domains (too obvi-

ous to be mentioned); but I also am aware of my hopeless ineptitude in other matters such as technology, finance, music and go-getting, to name a few. The epithet "brilliant" is a little redundant. Most monsters have shining appendages or eyes.

In its concern for memory and the recollection of specific detail, your writing reminds me of Proust's. Do you see any resemblance?
I see no resemblance whatever. Proust *imagined* a person (the "Marcel" of his long fairy tale *In Search of Lost Time*) who had a Bergsonian concept of past time and was thrilled by its sensual resurrection in sudden juxtapositions pertaining to the present. I am *not* an imaginary person and my memories are direct rays deliberately trained, not sparks and spangles.

You are now in your mid-seventies. How do you feel as you look back at your life? Have you accomplished all or most of the things you hoped to accomplish, or has some goal eluded you?
The literary line of my fate from 1920 to 1940 is what I expected at nineteen. I have written in Russian the kind of books I wanted to write. The English ones that followed in the next thirty-four years are a rare recompense for the trouble I took over my first compositions in my native language. If any goal has eluded me, it must be sought in another domain, that of lepidopterology. At the middle point of my life (1940–48) I used to devote many hours daily, including Sundays, to the working out of taxonomic problems in the laboratories of two great museums. Since my years at the Museum of Comparative Zoology in Harvard, I have not touched a microscope, knowing that if I did, I would drown again in its bright well. Thus I have not, and probably never shall, accomplish the greater part of the entrancing research work I had imagined in my young mirages, such as "A monograph of the Eurasian and American *machaon* group," or "The *Eupithecia* of the World." Gratitude for other pleasures leaves, really, no room in my mind for that ghost of regret.

Are you still an insomniac?
I had lately started jogging before turning in. Delightful! Keeping it up for a couple of hours, in the deepening dusk, along lakeside lanes, is both exhilarating and soothing. Except for a few pairs of lovers disen-

tangling themselves to watch my passage there is nobody to notice me. I wear tennis shorts and a heavy sweater which I usually shed after the first hour. I'm afraid I've made up this story *in toto,* but it shows how desperate I am beginning to be in my fight with insomnia. Harmless pills have ceased to affect me, and I decline to rely on brutal barbiturates. My afternoon siesta has stretched to almost three hours, and my night's sleep has dwindled to about the same length of time. At least two kind strangers have suggested a little warm milk with a spoonful of honey at bedtime.

Which of your books do you remember with the greatest pleasure? Of which character are you fondest?
Oh, *The Gift* and *Lolita,* of course, and also the novels I wrote in the Sixties and Seventies. And the four volumes of my work on *Eugene Onegin.* I am inordinately fond of those old books. (My weakest is certainly *Laughter in the Dark,* by the way.) As to the characters in them, I cannot love them separately, they are on a par with the fantasy and the fun and the moth on the mottled tree trunk.

If you had had a choice, what language would you have preferred to have been born with?
Russian.

Additional oral exchanges, Sept. 17, 1974:
    Nabokov offered him a drink—"A gin and tonic perhaps?"—"and professed amazement, shock, and incomprehension when I wanted instead a local Swiss beer, the agreeable but slightly acidic Feldschlösschen."
    "Feldschlösschen! . . . Feldschlösschen is for field mice! Try a German beer."
    "Maybe he likes light beer," Vera gently suggested.
    "It's not a question of light or dark. It's a question of good or bad."

If you ever do go back to America, where will you live?
California. California is one of my favorite states. I like the climate, the flora, and the fauna—the butterfly fauna. And it's close to Mexico and Alaska. I've never been to Alaska, unfortunately. It is the best place for butterflies.

Which part of California would you go to?
I like it all. I love Los Angeles, where we lived while I was writing the screenplay of *Lolita*. I had never seen jacaranda trees before, at least in bloom. Do you remember, darling? There was a whole street lined with jacarandas.

Whom do you most admire? (Clarke asked him again, "repeating one of the questions I had sent him, without getting, as his written reply shows, a very explicit response.")
Edmund White. He wrote *Forgetting Elena*. He's a marvelous writer. I'm also a great admirer of John Updike—the up, up, up Updike. J. D. Salinger is another writer I admire tremendously. Beautiful stuff! He's a real writer. I like some of Truman Capote's stuff, particularly *In Cold Blood*. Except for that impossible end, so sentimental, so false. But there are scenes in which he writes with true appetite, and he presents them very well.

Interview with Tibor Wlassics (1974)[*]

Dear Professor Wlassics,

Your *Galilei Critico Letterrario*, which arrived yesterday, is not only a charming gift but also a gentle reproach. I deserved a harsher one.

I now see that eons have elapsed since we met. An agonizing task, the correction of a French translation of *Ada*, with a deadline in January, has been consuming all my time. I take advantage of the brief ghost of a holiday to answer some of your questions (separate page).

Do you make a distinction between "human interest" and human interest?
Types of "human interest" are exemplified by the fashions of this or that season, such as the question did Byron acquire a clubfoot in result of his kicking his father in a fetal dream.

Re: your categorical denials of literary "influences" (Kafka, Proust, Joyce). Would it make any difference if one spoke of "tribute" to (rather than influence of) those masters in your narrative work?
Yes, tribute—and a comfortable feeling of belonging to the same club in a world where there are no other clubs.

---

[*] Apparently unpublished. Typescript and correspondence, in English, VNA Berg. Wlassics and his wife visited VN at the Montreux Palace on Aug. 26, 1974. The interview was intended as the introduction to a volume, *Vladimir Nabokov*, that Wlassics was to have had published in 1975 by La Nuova Italia, Florence. He had sent the questions on Aug. 20, 1974. VN sent Wlassics his apology (above) and answers on Dec. 27.

Interview with James Salter
for *People* (1975)[*]

Nabokov explains that he prefers to conduct interviews on paper, writing and rewriting the answers and some of the questions.

It has not been an unhappy marriage, then?
That is the understatement of the century.

On Ada
My fattest and most complex book.

On fame
I am not a famous writer. Lolita was a famous little girl. You know what it is to be a famous writer in Montreux? An American woman comes up on the street and cries out, "Mr. Malamud! I'd know you anywhere."

On dinner: someone comes in to cook, or Véra does.
We do not attach too much importance to food or wine.

On his liking bright people, "people who understand jokes"
Véra doesn't laugh, *he says resignedly.* She is married to one of the great clowns of all time, but she never laughs.

---

[*] "An Old Magician Named Nabokov Writes and Lives in Splendid Exile," *People*, March 17, 1975, 60–64. Correspondence, VNA Montreux. For the publication of *Tyrants Destroyed and Other Stories* on Jan. 27, 1975. Salter sent questions on Jan. 3, 1975, but VN had to cancel on Jan. 14, because of flu. Salter must have come to VN shortly afterward.

Mr. Nabokov's Acceptance Speech
(Essay, 1975)[*]

I am sorry not to be able to accept in person the National Book Award but I could not find a suitable boat to take me across the ocean and flying is for the birds.

To illustrate, through an amiable representative, my appreciation of this splendid prize allows me to dwell briefly on the bright side of a writer's life by listing the delights of the greatest of arts, the art of fiction. I enjoy, I have always enjoyed stressing the word "art." An unpopular intonation nowadays: art not as a profession, not as a summer commune of kindred minds, and not as a demonstration of topical ideas in a drizzle of politics, but Art with a capital A as big as the biggest Arch of Triumph, art careful and carefree, selfless and self-centered, art burning the brow and cooling the brain.

I have in view, naturally, my dedication to it not my achievement, which today is given a rich tangible prize and tomorrow may have to be content with a footnote in a survey of extinct authors—one of those suppositions that are permissible then only when one does not really believe them.

My sense of utter surrender to art started sixty years ago when my father's private librarian typed out for me and posted to the best literary review my first poem which, though as banal as a blue puddle in March,

---

* "Mr. Nabokov's Acceptance Speech," in case he won when the American National Book Awards, for which his *Look at the Harlequins!* was short-listed, were announced. Typescript, VNA Montreux. To his editor at McGraw-Hill, Fred Hills, he wrote on April 8, 1975, "I shall airmail express to you tomorrow the phantasm of an acceptance speech. . . . Dan Lacy or you would be kind to substitute for me if fancy becomes fact" (*Selected Letters, 1940–1977*, ed. DN and Matthew J. Bruccoli [New York: Harcourt Brace Jovanovich / Bruccoli Clark Layman, 1989], 545). His novel did not win.

was immediately accepted. Its printed image caused me much less of a thrill than the preliminary process, the sight of my live lines being sown by the typist in regular rows on the sheets, with a purple duplicate that I kept for years as one does a lock of hair or the bell tail of a rattler.

I must skip the later delight of writing a novel over which I took such fond trouble that I can still regurgitate it in my mind; and one always remembers the arrival of one's published book, the precious, the pure volume which one tenderly opens—to find a fatal misprint of the plausible kind that will keep up with the book's destiny through hard and soft, from one edition to another, like a tenacious ancestral wart. A much later bedazzlement was the Boxed Book, with its Order of the Ribbon affixed to the headband—and this touch of luxury leads me back to the thrill of a Literary Award.

And even if, at this eloquent point, to the stupefaction of the audience, a wild-eyed messenger on a real horse gallops onto the stage crying that it all had been a hideous mistake I would be delightfully recompensed by the embarrassed smile of the real winner waiting in the wings with his little speech.

149

Interview with Sophie Lannes
for *L'Express* (1975)*

What is exile, for a "cosmopolitan" who learned English before Russian?
What is exile? Well in my case (which isn't the first, by the way) it's not
at all my country that exiled me, but I who exiled Russia: it's very touching, it's almost official, but, like Pushkin's Tatiana, "I belong hencefor-
ward to another, and will remain faithful"—to my new passport, with
its golden eagle on an apple-green background, which Swiss, French,
Italian customs officers give back to me without even checking the
photo of a face still younger than mine each time.

Why Switzerland?
Why Switzerland? Why not? Its mountains, the diversity of its flora,
its smooth highways, its charming inns, remind me of my favorite
country, the American West. Really the only thing that irritates me in
Switzerland is that the beautiful mid-altitude meadows are mowed too
soon and too often—for I need the wildflowers—which all my translators rack their brains translating "savage flowers"[1]—I need them for my
entomological walks, the greatest pleasure in my life. But, naturally, I
can always climb in a magic chair to two thousand meters to find my
wild butterflies—taking care to avoid certain slopes of the high mountains, where cow dung replaces edelweiss. Dialogue on a mountain
pathway with a would-be "protector of nature": "He: You know it is
forbidden to hunt butterflies? I: What do you call a butterfly? (I show
him one, on the small side.) He: No, that's a sort of fly, I mean the ones

* "Portrait de Nabokov," *L'Express*, June 30–July 6, 1975, 22–25. Emended typescript with
VN's manuscript corrections, VNA Berg. For publication of the French *Ada*. Questions
submitted April 17, 1975, answers prepared by April 30.

they make jewels of, the big blue ones, you know." Poor man thought he was in Brazil.

You haven't settled anywhere for good. You have no house, no apartment, in Switzerland you even live in a hotel. Why this refusal to settle down?
A villa with all mod cons and an "inalienable view" cannot replace the *"château qui baignait ma Dore."*[2] A good hotel is enough for me; and I prefer countries where strikes don't happen every day. Like Marat, I like to write in a hot bath. His brother was a passionate butterfly hunter—an interesting little detail, don't you think?

I'll tell you frankly, as people say when frankness isn't their leading characteristic: frankly, then, the material side of life has never much interested me. The loss of an immense fortune, magicked away by Lenin (as I relate in my *Speak, Memory*), caused no more than a shrug of the shoulders in my family. On the other hand, this loss of precious things, of ancestral givens, explains my perfect indifference toward the material delights I could offer myself today.

You've spoken of America as the only country where you are truly happy. What has America represented and what does it represent for you? What are you attached to and what are you irritated by—for example, certain youth protest movements or the hippie spirit?
But the hippies and all that, the smells, the empty skulls, the guitars, the dirty feet, isn't that after all rather old-hat today? The hideous thunder of the motorbikes in Montreux isn't worse, psychologically, than the rattle of tram rails complained of by the English and Russians who came to the luxury hotels a hundred years ago. As for the word "protester," its meaning eludes me, and the term "the young" brings on a vague nausea. I don't know these people.

What do you feel in regard to Russia today? Do you still feel Russian?
What feeling does Russia inspire in me? Well, it's an exquisite miniature: the memory of a certain landscape, the savor of a few strands of old Russian literature, and that's it. Its churches in sculpted wood leave me still colder than the marbles of Rome. In the very depths of this sad Russia the muzhik whips his poor horse with as much enthusiasm as under the tsars of old.

As a child, I was Russian, my first muse was Russian. We speak only Russian in my family today, but hatred for the brutality, the ignoble baseness of Soviet tyranny, separates me forever from Russia's tender soil and its birches.

What language do you think in?

I don't think in any language; I think only in images. Of course there exist thoughts so close to speech that one almost pronounces them when one says to oneself, "Where could I have put it?" or "But I had it in my pocket just now."

Real meditation is silent. The stream of our daily routine burbles from time to time, but the sentence that inspiration releases is an underground torrent.

On his Russian versus his English

The afterword to the American edition of *Lolita* was written twenty years ago, when I rather naïvely thought that my Russian, which I was using only to compose a few poems from time to time, was a kind of beautiful cemetery well sheltered by the New World. Alas, much has changed since. My Russian prose has lost the suppleness I was so proud of. On the other hand—and it's a rather bizarre phenomenon—the few poems I have composed in my old age are incomparably more successful and original than all those of the first half of my life. A superb recompense, which I would like to compare to these exchanges of organs, those replacements of special membranes in the course of the evolution of certain creatures which find again the wings they have lost.

Yet I consider myself an American writer. There was a moment in the thirties when I could have tried to establish myself in England. Fate wanted me to choose the United States, and I'll never regret it. But there are people who won't forgive me. Or certain people in certain London weeklies rail against American readers who according to them have sheltered and coddled me instead of letting me write my books in England. When English reviewing gets angry, it turns itself into an obscene buffoon. As far as literature goes, America today has the upper hand over the British, and my unforgivable crime is to profit from what they call the American sycophantism that swells my reputation.

On elements of autobiography in his work
My seventeen novels—nine in Russian and eight in English—contain many echoes coming from a childhood preserved in my interior museum, a particularly precious relic. Here's why: I was describing, I was evoking my Russian childhood, in Russian, when I, the author, was about thirty. Well, show me a Russian today, aged thirty or even fifty, whose childhood was of the same type as mine. The creature no longer exists! So there's a certain exoticism as regards childhood that my Russian readers find in the memories I lend to my heroes. *Le château qui baignait ma Dore* is unknown to them, or very vaguely related to the dawns of a Tolstoy, a Turgenev. In other words my self, my past seems to be, because of this exotic side, more glittering than if all my young readers (everybody looks young from here) had also known *"et ma montagne et le grand chêne."*[3]

On memory and imagination
The two things—a simple memory and the simple movement of imagination—are easy to distinguish if one doesn't linger long (otherwise fantasy takes the upper hand). Let me give you an example. Leafing through an old diary, I suddenly recall the little café just before crossing the Villeneuve-Loubet Bridge, to the right of the road going from Nice to Grasse. That was ten years ago, but every detail is vividly colored. A fat tourist in front of me is eating a salad disgustingly. But this man I have just invented, just added to pure memory, for some literary need, and this invention scrambles the memory. So let's not trust fantasy, when the muse of memory gives us in passing a little gift.

On his dismissals of other writers
I am indifferent to general ideas. I have only a very vague idea of what, say, realism or existentialism is.

What pleases or displeases me isn't a team of writers, it's not even this or that writer, it's only certain books that I like or find boring and false. The didacticism of Gogol or the moralism of Dostoevsky are regions of thought where I avoid setting foot, but if you name Gogol's *The Carrick* or Tolstoy's *Death of Ivan Ilich*—ah, that's different, a flash of delight slides down my back—and even more if it was the original text we wanted to talk of, Gogol's *Shinel'* or Tolstoy's *Smert' Ivana Ilyicha.*[4]

But to turn to detestable books: reread, I ask you, Zola's *The Earth* or that other pile of rubbish by Balzac, whose title is, I think, *The Woman and the Panther*,[5] or the complicated and grotesque explanation of Raskolnikov's crime: sickening!

In your opinion, should literary creation be detached from every moral, social, and ideological intention?
If a critic finds a moral, social, or ideolotic side in a book I admire for other reasons, for other shivers, I don't read his criticism, that's all.

Do you have political opinions?
My political opinions come down to a few very simple principles that any gentleman, in the old sense of the term, does not display and does not discuss.

On Freud
Yes, this charlatan, this symbol repairer, this old umbrella-seller has caused much harm, and his disciples have made much money. But fashion passes, works appear where Freudianism is demolished in a magisterial and very heartening way. Let's speak no more of him.

What writers have influenced you? Those whose genius you recognize?
I love *Hamlet*, I love most of the chapters of Joyce's *Ulysses*, I love Proust's humor. I love a dozen Russian poems by different authors. I still love several works that I often allude to in my own work. What is called literary influence is a joke, since the solitude of the artist is the only thing that counts.

Is there an artistic reality opposed to the real?
"Reality" is one of the rare words which mean nothing without quotes. Without quotes the "real" is a griffin without grippers.[6] My "reality" and yours, and that of any other person, don't resemble one another and cannot be considered as a more or less homogenous mass. Our dearest friend is a creature of our imagination and vice versa—unless we drag ourselves along, he and I, like two shades interlaced through each moment of our two disparate lives, which would be macabre, absurd, and madly dull. All we know of the "reality" of the world around this

famous "we" is only a variable and rather insipid average. The density, the luster, the feel of a "reality" whose quotation marks come from our private printery are furnished by the artistic imagination.

Colored hearing

Yes, what's called colored hearing is developed to an extreme degree in me. Consonants, vowels, and diphthongs each have a special color that I see when I close my eyelids to concentrate my attention on the letter of my choice, in the luminous circle of thought. It can't be called a gift, since this palette has no artistic utility, and nor is it a medical condition. It seems that very few authors have spoken of this strange peculiarity. Rimbaud's famous sonnet[7] is suspiciously lyrical, with too many metaphors and not enough precise details. Besides, he describes only vowels, whereas it's the consonants that offer particularly mysterious and subtle nuances and distinctions.

A few years ago a Freudian psychiatrist gave an explanation of unbelievable imbecility. And yet real science should have developed a passion for this phenomenon. Are there for example two people whose letters in the same alphabet have exactly the same colors? And do these two people resemble each other in other respects?

Is your ear really deaf to music, even though your son is a singer, your brother, a conductor?

I like a few Puccini tunes, a few Russian romances, the song of the oriole, and the dawn chorus of blackbirds. My son is indeed an opera singer, but I have no "brother, a conductor."[8]

Eroticism in literature

The erotic theme is a theme like any other. It's one of the sensual facets of literary art. *Lolita* came at the right moment: a question of fashion, a lucky coincidence, a model little girl. Contemporary erotic production has the tremendous assistance of photography, and one finds a few caricaturists of genius among the descendants of Caran d'Ache.[9]

On chess

I am a good player but not a grandmaster. And although I have composed and published thirty or so chess problems, of which two or three enjoy a certain celebrity among the peaceful madmen who devote themselves to the art of problems, I've never gained a cent in this line. The rare combination, illusory solutions as complex as the only true solution—here are things that could be spoken about by a literary critic who was also an expert in chess problems (which differ from the game itself as a triolet differs from a series of novels), but this Siamese monster doesn't exist as far as I know.

How do you write, what do you read?
A pencil not too hard but sharpened as finely as a jewel; an eraser of my favorite brand xxxxxx;[10] medium-sized index cards; a half-bottle of Bordeaux; a lectern matching my elbow exactly; a little ball of red wax in each auditory channel; a rather strong light;—and the new book gets written bit by bit. For reading I read anything at all, little novels publishers send me, and even newspapers.

Expectations, regrets in life?
My life has corresponded to what I expected as an adolescent in a torrent of words and with a cornucopia of prodigious size. I have no right to regret anything at all.

One would feel inclined to say in reading you that life is a very entertaining and very cruel joke. What do you think of it yourself?
Read—or reread, I'm very polite—my novel *The Gift*, or my *Speak, Memory*, or my English commentary on *Eugene Onegin* in four volumes (which could well have been translated into French), and I believe that nothing would remain of the definition you attribute to me.

What do you detest most in the world?
Brutality, stupidity, noise.[11]

Interview with Bernard Pivot
for *Apostrophes* (1975)[*]

It is 9:47 p.m. and 47 seconds. Vladimir Nabokov, what are you usually doing at this hour?

At this hour I am under my eiderdown, with three pillows under my head, in a nightcap, in my modest bedroom which also serves me as study. A very strong bedside light, the lighthouse of my insomnias, is still burning on my night table, but will be turned off in a moment. I have in my mouth a black-currant lozenge and in my hands a New York or London weekly. I put it aside. I turn out the light. I turn it on again to stuff a handkerchief in my nightshirt's little pocket, and now starts

---

[*] "*Apostrophes:* Bernard Pivot rencontre Vladimir Nabokov" ("*Apostrophes:* Bernard Pivot Meets Vladimir Nabokov"), live television interview, Antenne-2 (Paris), May 30, 1975. Emended typescript with VN's manuscript corrections, VNA Berg; typed transcript, Dieter Zimmer collection; videotape cartridge (VHS Secam) (Paris: Vision Seuil). On the occasion of the publication of the French translation of *Ada,* June 1975. Although *Apostrophes* was one of the most-loved programs of its time in France, VN had to be cajoled into participating. All other *Apostrophes* interviews were impromptu, and with a group of critics involved in the discussion. Although this episode was also broadcast live and before a small audience, and there were critics present, VN was allowed to have the questions—only from Pivot himself— sent in advance, and to prepare his answers, which during the program he read from cards roughly concealed behind a stack of his books. VN was pleased afterward, and although some viewers deplored the absence of the program's usual spontaneity, Pivot later rebroadcast the episode twice, and regarded it as one of his finest accomplishments. He recalled: "He was really anti-TV. I went to see him in Montreux when I was starting to work for Two. I had to please him, and please Véra. . . . He received me in a large salon [at the Montreux Palace], where there was a piano. We started talking. The piano tuner came in. He set to work. We moved to another salon, where we hadn't noticed another piano. Our conversation resumed, and five minutes later, we saw the piano tuner come in. We left for a third salon, without a piano. It was a very Nabokovian scene. . . . To boost his courage [during the live broadcast], he wanted to drink whiskey. But he naturally didn't want to set a bad example for French viewers. We had poured a bottle of whiskey into a teapot. Every quarter of an hour, I would ask him: 'A little more tea, Monsieur Nabokov?' And he would drink with a broad smile. He was a great comedian, incredible for his joking, his warmth, his humor, his artful dodges, his impudence, and of course his intelligence. In my memory Nabokov is an icon. He spoke more than an hour. I have an almost religious feeling for that program." (Daniel Rondeau, "Pivot: Comment j'ai fait parler Nabokov" ["Pivot: How I Got Nabokov to Talk"], *Le Nouvel Observateur,* March 20, 1987.)

the interior debate: to take or not to take a sleeping pill? How delicious the positive decision is.

What is your routine on an ordinary day?
Let's choose a day in the middle of winter (in summer there's much more variety in my life). *(Remainder of answer omitted; see answers about VN's routine elsewhere.)*

When you were a little younger, did you already have this routine? Or did you have passions, fancies, impulses, that disturbed your days and nights?
Oh yes, at twenty-five, at thirty, energy, caprice, inspiration, all that kept me writing until 4:00 a.m. I would rarely get up before midday and wrote all day long, stretched out on a divan. The pen and the horizontal position have given way now to pencil and austere verticality. No more fits and starts, that's over. But how I would adore the birds' wake-up, the fluted and sonorous song of the blackbirds, who seemed to applaud the last sentences of the chapter I'd just finished composing.

So has writing always been the great love of your life? Can you imagine another life in which you didn't write?
Yes, I can very easily picture another life: a life in which I wouldn't be a novelist, the happy renter of an ivory Tower of Babel, but someone just as happy, in another fashion—which, by the way, I've tried—an obscure entomologist who spends the summer hunting butterflies in fabulous regions and the winter classifying his discoveries in a museum lab.

Do you feel more Russian, American, or, since you live in Switzerland, Swiss?
Here are a few details about the cosmopolitan aspect of my life. I was born in an old Russian family in St. Petersburg. My paternal grandmother was German in origin, but I never learned this language well enough to be able to read it without a dictionary. I spent my first eighteen summers in the country, on our estate not far from Petersburg. In autumn we went to the south, to Nice, Pau, Biarritz, Abbazia. In winter it was always Petersburg, which is now Leningrad, but our fine home of pink granite still exists in good condition, on the outside at least: tyrannies like the architecture of the past. Our estate was in the northern forest plain; it is rather close in its flora to the northwestern corner of

America: forests of bright aspens and dark pines, lots of birches, and splendid bogs with a multitude of flowers and more or less arctic butterflies. This totally happy phase lasted until the Bolshevik coup: the manor was nationalized. In April 1919 three Nabokov families, that of my father and those of his two brothers, were forced to leave Russia via Sebastopol, an old fortress of misfortune. The Red Army coming from the north was already invading the Crimea, where my father had been minister of justice in the provincial government during the brief liberal period before the Bolshevik terror. The same year, in October 'nineteen, I began my studies at Cambridge.

What's your preferred language: Russian, English, or French?
The language of my ancestors is still the one in which I feel perfectly at home, but I will never regret my American metamorphosis. French—or, rather, my French—doesn't align so well with the anguish of my imagination;[1] its syntax forbids me certain liberties that I take perfectly naturally with the other two languages. It goes without saying that I adore Russian, but English surpasses it as a work tool, it surpasses it in richness of nuance, in frenzied prose, in poetic precision.

... At three I spoke English better than Russian, and I read and wrote it before Russian; on the other hand, there was a whole period in my personal Russia, between ten and twenty, during which, while reading a prodigious crowd of English authors—Wells, Kipling, the magazine *The Boy's Own Paper*, to cite only a few summits—I spoke English only rarely, all the more so since at school there were no English classes (but we did have French—we took a whole winter to study Mérimée's tedious *Colomba*). I had learned French at six: my governess Mademoiselle Cécile Miauton stayed in our family until 1915! We began with *Le Cid* and *Les Misérables*. But the real treasures awaited me in my father's library.[2] At twelve I knew all the blessed poets of France.[3] *"Souvenir, souvenir, que me veux-tu? L'automne faisait voler la grive à travers l'air atone et le bois où la bise détone. ..."*[4] It's curious that at this tender age I already understood that Verlaine should not have been able to use such an incestuous rhyme: *atone, détone*. So there's the calendar of my three languages. Now a few details. Like most of the Nabokovs, and like many Russians (Lenin, for example), I spoke my native tongue with a little burr, which hardly hindered me in French (although it was far from the adorable rolled "r" of Parisian cabaret chanteuses) but which I hurried to get rid of in English—rather late, in America, after having heard my voice on radio for the first time. I said, horribly, "I am Russian" as if I came from Roussillon. I got rid of this flaw by disguising the dangerous letter with a little neutral vibration: "I am Wussian."

The French alphabet offers quite a different danger for a Russian, even if this Russian speaks French with a certain ease. The danger resides in the consonant "t" before an "i" or a "u." You always recognize a Russian of the *ancien régime* by his manner of pronouncing this softish "t" deriving from the Russian alphabet. He will say "*petz'it-à-petz'it*" [*petit-à-petit*, "little by little"] or "*c'est un tz'ype sympathz'ique*" [*c'est un type sympathique*, "he's a likable sort"]. Young Russians educated in France certainly don't have this habit, but their old parents don't even notice that neither habit nor study have firmed up for them this intimate softness. You could say that the Slavic consonant greets with a discreet smile the Gallic "i," melting with tenderness before it.

Isn't exile, however distressing, a stimulating thing for creators, a possibility of enrichment for the spirit and the sensibility?
[On his years in the Berlin and Paris emigration and the irritation of Nansen passports for the officially stateless.] But not all among us agreed to be bastards or phantoms. You could pass from Menton to San Remo very calmly by little mountain paths well known to butterfly hunters or absentminded poets.

The story of my life resembles less a biography than a bibliography. [In moving to America] I discovered a total incapacity to speak in public. So I decided to write in advance my hundred lectures a year on Russian literature. That makes two thousand typed pages of which, three times a week, I would recite twenty, having arranged them in a position not too obvious on my desk before the amphitheater of my students. Thanks to this procedure I never got muddled and the auditorium received the pure product of my knowledge. I repeated the same course each year, introducing new notes, new details.

Why do you live in Switzerland? And why in a hotel?
Why a Swiss hotel? Switzerland is charming and a hotel life simplifies a heap of things. I miss America greatly and hope to return there for another twenty-year stay. A quiet life in an American university town

would present no essential difference from Montreux, where, besides, the streets are noisier than in provincial America. On the other hand, since I am not rich enough—since no one is rich enough—to replay my whole childhood, it's not worth the trouble of settling anywhere. I mean, it's impossible to find the taste of Swiss milk chocolate from 1910 anymore. So I'd have to construct a whole factory. My wife and I have thought of a villa in France or Italy, but then the specter of postal strikes appeared in all its horror. People of settled professions, calm oysters firmly attached to their native mother-of-pearl, don't realize, perhaps, how regular and reliable mail, as in Switzerland, assuages the life of an author, even if this offering on an ordinary morning consists only of a few vague business letters and two or three autograph requests (warning to the audience). And the view from the balcony to the lake—this lake which is worth all the liquid silver it resembles.

Apart from exile and displacement, what are the main themes of your books?
Apart from displacement? But I am displaced everywhere and always. I'm at home in my very personal memories which have no connection with a Russia geographical, national, or physical. Émigré critics in Paris and my schoolteachers in Petersburg were right for once to complain that I wasn't Russian enough.

As for the principal themes of my books, well, there's a bit of everything.

But isn't a good novel above all an excellent story?
An excellent story, I perfectly agree. I would add, all the same, that my best novels don't have one, but several stories which interlace in a certain way. My *Pale Fire* has this counterpoint, and *Ada*, too. I like not only to see the main theme radiate through the whole novel but also to develop little secondary themes. Sometimes it's a digression that turns into a drama in a corner of the narrative, or the metaphors of an extended essay that join up to form a new story.

Do you think that stories invented by novelists—and I am thinking especially of a novelist called Vladimir Nabokov—are more interesting than life's true stories?
Let's be clear: the true story of a life has also been told by someone, and if it is an autobiography set down by the prudish pen of a person

without talent, it could well be that this life seems very insipid beside a marvelous invention like Joyce's *Ulysses*.

Nabokov is Lolita: *aren't you ultimately annoyed by the success of* Lolita— *which has been so emphatic that people have the impression that you are the father of this unique, slightly perverse daughter?*
Lolita isn't a perverse young girl. She's a poor child who has been debauched and whose senses never stir under the caresses of the foul Humbert Humbert, whom she asks once, "how long did [he] think we were going to live in stuffy cabins, doing filthy things together . . . ?" But to reply to your question: no, its success doesn't annoy me, I am not like Conan Doyle, who out of snobbery or simple stupidity preferred to be known as the author of *The Great Boer War*, which he thought superior to his Sherlock Holmes.

It is equally interesting to dwell, as journalists say, on the problem of the inept degradation that the character of the nymphet Lolita, whom I invented in 1955, has undergone in the mind of the broad public. Not only has the perversity of this poor child been grotesquely exaggerated, but her physical appearance, her age, everything has been transformed by the illustrations in foreign publications. Girls of eighteen or more, sidewalk kittens, cheap models, or simple long-legged criminals, are baptized "nymphets" or "Lolitas" in news stories in magazines in Italy, France, Germany, etc.; and the covers of translations, Turkish or Arab, reach the height of ineptitude when they feature a young woman with opulent contours and a blond mane imagined by boobies who have never read my book.

In reality Lolita is a little girl of twelve, whereas Humbert Humbert is a mature man, and it's the abyss between his age and that of the little girl that produces the vacuum, the vertigo, the seduction of mortal danger. Secondly, it's the imagination of the sad satyr that makes a magic creature of this little American schoolgirl, as banal and normal in her way as the poet *manqué* Humbert is in his. Outside the maniacal gaze of Humbert there is no nymphet. Lolita the nymphet exists only through the obsession that destroys Humbert. Here's an essential aspect of a unique book that has been betrayed by a factitious popularity.

Is Ada a cousin of Lolita?

Ada and Lolita are in no way cousins. In the world of my imagination—
for Lolita's America is ultimately as imaginary as the one in which Ada
lives—in these invented worlds the two young girls belong to different
classes and different intellectual levels. I have spoken of the first of the
two, the softer, the frailer, the nicer (Ada isn't nice at all).

I spoke of the abyss of time that separates Humbert from Lolita. On
the other hand, the good reader of *Ada* will find nothing particularly
morbid or rare in the case of a boy of fourteen who falls in love with
a young girl he plays with. They go too far, certainly, these two adolescents, and the fact that they are brother and sister is going to create
in time difficulties that the moralist foresees. What isn't foreseen is
that Ada and her lover after much disaster and distress are tranquilly
reunited in the radiance of an ideal old age.

A touch of parody appears here and there in the course of the novel,
as a circus always has its stumbling clown between the acrobat's show
and the illusionist's. I don't know why I have such a taste for mirrors
and mirages, but I know that at the age of ten or eleven I developed a
passion for conjuring, homely magic, whose various instruments—the
top hat with the double bottom, the wand starred with gold, the card
game that would turn into pigs' heads in your palm—all this would
arrive for you in a big box from the shop Peto on Caravan Street near
the Ciniselli circus in St. Petersburg. Included was a magic manual
showing how to make coins disappear or change denomination between
your fingers. I tried to reproduce these tricks, keeping myself in front
of a mirror, as the manual advised. My pale, serious little face reflected
in the mirror annoyed me, and I'd rig myself up in a *loup*, a black mask
which improved my looks. Alas, I didn't manage to match the skill of
the famous conjuror Mr. Merlin, who would be invited to children's
balls. I tried in vain to imitate his frivolous and deceptive patter that
my manual wanted me to spin out so as to obscure what I was up to
with my hands. "Frivolous and deceptive patter": there's a deceptive and
frivolous definition of my literary works. Anyway, my conjuring studies
didn't last long. "Tragic" is a very strong term, and yet there was a little
tragic side to the incident which helped me renounce my passion and
relegate my box to the lumber room, among defunct toys and broken
jumping jacks. So here's the incident. One Easter evening, at the last

children's party of the year, I couldn't stop myself from looking through a crack in the door—one of the live gills of world literature—to see how the preparations that Mr. Merlin was making for his opening routine in the grand salon were advancing. I saw him half-open a writing desk to slide in there calmly, coolly, a paper flower. The coolness, the familiarity, of his gesture was in atrocious contrast with the enchantments of his art.

And yet I knew all about, I knew so much about, what a magician's frock coat concealed and what it was capable of in the way of magic! This professional link, the link of bad faith, made me warn one of my little girl cousins in what hiding place the rose that Merlin would conjure with in one of his tricks would be found. At the critical moment the little traitress pointed with her finger to the desk, shouting out, "My cousin saw where you put it." I was still very young, but I remember very clearly noticing—or at least thinking I noticed—the atrocious expression which convulsed the features of the poor magician. I tell this incident to satisfy those of my shrewd critics who declare that in my novels dramas and mirrors are never far from one another. I must add, however, that when the drawer that the children indicated with derision was opened, the flower wasn't there: it was languishing under my little neighbor's chair!

When you come down to it, isn't there a good deal of eroticism in your work?
You can find a good deal of eroticism in the work of any novelist you can talk about without laughing. What is called eroticism is only one of the arabesques of the art of the novel.

What's striking—especially in Ada—*is your concern for detail, for the object in its place, for the exact reference. And in* Ada *one finds your fascination for butterflies.*
With the exception of a few Swiss butterflies, I have invented the species but not the genera featured in *Ada*. And I maintain that it's the first time that anyone has invented in a novel butterflies that are scientifically *possible*. You could reply: Very well, but in satisfying the expert, you're profiting a little from the reader's ignorance of butterflies, because if you had invented a new type of dog or cat for the manor folk, the trickery would only have irritated the reader, who would have to imagine a little mythological quadruped each time Ada takes the animal in her arms. It's a pity I didn't try to invent quadrupeds—I didn't think

of it—but I invented a new tree in the manor's orchard, that's already something!

Are you in favor of protecting nature?
The protection of certain rare animals is an excellent thing; it becomes absurd when ignorance or pedantry joins in. It's perfectly right to report a curio seller who collects for sale to amateurs a remarkable moth, the French race of a Spanish species, one of whose colonies risks extinction in the valley of the Durance, where these merchants go to harvest this beautiful creature's caterpillars on a common conifer. But it is absurd when a gamekeeper forbids an old naturalist to move about with his old net in a restricted area where a certain butterfly flies, whose sole food plant is the bladder senna—which means nothing to the gamekeeper—a bush with yellow flowers and large pods, which often grows around vineyards. Wherever the bush is, the butterfly can also be found, and it's the bush that should be protected, since a million collectors could not destroy this sky-blue insect if only the vineyardists stopped destroying, for some mysterious reason, the bladder sennas in their vineyards all along the Rhone.

In other cases the rarity of species varies with the seasons or else depends on a more or less sustained series of migrations. Farmers with their infernal pesticides, the cretins who burn tires and mattresses on no man's land—these are the real culprits, and not the scientist, without whom a policeman could not tell a butterfly from an angel or a bat.

Do you like football?
Yes, I've always adored the sport. I was goalie at school in Russia, at university in England, and in a team of White Russians in Berlin in the thirties. We played against very shady German workers, whom my Trinity College sweater annoyed. My last memory is from 1936. After a collision in the mud, I woke up on a pavilion cot. I had held the ball, I'd held it well, I still held it against my chest while impatient hands were trying to tear it from me.

You wrote this marvelous novel The Luzhin Defense: *are you a very good chess player? And what do you think of Fischer's attitude?*
Forty years ago I was a good enough player of chess, not a grandmaster, as the Germans say, but a club player sometimes able to set a trap for

a heedless champion. What has always drawn me in chess is the trick move, the hidden combination, and that's why I gave up live play to devote myself to composing chess problems.

I don't doubt that there exists an intimate link between certain mirages of my prose and the texture, at once brilliant and obscure, of enigmagic chess problems of which each one is the fruit of a thousand and one nights of insomnia. I especially like so-called suicide problems, where White forces Black to win.

Yes, Fischer is a strange being, but there's nothing abnormal in the fact of a chess player's not being normal. There was the case of the great player Rubinstein, at the start of the century: an ambulance would drive him each day from the insane asylum, his home, to the café room where the tournament was taking place, and then drive him back to his dark cell after the game. He didn't like to see his opponent, but an empty chair across the chessboard also irritated him, so they put a mirror there, and he saw his own reflection.

You don't seem to appreciate Freud?
That's not completely right. I appreciate Freud greatly as a comic author. The explanations he offers of the emotions and the dreams of his patients are incredible burlesque. I don't know how one could take them seriously. Enough about him, please.

Political writers aren't your bedside reading?
I am often asked whom I like and whom I hate among the politically committed or politically detached writers of my marvelous century. Well, first of all, I don't care at all for the writer who does not see the wonders of this century, little things—the free-and-easiness of male attire, the bathroom that has replaced the foul lavabo—and great things like the sublime liberty of thought in our double West, and the moon, the moon. I remember with what a shiver of delight, envy, and anguish I watched on the television screen man's first floating steps on the talcum powder of our satellite and how I despised all those who maintained it wasn't worth the expense of billions of dollars to walk in the dust of a dead world. So I detest, therefore, *engagé* scandalmongers, writers without mystery, the unfortunates who feed on the Viennese charlatan's elixirs. Those I love, on the other hand, are those who know, as I know,

that words alone are the real value of a masterpiece, a principle as old as it is true. I don't need to name anyone. One can be recognized by a language of signs through signs of language; or else, on the other hand, everything irritates us in the style of a contemptible contemporary, even his ellipses.

I am told you don't like Faulkner. I find that hard to believe.
I don't support regional literature, artificial folklore.

You play a lot with words? You make lots of puns?
One must draw everything one can from words, because it's the one real treasure a true writer has. Big general ideas are in yesterday's newspaper. If I like to take a word and turn it over to see its underside, shiny or dull or adorned with motley hues absent on its upperside, it's not at all out of idle curiosity, one finds all sorts of curious things by studying the underside of a word—unexpected shadows of other words, harmonies between them, hidden beauties that suddenly reveal something beyond the word. Serious wordplay, as I have in mind, is neither a game of chance nor a mere embellishment of style. It's a new verbal species that the marveling author offers to the poor reader, who doesn't want to look; to the good reader, who suddenly sees a completely new facet of an iridescent sentence.

Can I say of Vladimir Nabokov the novelist that he has the erudition of a scientist and the irony of a painter?
The "erudition of a scientist," OK. There's a little corner of ento-mological taxonomy where I used to know everything, where I was a complete master, in the forties at the Harvard Museum. But "the irony of a painter"? Irony is the method of discussion that Socrates used to confound invented sophists—and I can't take Socrates seriously. By extension, irony is a bitter laugh. But, really, my laughter is a good-natured fizz that's as much of the belly as the brain.

151

Interview with Willa Petchek
for *The Observer* (1976)[*]

On your working methods
I compose random parts of a novel while walking, indoors or in the woods, or lying in the bath and then write down the stuff on index cards in pencil. My characters are not supposed to move one step or indeed to breathe without my permission. The idea of using a typewriter seems to me as grotesque as "The Artist's Mother" built of tin cans and rags.

Your principal gift?
The strong, sweetly running engine of a first-rate imagination.

Your style?
Exceptionally limpid with innocent solecisms enlivening a somewhat monotonous rhythm.

On the theme of memory
One is always at home in one's past.

Does this suggest you dislike facing the future or contemplating the present?
What we perceive as the present is the bright crest of an evergrowing past and what we call the future is a looming abstraction ever coming into concrete appearance. I love and revere the present. As to the past, my dealings with it are more complex, ranging as they do from delicious

---

[*] "Nabokov Since Lolita," *The Observer*, May 30, 1976, 15–19. Emended typescript with VN's manuscript corrections, correspondence, VNA Berg. Petchek sent her questions on Feb. 11, 1976; VN had his answers ready by the date they met for the "interview," Feb. 26. Mostly a deft compilation of earlier writings and interviews.

gropings to blind angry fumblings. In a secret diary I have described my own self as "a vindictive person with a poor memory." And on the next page, under the heading "Jackals and jackasses to be remembered," I find a list of names belonging apparently to my detractors: Brougham, Condor, Croker, Jeffrey, Lockhard, Roberts, Thorn. Exactly what rot did they write about my books? Where? When? I shall never recall. *(He asks whether she recognizes those names.)* They were Byron's and Keats's critics *(he says "gleefully, screwing up his eyes with laughter").*

Authors' Authors (Questionnaire, 1976)*

Here are the three books I read during the three summer months of 1976 while hospitalized in Lausanne.

Dante's Inferno in Singleton's splendid translation (1970) with the Italian *en regard* and a detailed commentary.[1] What triumphant joy it is to see the honest light of literality take over again, after ages of meretricious paraphrase!

The Butterflies of North America by William H. Howe, coordinating editor and illustrator (1975). It describes and pictures in marvelous color all the nearctic species and many subspecies. Nothing like it has ever appeared here. The indifference of our philistine public to it is scandalous especially as all kinds of non-scientific coffee books—opalescent morphos and so on—are paraded yearly and presumably sell.

The Original of Laura. The not quite finished manuscript of a novel which I had begun writing and reworking before my illness and which was completed in my mind. I must have gone through it some 50 times and in my diurnal delirium kept reading it aloud to a small dream audience in a walled garden. My audience consisted of peacocks, pigeons, my long-dead parents, two cypresses, several young nurses crouching around, and a family doctor so old as to be almost invisible. Perhaps because of my stumblings and fits of coughing the story of my poor Laura had less success with my listeners than it will have, I hope, with intelligent reviewers when properly published.

---

* "Authors' Authors," *New York Times Book Review*, Dec. 5, 1976, 4. "The Book Review asked a number of authors, ranging from Vladimir Nabokov to John Dean, to tell us the three books they most enjoyed this year and to say, in a sentence or two, why."

Reputations Revisited
(Questionnaire, 1977)[*]

The Passionate Friends by H. G. Wells, is my most prized example of the unjustly ignored masterpiece. I must have been fourteen or fifteen when I went through its author's fiction after some five winters of tacit access to my father's library. Today at seventy-seven I clearly remember how affected I was by the style, the charm, the cream of the book, while not bothering about its "message" or "symbols" if any. (I have never reread it and now I see it as a colored haze leaving only some final details— growing a little closer to me in time—still coming through.)

The last meeting of the lovers takes place under legal supervision on a summer's day in a stranger's drawing room where the furniture is swathed in white covers. As Stephen, after parting with his mistress, walks out of the house in company with another person, he says to the latter:

Simply to say something and finding only a poor little statement concerning those chairs.

"Because of the flies."

A touch of high art refused to Conrad or Lawrence.

---

[*] "Reputations Revisited," *Times Literary Supplement*, Jan. 21, 1977, 66. On its seventy-fifth anniversary, *The Times Literary Supplement* "asked a number of writers, scholars and artists to nominate the most underrated and overrated books (or authors) of the past seventy-five years."

Interview with Hugh A. Mulligan
for *Ithaca Post* (1977)[*]

What is the Nabokov diet these days, both literary and caloric?
My caloric diet usually consists of bread and butter, transparent honey, wine, roast duck with red whortleberry jam, and similar plain fare.

My literary regime is more fancy, but two hours of meditation, between 2 a.m. and 4 a.m. (when the effect of a first sleeping pill evaporates and that of a second one has not begun), and a spell of writing in the afternoon, are about all my new novel (*The Original of Laura*) needs.

Somewhere I read that you have never flown across the Atlantic. Do long-distance flights frighten or bore you, and does the phasing out of the passenger liners account for your fewer trips to America?
The first ascent I made took place in a small cheap plane over Margate, Kent, in 1920. Nowadays my flights are limited to delightful hops from Montreux to Nice and back again. I shall certainly enjoy flying across the Atlantic when the last luxurious liner is extinct.

There was, I believe, a recent exchange of letters between you and Solzhenitsyn. What was the gist of them?
I praised the freedom and happiness of the West; he deplored the fact of his children not being able to get a Russian education abroad.

---

[*] "Vladimir Nabokov Discusses Writing, Politics, Russia . . . ," *Ithaca Post*, Jan. 30, 1977, 77. Holograph draft, Nov. 30, 1976, VNA Berg. Mulligan submitted his questions on Nov. 16, 1976. VN agreed to an interview on Nov. 30, but, still recovering after his long hospitalization, asked that the interview and especially the photographic session be short. Mulligan's published interview does not use VN's written answers but culls from previously published interviews.

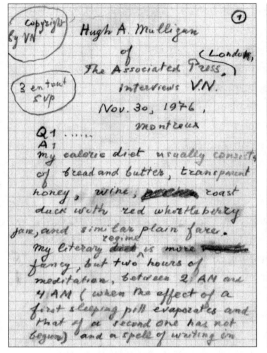
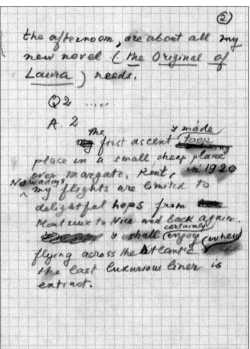

Fair copy manuscript of answers to interview by Hugh Mulligan, Associated Press, 1976. Nabokov said he wore out the erasers on his pencils faster than the lead at the other end.

As the father of Lolita and Ada, two of the glories of that gender, what do you think of the word changes brought about by Women's Liberation,—e.g. spokesperson, chairperson, snowperson, Ms., etc.?

I regard "Women's Liberation" as a joke. Let me add to your little list of word changes such combinations as: personure, persondolin and Hellperson.

You once gave your preference for celestial neighbors—Shakespeare laughing ribaldly at frying Freud. Does this indicate a belief in the hereafter and an insight into or presumption of your own future booking arrangements?

No. An infinite comic strip would soon become a dreadful bore.

I am polishing, dusting and perhaps even demolishing some of the statuary in my personal pantheon. Would you assist, please, with some pumice or a hammer for Willa Cather, Fitzgerald, Waugh, Mauriac and Capote?

Mauriac has written some wonderful stuff (e.g. *Le Noeud de vipères*). Are you sure you have not confused him with the execrable Malraux? Waugh's talent should also not be despised. The scene of the murder in Capote is great. You must have invented Willa Cather, and I don't remember *anything* of Fitzgerald's writings.

After the jolts and flaws of lost Vietnam and self-flagellating Watergate, do you worry about the future of America?

Political squabbles and awkward wars will be soon forgotten. Let us prepare new weapons and whistle softly as we work. Let me write my new novel in peace. That is my work, my duty. America does not need my worrying about her. The jitters I leave to other countries, and the worse they are the better.

On the 10th anniversary of the Bolshevik Revolution you wrote "An Anniversary," proclaiming 10 years of contempt for the Soviet political state and celebrating 10 years of freedom from it. The 60th anniversary is at hand next year. In the intervening half-century, has your contempt diminished?

My contempt for tyranny shall last forever. Things hidden from tourists—the terrible backroads, the jails, the concentration camps—cannot be compensated by a few more motorcars, stale sugar buns in redecorated shops, or the new fad, artificial caviar. Nothing has changed in these five decades. And thus it will remain until that dreary and diabolical regime is destroyed.

155

Interview with Robert Robinson
for BBC *Book Programme* (1977)[*]

First, sir, to spare you irritation, I wonder if you will instruct me in the pronunciation of your name.

Let me put it this way. There exists a number of deceptively simple-looking Russian names, whose spelling and pronunciation present the foreigner with strange traps. The name Suvarov took a couple of centuries to lose the preposterous middle "a"—it should be Suvorov. American autograph-seekers, while professing a knowledge of all my books—prudently not mentioning their titles—rejuggle the vowels of my name in all the ways allowed by mathematics. "Nabakav" is especially touching for the "a"s. Pronunciation problems fall into a less erratic pattern. On the playing fields of Cambridge, my football team used to hail me as "Nabkov" or, facetiously, "Macnab." New Yorkers reveal their tendency of turning "o" into "ah" by pronouncing my name "Nabarkov." The aberration, "Nobokov," is a favorite one of postal officials; now the correct Russian way would take too much time to explain, and so I've settled for the euphonious "Nabokov," with the middle syllable accented and rhyming with "smoke."[1] Would you like to try?

Mr. Nabokov.

That's right.

* "A Blush of Colour—Nabokov in Montreux," *The Listener,* March 24, 1977, 367, 369. Television interview for the BBC-2 *Book Programme.* VN received questions on Feb. 3, 1977, had answers ready by Feb. 6, and was filmed in Montreux on Feb. 14. His severe ill health had made composing *The Original of Laura* agonizingly slow and patchy, and he wrote in his diary on Feb. 6: "answered with pleasure and *entrain* the 24 BBC questions." After VN's death, Robinson recalled the scene, describing his frailty, and reprinted the interview, in "The Last Interview," in *Vladimir Nabokov: A Tribute,* ed. Peter Quennell (New York: William Morrow, 1980), 119–25.

You grant interviews on the understanding that they shall not be spontaneous.
This admirable method ensures there will be no dull patches. Can you tell me
why and when you decided upon it?
I'm not a dull speaker, I'm a bad speaker, I'm a wretched speaker. The
tape of my unprepared speech differs from my written prose as much
as the worm differs from the perfect insect—or, as I once put it, I think
like a genius, I write like a distinguished author and I speak like a child.

You've been a writer all your life. Can you evoke for us the earliest stirring
of the impulse?
I was a boy of fifteen, the lilacs were in full bloom; I had read Pushkin
and Keats; I was madly in love with a girl of my age, I had a new bicycle
(an Enfield, I remember) with reversible handlebars that could turn
it into a racer. My first poems were awful, but then I reversed those
handlebars, and things improved. It took me, however, ten more years
to realize that my true instrument was prose—poetic prose, in the special sense that it depended on comparisons and metaphors to say what
it wanted to say. I spent the years 1925 to 1940 in Berlin, Paris, and the
Riviera, after which I took off for America. I cannot complain of neglect
on the part of any great critics, although as always and everywhere there
was an odd rascal or two badgering me. What has amused me in recent
years is that those old novels and stories published in English in the
sixties and seventies, were appreciated much more warmly than they
had been in Russian thirty years ago.

Has your satisfaction in the act of writing ever fluctuated? I mean is it keener
now or less keen than once it was?
Keener.

Why?
Because the ice of experience now mingles with the fire of inspiration.

Apart from the pleasure it brings, what do you conceive your task as a writer
to be?
This writer's task is the purely subjective one of reproducing as closely
as possible the image of the book he has in his mind. The reader need
not know, or, indeed, cannot know, what the image is, and so cannot tell
how closely the book has conformed to its image in the author's mind.

In other words, the reader has no business bothering about the author's intentions, nor has the author any business trying to learn whether the consumer likes what he consumes.

Of course, the author works harder than the reader does; but I wonder whether it augments his—this is to say, your—pleasure that he makes the reader work hard, too.
The author is perfectly indifferent to the capacity and condition of the reader's brain.

Could you give us some idea of the pattern of your working day?
This pattern has lately become blurry and inconstant. At the peak of the book, I worked all day, cursing the tricks that objects play upon me, the mislaid spectacles, the spilled wine. I also find talking of my working day far less entertaining than I formerly did.

The conventional view of an hotel is as of a temporary shelter—one brings one's own luggage, after all—yet you choose to make it permanent.
I have toyed on and off with the idea of buying a villa. I can imagine the comfortable furniture, the efficient burglar alarms, but I am unable to visualize an adequate staff. Old retainers require time to get old, and I wonder how much of it there still is at my disposal.

You once entertained the possibility of returning to the United States. I wonder if you will.
I will certainly return to the United States at the first opportunity. I'm indolent, I'm sluggish, but I'm sure I'll go back with tenderness. The thrill with which I think of certain trails in the Rockies is only matched by visions of my Russian woods, which I will never revisit.

Is Switzerland a place with positive advantages for you, or is it simply a place without positive disadvantages?
The winters can be pretty dismal here, and my old borzoi[2] has developed feuds with lots of local dogs, but otherwise it's all right.

You think and write in three languages—which would be the preferred one?
Yes, I write in three languages, but I think in images. The matter of preference does not really arise. Images are mute, yet presently the silent

cinema begins to talk and I recognize its language. During the second part of my life, it was generally English, my own brand of English—not the Cambridge variety, but still English.

At any point do you invite your wife to comment on work in progress?
When the book is quite finished, and its fair copy is still warm and wet, my wife goes carefully through it. Her comments are usually few but invariably to the point.

Do you find that you reread your own earlier work, and if you do, with what feelings?
Rereading my own works is a purely utilitarian business. I have to do it when correcting a paperback edition riddled with misprints or controlling a translation, but there are some rewards. In certain species—this is going to be a metaphor—in certain species, the wings of the pupated butterfly begin to show in exquisite miniature through the wing cases of the chrysalis a few days before emergence. It is the pathetic sight of an iridescent future transpiring through the shell of the past, something of the kind I experience when dipping into my books written in the twenties. Suddenly, through a drab photograph, a blush of color, an outline of form, seems to be distinguishable. I'm saying this with absolute scientific modesty, not with the smugness of aging art.

Which writers are you currently reading with pleasure?
I'm rereading Rimbaud, his marvelous verse and his pathetic correspondence in the Pléiade edition. I am also dipping into a collection of unbelievably stupid Soviet jokes.

Your praise for Joyce and Wells has been high. Could you identify briefly the quality in each which sets them apart?
Joyce's *Ulysses* is set apart from all modern literature, not only by the force of his genius, but also by the novelty of his form. Wells is a great writer, but there are many writers as great as he.

Your distaste for the theories of Freud has sometimes sounded to me like the agony of one betrayed, as though the old magus had once fooled you with his famous three-card trick. Were you ever a fan?

What a bizarre notion! Actually I always loathed the Viennese quack. I used to stalk him down dark alleys of thought, and now we shall never forget the sight of old, flustered Freud seeking to unlock his door with the point of his umbrella.

The world knows that you are also a lepidopterist but may not know what that involves. In the collection of butterflies, could you describe the process from pursuit to display?
Only common butterflies, showy moths from the tropics, are put on display in a dusty case between a primitive mask and a vulgar abstract picture. The rare, precious stuff is kept in the glazed drawers of museum cabinets. As for pursuit, it is, of course, ecstasy to follow an undescribed beauty, skimming over the rocks of its habitat, but it is also great fun to locate a new species among the broken insects in an old biscuit tin sent over by a sailor from some remote island.

One can always induce a mild vertigo by recalling that Joyce might not have existed as the writer but as the tenor. Have you any sense of having narrowly missed some other role? What substitute could you endure?
Oh, yes, I have always had a number of parts lined up in case the muse failed. A lepidopterist exploring famous jungles came first, then there was the chess grandmaster, then the tennis ace with an unreturnable service, then the goalie saving a historic shot, and finally, finally, the author of a pile of unknown writings—*Pale Fire, Lolita, Ada*—which my heirs discover and publish.

Alberto Moravia told me of his conviction that each writer writes only of one thing—has but a single obsession he continually develops. Can you agree?
I have not read Alberto Moravia but the pronouncement you quote is certainly wrong in my case. The circus tiger is not obsessed by his torturer, my characters cringe as I come near with my whip. I have seen a whole avenue of imagined trees losing their leaves at the threat of my passage. If I do have any obsessions I'm careful not to reveal them in fictional form.

Mr. Nabokov, thank you.
You're welcome, as we say in my adopted country.

Acknowledgments

Since this book has been taking shape in my head from about the year of Nabokov's death, the acknowledgments range over old debts and much newer ones.

Véra Nabokov was VN's first bibliographer. Without the free access she allowed me to her husband's archive in 1979, and to the Library of Congress Nabokov papers in 1980, I would not have been able to produce such a comprehensive selection of Nabokov's "public prose."

Dieter E. Zimmer was Nabokov's second bibliographer. Drawing heavily on what Véra provided, as well as on his own meticulous work, he produced the first substantial Nabokov bibliography, published by Rowohlt in 1963 (*Vladimir Nabokov: Bibliographie des Gesamtwerks* [Reinbck bei Hamburg: Rowohlt, 1963, rev. 1964]). Zimmer, who not only interviewed Nabokov more than once himself, translated many of his works into German, and oversaw the first collected works (in twenty-five volumes) in any language, has edited, as volume 21 of the *Gesammelte Werke, Eigensinnige Ansichten* (Reinbek bei Hamburg: Rowohlt, 2004), a precursor of this volume, with many of the interviews, essays, and reviews gathered here. He also compiled a collection of print interviews and interviews in other media (radio and television), and generously chose to share them with me and others who cared about preserving Nabokov's legacy. Indeed, Zimmer has toiled selflessly on Nabokov for almost sixty years (while working at distinguished levels in quite other capacities), as translator, bibliographer, interviewer, editor, annotator, and hunter and pinner-down of butterfly references. All Nabokovians should be grateful to this indefatigable finder, checker, preserver, and disseminator of facts and documents.

The very ineptitude of Andrew Field's 1973 bibliography (*Nabokov: A Bibliography* [New York: McGraw-Hill]), despite building on Zimmer's, and on Véra and Vladimir Nabokov's help, inspired me, in the course of my Ph.D., and through the corrective efforts of the University of Toronto Library's Interloans section, to see how much needed to be done to find what Nabokov had written and said. Michael Juliar's vastly better 1986 bibliography (*Vladimir Nabokov: A Descriptive Bibliography* [New York: Garland]) became an invaluable tool and a way to organize the new discoveries I penciled in.

Thanks to Anastasia Tolstoy for providing the prompt to start the work on what had remained a project for the indefinite future, by proposing a collection of Nabokov's unpublished Russian reviews and essays to the Wylie Agency, the agent for the Nabokov Estate and now for the Vladimir Nabokov Literary Foundation; to Andrew Wylie for asking my advice; and to Anastasia, again, for her willingness to work with me and her help in translating and annotating the Russian material, and her calm patience while I attended to other projects.

My wife, Bronwen Nicholson, cheerily helped obtain through interlibrary loans and through the Berg Collection of the New York Public Library whatever I did not already have in both manuscript and published versions, and scanned and transcribed the texts. Thanks to the Interlibrary Loans section of the Auckland University Library, to the New York Public Library, including Isaac Gewirtz, and especially Carolyn Vega and Mary Catherine Kinniburgh, and to Edith A. Sandler, Manuscript Reference Librarian, Manuscript Division, Library of Congress.

For generous assistance with Russian texts and translations, our thanks go to Andrei Babikov, and for help with translations, to the late Gennady Barabtarlo. Especial thanks to Stanislav Shvabrin for his meticulous, precise, nuanced, erudite, and generous help with all the Russian translations and with suggestions for additional annotation.

Thanks also to Tommy Karshan and to Luke Parker for granting us permission to use their (in Tommy's case, his and Anastasia's) translations of, respectively, "Breitensträter-Paolino," here retitled "Play (Breitensträter-Paolino)" and "On Generalities," and to Paula Uzcudun for providing details about her grandfather Paulino Uzcudun (Paolino) and a translation of the relevant part of his autobiography. Thanks to

Maurice Couturier for supplying some of the more recherché French interviews, and to him and Marie Bouchet for help with occasional turns of French phrase or allusion. For assistance with Nabokov's version of his grandmother's Baltic German, my thanks again to Dieter E. Zimmer. And for assistance in checking translations from the Italian, my thanks to Chiara Montini. Brett Cooke unwittingly supplied a welcome prompt. Daniel Dor helped with a Hebrew detail.

Finally, thanks to Terry Zaroff-Evans for a brilliant and meticulous job as copy editor.

Notes

INTRODUCTION: THINKER, WRITER, SPEAKER, PERSON

1. *SO*, xi. Biographical information is based on Brian Boyd, *Vladimir Nabokov: The Russian Years* (Princeton, N.J.: Princeton University Press, 1990), and *Vladimir Nabokov: The American Years* (Princeton, N.J.: Princeton University Press, 1991).
2. VN to Stephen Jan Parker, Jan. 11, 1973, VNA Berg.
3. *SM*, 287. Boris Poplavsky (1903–35), Paris-based émigré poet and novelist who had published, however, only *Flagi* before dying accidentally from drugs laced with poison.
4. "Man and Things" (1928), p. 71.
5. See "On Opera" (1928), p. 74n.
6. *SM*, 35–36.
7. VN, *Invitation to a Beheading*, trans. DN with VN (New York: Putnam, 1959), 7.
8. "On Opera," pp. 74, 75.
9. "A. Znosko-Borovsky, *Capablanca and Alekhine*" (1927), p. 59.
10. See VN, *LTV.*
11. "Un Portrait: Vladimir Nabokoff Sirine, l'amoureux de la vie" ("Portrait: Vladimir Nabokoff Sirine, Lover of Life"), *Le Mois* 6 (June–July 1931), 141.
12. "Interview with Andrey Sedykh for *Poslednie novosti*" (1932), p. 113.
13. "Mr. Masefield and Clio" (1940), p. 148.
14. "Prof. Woodbridge in an Essay on Nature Postulates the Reality of the World" (1940), p. 152.
15. "The Innocence of Hilaire Belloc" (1941), p. 186.
16. VN, *Bend Sinister* (1947; New York: Vintage, 1990), xiii.
17. *V&V*, 2–11.
18. Published as "The Art of Literature and Common Sense," in VN, *Lectures on Literature*, ed. Fredson Bowers (New York: Harcourt Brace Jovanovich/Bruccoli Clark, 1980), 371–82; the omission is noted on p. 377; the reinstatement extends from p. 197 to p. 199.
19. VN, *Nabokov's Butterflies: Unpublished and Uncollected Writings*, ed. Brian Boyd and Robert Michael Pyle (Boston: Beacon, 1999).
20. "[On Democracy]" (1942), p. 203.
21. "In Memory of Iosif Hessen" (1943), pp. 208–9.
22. "The Place of Russian Studies in the Curriculum" (1948), p. 228.
23. "Interview with Mati Laansoo for Canadian Broadcasting Corporation" (1973), p. 422.
24. "Interview with Gerald Clarke for *Esquire*" (1974), p. 443.

25. "Interview with Robert Robinson for BBC *Book Programme*" (1977), p. 478.
26. *SO*, 312.
27. Transcript of "Interview with Pierre Burton and Lionel Trilling for Canadian Broadcasting Corporation," 1958, Dieter Zimmer collection.
28. Appel speaking at the Nabokov centenary tribute, Town Hall, New York, Apr. 15, 1999.
29. *SO*, 34.
30. *SO*, 20.
31. "Interview with Maurice Dolbier for *New York Herald Tribune*" (1962), p. 316.
32. VN to Robert Hughes, National Educational Television, Nov. 9, 1965, in VN, *Selected Letters 1940–1977*, ed. DN and Matthew J. Bruccoli (New York: Harcourt Brace Jovanovich / Bruccoli Clark Layman, 1989), 382.
33. Helga Chudacoff and VN, typescript report of interview conducted on June 20, 1974, VNA Berg.
34. "Interview with James Salter for *People*" (1975), p. 449.
35. Andrew Field, *Nabokov: His Life in Part* (New York: Viking Press, 1977), 180.
36. Alexander Dolinin, "Nabokov as a Russian Writer," in *The Cambridge Companion to Vladimir Nabokov*, ed. Julian W. Connolly (Cambridge, U.K.: Cambridge University Press, 2005), 53.
37. Ibid., 54, 56.
38. See Brian Boyd, *Stalking Nabokov: Selected Essays* (New York: Columbia University Press, 2011), 176–91.
39. "Interview with Sophie Lannes for *L'Express*" (1975), p. 454.
40. "Interview with Bernard Pivot for *Apostrophes*" (1975), p. 461.
41. "Interview with Martha MacGregor for *New York Post*" (1958), p. 243.
42. "Interview with Gerald Clarke for *Esquire*" (1974), p. 446.
43. "Interview of Vladimir Nabokov and Alain Robbe-Grillet with André Parinaud, Roger Nimier, and Paul Guimard for *Arts* (Paris)" (1959), p. 271.
44. "Interview for *Newsweek*" (1962), p. 320.
45. "Interview with Gerald Clarke for *Esquire*" (1974), p. 445.
46. Maurice Couturier, *Nabokov, ou la tyranne de l'auteur* (Paris: Seuil, 1993), 350, 382.
47. "Interview with David Holmes for BBC Radio" (1959), p. 288.
48. "Interview with Robert Robinson for BBC *Book Programme*" (1977), p. 479.
49. "Unidentified Interview" (1962), p. 314.
50. "Interview with Dieter E. Zimmer for Norddeutscher Rundfunk" (1966), p. 357.
51. "Mr. Masefield and Clio" (1940), p. 148.
52. "Questionnaire on Proust" (1930), p. 90.
53. "The Triumph of Virtue" (1930), p. 92.
54. "Interview with Alberto Ongaro for *L'Europeo*" (1966), pp. 345, 346–47.
55. "Writers and the Era," p. 106.

2. RUPERT BROOKE (1921)

1. Rupert Brooke, "The Fish," 1911, in Rupert Brooke, *Collected Poems* (London: Sidgwich & Jackson, 1918).
2. Rupert Brooke, "Heaven," 1913.
3. Rupert Brooke, "Tiare Tahiti," 1914.
4. Rupert Brooke, "The Life Beyond," 1910.
5. Rupert Brooke, "Dust," 1909–10.

6. Rupert Brooke, "Sonnet: 'Oh! Death will find me, long before I tire,' " 1909.
7. Rupert Brooke, "Clouds," 1913.
8. Rupert Brooke, "IV. The Dead," 1914.
9. Rupert Brooke, "V. The Soldier," 1914.
10. Rupert Brooke, "Mary and Gabriel," 1912.
11. Rupert Brooke, "The Great Lover," 1914.
12. Ibid.
13. Rupert Brooke, "Mutability," 1913.
14. Rupert Brooke, "The Call," 1907.
15. "Le grand peut-être," Rabelais's famous term for the hereafter, famously echoed in John Shade's "Your great Maybe, Rabelais: The grand potato" (*Pale Fire* [1962; New York: Vintage, 1989], 52, lines 500–501).
16. Rupert Brooke, "Thoughts on the Shape of the Human Body," 1911.
17. Rupert Brooke, "Menelaus and Helen," 1911.
18. Rupert Brooke, "Jealousy," 1907.
19. Rupert Brooke, "A Channel Passage," 1909.
20. Rupert Brooke, "The Voice," 1909.
21. Rupert Brooke, "Sonnet: 'I said I splendidly loved you; it's not true,' " 1910.
22. Rupert Brooke, "Home," 1913.
23. The courtesan Zuliette, in book 7 of Rousseau's *Confessions*, trans. W. Conyngham Mallory (The Floating Press, 2012), 368–70.
24. Rupert Brooke, "The Jolly Company," 1908.
25. Rupert Brooke, "Failure," 1906.
26. Rupert Brooke, "The Vision of the Archangels," 1906.
27. Russian painter Mikhail Vrubel' (1856–1910), whose befeathered angels (e.g., *Six-Winged Seraph [Azrael]*, 1904) and demons (e.g., *Demon Downcast*, 1902) VN would later extol, in, for instance, *Ada*.
28. Now called *Victoria amazonica*, Queen Victoria's water lily, with white swanlike flowers and leaves up to three meters wide.
29. Rupert Brooke, "Lines Written in the Belief That the Ancient Roman Festival of the Dead Was Called Ambarvalia," 1910.
30. Ambarvalia: Roman private and public field lustration, or ceremony of purification and of averting evil, held in May (*Oxford Classical Dictionary*).
31. Rudyard Kipling, "Sussex," 1902.
32. Alexander Pushkin, "Fragments of Onegin's Journey," xviii.3 in *EO*, I, 339 ("before a small isba two rowans").
33. Mikhail Lermontov, "Otchizna" ("My Native Land," 1841), in *V&V*, 291.
34. Rupert Brooke, "The Old Vicarage, Grantchester," 1912.

3. LAUGHTER AND DREAMS (1923)

1. Compare this with the mature VN's description of Catkin Week, *SM*, 239.

5. ON POETRY (1924)

1. These poets included Valery Bryusov (1873–1924), Konstantin Balmont (1867–1942), and especially Aleksandr Blok (1880–1921).
2. The Guild of Poets, a group of poets, including Nikolay Gumilyov and Sergey Gorodetsky, formed in 1912. In opposition to the diffuse suggestiveness of the Symbolist poets, they stressed crisp form and cool craft.
3. VN crossed out "like *masterov* [masters] and *bogov* [gods]." In this example, the words rhyme only because they both share the same *-ov* case ending (genitive

plural), as weak a rhyme as if one were to "rhyme" "Aldanov" and "Nabokov," whereas "Bulgakov" and "Nabokov," with the supporting "k" sound, would be less impoverished a rhyme.

6. PLAY (BREITENSTRÄTER–PAOLINO) (1925)

1. In fact it was Arthur Wellesley, Duke of Wellington, who is supposed to have said, "The battle of Waterloo was won in the playing fields of Eton," according to Montalembert, *De l'avenir politique de l'Angleterre,* 1855.
2. Thumbs down.
3. *Cashel Byron's Profession* (1883).
4. The novels *The Game* (1905) and *The Abysmal Brute* (1911) and the stories "A Piece of Steak" (1909) and "The Mexican" (1911).
5. The novel *Rodney Stone* (1896).
6. The story "Boks" ("Boxing"), 1913.
7. James Figg, first English champion, 1719–30; James Corbett, first American world champion, 1892–97; Tom Cribb, English champion, 1809–22.
8. American John Sullivan, world champion 1882–92; Canadian Tommy Burns, world champion 1906–8; American James Jeffries, world champion, 1899–1905.
9. American Jack Johnson, world heavyweight champion, 1908–15.
10. In fact the bout took place on July 4, 1910.
11. Smith: unclear which of several boxers of this name active in the 1910s and 1920s VN means; Billy Wells, English champion, 1911; Frank Goddard, English champion, 1919; Englishman Jimmy Wilde, flyweight champion of the world, 1916–23; Joe Beckett, English champion, 1919; Frenchman Georges Carpentier, world light-heavyweight champion, 1920–22.
12. The fight took place on Dec. 4, 1919; the knockout came after seventy-seven seconds.
13. Paulino Uzcudun (1899–1985), known in the ring as Paolino, was European champion in 1926 and 1933, and claimed world championship in 1933. The match Nabokov describes took place in the Sport Palast.
14. Hans Breitensträter (1897–1972), German champion 1920–23, 1925.
15. This and the next quotation echo Lermontov's "Song about Tsar Ivan Vasilyevich: A Young *Oprichnik* and the Valiant Merchant Kalashnikov," 1837. The *oprichniks* were Ivan the Terrible's notorious enforcers.
16. Paulino Uzcudun recalls the fight in his autobiography: "My fight against Breitensträter took place at the very large Sport Palast, which, on the occasion of my fight against the local idol, the public had packed. Breitensträter boxed well and had a magnificent right, which he made reach its destination with wonderful speed; but I could tell from the first moment that sooner or later I would hunt him down and, that as soon as it happened, the fight would be over. And so it was, in effect: in the ninth round, one of my strong hooks exploded against his jaw and Breitensträter fell to the ground, and he remained on the floor while the referee counted out the regulation seconds. The public, who throughout the fight had not ceased to encourage the German, urging him not to lose faith and to defeat me, as soon as they saw me victorious rewarded me, with magnificent sportmanship, with one of the most unanimous and clamorous ovations that I have received in my life" (*Mi Vida* [Madrid: Espasa Calpe, 1934], 67–68, translation by his granddaughter Paola Uzcudun).

7. LETTER TO THE EDITOR, *ZVENO* (1926)

1. Konstantin Mochulsky, review of *Mashen'ka*, *Zveno*, April 18, 1926. Mochulsky (1892–1948), historian and literary critic, frequently wrote for the émigré newspapers *Zveno* and *Poslednie novosti*. He would later take up a professorship at the Sorbonne.

8. A FEW WORDS ON THE WRETCHEDNESS OF SOVIET FICTION AND AN ATTEMPT TO DETERMINE ITS CAUSE (1926)

1. "Predskazanie" ("A Prophecy," 1830).
2. The text corresponding to the next two lines (*"yavlenie ne strashnoe—ona proydyot—eta seraya pora—i shkol'niki gryadushchikh vekov,"* msp. 1) is omitted in Dolinin's edition of this essay, p. 9, although Dolinin notes the ungrammaticality of the text as he had transcribed it. Since Dolinin's edition is the only published version of the essay in the original Russian, we will note where the translation follows the manuscript and not his omissions and misreadings.
3. As Russians called literary-intellectual journals, some of which might actually be thin.
4. Dolinin, p. 9, omits *etot*, "this" (msp. 2).
5. Fyodor Gladkov (1883–1958), *Tsement* (*Cement*), published serially in *Krasnaya nov'* 1–6 (1925), and in book form (Moscow, Leningrad) in 1926. The book form is cited in notes that follow.
6. *Tsement*, 26. Here, as elsewhere, VN sometimes omits occasional words from his source; Dolinin marks the elisions and one or two misquotations.
7. Ibid., 24.
8. Dolinin, p. 10, misreads *kamore* ("chamber") (msp. 4) as *kamorke* ("cubbyhole").
9. *Tsement*, 32, 33, 34, 35.
10. Ibid., 12.
11. Ibid.
12. Thomas Mayne Reid (1818–83), Scots-Irish-American novelist whose Westerns were particularly popular in Russia, and with VN as a boy (see *SM*, 195–207). VN's reference to Mayne Reid harks back to a joke a couple of lines earlier that he deleted in the course of his hasty revision.
13. In *Tsement*: "How in the cooperages the saws used to sing like wenches in springtime."
14. Ibid., 15.
15. Ibid., 46.
16. Dolinin, p. 11, omits *akhnulo*, "gasped."
17. *Tsement*, 47.
18. Dolinin, p. 11, omits *milym*, "nice" (msp. 7).
19. David Margot, *Grammaire théorique et pratique de la langue française: À l'usage des classes supérieures des écoles*, 1877.
20. *Tsement*, 84.
21. Ibid., 92.
22. Ibid., 313.
23. Dolinin, p. 12, reads *dolgo* ("long") rather than *dole* ("longer") (msp. 9).
24. Soviet writer Lydia Seifullina (1889–1954).
25. Short story, 1924.
26. Evdokia Nagrodskaya (1866–1930), Russian novelist, whose highly popular first novel, *Gnev Dionisa* (1910), translated into English by Louise McReynolds as *The Wrath of Dionysus* (Bloomington: Indiana University Press, 1997),

focuses on sexual identity and gender roles; Lidia Charskaya (1875–1938), actress and prolific popular novelist. In his afterword to his Russian translation of *Lolita*, VN describes *Doctor Zhivago* as a book about a "lyrical doctor with penny dreadful mystical urges and philistine turns of speech and an enchantress straight out of Charskaya" (*Lolita*, trans. VN [New York: Phaedra, 1967], 298). Simon Karlinsky, quoting and translating this, explains, "Lydia Charskaya wrote widely popular treacly novels for and about teen-aged girls in pre-revolutionary Russia" (*Dear Bunny, Dear Volodya: The Nabokov-Wilson Letters, 1940–1971*, rev. ed., ed. Simon Karlinsky [Berkeley and Los Angeles: University of California Press, 2001], 27).

27. VN misquotes, writing *I znachitel'no* ("And significantly") instead of *Iznachal'no* ("Primordially").

28. L. N. Seifullina, *Sobranie sochineniy* (Collected Works), 3rd ed. (Moscow, 1925), vol. 2, pp. 18–19, 53.

29. Ibid., 25.

30. Dolinin, p. 13, omits msp. 11, "X . . . X's."

31. Claude Anet (1868–1931), pen name of Jean Schopfer, a French writer and journalist who lived in Russia for several years and set several of his novels there.

32. Seifullina, *Sobranie sochineniy*, vol. 2, p. 143.

33. Dolinin, p. 14, omits msp. 13's *i* ("and") and starts a new sentence here.

34. Soviet writer Mikhail Zoshchenko (1894–1958).

35. Dolinin (p. 22, n. 23) notes that this story, published in the Soviet *Literaturnaya nedelya* 9 (1922), was not included in Zoshchenko's collections between 1922 and 1926, so must have been encountered by VN in an émigré reprint.

36. Dolinin, p. 14, reads *nashi* ("ours") rather than *natsiya* ("nation") (msp. 14).

37. Seifullina, *Sobranie sochineniy*, vol. 1, p. 251.

38. "Lyal'ka pyat'desyat'," *Krasnaya nov'* 1 (1922), 35.

39. Stories from the collection *Vesyolaya zhizn'* (Leningrad, 1924).

40. First novel (1924) of the Soviet writer Leonid Leonov (1899–1994).

41. Soviet writer Konstantin Fedin (1892–1977).

42. S. F. Bystrov and V. Puzanov are two little-known "peasant" writers VN must have encountered, Dolinin (p. 22, n. 28) suggests, in the eighth number of *Krasnaya nov'* for 1925.

43. Soviet writer Boris Pilnyak (1894–1938).

44. Dolinin, p. 15, reads *kak* ("how") instead of *kogda* ("when") (msp. 16).

45. Boris Pilnyak, *Sobranie sochineniy* [Collected Works] (Moscow and Leningrad, 1925), vol. 5 (*Mat' syra-zemlya*), p. 8.

46. Dolinin, p. 15, omits *vovse*, "at all" (msp. 17).

47. VN begins to waver between the correct "Nekuliev" and his more frequent (but erroneous) "Nikulin."

48. Dolinin, p. 16, misreads *voennaya khitrost' s soboyu; oni* ("strategic maneuver with themselves; they") (msp. 17) as *vesyolaya khitrost';—s soboyu oni* ("jolly tactics;—with themselves, they").

49. Pilnyak, *Sobranie sochineniy*, vol. 5, p. 66.

50. P. N. Krasnov, lowbrow, anti-Semitic, and monarchist émigré writer.

51. Dolinin, p. 16, misreads *Vozvrashchayus'* ("I'm going back") as *Vozvrashchayas'* ("Going back") (msp. 19).

52. Lvov: in Chekhov's play *Ivanov*, 1887. Bazarov: in Turgenev's novel *Fathers and Sons*, 1862. Sanin: in Mikhail Artsybashev's novel *Sanin*, 1907.

53. Dolinin, p. 17, omits *tem* ("of the themes") (msp. 20).

54. *Kavkazskie ocherki* (Caucasian Sketches, 1834–1836), a five-story cycle by Alexander Bestuzhev-Marlinsky.

55. Dolinin (p. 22, n. 35) identifies this 1903 story as the best known of Lidia Charskaya's schoolgirl tales.
56. Vsevolod Ivanov, "Pustynya Tuub-Koya," *Krug* (Moscow) 4 (1925), 199.
57. Pilnyak, *Sobranie sochineniy*, vol. 5, pp. 145–250. The Pomors (Russian *Pomory*) are long-established Russian settlers (originally from Novgorod) in the White Sea area.
58. VN admired Vladimir Dahl (1801–1872) as a lexicographer but was less interested in his folklore and ethnographic work.
59. Russian writer (1871–1919). VN has in mind the well-known comment of Lev Tolstoy on Leonid Andreev's story "Bezdna" ("The Abyss"), which also features rape piled on rape: "He frightens, but I'm not scared."
60. Dolinin, p. 18, misreads *etakaya* ("such a") as *takaya* ("this") (msp. 22).
61. Dolinin, p. 18, misreads *avtomobili* ("cars") as "car" (msp. 22).
62. Boris Pilnyak, *Angliyskie rasskazy* (*English Stories*, Moscow-Leningrad, 1924), 7.
63. Wolfgang E. Groeger (1882–?), a German translator of Russian literature.
64. Dolinin, p. 18, omits *v obshchem*, "at all, in general" (msp. 23).
65. Fedin, *Goroda i gody* (*Cities and Years*) (Leningrad, 1924), 26.
66. Olga Forsh, author of the story collection *Obyvateli* (Ordinary Folk [Moscow-Petersburg, 1923]).
67. Despite the context, Dolinin, p. 20, misreads *upoitel'noy* ("entrancing") as *unizitel'noy* ("humiliating") (msp. 28).
68. Vladimir Lidin (1894–1979), Soviet writer highly prolific in the early 1920s.
69. Alexander Yakovlev (1886–1953), Soviet writer known for *October*, 1923, and other propagandistic works.
70. Dolinin, p. 21, omits *nasmeshlivoy*, "mocking, scornful" (msp. 28).

9. ON GENERALITIES (1926)

1. Alexander Dolinin suggests this refers to the émigré historian Nikolai Berdyaev's 1923 essay on the postwar era, "Novoe srednevekov'e" ("The New Middle Ages,"), collected in his *The End of Our Time*, 1933 ("Clio laughs last: Nabokov's answer to historicism," in Julian W. Connolly, ed., *Nabokov and His Fiction: New Perspectives* [Cambridge, U.K.: Cambridge University Press, 1999], 197–215, p. 204).
2. As a deleted fragment indicates, VN has in mind the presumably apocryphal anecdote about Sir Walter Raleigh, who completed only one of the five projected volumes of his *History of the World* (Milton Waldman, *Walter Raleigh* [London: 1950], 189).
3. In Oct. 1925, multilateral international treaties settling the borders of Western Europe after World War I were negotiated in Locarno, Switzerland.
4. The Charleston, wildly popular as a dance in 1925 and 1926, incorporated some highly modified African American elements. The African American dancer Josephine Baker popularized it in France in her skimpily clad erotic dances, including "Danse sauvage," in Paris's *La Revue nègre*, 1925.
5. Pageboy haircuts, at the peak of their popularity in 1926. Dolinin notes a letter of Madame de Sévigné of March 18, 1671, describing a short-cut, straight, wigless women's hairdo.
6. A "little tragedy" in verse, 1830, by Alexander Pushkin.
7. A Russian team sport played with bat and ball, and not unlike cricket or baseball in involving running between marked zones. VN evokes it in *The Defense* (explained as "Russian baseball," chap. 2), *Glory* (as "tag-bat," chap. 42), and even in his Russian translation of *Lolita*, where "the crack of a bat" (II.36) in an American school playing field becomes *bryak lapty* ("the crack of *lapta*").

8. "The young postwar generation." Dolinin cites as examples Jacques de Lacretelle, *La Vie inquiète de Jean Hermelin*, 1920; Philippe Soupault, *Le Bon Apôtre*, 1923, and *À la dérive*, 1923; André Obey, *L'Enfant inquiet*, 1920.

9. Lenin's real surname.

10. A. ZNOSKO-BOROVSKY, *CAPABLANCA AND ALEKHINE* (1927)

1. Invented as the goddess of chess in the poem *Scacchia Ludus* (1527) by Hieronymus Vida (1485?–1566).

11. ANNIVERSARY (1927)

1. The Lenin variant of the Marx species of ant.
2. Anastasia Verbitskaya (1861–1928), best-selling Russian popular novelist.
3. In Russian, *seriy, eseseriy yubiley*, "gray USSR jubilee."

12. VLADISLAV KHODASEVICH, *COLLECTED POEMS* (1927)

1. The epigraph to Khodasevich's 1920–23 poem "Brenta," from Alexander Pushkin, *Eugene Onegin*, I.xlix.1–2. In *EO*, I, 116: "Adrian waves, / O Brenta!").
2. "Brenta," line 1: "Brenta, rusty little stream."
3. Closing lines (17–18) of "Brenta": "From that time I love, Brenta, / Prose in life and in verse."
4. In Russian, *"Adriaticheskie volny."*
5. "Tak byvaet pochemu-to" ("This Is How It Happens for Some Reason," 1920).
6. "Mel'nitsa," 1920–23.
7. "Ballada" ("Sizhu, osveshchaemiy sverkhu"), 1921, trans. by VN as "Orpheus" in *V&V*, 345–47.
8. *V&V*, 345, lines 25–26. More literally: "And music, music, music, / threads its way into my singing," trans. David Bethea, *Khodasevich: His Life and Art* (Princeton, N.J.: Princeton University Press, 1983), 239.
9. *V&V*, 347, lines 37–40; more literally, "And in a flowing, revolving dance / my entire room moves rhythmically, / and someone hands me / a heavy lyre through the wind" (Bethea, *Khodasevich*, 240).
10. "Okna vo dvor" ("Windows onto a Courtyard," 1924).
11. "Ballada" (*"Mne nevozhmozhno byt' soboy,"* "I can't be myself") 1925, lines 16–23, in Vladislav Khodasevich, *Sobranie sochineniy*, ed. John Malmstad and Robert Hughes (Ann Arbor, Mich.: Ardis, 1983), 164–66.
12. "Pod zemley" ("Underground," 1923).
13. Masturbation in the men's room of a subway public lavatory.
14. "Avtomobil'" ("The Automobile," 1921).
15. "Pokrova Mayi potayennoy" ("The Cloak of Undercover Maya," 1922).
16. "U morya. I" ("By the Sea: I," 1922–23).
17. "Khranilishche" ("The Storehouse," 1924).
18. "O, esli b v etot chas zhelannogo" ("Oh, If Only in That Hour Desired," 1915).
19. "Iz dnevnika" ("From the Diary," 1921).
20. "Probochka" ("The Cork," 1921).
21. "Pro sebya. II" ("About Myself: II," 1919).
22. "So slabykh vek" ("From Weak Eyelids," 1914).
23. "Epizod" ("The Episode," 1918). In the Russian VN emphasizes *"Iznemogaya v istome tuskloy, kotoraya menya* tomila."
24. "Pro sebya. I" ("About Myself: I," 1919). In the Russian VN emphasizes "chto znachit znak *ego spiny mokhnatoy.*"

25. "Obo vsem v odnikh stikhakh ne skazhesh'" ("You Can't Speak of Everything in Verse Alone," 1915).
26. "Na tuskneyushchie shpili" ("On Dimming Spires," 1921).
27. "Burya" ("Tempest," 1921).
28. "2-go noyabrya" ("November 2," 1918).
29. "Glyazhu na grubye remesla" ("I Look at Coarse Trades," 1922).
30. "Kogda b ya dolgo zhil na svete" ("When I've Lived a Long Time on Earth," 1921).

13. MAN AND THINGS (1928)

1. VN misremembers who says this: not the doctor, Chebutykin, who will drop the gift, but Vershinin. Dolinin compounds the error by identifying the wrong speech from Chebutykin.
2. A "river of diamonds," a diamond necklace.
3. In prerevolutionary Russia, *Chelovek!* ("Man!") was a way of summoning a waiter, like the French *Garçon!*, whose literal meaning, "Boy!," has similarly made the expression now offensive and obsolete in restaurants and bars.
4. Kaiser Wilhelm II (1859–1941), German emperor 1888–1918.
5. All are natural diminutives in Russian.
6. *Nosik,* "little nose."

15. OMAR KHAYYÁM TRANSLATED BY IVAN TKHORZHEVSKY (1928)

1. Edward FitzGerald (1809–83), *The Rubáiyát of Omar Khayyam* (1859).
2. Jean-Baptiste Nicolas, *Les Quatrains de Khayyam* (Paris: Duprat, 1863).

16. ALEKSEY REMIZOV, *THE STAR ABOVE STARS* (1928)

1. Aleksey Remizov (1877–1957), medievalizing Russian writer.

18. IVAN BUNIN, *SELECTED POEMS* (1929)

1. VN here paraphrases a line from Alexander Blok's poem "Za grobom" ("Behind the Coffin").
2. *Niva* (Cornfield), Russian illustrated weekly magazine (1870–1918), the most popular of its time and a "thin journal" in contrast to the "thick journals" (of which the émigré *Sovremmennye zapiski,* for instance, was a descendant) with more heavyweight literary and political contributions.
3. "Ogon' na machte" ("Fire on the Mast," 1905).
4. "Val's" ("Waltz," 1906).
5. "Diya" ("Dia," 1907).
6. "Karavan" ("Caravan," 1908).
7. "Knyaz' Vseslav" ("Prince Vseslav," 1916).
8. "Shchegly, ikh zvon, steklyanny, nezhivoy" ("Goldfinches, Their Peal, Glassy, Unliving," 1917).
9. "Sobaka" ("Dog," 1909).
10. "Kray bez istorii. Vsyo les da les, bolota" ("A Land Without History. All Forest After Forest, Bogs," 1916).
11. "Germon" ("Hermon," 1907).
12. "Posle Messinskogo zemletryaseniya" ("After the Messina Earthquake," 1909).
13. "V arkhipelage" ("In an Archipelago," 1908).

14. "Mogila v skale" ("Grave in Rock," 1909).
15. "Indiyskiy okean" ("The Indian Ocean," 1916).
16. "Tseylon" ("Ceylon," 1916).
17. "Liman peskom ot morya otdelen" ("Liman Is Separated from the Sea by Sand," 1916).
18. "Lyublyu tsvetnye stekla okon" ("I Love Windows' Colored Glass," 1906).
19. "Ogromniy, krasniy, stariy parokhod" ("A Huge Old Red Steamer," 1906).
20. "Raskrylos' nebo goluboe" ("A Blue Sky Opened," 1901).
21. "Petukh na tserkovnom kreste" ("The Cock on a Church Cross," 1922).
22. "Grobnitsa Rakhili" ("Rachel's Tomb," 1907).
23. "Rastyot, rastyot mogilnaya trava" ("The Grave Grass Grows, Grows," 1906).
24. "Kanun kupali" ("The Eve of Kupala," 1903).

19. ALEXANDER KUPRIN, *THE GLADE: SHORT STORIES* (1929)

1. Alexander Kuprin (1870–1938), a writer well recognized in Russia from around 1900, but impoverished in the emigration. For VN's later fondness for him as a person, see *LTV,* 230–31.

21. THE TRIUMPH OF VIRTUE (1930)

1. *Otvetstvennyi rabotnik* literally means simply "responsible worker," but in Soviet usage meant an executive within the Soviet system. VN invokes this type as a Soviet's idea of how the role of a Western "bourgeois" has been transformed in the Soviet world. (We owe this nuance to Stanislav Shvabrin.)
2. In prerevolutionary Russia, an intellectual not belonging to the gentry.
3. In Gogol's *Dead Souls.*
4. Rich peasant exploiting others.
5. The Communist Youth League (*Kom*munisticheskiy *soyuz molo*dyozhi) referred to two paragraphs previously.

23. BORIS POPLAVSKY, *FLAGS* (1931)

1. "Sentimental'naia demonologia" ("Sentimental Demonology"). Translations follow Boris Poplavsky, *Flags,* trans. Belinda Cooke and Richard McKane (Bristol, U.K.: Shearsman Books, 2009).
2. "Devochka vozvratilas', angel zapel naugad" ("The Little Girl Returned, the Angel Began to Sing at Random").
3. "Solntse niskhodit, eshche tak zharko" ("The Sun Sinks, It's Still So Hot").
4. "Morella I" / "Morella I." VN misremembers: the line is *"O, Morella, usni, kak uzhasny ogromnyie zhizni,"* where he has *"orlinnye zhizni"* ("aquiline lives" instead of "huge lives"). He retained this incorrect version of the line for the rest of his life.
5. "Don Kikhot" ("Don Quixote") (translation amended).
6. Note the sound play: *"Khokhotali motory, grokhotali monokli."*
7. Note the sound play: *"Sineveli dni, sireneveli."*
8. VN is here alluding to the poetry of Igor Severyanin, and to the poems "Kenzeli" ("Quinzels") and "Russkaya" ("Russian"), respectively.
9. VN here quotes from the songs of Alexander Vertinsky, "Oloviannoe serdtse" ("Tin Heart") and "Bal Gospoden" ("The Lord's Ball").
10. "V bor'be so snegom" ("A Struggle with the Snow": note sound play in *"se slov igra mogla slomat' osla, / no ya osel zhelezeniy, ya zhele,/ zhalel vsegda, zhalel, no an oslab"*).

11. Word used to reinforce opposition to what has been proposed, something contrary or in contrast.
12. "Volshebnyi fonar'" ("The Magic Lantern").
13. "Bor'ba so snom" ("A Struggle with Sleep").
14. "Astral'nyi mir" ("Astral World").
15. "Don Quixote"; Cooke and McKane translate it as "African style."
16. "Angélique."
17. "Astral'nyi mir" ("Astral World"); Cooke and McKane translate it as "stylish hall."
18. "Otritsatel'nyi polyus molchit i siyayet" ("The Negative Pole Is Silent and Shines").
19. "Dvoetsarstvie" ("Joint Reign").
20. Rather than the correct *oktyabr', pyupitr, dirizhabl', korabl'*.
21. Grand Duke Konstantin Konstantinovich of Russia (1858–1915), a grandson of Emperor Nicholas I of Russia, a poet and playwright who wrote under the pen name "K.R.," initials of his given name and family name, Konstantin Romanov. His poetry is mocked in *Ada*, at the end of pt. 1, chap. 38.
22. Antonin Ladinsky (1895–1961), émigré poet, whose volume *Chornoe i goluboe* VN had very recently reviewed (*Rul'*, Jan. 28, 1931, 2–3).
23. "Morella I" / "Morella I." VN misquotes here, as before.

26. NINA BERBEROVA, *THE LAST AND THE FIRST* (1931)

1. Nina Berberova (1901–93), émigré novelist and short-story writer, based in Paris.

27. IN MEMORY OF A. M. CHORNY (1932)

1. Allusion to the logo of the Koh-i-Noor Hardtmuth brand of erasers, still in production.
2. Therefore, across Russia, or Europe; *chorniy* means "black." An echo of line 9 of Gavriil Derzhavin's 1795 variation, "Pamyatnik" ("The Monument"), on Horace's famous poem "Exegi Monumentum," which Pushkin in turn famously de-solemnized (see *V&V*, 32–33).
3. *Gorniy put'* (The Empyrean Path) (Berlin: Grani, 1923).

28. INTERVIEW WITH ANDREY SEDYKH FOR *POSLEDNIE NOVOSTI* (1932)

1. Alexander Alekhine (1892–1946), Russian émigré from 1921, world chess champion 1927–35, 1937–46. Saviely Tartakower (1887–1956), Polish and French grandmaster.
2. Mark Aldanov (1886?–1957), émigré novelist. His *Begstvo* (*The Escape*) began serial publication in 1930 and was published in book form in 1932.

29. IN MEMORY OF AMALIA FONDAMINSKY (1937)

1. Fyodor Stepun (1884–1965), émigré writer and philosopher based in Germany.
2. The novel *Nikolai Pereslegin* (1929).
3. From the untitled poem beginning "*Svoenravnoe prozvan'e / Dal ya miloy v lasku ey*" (1834), by Evgeny Baratynsky (1800–1844), translated by VN as "To His Wife." Opening lines in VN's rhymed and approximate translation: "I have given her a nickname, just a fanciful caress," *V&V*, 225.

30. PUSHKIN, OR THE TRUE AND THE SEEMINGLY TRUE (1937)

1. DN note (from a longer introduction): "While my translation of the prose is as literal as I could make it, it is true that the special personality of the French language, where a nuance lurks behind the turn of every phrase and a botched idiom is idiotic, requires minor adjustments in order to obtain at least plausible English. A separate problem was what to do about Nabokov's examples of Pushkin's verse in French. Together with his considerations regarding the translation of Pushkin from Russian into French, they are specific and intimately related to the character of both the 'from' and 'into' languages. At the same time they reflect a general approach to translation that was to evolve substantially in the years that followed. Therefore I retained the French examples for the bilingual reader, and hoped to provide the ideal supplement: Nabokov's own English versions from various periods. A search of readily accessible manuscripts and typescripts amid a treasure-trove of his translations revealed, alas, that he seems to have Englished only one of the four samples—the stanza which is misidentified, through an editorial error or a rare absentminded lapse of the author's, as being from *Eugene Onegin*, but which is actually from 'Yezerski' (begun by Pushkin in 1830, when he was finishing *Onegin*).

   "Nevertheless, this excerpt does make it possible to present, alongside Nabokov's French illustrations of what he explains in his text, an additional peek into the evolution of his theory and technique as applied to the translation of Pushkin's poetry, and poetry in general. Presumably done in connection with his U.S. university courses, this English fragment reflects a partial transition from the accommodations, made in the name of rhyme and musicality in the French verses and in other early translations, to the unflinching fidelity of his *Onegin* (which Nabokov deliberately conceived as an uncompromisingly literal 'crib').

   "I have inserted in the text, together with Nabokov's translation of a section of 'Yezerski,' my English versions of the other three examples. They are based on the Russian originals, with occasional assists from the solutions adopted in Nabokov's French (e.g., the substitution of the Fate Lachesis for Pushkin's generic Parca). One stringent test of rhymed translations, and of rhymed poetry in general (although most versifiers seem to prefer playing on a netless, unlined court these days), is to check how obvious it is that one part of a rhyme came first, and to what degree the other part protrudes like a sore toe of the prosodic foot. 'Sing not, my fair' best lent itself to an attempt at preserving not only meter but also rhyme, or at least assonance, and is to a degree analogous to the general method used in Nabokov's somewhat freer French samples, which seem to pass that test with flying colors.

   "In the remaining two poems I made no compromise whatever for the sake of rhymes, welcoming them only if they tumbled of their own accord into my lap, while the relative simplicity of the Russian originals allowed literality to cohabit pretty well with meter. Even though his English version of *Onegin* codified a rhymeless and meterless scholarly precision, what Vladimir Nabokov had indicated elsewhere about poetic translation suggests that, even in later years, he, too, might have chosen to retain at least the meter of these particular poems. Would that there were a Volapük or Esperanto rich enough for poetry."

2. During the Crimean War, the Russians retreated from Sebastopol on Sept. 9, 1855, after a siege by the French, Ottoman, and English allies begun in Oct. 1854.

3. DN note: "A hotbed of counterrevolutionary insurrection in 1793."

4. Iron Chancellor: Otto von Bismarck (1815–98), first chancellor of the German Empire, 1871–90.
5. French name of Tchaikovsky's opera *The Queen of Spades*.
6. Nightclub (literally, "box of night").
7. Heelless North African and Middle Eastern slipper, usually leather.

33. DEFINITIONS (1940)

1. *Prestataire*, French for a person liable to statute labor. In accordance with the decrees issued by French Prime Minister Édouard Daladier, in Jan. 1940, all refugees and those without citizenship were to become members of the unarmed auxiliary force and serve alongside the French army.
2. "Philistine vulgarity," or "smug Philistinism," as Nabokov translates it. For detailed discussions of this very Russian term, see his *Nikolai Gogol* (New Directions, 1944), pp. 63–74, and *Lectures on Russian Literature*, ed. Fredson Bowers (New York: Harcourt Brace Jovanovich/Bruccoli Clark, 1981), 313.
3. Now Chişinău, Moldava. Pushkin spent three years in exile in Kishinev.
4. Where Pushkin and then Lermontov were exiled.
5. The grand central street of St. Petersburg, made strange by Gogol, Dostoevsky, and Bely.
6. VN probably has in mind Alexei Tolstoy's historical novel *Peter the First* (1929–34), which suggested analogies between Peter I and Stalin, and which would win the Stalin Prize in 1941.

35. CRYSTAL AND RUBY (1940)

1. Stalin was born in Georgia and of Georgian ethnicity.

36. HELP, PEOPLE! (1940)

1. A Russian summer soup made with raw vegetables and kvass (a drink made from rye bread), typically served cold.

37. MR. MASEFIELD AND CLIO (1940)

1. The Ballets Russes de Monte Carlo were formed in 1932, after the death of Diaghilev.

38. PROF. WOODBRIDGE IN AN ESSAY ON NATURE POSTULATES THE REALITY OF THE WORLD (1940)

1. Woodbridge (1867–1940) spent most of his career at Columbia University.

40. SOVIET LITERATURE 1940 (1941)

1. Alfred Rosenberg (1893–1946), theorist and Nazi Party ideologue. VN misspelled the name "Rozenberg."
2. Alluding to Hamlet's lament for his dead jester, "Alas, poor Yorick, I knew him, Horatio" (*Hamlet* 5.1.180) and its echo in Laurence Sterne's *Tristram Shandy*. Karl Radek was accused of treason in Stalin's Great Purge, and sentenced in the Second Moscow Trial, 1937, to ten years' hard labor, but was killed by an NKVD agent in 1939.

3. Vicki Baum, *Grand Hotel* (1929); the original, *Menschen im Hotel,* was the basis for the Edward Goulding film *Grand Hotel* (1932), which won the Academy Award for Best Picture. In his recent (and not yet published) first novel in English, *The Real Life of Sebastian Knight,* VN had written of "the fashionable trick of grouping a medley of people in a limited space (a hotel, an island, a street)" (chap. 10). Later, in his lectures on *Don Quixote,* he would note: "Cervantes has hit on the convenient 'island' device which consists in grouping characters in some isolated limited locus—an island, a hotel, a ship, an airplane, a country-house, a railway car. As a matter of fact, it is also Dostoevski's device, in his completely irresponsible and somewhat antiquated novels, where a dozen of people have a tremendous row in a roomette on a train—a train that moves not. And to move still further, the same trick of grouping people in one place is, of course, used in the modern mystery story where a number of potential suspects are isolated in a snowbound hotel, or in a solitary country-house, et cetera, so as to neatly limit possible clues in the little reader's mind." (*Lectures on Don Quixote,* 147.)
4. Ilf (Ilya Feinsilberg, 1897–1937); with Evgeniy Petrov (1903–42), he formed the satiric writing duo Ilf and Petrov, whom VN rated highly.
5. Ruvim Freierman, *Dikaya sobaka Dingo: ili, povest o pervoy lyubvi* (*Dingo the Wild Dog: or A Tale of First Love*).

41. FAINT ROSE, OR THE LIFE OF AN ARTIST WHO LIVED IN AN IVORY TOWER (1941)

1. English-born painter Charles Conder (1868–1909) lived in Australia 1884–90, and thereafter in Europe, especially England and Paris.
2. French novelist Édouard Dujardin (1861–1949), whose 1888 novel, *Les Lauriers sont coupés,* is often seen as the first extensive use of stream-of-consciousness technique. When VN met Dujardin is not otherwise known.
3. Conder died of syphilis.

42. INTERVIEW WITH BETH KULAKOFSKY FOR *WELLESLEY COLLEGE NEWS* (1941)

1. Where VN had never been.

43. ONE HUNDRED YEARS OF ENGLAND IN A WORK BOTH SCHOLARLY AND TIMELY (1941)

1. Allusion to the underground, nocturnal species which has devolved from the working class in the distant future of H. G. Wells's *The Time Machine* (1895), the upper classes having evolved into the effete Eloi.
2. The 1840s and the 1860s were particularly active periods of radical debate in the presses of imperial Russia.

44. ON THE OCCASION OF M. ZHELEZNOV'S REVIEW, *NOVOE RUSSKOE SLOVO* (1941)

1. VN's *Sobytie* (*The Event*), which had premiered in Paris on March 4, 1938, in the Salle des Journaux of the Bibliothèque Nationale, was staged on April 4, 1941, in New York at the Heckscher Theatre. The actor Dolmatov played the role of "The Famous Writer" Pyotr Nikolaevich, in whom some contempo-

raries detected a caricature of Ivan Bunin. Zheleznov was the pseudonym of poet and journalist M. K. Aisenshtadt (1900–1970). For the first re-publication of Nabokov's letter, and a brief discussion of the Paris and New York performances of *The Event*, see Vladimir Nabokov, *Tragediya gospodina Morna, P'esy, Lektsii o drame*, ed. Andrei Babikov (St. Petersburg: Azbuka-klassika, 2008), 591.

45. [SHAKESPEARE, THE PROFESSORS, AND THE PEOPLE] (1941?)

1. Bavarian town above which Hitler had built his Berghof in 1935.
2. *Unser:* German, "our."
3. Alwin Thaler, *Shakespere's Silences* (Cambridge, Mass.: Harvard University Press, 1929).
4. John Bourchier, second Baron Berners (1467–1533), *Huon of Burdeuxe*, c. 1540.
5. W. W. Greg, "Hamlet's Hallucination," *Modern Language Review* 12, no. 4 (1917), 393–421.
6. John Dover Wilson, *What Happens in Hamlet* (Cambridge, U.K.: Cambridge University Press, 1935).

46. SICKLE, HAMMER AND GUN (1941?)

1. First name and patronymic of Lenin; by itself the patronymic, "Ilyitch," was often used as an affectionate name by his Soviet admirers.

47. MR. WILLIAMS' SHAKESPEARE (1941)

1. City in the Volga region, between Nizhniy Novgorod and Kazan', now known (since 1928) as Yoshkar-Ola.

49. THE INNOCENCE OF HILAIRE BELLOC (1941)

1. "Caress the sentence, it will smile at you." Anatole France's phrase was actually *"Caressez longuement votre phrase et elle finira par sourire"* ("Caress your sentence at length and it will end up smiling").
2. Probably Margaret Mitchell, *Gone with the Wind*, 1936 (possibly blurred with Norman Douglas, *South Wind*, 1917); Ernest Hemingway, *For Whom the Bell Tolls*, 1940; and James Joyce, *Finnegans Wake*, 1939.

51. THE CREATIVE WRITER (1941)

1. Cesare Lombroso (1835–1909), Italian criminologist and physiognomist. His *Genio e Follia* (1864) and *L'uomo di genio* (1888) explained genius as a form of insanity.
2. British bacteriologist Frederick Griffith (1879–1941) in 1928 showed in mice, not rats, that bacterial strains could transform.
3. Johann Ludwig Rhumbler (1864–1936), German cell biologist.
4. VN ignores the letter-for-letter correspondence customary in transliteration (*vdokhnovenie*) to offer an Anglophone reader a closer approximation of the sound.

54. INTERVIEW WITH KATHLEEN LUCAS
FOR *WELLESLEY COLLEGE NEWS* (1942)

1. VN may in fact have said "Primitive art—that's Mr. Boubou!" He disliked "primitive art" or "tribal art." "Mr. Boubou" is a French term for a generic African.

55. IN MEMORY OF IOSIF HESSEN (1943)

1. The Constitutional Democratic Party, known by the nickname Kadet Party. VN's father, V. D. Nabokov, was a leading Kadet in and outside the Russian Duma (parliament), and Iosif Vladimirovich Hessen (1865–1943), a lawyer and journalist, was also a Central Committee member.
2. Hessen was five years older than VN's father.
3. *Pravo* (Law), a leading liberal journal, advocating legal and constitutional reforms, founded in 1898; V. D. Nabokov and I. V. Hessen were on its board from 1899; Hessen became editor-in-chief in 1906.
4. *Rech'* (Speech), Russia's leading liberal daily, 1906–17. The Kadet leader Pavel Milyukov and I. V. Hessen were founding coeditors, Hessen being in practice the editor-in-chief; V. D. Nabokov was a third on the editorial board of four.
5. *Rul'* (The Rudder), émigré liberal daily founded in Berlin in 1920 by V. D. Nabokov, I. V. Hessen, and Avgust Kaminka; after V. D. Nabokov's assassination on March 28, 1922, I. V. Hessen served as the sole editor until the newspaper folded in 1931.
6. Hessen was Jewish and, like the Gentile V. D. Nabokov, had been a champion of Jewish rights in Russia.
7. Elena Polevitskaya (1881–1973), leading stage actress in Russia, the emigration, and the USSR. Nadezhda Plevitskaya (1884–1940), Russian popular singer and from 1930 a Soviet agent, involved in the 1937 abduction of the White General Miller (as VN records in his 1943 story "The Assistant Producer").
8. The so-called Hegelian triad of thesis-antithesis-synthesis, popular in Russian schools. A few years later, VN would blend it with the image of a spiral to summarize the phases of his own life to date in chap. 14 of his autobiography, *Speak, Memory.*
9. Hessen died on March 22, 1943.

59. ON LEARNING RUSSIAN (1945)

1. The "h" here indicates Russian pronunciation, for Anglophones, rather than Russian spelling.
2. Again, VN here indicates approximate pronunciation rather than spelling. The usual transliteration (including VN's elsewhere) is *govorit'*, the "t' " ("t" and soft sign in Cyrillic) indicating that the "t" is palatalized (as most consonants can be in Russian), which does make it sound rather like an English "tz."

61. THE PLACE OF RUSSIAN STUDIES IN THE CURRICULUM (1948)

1. Reference point.
2. VN had accepted the offer of a position as professor of Russian literature at Cornell by Nov. 14, 1947, after the president of Wellesley declined to make a counteroffer to Cornell's.

62. THOMAS MANN, "THE RAILWAY ACCIDENT" (1950)

1. By Lynd Ward (1905–1985).
2. Helen Tracy Lowe-Porter (1876–1963).
3. "Das Eisenbahnunglück," published 1909. "The Railway Accident," one of three stories in *Nocturnes*, takes up pp. 28–44, with illustrations by Ward on pp. 28 and 34.
4. *Die Verwandlung*, published 1915.
5. Nabokov does not quote verbatim. The translation (pp. 30–31) reads "that guard with the leather cartridge belt, the prodigious sergeant-major's moustache and the inhospitable eye. Watch him rebuking the old woman in the threadbare black cape—for two pins she would have got into a second-class carriage."
6. The translation of Mann's text here (p. 35) reads: "I heard his immediate and elemental burst of rage. 'What do you want?' he roared. 'Leave me alone, you swine.' He said swine. It was a lordly epithet, the epithet of a cavalry officer—it did my heart good to hear it.... Just as I stepped into the corridor to get a better view the door of the compartment abruptly opened and the ticket flew out into the attendant's face; yes, it was flung with violence straight in his face. He picked it up with both hands, and though he had got the corner of it in one eye, so that the tears came, he thanked the man, saluting and clicking his heels together."
7. The translation of Mann's text reads here (pp. 43–44): "And inside of an hour we were all stowed higgledy-piggledy into a special train.

    "I had my first-class ticket—my journey being paid for—but it availed me nothing, for everybody wanted to ride first and my carriage was more crowded than the others. But just as I found me a little niche, whom do I see diagonally opposite to me, huddled in the corner? My hero, the gentleman with the spats and the vocabulary of a cavalry officer. He did not have his dog, it had been taken away from him in defiance of his rights as a nob, and now sat howling in a gloomy prison just behind the engine.... And with a sour smile my gentleman resigned himself to the crazy situation.

    "And now who got in, supported by two firemen? A wee little old grandmother in a tattered black cape, the very same who in Munich would for two pins have got into a second-class carriage. 'Is this the first class?' she kept asking. And when we made room and assured her that it was, she sank down with a 'God be praised!' onto the plush cushions as though only now was she safe and sound."

63. INTERVIEW WITH HARVEY BREIT
FOR *NEW YORK TIMES BOOK REVIEW* (1951)

1. Reuben Fine (1914–93), American psychologist and chess master and author in both fields.
2. Samuel Reshevsky (1911–92), Polish-born American chess grandmaster.
3. Not his first novel, which was *Mashen'ka* (1925; translated as *Mary*, 1970), but his first novel published in America.

65. SALUTATIONS (1956)

1. Mark Aldanov (Nov. 7, 1886–1957), Russian émigré historical novelist.
2. The victim of such a celebration: in Russian, *"zhertva takogo torzhestva"* (where *takogo* is pronounced "takova").
3. *Svyataya Elena, malen'kiy ostrov* (1921).

67. INTERVIEW IN *NEW YORK POST* (1958)

1. A 1956 novel by Grace Metalious (1924–64), one of the fastest-selling novels of all time, on *The New York Times* best-seller list for fifty-nine weeks, and considered at the time almost scandalously steamy. In 1957, it was made into a film produced by Twentieth Century–Fox and directed by Mark Robson.

73. "A G.S. MAN," *CORNELL DAILY SUN* (1958)

1. Because there was no Department of Russian Literature at Cornell, Nabokov's courses were all part of the Division of Literature, based in Goldwin Smith Hall, and specifically of its Department of Romance Literature, headed by Morris Bishop, who had recruited him for Cornell. Morrill Hall housed the Division of Languages, whose methods of teaching Russian Nabokov deplored, as the satire in *Pnin* also reveals.

76. INTERVIEW WITH THOMAS B. TURLEY FOR *NIAGARA FALLS GAZETTE* (1959)

1. In fact *Mashen'ka (Mary)* was published in 1926.

81. INTERVIEW OF VLADIMIR NABOKOV AND ALAIN ROBBE-GRILLET WITH ANDRÉ PARINAUD, ROGER NIMIER, AND PAUL GUIMARD FOR *ARTS* (PARIS) (1959)

1. He would have gone on to explain that *fou* can mean "madman" or a chess bishop.
2. If the conversation was correctly transcribed, VN said "authors . . . translate" when he clearly meant "publishers . . . publish."

84. INTERVIEW WITH PIERRE MAZARS FOR *LE FIGARO LITTÉRAIRE* (1959)

1. In French, *"Les senteurs et les sentiers."*
2. Robbe-Grillet's kind, that is.

87. INTERVIEW WITH ANNE GUÉRIN FOR *L'EXPRESS* (1959)

1. On the last page of the novel, Humbert writes: "Dolly Schiller will probably survive me by many years. The following decision I make with all the legal impact and support of a signed testament: I wish this memoir to be published only when Lolita is no longer alive."
2. Eugène Scribe (1791–1861), French dramatist, known as the model author of the "well-made play."
3. Henri-René Lenormand (1882–1951), French dramatist.

89. INTERVIEW WITH JOHN COLEMAN FOR *THE SPECTATOR* (1959)

1. The novel (or linked short stories) *Memoirs of Hecate County* (1946) was quickly banned in the United States and remained so until 1959.

2. "Notes on Neotropical Plebejinae (Lycaenidae, Lepidoptera)," *Psyche* 52, no. 12 (March–June 1945), 1–61. Kurt Johnson and Steve Coates, in *Nabokov's Blues: The Scientific Odyssey of a Literary Genius* (Cambridge, Mass.: Zoland, 1999), dwell at length on the originality and continued impact of this paper.

91. "OLYMPIA PRESS," *NEW YORK TIMES BOOK REVIEW* (1960)

1. Henry Popkin, "The Famous and Infamous Wares of Mr. Girodias," *New York Times Book Review*, Apr. 7, 1960, 4.

101. INTERVIEW WITH MAURICE DOLBIER FOR *NEW YORK HERALD TRIBUNE* (1962)

1. So Dolbier noted. The correct text is: "The moon's an arrant thief, / And her pale fire she snatches from the sun."

108. LETTER TO THE EDITOR, *RUSSKAYA MYSL'* (1963)

1. Rodion Berezov, "Pamyati Anny Leonidovny Shakhovskoy," *Russkaya mysl'*, September 17, 1963, 6. Rodion Akulshin (1896–1988), pen name Berezov, emigrated to the United States after release from a German prisoner-of-war camp in 1945, rather than face prison or execution in the USSR.

110. INTERVIEW WITH DOUGLAS M. DAVIS FOR *NATIONAL OBSERVER* (1964)

1. "Stopping by Woods on a Snowy Evening (1922)."

111. INTERVIEW WITH HORST TAPPE FOR *DIE WELT* (1964)

1. Unfinished, after his British publisher, George Weidenfeld, backed out of VN's ambitious plans. For some of the material, see Brian Boyd and Robert Michael Pyle, eds., *Nabokov's Butterflies: Unpublished and Uncollected Writings* (Boston: Beacon, 1999).

113. INTERVIEW WITH GORDON ACKERMAN FOR *WEEKLY TRIBUNE* (1966)

1. Lollobrigida.

115. INTERVIEW WITH PENELOPE GILLIATT FOR *VOGUE* (1966)

1. To the USSR.
2. *Love's Labor's Lost*, 5.2.912.
3. From this point on, he is talking of *Lolita*, not *The Enchanter*.

116. INTERVIEW WITH DIETER E. ZIMMER FOR NORDDEUTSCHER RUNDFUNK (1966)

1. "I love and I hate," echo of Catullus, poem 85.
2. Butterfly hunter.

117. INTERVIEW WITH PAT GARIAN FOR GERMAN *HARPER'S BAZAAR* (1967)

1. Should be *"Aber bitte schön mit doppelten Türen"* ("But please, with double doors").

119. INTERVIEW WITH PIERRE DOMMERGUES FOR *LES LANGUES MODERNES* (1967–68)

1. Bertrand Russell.
2. There are forty members at any one time of the prestigious Académie Française, writers and thinkers chosen to guard over the traditions of the French language and literature. Their nickname is "the immortals."
3. Painter Jean Holabird, without knowing this passage, proposed and executed *AlphaBet in Color* (*Vladimir Nabokov: AlphaBet in Color* [Corte Madera, Calif.: Ginkgo Press, 2005]), which takes VN's description of the colors he associates with letters in Russian, English, and French and devotes a page to each, with the edges of the gradually wider pages forming a rainbow effect.
4. Alain Robbe-Grillet, *Le Voyeur* (Paris: Éditions de Minuit, 1955).

122. INTERVIEW WITH GAETANO TUMIATI FOR *LA STAMPA* (1969)

1. The Nabokov family estate and summer residence of VN's Russian childhood, celebrated in *Speak, Memory*.
2. Yuri Olesha (1899–1960) and Mikhail Bulgakov (1891–1940), writers who remained in the Soviet Union yet wrote works of integrity without falling fatally foul of Soviet censorship.

124. INTERVIEW WITH CONSTANZO COSTANTINI FOR *IL MESSAGERO* (1969)

1. "La pioggia nel pineto" (1902).

128. INTERVIEW WITH HANSPETER RIKLIN (1970)

1. Jacques Martin (1933–2007) and Danièle Gilbert (1943–) were hosts of the Monday-to-Friday television variety show *Midi magazine* (1968–69), which changed its name to *Midi chez vous* (1969–71) on ORTF's Channel 1.
2. Mao's *Little Red Book* was a fashionable accoutrement within the youth counterculture.

129. INTERVIEW WITH ANDREW FIELD FOR HIS BIOGRAPHY (1970)

1. Nabokov's younger sister (1906–2000), then living in Geneva.
2. *All Petrograd*, an address directory.
3. Tauride Garden.
4. "Shaken off the soft dust of Russia." A pseudo-citation?
5. Horst Tappe.
6. VN's cousin and best friend, Baron Georgiy Evgenievich (Yuri, Yurik) Rausch von Traubenberg (1897–1919).

7. VN's misremembering of Chorny's real name, Alexander Glikberg. For VN's recollection of Chorny's kindness toward his early verse, see pp. 111–12.
8. Museum of Comparative Zoology, Harvard, where Nabokov was de facto curator of Lepidoptera, 1941–1948.
9. In fact producer David O. Selznick (1902–65).
10. Not house-trained.
11. Concert-chamber singer.

131. INTERVIEW WITH ALAN LEVY FOR *NEW YORK TIMES MAGAZINE* (1970–71)

1. Karel Kramář (1860–1937), Czech nationalist politician, prime minister, 1918–19.
2. VN suspected, in other words, that the comment was Edmund Wilson's. Wilson certainly made similar comments.
3. Alfred Appel, Jr. (1934–2009) had recently prepared, with VN's help, *The Annotated Lolita* (New York: McGraw-Hill, 1970).
4. This response is from Alan Levy, *Vladimir Nabokov: The Velvet Butterfly* (Sag Harbor, N.Y.: Permanent Press, 1984), 34.
5. *Pieris bryoniae*, common name usually dark-veined or mountain green white, prized by collectors.

132. HOMAGE TO FRANZ HELLENS (1971)

1. Maiden and pen name, Zinaida Shakhovskoy.
2. *Oeil-de-Dieu* (*Eye of God*, 1925).
3. *La Femme partagée* (The Shared Woman, 1929).

134. INTERVIEW WITH STEPHEN JAN PARKER (1971)

1. The novella "Rasskaz o semi poveshenykh" ("The Story of the Seven Hanged") (1908), known in English as "The Seven Who Were Hanged."

137. INTERVIEW WITH SETH GOLDSCHLAGER FOR *NEWSWEEK* (1972)

1. Alluding to the famous madeleine dipped in tea whose taste brings the past back in a rush for Marcel in the *Swann's Way* section of Proust's *In Search of Lost Time*.
2. Rest of answer omitted, since VN's introductions to the translated novels spell out these details.

139. INTERVIEW WITH MATI LAANSOO FOR CANADIAN BROADCASTING CORPORATION (1973)

1. Now in *SO*.

142. INTERVIEW WITH HELGA CHUDACOFF FOR *DIE WELT* (1974)

1. *SO*, 120.

149. INTERVIEW WITH SOPHIE LANNES
FOR *L'EXPRESS* (1975)

1. Instead of the idiomatic *fleurs des champs* (lexically, "flowers of the fields"), *fleurs sauvages*, "savage flowers."
2. "The castle that my [River] Dore bathed," a famous line from the poem "Le Montagnard émigré" ("The Émigré Highlander," 1806, also known as "Romance à Hélène," later incorporated into *Les Aventures du dernier Abencérage*, 1826) by the famously nostalgic François-René de Chateaubriand, one of VN's favorite French authors; the poem is echoed and reworked in *Ada* (pt. 1, chap. 22), and this line was even once suggested by VN as the possible title for a French translation of his autobiography.
3. Another line ("and my mountain, and the big oak") from Chateaubriand's poem, also evoked and varied in *Ada*.
4. "The Carrick" ("The Overcoat") and "The Death of Ivan Il'ich."
5. Actually *Une Passion dans le Désert* (1830).
6. In French, *"un gryphon sans griffes,"* "a griffin without claws."
7. "Voyelles" ("Vowels"), 1883.
8. Lannes's confusion was with VN's cousin Nicolas Nabokov, a composer, not a conductor, whose photograph often wrongly illustrated articles about VN.
9. "Pen" name of the French political cartoonist Emmanuel Poiré (1858–1909), from the Russian *karandash*, "pencil."
10. VN crossed out the brand name.
11. In French, *"La brutalité, la bêtise, le bruit."*

150. INTERVIEW WITH BERNARD PIVOT
FOR *APOSTROPHES* (1975)

1. *". . . ne se plie pas si bien aux supplices de mon imagination."*
2. Crossed out: "in my grandfather's library in the country and my father's library in town."
3. A play on the "accursed poets": Verlaine, Rimbaud, Mallarmé.
4. The first two lines and an approximation of the fourth of the sonnet "Nevermore" (1866), by Paul Verlaine (1844–96): *"Souvenir, souvenir, que me veux-tu? L'automne / Faisait voler la grive à travers l'air atone, / Et le soleil dardait un rayon monotone / Sur le bois jaunissant où la bise détone."* ("Memory, memory, what do you want from me? I remember / Autumn made the thrush fly through the lifeless air, / And the sun launched a monotonous ray where / The north wind exploded in a wood growing yellower.") (Translation, perhaps by Sydney Charles Nathan, at https://larencontrepoetique.com/2016/10/13/verlaine-rencontre-schiele/).

152. AUTHORS' AUTHORS (1976)

1. Dante Alighieri, *The Divine Comedy*. Trans. with commentary by Charles S. Singleton. 6 vols. Bollingen Series LXXX, Princeton: Princeton University Press, 1970.

155. INTERVIEW WITH ROBERT ROBINSON
FOR BBC *BOOK PROGRAMME* (1977)

1. Very much a compromise for Anglophone tongues rather than an echo of the Russian. Much closer would be "a mock of": In despair at mispronunciations, "Nabokov makes a mock of" his own name.
2. His parents had owned dachshunds, but VN himself never owned a dog.

Index

Unless otherwise identified, all literary works are by VN, who is also the default referent: "Ackerman, Gordon, interview with" refers to Ackerman's interview with VN and "Basilissa (Masefield), review of" to VN's review of Masefield's novel. Where possible, interviews are listed both by interviewer and by periodical or broadcaster, reviews both by title of books reviewed and by review title. Page references to texts published here are in bold, and their genre (essay, interview, lecture, letter to editor, questionnaire, review) is noted; other VN texts are identified only by title. References to aspects of Nabokov's life, character, and thought are under "Nabokov, Vladimir Vladimirovich." References to endnotes take the form 491n28.1 (page 491, section 28, note 1). Italics identify particularly important entries.

Illustration Credits

All photographs of VN manuscripts supplied from the Henry W. and Albert A. Berg Collection of English and American Literature, The New York Public Library Astor, Lenox, and Tilden Foundations, and photographed by the photographic studio of The New York Public Library. All material reproduced with the permission of the Vladimir Nabokov Literary Foundation; the typescript on p. 324 also with the permission of the Jacob Bronowski Estate.

A NOTE ABOUT THE AUTHOR AND EDITORS

VLADIMIR NABOKOV studied French and Russian literature at Trinity College, Cambridge, then lived in Berlin and Paris, writing prolifically in Russian under the pseudonym Sirin, including the brilliant novels *The Defense* (1930), *Invitation to a Beheading* (1934) and *The Gift* (1938). In 1940, he left France for America, where he taught at Stanford, Wellesley, Cornell, and Harvard, and wrote some of his greatest works, *Speak, Memory* (1951), *Lolita* (1955), and *Pnin* (1957). In 1959 he returned to Europe, where he wrote more masterpieces, *Pale Fire* (1962) and *Ada* (1969), and translated his earlier Russian work into English. He died in Montreux, Switzerland, in 1977.

BRIAN BOYD, University Distinguished Professor of English, University of Auckland, has published on literature (American, Brazilian, English, Greek, Irish, New Zealand, Polish, Russian), from epics to comics, art from the Paleolithic to the present, philosophy, anthropology, and psychology, but most of all on Vladimir Nabokov, as annotator, bibliographer, biographer, critic, editor, translator, and more. His works have appeared in nineteen languages and won awards on four continents.

ANASTASIA TOLSTOY, a Junior Research Fellow at Wolfson College, University of Oxford, holds a doctorate from Oxford, where she completed a D.Phil. on "Vladimir Nabokov and the Aesthetics of Disgust." She is the cotranslator, with Thomas Karshan, of Nabokov's neo-Shakespearean blank verse drama *The Tragedy of Mister Morn*.

A NOTE ON THE TYPE

This book was set in Janson, a typeface named for the Dutchman Anton Janson, but is actually the work of Nicholas Kis (1650–1702). The type is an excellent example of the influential and sturdy Dutch types that prevailed in England up to the time William Caslon (1692–1766) developed his own incomparable designs from them.

Composed by North Market Street Graphics,
Lancaster, Pennsylvania

Printed and bound by Berryville Graphics,
Berryville, Virginia

Designed by Cassandra J. Pappas